Ethics and the Orator

Ethics and the Orator

THE CICERONIAN TRADITION
OF POLITICAL MORALITY

Gary A. Remer

The University of Chicago Press   CHICAGO & LONDON

The University of Chicago Press, Chicago 60637

The University of Chicago Press, Ltd., London

© 2017 by The University of Chicago

All rights reserved. No part of this book may be used or reproduced in any
manner whatsoever without written permission, except in the case of brief
quotations in critical articles and reviews. For more information, contact
the University of Chicago Press, 1427 E. 60th St., Chicago, IL 60637.

Published 2017.

Printed in the United States of America

26 25 24 23 22 21 20 19 18 17   1 2 3 4 5

ISBN-13: 978-0-226-43916-7 (cloth)

ISBN-13: 978-0-226-43933-4 (e-book)

DOI: 10.7208/chicago/9780226439334.001.0001

Library of Congress Cataloging-in-Publication Data

Names: Remer, Gary, 1957–author.

Title: Ethics and the orator : the Ciceronian tradition of political morality / Gary A. Remer.

Description: Chicago ; London : The University of Chicago Press, 2017. |
Includes bibliographical references and index.

Identifiers: LCCN 2016032946 | ISBN 9780226439167 (cloth : alk. paper) |
ISBN 9780226439334 (e-book)

Subjects: LCSH: Cicero, Marcus Tullius. | Cicero, Marcus Tullius—Influence. |
Political ethics. | Rhetoric—Political aspects. | Rhetoric—Moral and
ethical aspects. | Political science—Philosophy.

Classification: LCC JA79 .R458 2017 | DDC 172—dc23

LC record available at https://lccn.loc.gov/2016032946

♾ This paper meets the requirements of ANSI/NISO z39.48-1992
(Permanence of Paper).

For my wife, Toni
my mother, Jacky
and my father, Nate ז״ל

CONTENTS

ACKNOWLEDGMENTS

Cicero has been a virtual companion of mine for over thirty years now. For a not-insignificant part of that time, I have been thinking about Cicero's approach to political morality and its relationship to his rhetorical outlook—the subject of this book. At times, I have *almost* felt like Machiavelli, who, in his letter to Francesco Vettori, describes his internal dialogues *about* ancient political decisions as actual dialogues *with* ancient political figures. Machiavelli describes himself—during the evenings of his enforced retirement—as "taking off the day's clothing covered with mud and dust [to] put on garments regal and courtly," so that after being properly garbed, "he may enter the ancient courts of ancient men . . . to speak with them and to ask them the reason for their actions; and they in their kindness answer." Unlike Machiavelli, however, I never clothed myself in royal attire. Perhaps if I had only followed the Florentine's practice, Cicero would have yielded answers to my questions sooner, and I could have completed *Ethics and the Orator: The Ciceronian Tradition of Political Morality* in a timelier fashion.

Cicero, however, has not been my only companion in the research and writing of this book. I have many friends and colleagues—the two are not mutually exclusive—to thank for their help over the years. I begin by thanking my editor, Douglas Mitchell, for his unwavering support of and confidence in me and my project. I am deeply indebted to those who have read and commented on the manuscript in its entirety or sections thereof: Mark Vail, Susan Tarcov, Nathan Tarcov, Clifford Orwin, Daniel Kapust, Walter Nicgorski, Michael Walzer, Dean Hammer, Michele Lowrie, Beth Theiss-Morse, David Estrin, Eugene Garver, Richard Kraut, the late Elaine Fantham, Jan Papy, Christina

Kraus, Julien Talpin, Philippe Urfalino, and Jane Mansbridge. I am grateful to Cary Nederman, Ben Fontana, the late Michael Leff, Elizabeth Asmis, Peter White, Joy Connolly, Bryan Garsten, Bob Hariman, Daniela Cammack, John McCormick, Richard Fallon, Kathleen Behme, Ben Laurence, Oliver Sensen, David Konstan, and Gordon Schochet for taking the time to talk and correspond about the ideas and arguments that appear in my book—sometimes in the context of conferences (the Annual Meeting of the American Political Science Association, the Midwest Political Science Association Annual Conference, and the Northeastern Political Science Association Annual Conference), oftentimes not. I also owe a debt of gratitude to Molly Rodin, Chiara Graf, Martin Baeumel, Leigh Hansen, and Rachel Hullett for their assistance in translating some of the primary sources.

Thanks are due to the individuals and their institutions for inviting me to present my work outside the typical venues for political scientists: Emanuel Richter, Rüdiger Voigt, Helmut König, and the *Zentrum für interdisziplinäre Forschung*, Universität Bielefeld, for inviting me to present at a conference on "Res publica und Demokratie: die Bedeutung von Cicero für das heutige Staatsverständnis," Bielefeld, Germany (2005); Filiz Katman and Aydin University for inviting me to present at the First International Deliberative Democracy Symposium, Istanbul, Turkey (2009); Bertjan Wolthuis, Wouter Werner, and Vrije Universiteit Amsterdam for inviting me to present at the Conference on World Legislation (2010); Elinor Ochs, the late Jennifer Jackson, and UCLA's Center for Language, Interaction, and Culture (CLIC) for inviting me to present at the interdisciplinary symposium on "Political Language and Crises of Democracy," Los Angeles (2013); Paula Cossart and Université de Lille III for inviting me to present at two meetings—the General Conference of the European Consortium for Political Research (ECPR), Bordeaux, France (2013); and a conference on "Participation et délibération au prisme de l'histoire" at *Maison de Sciences de l'Homme de de la Société*, Lille, France (2013).

I acknowledge the Earhart Foundation for their generous grant, which allowed me to use my full sabbatical year to work on my book. I also acknowledge my home institution, Tulane University, its School of Liberal Arts, and Dean Carole Haber for awarding me the Lurcy Grant and the Sizeler Professorship, which facilitated the writing of this volume. I relied on several libraries for my research, primarily Tulane University's Howard-Tilton Memorial Library, the University of Chicago's Regenstein Library, and UCLA's Young Research Library. My ability to work effectively at the latter two libraries was assisted by my being granted visiting scholar status by the University of Chicago and UCLA, and by the help of my faculty sponsors at these universities—Nathan

Tarcov and the late Iris Marion Young (University of Chicago) and David Rapoport (UCLA). In addition, the staff at these libraries deserve credit for their assistance, especially the Regenstein's Vicki Burwell-Rankin, who provided me with a comfortable faculty study in which to research and write.

Substantial portions of four chapters originally appeared as journal articles. I am grateful to the journals, their editors, and their presses for the permission granted to incorporate these materials into the book. A version of chapter 1 appeared as "Rhetoric, Emotional Manipulation, and Political Morality: The Modern Relevance of Cicero vis-à-vis Aristotle," *Rhetorica: A Journal of the History of Rhetoric* 31 (2013): 402–43. Copyright © 2013, University of California Press.

A version of chapter 3 appeared initially as "Rhetoric as a Balancing of Ends: Cicero and Machiavelli," *Philosophy and Rhetoric* 42 (2009): 1–28. Copyright © 2009. This article is used by the permission of the Pennsylvania State University Press.

A version of chapter 4 appears as "Justus Lipsius, Morally Acceptable Deceit and Prudence in the Ciceronian Tradition," *History of Political Thought* 37 (2016): 238–70. Copyright © 2016, Imprint Academic.

A version of chapter 5 appeared originally as "The Classical Orator as Political Representative: Cicero and the Modern Concept of Representation," *Journal of Politics* 72 (2010): 1063–82. Copyright © 2010, Cambridge University Press.

I am indebted to friends, whose support was more moral than academic.

I have shared an apartment in Chicago for several summers with my friend Heather Vincent, a classicist whose company and bonhomie during my most difficult periods enabled me to focus on my work and not my loneliness. I have had the good fortune to find a group of friends in Chicago who belong to the Lake Shore Drive Synagogue. I am grateful to all my newfound friends at the synagogue for their camaraderie and, especially, Walter and May March for hosting me and the guys for drinks and snacks on Friday afternoons. I have only recently finished reciting Kaddish for my father of blessed memory. Although Jewish tradition requires the mourner to recite Kaddish at morning, afternoon, and evening services, a close friend of both my father and me, Aviad Tabory, assumed my responsibility to recite Kaddish for the afternoons and evenings of summer 2015, thereby permitting me to complete the first draft of the book before teaching resumed.

Finally, there is my family. I am grateful for the encouragement I received from my sister, Rebecca Alexander, and my brother-in-law, Sam Alexander. I offer my sincerest thanks to my mother and late father for the full range of help they provided. The innocent victims of my book-induced moodiness were those with whom I share a home. I thank my children—Jordan, Tova, Amos, Gerhardt, and Ezra—for tolerating me when I was intolerable and for supporting me in my work even when doing so was against their interests. Finally, I wish to single out my wife, Toni, who was both the greatest victim and the most unflagging supporter of my research and writing. Her love and patience, her willingness to allow me to devote myself single-mindedly to my work while she assumed all other responsibilities, including the thankless job of prodding me to work when I wanted to avoid working, have made this book possible. Thus, I dedicate *Ethics and the Orator* to her and my parents.

Politics and politicians have long been condemned as immoral. Thus, some twenty-five hundred years ago, Plato deemed politics evil and judged its practitioners (in contrast to true statesmen) responsible for corrupting rather than morally improving their citizenry (Wolin 2004, 39).[1] Instead of hailing the political heroes of ancient Athens—Themistocles, Pericles, and Cimon—for their contributions to their polis, Plato savages them for manipulating and playing on the desires and opinions of the citizens: "They had never risked the loss of power and esteem by attempting to transmute popular wants and opinions into something loftier; nor had they been willing to impose a correct but unpopular policy" (41; Plato 1979, 515c–522a). Paradoxically, as Sheldon Wolin observes, Plato tasked political philosophy, whose objective was the creation of the good society, with ridding the community of politics (Wolin 2004, 39).[2]

As recent opinion polls indicate, today's politics and politicians are not regarded more highly by the public.[3] In Great Britain, for example, a survey by Ipsos MORI reports that the public believes "[p]oliticians are now the group of professionals least likely to tell the truth. . . . Only 13% of people trust politicians to tell the truth . . . , while 82% think they do not tell the truth. . . . That 13% score is the worst MPs have recorded in the poll's twenty-six-year history and means they are now the group people most mistrust" (*The Guardian*, September 27, 2009). Results of current polling in the United States reflect similar attitudes.[4]

Ironically, if the current public is especially mistrustful of politics and politicians, an increasing number of scholars, beginning in the 1970s with the publication of Michael Walzer's seminal article "Political Action: The Problem of

Dirty Hands" (1973), have defended the morality—or at least the moral neces- sity—of politicians engaging in activities that are ordinarily judged as morally unacceptable. Walzer and other like-minded political thinkers[5] have argued that doing the right thing politically (and in a certain sense morally) requires politicians to dirty their hands when the consequences demand it. To use an example from Walzer, a politician who authorizes the torture of a captured rebel leader, "convinced that he must do so for the sake of the people who might otherwise die in the explosions," commits a moral crime. Yet Walzer maintains that this same politician, if he acknowledges and bears his guilt, is a *moral politician*: "Here is the moral politician: it is by his dirty hands that we know him. If he were a moral man and nothing else, his hands would not be dirty; if he were a politician and nothing else, he would pretend that they were clean" (1973, 166–68).

In the decades following Walzer's initial discussion of "dirty hands," a host of books and articles have appeared that, despite their profound differences in method, focus, and outlook, share the common position that absolutist moral- ism in politics is not tantamount to moral politics.[6] Without reaching a consen- sus on how to arrive at a balance between what Ruth Grant (1997) terms "an unethical pragmatic realism on the one hand and a principled idealism (unethi- cal too in its political irresponsibility) on the other" (4), these authors agree that political morality demands *both* political practicality and moral commitment.[7] For example, many of the essays in Stuart Hampshire's edited work *Public and Private Morality* (1978b) and in Paul Rynard and David P. Shugarman's ed- ited book *Cruelty and Deception: The Controversy over Dirty Hands in Politics* (2000) build on (though sometimes take issue with) Walzer's account of "dirty hands" to defend a pragmatic political morality.[8] C. A. J. Coady's *Messy Moral- ity: The Challenge of Politics* (2008) upholds the relevance of morality in politics while justifying the need, at times, to depart from conventional morality, for example, by lying. Michael Ignatieff's *The Lesser Evil: Political Ethics in an Age of Terror* (2004) considers how democracies can combat terrorism success- fully without abandoning their morality. As Ignatieff explains, "I try to chart a middle course between a pure civil libertarian position which maintains that no violations of rights can ever be justified and a purely pragmatic position that judges antiterrorist measures solely by their effectiveness" (viii). And Avishai Margalit's *On Compromise and Rotten Compromises* (2010) vindicates a range of political compromises that under ordinary circumstances would be immoral, like Churchill's decision in World War II to side with Stalin against Hitler, even though both were mass murderers. Churchill's choice to align Great Brit- ain with Stalin's Soviet Union was morally correct under the circumstances,

Margalit explains, "because Hitler's evil was radical evil, undermining morality itself. Stalin's monstrous evil was different, and Churchill correctly sensed the difference" (177–98).

The writings listed above make their case for greater moral flexibility in politics without substantially incorporating the arguments of earlier political thinkers.[9] Other authors, however, have composed books suggesting the need for a more realistic outlook on politics and morality that embed their own views within their analyses of previous political thinkers' works. Take hypocrisy as an example. Hypocrisy is widely regarded as a vice in "the forefront of political sins" (Shklar 1984, 48). But Ruth Grant and David Runciman have each composed books that take issue with this moralistic approach to hypocrisy, identifying their more accommodating attitude to political hypocrisy with distinct intellectual traditions.[10] Grant in *Hypocrisy and Integrity: Machiavelli, Rousseau, and the Ethics of Politics* (1997) groups Machiavelli and Rousseau together as representatives of an antiliberal tradition, which, contrary to the liberal tradition of Thomas Hobbes, John Locke, and Adam Smith, appreciates the need for political hypocrisy (177, 13). According to Grant, Machiavelli and Rousseau treat hypocrisy as more than a political expedient. For them, she contends hypocrisy plays a moral role in the polity as the respect vice pays to an unattainable virtue (13).

Runciman, in *Political Hypocrisy: The Mask of Power, from Hobbes to Orwell and Beyond* (2008), finds in the liberal tradition—the same tradition that, according to Grant, is implacably opposed to hypocrisy—a kind of defense of some varieties of hypocrisy. Identifying a (predominately English) liberal tradition regarding hypocrisy, which runs from Hobbes through Bernard de Mandeville, American Revolutionary writers (including Benjamin Franklin, John Adams, and Thomas Jefferson), Jeremy Bentham, the Victorians (Anthony Trollope, John Morley, and Henry Sidgwick), and George Orwell, Runciman explains that this tradition does a better job of distinguishing between beneficial and harmful forms of hypocrisy than does antiliberalism, which is inclined to deem hypocrisy uniformly immoral. Ironically, Runciman adopts the "liberal" stance—for Grant, it was the antiliberal stance—that hypocrisy as an act of concealment is "the tribute that vice pays to virtue" (10). Thus Runciman acknowledges that hypocrisy may be "a coping mechanism for the [inescapable] problem of vice itself, in which case it may be that hypocrisy is not a vice at all" (10).

Like most authors who adopt a morally pragmatic approach to politics, Grant and Runciman do not substantially associate their arguments with thinkers before Machiavelli.[11] But a problem with restricting one's purview to

modernity or even to the Renaissance and beyond is that age-old strains between politics and morality *and* the enduring attempts to reconcile them are
ignored. Political theorists long before the sixteenth century recognized that,
when dealing with politics, the best that can be hoped for is, in Coady's words, a
"messy morality"—messy, at least, when compared with the absolutist morality
commonly associated with Immanuel Kant. Recent studies of political morality,
even those that adopt a historical perspective, overlook the continuity of arguments made by theorists for over two thousand years—arguments emphasizing
prudential reasoning, decorum, and the balancing of the moral and beneficial—
that constitute a particular tradition within the history of political thought. As
I demonstrate in the present book, this tradition of pragmatic political morality
is grounded in the theory and practice of classical rhetoric, by which I mean the
art of persuasion developed by the Greeks and Romans of the classical period.
And the classical rhetorician who is chiefly responsible for initiating this tradition of pragmatic political morality is Marcus Tullius Cicero (106–43 BCE),
who explicates his conception of political morality in his rhetorical and philosophical writings, speeches, and letters.

   That the most long-standing and significant tradition defending the morality of real-life politics is derived from classical rhetoric should come as no
surprise. Politics and rhetoric in democratic Athens and republican Rome
were inseparable. In fourth-century Athens, *rhētōr* was the most common term
for orator *and* expert politician because the politician in democratic Athens
practiced his art *through* public speech, addressing the assembly frequently
and competing in political trials with other *rhētores* (Ober 1989, 105). In both
his *Rhetoric* (written ca. 330 BCE) and *Nicomachean Ethics*, Aristotle ties
rhetoric to politics, referring to rhetoric as "a certain kind of offshoot" (1991,
1.2) and a part of politics (1984b, 1094b1–5). And in republican Rome, Cicero
emphasizes the political nature of rhetoric and of its practitioner, the orator,
by "associat[ing] eloquence with the authority to determine public policy"
and by "fus[ing] the concept of the orator with that of the statesman" (Fantham 2004, 313). Accordingly, in the dialogue *De oratore* (written in 55 BCE),
Cicero has the interlocutor Crassus describe the ideal orator as "an author of
public policy, a guide in governing the community, and a leader who employs
his eloquence in formulating his thoughts in the Senate, before the people,
and in public court cases" (2001a, 3.63). Even while delivering legal speeches,
the Ciceronian orator is often engaging, de facto, in political oratory, given
the political character of Roman legal cases.[12] Thus, while the judicial genre
dominated Roman oratory and Cicero emphasized judicial rhetoric in his own

work, Roman forensic (judicial) speech was not easily distinguished from deliberative (political) speech.[13]

Rhetoric and politics are not only conjoined by their advocates, like Aristotle and Cicero, but by their critics too, most famously Plato. In the *Gorgias*, which remains the classic critique of rhetorical norms to this day, Plato condemns rhetoric *and* politics. As Brian Vickers explains, the attitude of the *Gorgias* to rhetoric cannot be divorced from its discussion of politics: "This is because . . . [i]n the *Gorgias* rhetoric is treated as subservient to politics, being indeed the main tool of politics in Athenian democracy" (Vickers 1988, 84). In this dialogue, Plato evinces his antipathy to both "the democracy of Athens . . . and to the medium which sustained that system—the oratory of the *rhetores* or public speakers in the Council, the Assembly, and the lawcourts" (85). Similarly, Ryan Balot writes that through their conversation in the *Gorgias*, Socrates's speakers come to recognize a crucial Platonic point: "To investigate rhetoric is also to explore the nature and ends of political debate, the aspirations of political leaders, and the relationship between politics, ethics, and philosophy" (2006, 191).

Among the major moral problems encountered in politics and rhetoric are manipulation, deception,[14] violence, and hierarchy. The definitions and explanations of these concepts that I provide are not intended to be authoritative or exhaustive. Instead, they are offered to clarify how these concepts will be used in this book. Thus, manipulation may be said to arise "when (1) agent A uses hidden or irrational force to affect agent B's choices and (2) agent A acts intentionally" (Klemp 2011, 59–60). I take deception to involve "intentionally or negligently causing someone to believe something that the deceiver knows or should know to be false" (Gutmann and Thompson 2006, 72).[15] Manipulation may often be seen as a subset of deception, although an audience may sometimes knowingly consent to being manipulated (Garver 1994, 161). What distinguishes manipulation from generic deception is that deception is "typically a defensive, protective strategy; it is intended to deflect others from interfering with your plans." Manipulation, however, is more offensive in the sense that "it is intended to induce others to do your bidding" (Gutmann and Thompson 2006, 160). Although violence is generally defined as "the deliberate exercise of physical force against a person" or property (*Oxford English Dictionary*, 3rd. ed.), the violence discussed in this book is of the sort that is usually deemed immoral (e.g., torture) but is considered defensible, by some, under exceptional situations. (It is the violence of "dirty hands.") By hierarchy I mean the unequal structural relationship between politician and ordinary citizen, which supplies the former political power unavailable to the latter.

That the first three classifications of morally dubious or condemnable actions (manipulation, deception, and violence) are commonly associated with politics is indicated by Amy Gutmann and Dennis Thompson, who highlight this association by devoting separate chapters in their casebook *Ethics and Politics: Cases and Comments* (2006) to each aforementioned category—"the morally questionable means that are most commonly used in the political process" (xi). Like Gutmann and Thompson, I accept that a broad consensus exists condemning the speech and actions included in the initial three categories, at least under ordinary circumstances.[16] Gutmann and Thompson, however, do not discuss asymmetry between politicians and regular citizens. Although no consensus exists opposing the immorality of political hierarchy per se, there is wider agreement against the perceived immorality of a certain kind of political hierarchy—that is, an asymmetrical political system that denies its citizens the de facto opportunity to engage in political discussion and to affect political decision making.[17]

As with the previous three categories, I do not present a fully developed criticism of political hierarchy here. Rather, I focus more on how the arguments asserting the immorality of all four categories—manipulation, deception, violence, and hierarchy in politics—are linked, either explicitly or implicitly, to the critique of rhetoric's immorality. (Showing that rhetoric is criticized, however, entails also shedding light on why rhetoric is criticized.) And just as the criticism of political immorality is exhibited in the reaction to rhetoric so, too, the defense of politics against charges of immorality is grounded in rhetoric, especially Ciceronian rhetoric. Before outlining the rhetorical case for the morality of politics, however, we shall first turn to the arguments against rhetorical immorality.

THE CASE AGAINST RHETORIC

In the *Gorgias*, Plato portrays Socrates as attacking rhetors for emotionally manipulating their hearers through flattery and providing "gratification and pleasure," which yields bad consequences for the people. Rhetorical manipulation does not instruct audiences about "the just and unjust," instead substituting the "apparent good" for the true good (Plato 1979, 447a–466a).[18] And though we are likely to differ with Plato about which goods (consequences) orators deny their audiences (i.e., most people today would probably disagree with Plato that orators are guilty of denying their listeners knowledge that would better their souls), we are likely to accept Plato's more general claim that politicians emotionally manipulate audiences into making bad decisions about what is good for their members. Instead of identifying the bad consequences of emotional manipulation with ignorance of abstract truths, we today might say that politicians' emotional appeals sometimes lead to negative consequences, for example, citizens voting against their economic interests or adopting political positions that conflict with their deeply held convictions.

Rhetoric, as Plato has Socrates describe it in the *Gorgias*, is irrational, lacking any "rational account (*logos*) by which it applies the things it applies . . . , so that it cannot say what is the explanation of each thing"; it is not a craft or art (*techne*), Socrates says, because it is "unreasoning (*alogon*)" (465a). Not bound by rational argument, orators can argue as easily for falsehood as for truth, for right as effortlessly as for wrong. And they are likelier to deceive than tell the truth because the *demos*, to whom they cater, would rather hear lies that reinforce their pursuit of the appetites than uncomfortable truths (517b).[19]

Socrates categorizes both rhetoric and cookery as knacks of "producing pleasure and gratification" (462c–e). Although rhetoric, like cookery, conceals itself as a craft (465d), it is actually "crooked, *deceptive*, mean" (465b); it "lures and *deceives* foolishness with what is pleasantest at the moment," denying its listeners knowledge of the just and unjust (464d; emphasis added).[20] Deluding Athenians into believing that rhetoric is the cause of their city's greatness, the illustrious practitioners of this knack have instead, Socrates relates, left the city "swelling and festering," bereft of justice and temperance, but "full of harbours and dockyards and walls and tribute and that sort of rubbish" (518e–519a).

While Plato considers the consequences of rhetorical manipulation and deception, Kant criticizes only the inherent wrongs of manipulation and deceit, which he knowingly attributes to rhetoric, and of violence, which he implicitly connects to rhetoric. As we shall see interspersed through the book's chapters, rhetoric is predisposed to evaluate the morality of means by their ends. Thus, public speakers employ a panoply of oratorical means—many regarded as ethically dubious—to persuade their audiences. Moreover, in aiming to best their opponents, orators treat their hearers as means to that goal. Victoria Kahn (1994) elucidates this morally questionable side of rhetoric in speaking of Machiavelli's deeply rhetorical politics, which emphasizes the tension between a morally neutral, instrumental rhetoric and a prudential rhetoric subordinated to ethics. Although Machiavelli chose the former over the latter (contrary to Cicero, as we shall see in chapter 3), the Florentine's rhetorical politics underscores the moral problems intrinsic to rhetoric—its tensions between means and ends, "its ethical indeterminacy, its concern with success, its use for the purpose of force and fraud, violence and misrepresentation" (1994, 8–9).

Kant's absolutist moral framework stands diametrically opposed to rhetoric's justification of employing immoral means for beneficial, even noble, ends.[21] In the *Critique of the Power of Judgment* (2000), Kant terms rhetoric *Beredsamkeit*, which also denotes "a practice that entails manipulation" (Stroud 2014, 41–43; Kant 2000, 5:327). He indicts rhetoric there as the "art of deceiving by means of beautiful illusion (as in *ars oratoria*)" (2000, 5:327). And he accuses rhetoric of "bring[ing] to bear the machinery of persuasion, which, since it can also be used for glossing over or concealing vice and error, can never entirely eradicate the deep-seated suspicion of artful trickery" (5:327).

Because rhetoric manipulates and deceives its audience, it violates Kant's "Formula of Humanity," which expresses our duty to act respectfully toward the freedom of others or even ourselves: "*So act that you use humanity, in your own person as well as in the person of any other, always at the same time as an end, never simply as a means*" (Kant 2011, 4:429; emphasis in original). Treating persons as means and not ends presupposes that "we respect the freedom of others in our actions. . . . Acting in accord with this formula demands that we act towards others in ways they could assent to" (Klemp 2011, 76). For Kant, freedom is connected with our ability to choose our ends and to reason for ourselves (76). Like Locke and Rousseau before him, Kant believes that for an act to be considered moral, it must be freely chosen. Rhetoric, however, treats listeners as means, depriving them of their autonomy. It seeks "to win minds over to the advantage of the speaker before they can judge and to rob them of their freedom" (2000, 5:327). Commenting on the orator's denial of the listener's autonomy, particularly through manipulation, Kant confesses that "reading the best speech of a Roman popular speaker or a contemporary speaker in parliament . . . has always been mixed with the disagreeable feeling of a deceitful art, which understands how to move people, like machines, to a judgment in important matters which must lose all weight for them in calm reflection" (5:327–28).[22] Alluding to rhetoric's treatment of listeners as means and not ends, Kant blames rhetoric for "taking someone in for the advantage of someone else" (5:327). Likewise, speaking not of the orator but of "someone who has it in mind to make a lying promise to others," Kant presumes that this deceiver "will see at once that he wants to make use of another human being *merely as a means*, who does not at the same time contain in himself the end" (Kant 2011, 4:429–30; emphasis in original).[23]

In appendix I to *Perpetual Peace: A Philosophical Sketch*, Kant tackles the question of violence (as dirty hands). He does not directly address the question in terms of rhetoric but in relation of means to ends—an important element in the debate over the morality of rhetoric. There he contrasts the moral politician ("someone who conceives of the principles of political expediency in such a way that they can co-exist with morality") with the political moralist ("one who fashions his morality to suit his own advantage as a statesman") (Kant 1991, 118). Kant does not believe all violence is immoral. Even the moral politician may engage in violence: Kant approves killing in a "just" war, and he backs capital punishment for murder (Hill 1997, 105–6). Rather than condemn violence per se, he denounces immoral violence that the political moralist might justify by its acceptable end. For Kant, no means that contravene a moral duty are justifiable, even if the end is itself a moral duty.

Thus, he observes: "For morality, with regard to its principles of public right (hence in relation to a political code which can be known *a priori*), has the peculiar feature that *the less it makes its conduct depend upon the end it envisages (whether this be a physical or moral advantage), the more it will in general harmonise with this end*. And the reason for this is that it is precisely the general will as it is given *a priori* . . . which alone determines what is right among men" (1991, 123; emphasis added). Consistent with this observation, Kant elucidates the meaning of the proverb *fiat iustitia, pereat mundus*, "Let justice prevail even if the world perish." Contra rhetoric's focus on ends, he adopts an absolutist position on political action. Explicating the proverb on justice, he states: "This proposition simply means that whatever the physical consequences may be, the political maxims adopted must not be influenced by the prospect of any benefit or happiness which might accrue to the state if it followed them, *i.e., by the end which each state takes as the object of its will* [emphasis added] (as the highest *empirical* principle of political wisdom); they should be influenced only by the pure concept of rightful duty, i.e. by an obligation whose principle is given *a priori* by pure reason" (123–24). For Kant, the moral ends that direct the political moralist's violent (immoral) means can redeem neither him nor his actions. (The political moralist treats "the problems of political, international, and cosmopolitan right as mere *technical* tasks" [122].) In contrast, by bending his knee before right—including the apparently beneficial use of violence—the moral politician, like his politics, "may hope in return to arrive, however slowly, at a stage of lasting brilliance" (125).

For the critique of rhetoric as creating an unjust hierarchy between speaker and audience, we return again to Plato's *Gorgias*. As Peter Euben (1997) interprets the *Gorgias*, Socrates, though a critic of democracy, rejects the asymmetry between speaker and audience that typifies political oratory. In the dialogue, Plato uses Socrates to criticize the orator as a demagogue, that is, as a leader who pretends to be a friend of the people, while secretly despising them. And this criticism of the orator qua demagogue raises questions about rhetoric's elitism—questions that are morally troubling for contemporary democrats who define equal political participation as a moral requirement.[24] Plato points up rhetoric's elitism through his characterization of Callicles. As a politician in a democracy, Callicles must rely on the common people for support; he gains their favor by gratifying them, without making them better. Although he needs the people, Callicles makes plain his disdain for them. He refers to the masses as "a rabble of slaves and all sorts of people worth nothing, except perhaps in bodily strength" (Plato 1979, 489c). He accepts the superiority of a natural elite to rule over "the lower men" (1979, 490a). (Although Callicles's contempt for the masses may not reflect the feelings of most orators, his desire to manipulate the people into doing what he wants *is* typical of orators.) Callicles's example shows that, even in a democracy, the relationship between orator and audience is hierarchical. And Socrates, though he may criticize democracy, offers in his dialectic a model of conversation that is more egalitarian than rhetoric.[25] Euben gives voice to this perspective: "Rhetoricians and sophists tell people what they want to hear as a way of gaining power over them" (1997, 215). In contrast to rhetoricians, who place themselves above the people, Socrates attempts "to educate every Athenian to be a leader" (215).[26] Oratory is performed *before* the public, not *by* the public, but dialectic can be taught and practiced by everyone (215).

THE *CICERONIAN* TRADITION OF POLITICAL MORALITY

Having just presented the critique of rhetoric as the cause of political immorality, we shall now reflect on the defense of rhetoric as the cause of political morality. But which defense of rhetoric? Like Bryan Garsten, who eschews the ancient sophists' vindication of rhetoric in his masterful defense of rhetoric and judgment, *Saving Persuasion* (2006), I too shall avoid their justification of rhetoric in my present work, *Ethics and the Orator: The Ciceronian Tradition of Political Morality*.[27] As Garsten correctly notes, the sophists seem to have praised rhetoric unreservedly, without taking the moral critique of rhetoric seriously (2006, 13, 19). Garsten turns instead to Aristotle and Cicero, whom he perceives as more sober proponents of rhetoric "who both reflected on the limited power of speech and on the harm that orators and demagogues could do and who therefore devoted attention to domesticating persuasion as well as accommodating it" (13).[28]

Unlike Garsten, however, I center my book on Cicero's and not Aristotle's rhetorically based defense of political morality—not the obvious choice, as we shall soon see. Over the last thirty years, Aristotle's *Rhetoric* has emerged as the central classical figure in the quest to integrate rhetoric and politics with ethics (Leff 1993). Much of the recent scholarly literature on Aristotle's *Rhetoric* responds to Plato's attack on rhetoric in the *Gorgias*.[29] Although scholars reading the *Rhetoric* as a rejoinder to Plato's criticisms differ significantly in their interpretations of Aristotle's response, many, perhaps most, accept that Aristotle succeeds in giving an account of rhetoric (contrary to Plato) as an ethically defensible art. We shall now review some of the primary responses to the moral difficulties of rhetoric and, by implication, politics that are attributed to Aristotle. William Grimaldi denies that Aristotle's rhetoric is a form of manipulation by arguing that for Aristotle, as for the ancient Greek rhetoricians more generally, rhetoric "is centered on the character, nature, and use of language as the vehicle of communication" (Grimaldi 1972, 1). Rather than being indifferent to the truth, Grimaldi argues that rhetoric prevents us from making wrong judgments and in doing so "protects truth and justice" (Grimaldi 1978, 176). According to Grimaldi, "Aristotle is saying quite pointedly [that rhetoric] is supposed to re-present the real (i.e., truth and justice) in any situation for an auditor" (176).

While Grimaldi vests Aristotle's rhetoric with intrinsic moral significance, other writers deny that the Stagirite conceives of rhetoric as moral in itself. Instead, they argue, his rhetoric, as an art, possesses its own artistic (as opposed to moral) rules, which increase the likelihood that rhetoric will be practiced, de facto, morally. For example, Eugene Garver (1994), Mary Margaret McCabe (1994), and Garsten (2006, 115–41) interpret Aristotle as focusing his rhetoric qua art on argumentation rather than winning, which excludes manipulation from the *art* of rhetoric.[30] Similarly, Troels Engberg-Pedersen (1996) contends that the moral status of Aristotle's rhetoric is partially shielded from accusations of manipulation and deception because of Aristotle's assumptions that rhetoric's purpose is *Wahrheitsfindung*, that is, truth finding, *and* that, "speaking generally, the truth and the better are by nature more convincing" (128). Thus Engberg-Pedersen concludes that, taken by itself, Aristotelian "rhetorical skill is morally neutral" and that "it can be used morally badly without detriment to its intrinsic character," but that it is also a "genuine good" because "it helps to find the true and the good" (130).

A growing number of scholars vindicate rhetoric by pointing to the parallels between the rhetorical process, as delineated in the *Rhetoric*, and the process of practical wisdom (*phronesis*), as explained in the *Nicomachean Ethics* (Leff 1993, 318): "Rhetoric is the counterpart in the realm of speech to what *phronesis* is in the realm of *praxis*" (Beiner 1983, 88). Lois Self (1979) takes note of the similarity between rhetoric and *phronesis* by observing that Aristotle uses the same word, *bouleusis*, "to characterize the process of deliberation in the *Rhetoric* as he uses to describe the faculty of the man of practical wisdom in the *Nicomachean Ethics*"—a word that may also be translated as "to counsel" (137).

Because Aristotle asserts, in the *Nicomachean Ethics*, that "it is impossible to be practically wise without being good" (1984b, 1144a36–37), his linking of rhetoric to practical wisdom suggests to some that rhetoric partakes of the moral quality of practical wisdom (Self 1979, 143). Moreover, because "[p]ractical wisdom is the only excellence peculiar to the ruler" (1984c, 1277b26–29), the nexus between rhetorical and political morality is underscored.[31] The orator/politician possessing practical wisdom is characterized, above all, by "his ability to deliberate well." Therefore, "it is apparent that he would be able to marshal the arguments necessary for effective deliberative oratory—to 'counsel' audiences toward *right choices*" (137; emphasis added). Likewise, Ronald Beiner explains that Aristotelian *phronesis* is to be found in the orator, who in choosing the appropriate manner of speech, "*shows himself to be a man of moral purpose*, and a man of judgment" (1983, 87, 97; emphasis added). And Christopher Johnstone (1980), who identifies rhetoric's function, for Aristotle, as "guiding practical decisions and hence join[ing] [rhetoric] with the activities of deliberation and practical judgment" (5–6), finds, in Aristotle's treatment of rhetoric, "a vital link between the exercise of moral virtue and excellence in persuading" (10).

If rhetorical calculation is analogous to practical wisdom, as these authors contend, then the *rhetor*, like the *phronimos* (the person of practical wisdom), is well equipped to judge how best to speak or act morally according to circumstance. The rhetor's practical judgment would enable the orator/politician to determine the moral means of engaging in violence—in Garsten's words, "to respond to each situation in all of its particularity" (2006, 115)—despite the general moral prohibition against certain forms of violence like torture. Although Kant would have rejected such situational reasoning, Aristotle's rhetorical and ethical deliberation concerning particulars, as described by these authors, might appeal to an audience for whom Kant's absolutism is untenable.[32]

And what of the asymmetry between speaker and audience that critics of rhetoric find morally objectionable? For some proponents of Aristotle, no such asymmetry exists in Aristotle's rhetorical situation. As Danielle Allen (2004) interprets Aristotle, "the hierarchical model is nowhere to be found in the *Rhetoric* as example, explanation, or justification for the art of rhetoric; persuasion is treated solely as the speech of a friend" (142).[33]

Returning again to the charge that rhetoric is manipulative, we find that one of the fundamental reasons why many contemporary scholars embrace

Aristotle as *the* defender of a moral political rhetoric is his stance concerning the emotions. Particularly in the *Rhetoric*, Aristotle's response to the immorality of emotional manipulation is his cognitive approach to the emotions, in which thought or belief is construed as the efficient cause of emotion (Fortenbaugh 1975, 17). "In Aristotle's view, emotions are not blind animal forces, but intelligent and discriminating parts of the personality, closely related to beliefs of a certain sort, and therefore responsive to cognitive modification" (Nussbaum 1996, 303). By grounding emotion in thought, Aristotle rejects the dichotomy of reason and passion that has dominated post-Cartesian philosophy in the West (Konstan 2006, 43). And for votaries of Aristotle, this joining of emotion with reason obviates the irrationalism that often gives rise to emotional manipulation (see Garsten 2006, 238n24; Klemp 2011, 68–69).

By pairing Aristotle and Cicero in his defense of rhetoric, Garsten suggests sufficient consistency between the two to develop a single antidemagogic theory of political persuasion.[34] In choosing to present a theory of political morality derived from Cicero's, not Aristotle's, rhetoric, however, I focus more on their differences than similarities, finding Cicero—because of some of these differences—a more suitable source for a rhetorically based political morality than Aristotle. Nevertheless, I acknowledge the substantial similarities between the two classical rhetoricians, which include their connecting politics with rhetoric, their shared belief in the essential morality of politics, their common affirmation that rhetoric can be used morally, and their linking the political virtue of *phronesis* or prudence to rhetoric.

Why Cicero not Aristotle? Although Aristotle's *Rhetoric* is commonly seen today as *the* major text in the tradition of classical rhetoric, Cicero's rhetorical writings were far more influential from antiquity through modernity—at least through the late nineteenth century.[35] And unlike Aristotle who was a philosopher disengaged from political activity, Cicero was both a political thinker *and* a politician—for example, he was elected as consul, the highest office in the Republic, at the youngest possible age—suggesting the possibility, even probability, that Cicero's conception of political morality was more affected by the practice of politics than was Aristotle's political ethics. Nevertheless, although suggestive, neither the longevity of Cicero's influence nor his role as a leading politician demonstrates his greater relevance for us today. The case for Cicero above Aristotle must be based on his ideas, not extraneous factors.

Let us revisit the question of the morality of rhetoric/politics. When I introduced the contemporary scholarship on Aristotle's rhetoric, I said that it presents his rhetoric as an "ethically defensible art," suggesting the possibility that rhetoric is not intrinsically an "ethical art." Although some writers, like

Grimaldi, recognize Aristotle's rhetoric as inherently moral, most scholars—even those who read the *Rhetoric* as offering an ethically defensible art, like Garver, Garsten, and Engberg-Pedersen—situate Aristotle's ethics outside his rhetoric. Thus, for Garver and Garsten, Aristotle's rhetoric has artistic norms, which are not themselves ethical norms. In Garver's words: "There is no ethics of rhetoric, there is only an ethics of rhetoricians, and that is just ethics itself" (1994, 229).[36]

The ethical neutrality of Aristotle's *Rhetoric* can be set within the context of Richard Lanham's division between "weak" and "strong" defenses of rhetoric (1993, 155–56). As Michael Leff explicates Lanham's distinction, the weak defense is instrumental and ethically neutral; good rhetoric is distinguishable from bad, but not because of anything "intrinsic to rhetoric" (1998, 62). And, Leff further states, "Aristotle offers one of the oldest and best known versions of this position." His ethics of rhetoric, according to Leff, "must come from sources outside the art, since the art deals with persuasion as an instrumental and not as an ethical force" (62).

The strong defense is a view of rhetoric in which priority is given to practice over theory. From the perspective of the strong defense, "ethical and political knowledge is not based in a priori, abstract truth but is formed through rhetorical engagement in concrete situations" (Lanham 1993, 166, 186–89; Leff 1998, 62–65). Like Leff, I identify Cicero as the exemplar of the strong defense. As we shall see through the book, this engagement with the concrete imparts a pragmatic bent to Cicero's approach to political morality, imposing a moral duty on the orator/politician to speak and act with decorum, that is, according to what is fitting to the given circumstance (Leff 1998, 61–88; Lanham 1993, 189; Cicero 1939b, 123).

I develop the argument for an intrinsic over an extrinsic rhetorical morality—for Cicero over Aristotle—in chapter 1, in relation to emotional manipulation. At first blush, Cicero appears to have less to tell us about the moral use of emotions in rhetoric than does Aristotle. In contrast to Aristotle, who reconciles reason and emotion, Cicero seems to set emotion against reason, openly praising the use of emotions to thwart rational decision-making. In *De oratore*, Cicero has the character Marcus Antonius, the interlocutor primarily charged with explicating the rhetorical emotions, affirm that "nothing in oratory . . . is more important than . . . for the audience itself to be moved in such a way as to be ruled by some strong emotional impulse rather than by reasoned judgment" (Cicero 2001a, 2.178).[37] Soon after, Antonius boasts that he acquitted a defendant, "not so much because the jurors were informed, but because their minds were affected" (Cicero 2001a, 2.201). It should not be surprising, then, that even though Garsten, in *Saving Persuasion*, devotes a chapter to Aristotle and a chapter to Cicero as still-relevant champions of rhetoric, he turns only to Aristotle for counsel on rhetorical appeals to emotions (Garsten 2006, 115–41). Likewise, Jakob Wisse (1989), though he views both Cicero and Aristotle as expounding a morally neutral rhetoric, concedes that Aristotle's *Rhetoric* "gives those who try to whitewash him more opportunities to confuse the issue" and that "less (uneasy) attempts at removing a suspicion of immorality have been made in the case of [Cicero's] *De oratore* than in that of the *Rhetoric*" (297). Even scholars such as Wisse, who consider Aristotle's rhetoric morally neutral, concede that it assumes the guise of morality vis-à-vis Ciceronian rhetoric—Cicero appearing less worthy of emulation for the emotional manipulation he recommends in *De oratore*.

Notwithstanding the widespread assumption that Aristotle forges a better relationship among rhetoric, the emotions, and political morality than Cicero, I propose in the first chapter that Cicero, not Aristotle, offers a more relevant account of the relationship among these terms.[38] As I demonstrate there, for Aristotle, rational but false arguments can also be used to induce emotions in an audience. Moreover, Aristotle's approach to emotional appeals in politics is, compared to Cicero's, static, unable to adapt to new political circumstances. Therefore, I submit that Cicero's approach to the rhetorical emotions, if given a fair hearing, will be more acceptable to a modern audience than Aristotle's because it is ethically based while also responsive to political realities. Cicero accommodates emotional appeals to circumstance based on his belief in decorum as a moral principle. The flexibility of the Ciceronian path allows it to be adapted to our present political state of affairs, as opposed to the Aristotelian approach, which cannot.

Although Aristotle has garnered the lion's share of interest among scholars seeking to unify politics, persuasion, and ethics, a not-insubstantial number of writers have recently turned to Cicero, rather than Aristotle, for his approach to the union of rhetoric, politics, and morality.[39] Not all writers who direct their attention to the morality of rhetoric in Cicero, however, believe that he succeeded in making rhetoric moral. For example, Michelle Zerba, in *Doubt and Skepticism in Antiquity and the Renaissance* (2012), points up what she characterizes as Cicero's "pantomimic morality" (particularly in his *De oratore*), that is, a morality that is only apparent, masking pretense and dissimulation (170–76).[40] Within the last decade, however, several books have been published devoted, in part, to what the authors see as Cicero's effective synthesis of rhetoric, politics, and morality. Three of the books are Garsten's *Saving Persuasion*, Joy Connolly's *The State of Speech* (2007), and her more recent *The Life of Roman Republicanism* (2015).[41]

Of these three books, Garsten's, superficially at least, most resembles my present work. Like my book, *Saving Persuasion* defends the morality of rhetoric cum politics from a Ciceronian perspective. Garsten develops his account of Cicero in a single chapter—the first half of his book is devoted to the modern attack on rhetoric advanced by Hobbes, Rousseau, and Kant, with chapters on Aristotle and Cicero dedicated to the prorhetorical case. Although *Saving Persuasion* may appear similar to my own book, the approaches differ significantly. First, Garsten's Cicero is a more morally congenial advocate of rhetoric than the Cicero presented in my study. As just seen, Cicero in *De oratore* presents himself, through his interlocutors, as much more manipulative than the Cicero that Garsten describes—for Garsten, Cicero was an orator who "did not agree with those who viewed oratory as nothing more than emotional manipulation and pandering demagoguery" (169). (Although Cicero viewed oratory as *something more* than emotionally manipulative, Cicero did not eschew emotional manipulation when he considered it a necessary means of persuasion.) *Pace* Garsten, the actual Cicero (as observed in his rhetorical works, orations, letters, and deeds) was prepared to engage in speech and behavior more immoral, by conventional standards, than the morally unobjectionable Cicero that appears in *Saving Persuasion*. Garsten's more ethically presentable Cicero does not require the same degree of moral justification for his speech and actions as is demanded of the more morally complicated Cicero depicted in these pages.

Second, Cicero's defense of rhetoric, à la Garsten, is not a strong defense. His defense, as Garsten presents it, is based not on ethical values intrinsic to rhetoric but on the importation of "a substantial set of firm moral and political convictions" from Stoicism, which could serve as "a source of guidance distinct from the immediate approval of his listeners and therefore [could provide] a check on the orator's natural tendency to pander" (2006, 143). As an Academic skeptic, Cicero asserted his right to appropriate other philosophies, including Stoicism, as he saw necessary. For Garsten, Cicero obtained from Stoicism—not from rhetoric—a moral framework that protected oratory from demagogy,[42] that is, Stoic moral ideals provided a deliberative space for orators and audience.[43]

Closer to my own examination of Cicero's conception of political morality than Garsten's is Connolly's analysis of Cicero in her magisterial *The State of Speech*. Although this book is about rhetoric and political thought in ancient

Rome and not solely about Cicero, *The State of Speech* focuses more on Cicero than on any other thinker. This book covers a range of themes that are contained in my book: decorum as a rhetorical norm (169–75); the "balanc[ing] of honor and interest, aristocratic dignity with popular approval, reason and emotional engagement" (76); and the mutual interaction of orator and audience (147). Like *Saving Persuasion* and my own book, *The State of Speech* is also concerned with the Ciceronian legacy, the possibility "that the Roman rhetorical tradition provides a model" for liberal democracy (193). (Additionally, she discusses an assortment of important themes that neither Garsten nor I examine—at least in detail—including gender, the body, performance, and the theater.) In contrast to Garsten, she seeks to link political ethics to their rhetorical roots. She maintains that, for Cicero, "rhetoric offers a more robust version of ethical education" than philosophy, while also recognizing that although rhetorical theory "makes strong claims to teach performative ethics, oratorical persuasion must also be flexible, changeable, contingent on circumstances" (267).[44] Moreover, she maintains that Cicero presents the *orator perfectus* as the ideal republican citizen, an ethical model for the political community (145). But Connolly's inquiry into the rhetorical roots of Ciceronian ethics, in *The State of Speech*, in contrast to mine, is not systematic. It would be difficult if not impossible to discern, in this work, a coherent account of Cicero's approach to political morality. Although this book concerns itself with the moral status of rhetoric and the Republic, the reader does not find much sustained attention given to Ciceronian political morality per se. In place of morality, Connolly more often speaks of moralism, which she treats as a smokescreen for power inequalities. Thus, she argues that moral judgment is the "mainstay of republican oratory" because it "conceals signs of instability in the political order" (58–59). Similarly, the "common norms of justice and morality agreed on in any given community"—for Cicero, "the bonds that link the *res publica*"— tend "to enable moral and political tyranny, at the hands of either the majority or a powerful minority" (137–38). Because Connolly does not investigate here Cicero's rhetorically based political morality methodically, we are left with little sense of the unity of Cicero's conception of political morality contained in, and assembled from, a broad spectrum of his writings, which are examined in detail in my book.

In *The Life of Roman Republicanism*, Connolly examines the significance of conflict in Cicero's conception of republicanism. Although Cicero is generally viewed as regarding political and social conflict as disadvantageous and morally evil—in contrast to that other republican, Machiavelli, who values conflict as beneficial (Machiavelli 1996, 1.4)—Connolly argues otherwise. Thus, in

The Life of Roman Republicanism, she expounds on Cicero's conviction that antagonism is both necessary and productive, a theme she introduces in her earlier *The State of Speech* (2007, 73). (Additionally, as in *The State of Speech*, Connolly does not focus solely on Cicero in her latest book—he shares space with Sallust and Horace, with chapters devoted to each of the two; nevertheless, as in her earlier book, Cicero is the dominant figure.) Her uncommon reading of Cicero highlights his relevance for politics today because of its implications for greater political inclusiveness—implications consistent with the understanding of Cicero I develop in the present book. Nonetheless, as I explain, what I see as Connolly's exaggeration of Cicero's defense of conflict leads her to reject any notion of a stable conception of moral consensus in Cicero, which is at odds with the account of Ciceronian political morality presented in *Ethics and the Orator*.

Connolly supports her case for Cicero's continued importance by rejecting the standard views of Cicero as an unambiguous advocate of concord based on the domination of the ruling classes (*concordia ordinum*) and as an uncomplicated "spokesman of conservative aristocratic privilege" (2015, 14)—views of Cicero that are, "to most modern readers, unsavory" (34). Instead, she proposes a construction of Cicero as an advocate of "unsettling institutions so that they do *not* become unyielding fortresses of elite domination" (35) and as espousing a rhetorical perspective that also welcomes the speech of "nontraditional members of the community, even 'the uninitiated'" (58).[45] (As in her previous book, her interpretation of Cicero is largely informed by his rhetorical outlook.) Similarly, Connolly states that though many critics have concluded that Cicero's orator serves as "a model for oligarchic domination, a driver of false consensus that enacts the will of the rich and noble senatorial order," she maintains that "his ideal orator devotes himself to a life of conflict. . . . He speaks to all, he speaks for those who have no voice" (159–60). Connolly does not deny that Cicero is a partisan of the senatorial elite, but he is more than that. Rather than simply siding with defenders of senatorial authority, she holds that Cicero conceives of political authority as "a product of communal recognition in an antagonistic context" (46). Likewise, she contends that "[s]enatorial domination is not authoritarian or eternal; it is one condition of agonistic confrontation" (161), representative of the rhetorical situation.

As I noted above, Connolly's claim that Cicero cannot be reduced to a mouthpiece for the elites is consistent with my book's viewpoint. Like Connolly, although I cannot disregard Cicero's political support for the ruling classes, I identify the significance of his political ideas chiefly in their significance for the citizenry at large—those of Ciceronian Rome *and* our own; as

Connolly notes, "my point is not Cicero's personal political commitments" (168). In line with Connolly, I point out in my conclusion that Cicero makes room for political conflict between his own side and that of his opposition, so long as the conflicting parties are both motivated by the well-being of the Republic. As I see it, Cicero's legitimation of political difference derives from the political community's moral consensus, which accepts the agonistic structure of public oratory. Consensus itself is Cicero's standard—moral and otherwise—because it is the community's agreement or sense (*communis sensus*) that orators rely upon when seeking to persuade their audiences. (See chapter 5.)

In *The Life of Roman Republicanism*, however, Connolly presents political and moral consensus as evanescent. For Connolly, class conflict negates any stable core of political-moral values approved by all (or nearly all) citizens of the Republic. And the Cicero to which she draws attention denies the reality of consensus in a republic divided by sociopolitical antagonisms. Thus, she sees her book as rebutting the widespread claim "that Cicero's thought holds as the main goal of politics the common good as articulated through a consensus made possible in conditions of concord" (26).[46] Connolly further suggests that we see freedom in Cicero not as "the formation of consensus but its opposite, the division of the community into parts, that is the common ground of the community" (33). Her focus on societal antagonism to the exclusion of communal consensus leads her to declare: "I am not interested in values but in the repertoire of strategies that make the perpetuity of contest easier to bear" (168). This rejection of consensual values in Cicero (and in the political actuality of late republican Rome) stands in opposition to a fundamental claim of my book, that Cicero proposes a conception of political morality based on community values. Though I do not deny that political morality develops, in part, through a process of conflict, I maintain that for Cicero (and for republican Romans) there is a core political morality that is largely stable at any specific point in time.[47] By core political morality, I do not suggest a set of ideals that the political community interprets univocally. These ideals "could be interpreted in widely divergent ways and brought forward to justify the most diverse policies" (Brunt 1988, 49). Disagreement about the specific meaning of moral ideals, however, does not negate consensus on these ideals. Liberty and equality, for example, are moral ideals in most societies today, despite being construed differently by opposing groups and individuals within each society. Daniel Kapust's *Republicanism, Rhetoric, and Roman Political Thought: Sallust, Livy, and Tacitus* (2011b) serves as an important corrective to Connolly's *The Life of Roman Republicanism* when Kapust points up that "Cicero's commonwealth is rooted in consensus—'a shared sense of justice reflected in the moral life and institutional arrangements of a society'" (104; Schofield 1995, 72, cited in Kapust 2011b, 104).[48] Similarly, Robert Morstein-Marx, a noted scholar of the late Republic, observes in his discussion of *contiones* in Ciceronian Rome,[49] "a broad consensus on fundamental republican values and principles reigned rather than conflict—an ideological consensus that might best be described as . . . 'contional' or even simply 'republican'" (2013, 43).

Now, after distinguishing *Ethics and the Orator* from several other recent books that treat the nexus between rhetoric, politics, and morality in Cicero's thought, I turn to address directly what *is* discussed in this book. The characteristics of Cicero's rhetorically grounded political morality examined in my book include the following: true rhetoric/politics as a moral activity; decorum (or prudence) as a moral imperative; decorum's roots in the sense of the community (*communis sensus*); the distinct moral status of the politician; the balancing of the demands of the moral (*honestum*) and the useful (*utile*); the (explicit or implicit) recognition that moral ends may sometimes justify the employment of ordinarily immoral means; the common benefit, especially the safety of the *res publica*, as the ultimate moral good; the use of argument *in utramque partem,* on either side of a question, to arrive at the probable truth and to facilitate change; and the determination of the proper equilibrium between the political liberty of the people, on the one hand, and the politician's obligation to counsel and lead the people, on the other hand. These elements of Cicero's political morality are not discrete but, as I show, interrelated.

While chapter 1 is concerned with Cicero's response to the moral problem of emotional manipulation, chapter 2 focuses on deception and, in particular, the problem of dirty hands associated with conventionally immoral violence. This chapter looks to Cicero's theory of the four *personae* in *De officiis* (written in 44 BCE) in laying out a doctrine of distinct political and nonpolitical morality, examining, specifically, how Cicero understands the distinctive morality of the politician in relation to the safety of the Republic. It further shows how the morality of the politician is rooted in decorum. Because decorum is grounded in the values of the political community, not the politician's own private opinions, the chapter concludes by considering the means by which the citizenry may sanction politicians' actions—ordinarily immoral—that are carried out under exceptional circumstances.

As the title of my book suggests, this work is not a study of only *Cicero's* political morality but of political morality in the *Ciceronian tradition*. Thus, in chapters 3 through 6, Cicero is not analyzed in isolation but in tandem with other political thinkers. The focus of chapters 4 and 5 is to explicate both

Cicero's ideas and the ideas of later thinkers who stand in the Ciceronian tradition, while the focus of chapters 3 and 6 is to elucidate this tradition by examining the ideas of Cicero and those outside the Ciceronian tradition. The tradition that I explain and largely defend is a tradition that remains faithful to the characteristics of Cicero's own conception of political morality, a tradition that espouses a morally pragmatic approach to politics.[50] I do not expect that members of this tradition adopt every characteristic that I associate with Cicero's own conception of political morality. I assume, instead, that theorists following in the Ciceronian tradition adopt the elements of Ciceronian political morality in varying degrees, suggesting, accordingly, their stronger or weaker relationship to the tradition.

Although Niccolò Machiavelli is usually juxtaposed with Cicero to emphasize their differences (Hulliung 1983, 28–29, 131–33, 195, 215; Kahn 1994; Barlow 1999), some contemporary scholars point up the similarities between their approaches to politics and morality (Jossa 1964; Colish 1978; Zerba 2012, 184–207). Though the influence of Roman republican, especially rhetorical, beliefs is common to both Cicero and Machiavelli, chapter 3 is intended to demarcate Ciceronian moral politics from Machiavelli's utilitarian politics, excluding Machiavelli from the Ciceronian tradition of political morality. The division between Cicero and Machiavelli on morality and politics is based on their distinct positions regarding the *honestum* and the *utile*: Cicero balances the moral and the beneficial; Machiavelli discards the moral while maintaining the useful. (Machiavelli's theory is pragmatic but not moral.) For Cicero, as opposed to Machiavelli, politics is truncated when it surrenders the duty to pursue the moral *and* the beneficial. By affirming an obligation to the *honestum* grounded on the moral sense of the community, Cicero adheres to the principle of decorum. By rejecting a political duty to the *honestum*, however, Machiavelli abandons decorum, which includes a responsibility to follow communal norms.

While Machiavelli stands outside the Ciceronian tradition of political morality, I show in chapter 4 that Justus Lipsius, another important political theorist of the Renaissance, stands squarely within the Ciceronian tradition. This interpretation of Lipsius, however, opposes the scholarly consensus in which Lipsius begins his humanist career as a Ciceronian who, during maturity, breaks with his youthful Ciceronianism, repudiating the Roman orator's moral politics for the Roman historian Tacitus's realist politics. Supporters of this account, however, have not actually compared the younger Lipsius's works with those of the middle-aged Lipsius. In this chapter, the younger and older Lipsius's attitudes toward Cicero's political and moral ideals are both evaluated, showing the Ciceronian continuity in Lipsius's attitudes to political morality. And a careful reading of Lipsius's mature political text, the *Politica*, substantiates his fidelity to the Ciceronian tradition of political morality. There, he embraces Cicero's defense of a political morality that judges political deception to be morally justifiable according to context.

Like other intellectual traditions, the Ciceronian tradition is not stagnant. Alasdair MacIntyre captures this idea of an evolving tradition when he writes that "when a tradition is in good order, when progress is taking place, there is always a certain cumulative element to a tradition" (MacIntyre 1984, 146). The rhetorical Cicero is ideally suited for conceiving of tradition as changeable. Because decorum is at the core of Cicero's rhetorical theory, he recognizes that the truth and, certainly, the form in which truth is expressed do not remain static. Desiderius Erasmus backs this interpretation of Cicero by identifying the true Ciceronian with someone, like Cicero, who "spoke in the best possible way in the age he lived in" (1986, 381). In the *Ciceronianus*, his critique of rigid and doctrinaire Ciceronians who aped Cicero's style in their own writings, Erasmus has one interlocutor, Bulephorus, ask the other interlocutor, Nosoponus, the following question: "[D]o you think the world as it is now has anything in common with the situation at the time when Cicero delivered his speeches?" Bulephorus continues: "Everything has been completely altered— religion, empire, government, constitution, law, customs, pursuits, even men's physical appearance" (1986, 383). Bulephorus concludes that, paradoxically, "[i]t may well be that the most Ciceronian person is the one least like Cicero, the person, that is, who expresses himself in the best and appropriate way, even though he does so in a manner very different than Cicero's, . . . considering that everything has been completely altered" (399).

Like Erasmus's Bulephorus, Lipsius decides, on Ciceronian grounds of decorum (or prudence), that his approach to political morality must reflect the changes in government and religion over the previous sixteen hundred or more years. Thus, Lipsius addresses the politics and morality of monarchies, not republics—consistent with his own time, if not our own. He also accommodates Cicero's political morality to a Christian or postclassical world. (Once again, Erasmus: "I won't have it that a man is speaking in Ciceronian manner, if, being a Christian, he speaks to Christians on a Christian subject in the way that Cicero, being a pagan, once spoke to pagans on non-Christian subjects" [392].) Therefore, Lipsius moderates pagan Rome's apotheosis of the political community, adjusting a morality that was communal, not individualistic, to a morality that shows greater respect for the individual.

Chapter 5 explores how Cicero fashions a condition of equilibrium between the prerogatives of the people and the orator-statesman, between the political rights of the *populus* and the orator-statesman's privileges of leadership and guardianship—Cicero's response to the criticism of rhetoric/politics as immorally hierarchical. We see in this chapter how representation and, specifically, the distinction between trustee and delegate are not modern concepts but have their roots in the Ciceronian conception of the orator as representative. Against the argument that representation is not a moral concept, chapter 5 illustrates how, for Cicero, the orator qua representative is both morally obligated to uphold the "sense of the community" and to act for the people's welfare. As in chapter 4, I delineate Cicero's ideas together with those of later Ciceronian thinkers in chapter 5—Edmund Burke, the authors of the *Federalist*, and J. S. Mill. Notwithstanding the difference between Cicero's orator not being formally elected and the modern representative being selected through suffrage, the chapter emphasizes the deeper similarities between the two. For example, both are expected to act prudently, and both are distinguished from ordinary citizens by their innate capacities as "natural aristocrats."

Although Cicero, Burke, the authors of the *Federalist*, and J. S. Mill sought to balance the powers of the people and politicians, power—exemplified by speech—was for them still dyadic, with communication divided between an (active) speaker and a (mostly, but not altogether, passive) audience. In chapter 6, however, the focus is on communication between ordinary citizens. The *dramatis personae* in this chapter are Cicero and the deliberative democrats, the latter who contend that democratic decision making is not fully legitimate without popular deliberation. Proponents of deliberative democracy would like to replace mass oratory (speaker opposite audience) with deliberation, which they envision as a kind of conversation between citizens. The deliberative democrats' conception of conversation is anticipated by Cicero's own conception of conversation, which is strikingly similar to the political discourse described by deliberative democrats some two millennia after Cicero. Unlike the deliberative democrats, however, Cicero does not hold up conversation as the primary model of political communication. In the second half of this chapter I consider why not. This question is answered by citing Cicero's own arguments supported by empirical evidence, which suggest that the ideals of deliberative democracy, while perhaps laudable in the abstract, do not comport with political experience—ancient or modern. Thus, like Machiavelli, the proponents of deliberative democracy stand outside the Ciceronian tradition of political morality. But, while Cicero's moral pragmatism for Machiavelli is insufficiently realist, for the deliberative democrats it possesses too little idealism.

Part of the goal of situating Cicero within a larger tradition is to highlight the continuing relevance of his ideas. But Cicero's contemporary relevance is complicated by his distance from our political world. Even the most cursory comparison of late republican Rome with current liberal democracies makes clear the profound differences between them. As opposed to present-day liberal democracies, the Republic excluded slaves and women from political participation, and the vote of working-class male citizens, relative to their wealthier counterparts, was diluted in Rome's legislative assemblies (Vishnia 2012, 127–29). Moreover, Cicero himself was, probably for most of us today, on the wrong side of the policy debates of the late Republic: he opposed virtually all land reform; he sided with the elite of wealth and birth against the common people; and he opposed the secret ballot because it weakened the control of the upper classes over the *populus*, acceding to the secret ballot only as a necessary evil foisted by the poor on the rich. How, then, can the deeply conservative Cicero—or his tradition—be viewed as relevant today when, contra Cicero, even contemporary ultraconservatives largely accept the principle of one person, one vote?

The answer, I believe, lies in distinguishing between Cicero and the Ciceronian tradition in general, and Cicero and the Ciceronian tradition on political morality. The fundamental elements of Ciceronian political morality have broad appeal, at least wider-ranging appeal than many of his pro-*optimate* political opinions.[51] Although Cicero does not separate his political positions into distinct categories or traditions, we who come after Cicero can speak of different Ciceronian traditions, his tradition of political morality being only one of them. For example, we might also recognize a Ciceronian tradition of republicanism, private property, natural law, and so on. The recognition of a specific political, moral, or rhetorical tradition (e.g., a particular tradition within a broader Ciceronian, Platonic, Aristotelian, or Tacitist tradition) depends on whether we can identify common principles that compose the specific tradition *and* whether subsequent thinkers (i.e., those succeeding Cicero, Plato, Aristotle, Tacitus, or other typically unwitting founders of traditions) participate in a conversation with the arguments of the tradition's founder and/or the related arguments of other "borrowers" from the tradition's founder.[52] What do I mean? As we shall see in chapter 4, when Lipsius explains his conception of political morality, he parts ways with Cicero on a range of issues—we might say that he turns away from other Ciceronian traditions—but he accepts the basic characteristics of Cicero's conception of political morality and develops his own viewpoint while in conversation with Cicero, as manifested in a host of citations from Cicero on the subject. And in chapter 5, Burke, the authors of the *Federalist*, and J. S. Mill are presented as part of the Ciceronian tradition of political morality because they too adopt the primary elements of that tradition and engage in conversation with the arguments they "borrowed" from Cicero, directly or indirectly.

Cicero was committed to Roman values, believing (like most Romans) that his nation's values were superior to those of other nations. Thus, when I present his conviction that decorum is rooted in the values of "the community" as one of the characteristics of Ciceronian political morality, Cicero himself would have understood those values to be Roman. But like all other political theorists writing in and for a different context than our own, Cicero must be untethered, to some extent, from his context-specific political and moral beliefs, if he is to be made relevant to different political and moral contexts. Therefore, political and moral traditions cannot be restricted to the specific content of even the tradition's founder, for example, by delimiting Ciceronian political morality by its adherence to the moral values of late republican Rome.

The centrality of decorum in Cicero's rhetorical, political, and moral thought—as noted by Erasmus—further legitimates extending the Ciceronian tradition beyond the content of distinctively Roman beliefs and values. Unlike other thinkers whose ideas *we* need to adapt to new conditions, Cicero is himself committed to adapting his own beliefs to different situations; his duty to speak and act with decorum requires him to accommodate his speech and action to conform to the requirements of context. From this perspective, it might be said that Cicero adheres to Roman values because that is what seemliness or decorum dictates (Cicero 1991a, 1.93; Kapust 2011b, 101–2) as much as because he has discovered, through impartial analysis, that Roman values embody the immutable truth. There is little reason to think that Cicero expected non-Romans to abandon their own mores for Roman mores. Presumably, even for Cicero, each nation has an obligation to obey its own values, not those of another nation.

Quintilian and John of Salisbury in the Ciceronian Tradition

Although I cannot demonstrate the longevity and robustness of the Ciceronian tradition of political morality in this single volume, I seek support for the tradition's endurance and vigor by turning, in this prologue, to the thought of Quintilian and John of Salisbury, who were profoundly influenced by Cicero. Although I do not analyze their works sufficiently to show the full extent of their participation in the Ciceronian tradition of political morality, I indicate their association with the tradition by pointing up their espousal of some of the key elements identified earlier with the tradition. I have intentionally chosen these examples from a period before the Renaissance because Cicero's influence is frequently expected to be weaker (or less genuinely Ciceronian) before the fourteenth and fifteenth centuries.[1] As Cary Nederman observes, "one commonly encounters some version of the claim that, until the dawn of the Renaissance, the full significance of Cicero's work was not, and perhaps could not be, adequately appreciated" (Nederman 1992, 76). Typical of this commonplace is Jerrold Seigel's view of the early-Renaissance humanists who, he explains, considered Cicero "the central figure of classical culture, the inspiration and guide for those who sought to return to the classical world" (Seigel 1968, 3). Therefore, I introduce pre-Renaissance Ciceronians to suggest what should be more widely known, at least in the academic world, that is, that the tradition of Ciceronian political morality also persists from Cicero's own time until the Renaissance or, as Nederman comments on Cicero's influence more generally, that "few educated individuals in the West between the end of the Roman Republic and the beginning of the *cinquecento,* regardless of intellectual orientation or spiritual commitment, escaped the impact of the Ciceronian tradition" (1992, 76).[2] Quintilian will, perforce, be discussed in greater detail than John of Salisbury, as Cicero's imprint on Quintilian is the more apparent. John's adoption of elements of Ciceronian political morality, however, will also be adumbrated.

Given the lengthy gap between Quintilian and John of Salisbury (about eleven hundred years), as well as that between John of Salisbury and Justus Lipsius, (about four hundred years), it is only reasonable to expect important political, moral, and religious differences between these writers. But by discussing Quintilian and John with some degree of specificity—followed by analyses in subsequent chapters of Lipsius, the authors of the *Federalist*, Edmund Burke, and J. S. Mill—we can also see the degree of commonality existing between the thinkers who constitute the Ciceronian tradition. Their shared conceptions of political morality indicate not only the common moral dilemmas faced by politicians since the classical period but also the similarly pragmatic manner in which Ciceronians from antiquity into the nineteenth century have responded to these dilemmas. That the Ciceronian responses to these dilemmas have been so durable implies that the tradition still has something to teach us today about the perennial ethical problems of politics—a theme that runs through *Ethics and the Orator*. We shall consider the contemporary relevance of the Ciceronian approach in the book's individual chapters but, more generally, in the conclusion to *Ethics and the Orator*.

Quintilian (ca. 40 CE–ca. 96 CE) is perhaps the thinker, besides Cicero himself, who best exhibits the characteristics of the Ciceronian tradition of political morality. He was a Roman citizen of Spanish birth, a teacher of rhetoric, living some one hundred years after Cicero, during the Julio-Claudian and Flavian imperial dynasties. Quintilian, for whom Cicero is the exemplary orator (Quintilian 2001d, 12.1.14; 2001a, 2.16.7; Kennedy 1969, 110–12), argues even more vocally than Cicero that rhetoric is an ethical art and that the orator is a moral figure, while defending, like Cicero, the orator's need to manipulate and deceive audiences.

Because Quintilian writes during the Imperial period when public political oratory like that practiced by Cicero is unfeasible, the focus of his twelve-volume rhetorical masterwork, the *Institutio oratoria* (published ca. 94 CE) is judicial oratory. Nevertheless, Quintilian still embraces Cicero's ideal of the orator as a statesman: "The man I am educating is . . . to guide the counsels of the senate or lead an erring people into better ways" (2001d, 12.1.25–26). Quintilian even holds out hope that the orator he is training will "be able to play the part of the real statesman not in private seminars but in the experience of and activity of real life" (2001d, 12.2.7–8; see also Kennedy 1969, 131–2).

Quintilian's orator, reflecting Cicero's paradigm, is (in the words attributed to Cato the Censor) a *vir bonus, dicendi peritus*, "a good man skilled in speaking" (2001d, 12.1.1). Quintilian emphasizes the moral virtue of the orator, especially in book 12 of the *Institutio* (Winterbottom 1964, 90–97; Brinton 1983, 167–84). Similarly, he defines rhetoric as *bene dicendi scientiam*, "the science of speaking well" (2001a, 2.15.34), which suggests not only effective but, more importantly, ethical speech (Mendelson 2002, 185).[3] But, like Cicero, Quintilian upholds the morality of the orator who must engage in conventionally immoral speech and behavior when it promotes good ends. Thus, he writes: "I am not arguing that the orator I am shaping will often have to do [what is ordinarily immoral], only that, if some such reason compels him to do so, the definition of an orator as 'a good man skilled in speaking' still holds good" (2001d, 12.1.44).

Quintilian justifies the orator's departures from traditional morality by evaluating the orator's unsavory means in terms of their noble ends and good intentions: "We, on the other hand, have to compose speeches for others to judge, often before people who are quite untrained and certainly ignorant of that sort of scholarship; and unless we can entice them with delights, drag them along by the strength of our pleading, and sometimes disturb them by emotional appeals, *we cannot make even a just and true cause prevail*" (2001b, 5.14.29; emphasis added). To those who allege "that rhetoric makes uses of vices, which no art does, in speaking falsehoods and exciting emotions," Quintilian responds: "neither of these is disgraceful *when done for a good reason*; therefore it is not a vice either" (2001a, 2.17.27–28; emphasis added). Likewise, echoing Cicero in *De officiis* (e.g., 1991a, 2.51), Quintilian asserts "that there are many actions which are made honourable or the reverse not so much because of what was done as because of the motive" (2001d, 12.1.36–37).

Quintilian is especially inclined to subordinate means to ends when the end in question is the political community's welfare or safety, which for Quintilian as for Cicero is the supreme moral standard. It is in the orator's role as defender of the state's well-being, whether as courtroom advocate or, ideally, statesman, that Quintilian recognizes his prerogative to act in conventionally immoral ways for the common interest—privileges denied ordinary citizens.[4] Quintilian's examples of morally justifiable deception abound. Orators may legitimately lie to defend someone who has conspired against a tyrant because the orator is benefitting the state (2001d, 12.1.40–41). Or, Quintilian asks, "suppose we know that certain acts, though naturally just, are *against the public interest* [inutilia civitati] *in the present circumstances*: shall we not use a skill in speaking which is indeed honourable, but which looks like dishonest practice?" (2001d, 12.1.41–42; emphasis added). Would it not also be permitted, Quintilian inquires, for an orator to do what he can to acquit a guilty general "without whom the state cannot defeat its enemies?" (2001d, 12.1.43). Moreover, he sanctions the defense of guilty parties who "can somehow be converted to a right way of thinking"; "it is more in the public interest [*communis utilitas*] that they should be acquitted than that they should be punished" (2001d, 12.1.42; see also 12.1.36–44; Ussani 2003, 295–301).

What of the other elements fundamental to Ciceronian political morality? Quintilian conceives of speaking or acting with decorum as a moral duty, arguing that "what is always and in all circumstances becoming [*deceat*] is to act and speak in an honorable way [*facere ac dicere honeste*]," while "it is never becoming for anyone ever to act or speak dishonorably in any circumstances" (2001d, 11.1.11–15; Mendelson 2002, 176–77; López 2007, 318). For Quintilian, like Cicero, decorum and morality are virtually indistinguishable (Cicero 1991a, 1.93–94), and the source of both is the values of the community. Writing during the late Republic, Cicero associated these values more overtly with the Roman *populus*—at least, when speaking before their public meetings. But Quintilian, composing the *Institutio* during the most tyrannical period of Emperor Domitian's rule, identifies moral values with the community in general, not specifically the common people. Moreover, for Quintilian, the community's values are revealed in the "consensus of the good" (2001a, 1.6.45) and discovered in the *communis sensus*, as manifested in the "courage, justice, loyalty, self-control, frugality, or contempt for pain and death" of virtuous Romans like "Fabricius, Curius, Regulus, Decius, Mucius, and countless others" (2001d, 12.2.29–30; Ussani 2003, 295). As for the balancing of the *honestum* and the *utile*, Quintilian classifies the ends of deliberative oratory as the honorable and the useful (2001b, 3.8.22–26), acknowledging, however, that "if one had to find a single object for [deliberative speeches], I should have preferred Cicero's view that the essential feature of this type of theme is dignity," that is, the *honestum* (2001b, 3.8.1). Nevertheless, Quintilian (like Cicero) does not diminish the role of *utilitas*, counting it as "one of the virtues of eloquence" (2001b, 5.12.23). Quintilian's solution to the tension between morality and usefulness is to balance the two ends, "promoting in rhetoric an alignment of honor and practicality, *honestum* and *utile*" (Mendelson 2002, 204). Finally, Quintilian relies throughout the *Institutio* on argument *in utramque partem* as a means of highlighting probable truths and of using conflicting probabilities to retain what is best in the traditional doctrines, while enabling the orator to make "whatever changes, additions, or omissions seem desirable" (2001a, 2.13.17; 2001d, 12.2.25, 12.1.34–35; Mendelson 2002, 181–87, 206–209).

If the Renaissance is commonly viewed as the apex of the Ciceronian rhetorical revival, the Latin Middle Ages is generally viewed as the nadir of Cicero's rhetorical influence (Nederman 1988, 76–78). Seigel explains what he sees as the diminished role of authentic oratory in the Middle Ages: "Whereas Cicero's orator had derived his identity from his practice of rhetoric and thus had tended to regard many other aspects of life and thought from the viewpoint of oratory, most medieval practitioners of rhetoric had some other primary identity and hence regarded rhetoric as an adjunct to some other task" (Seigel 1968, 178). If the Middle Ages were as bereft of full-fledged oratory as Seigel and other scholars maintain, it would be an unlikely period to encounter any version of Cicero's pragmatically moral orator. The participation of John of Salisbury (ca. 1120–1180) in the Ciceronian tradition of political morality, however, indicates that the medieval era was not as devoid of Cicero's rhetorical outlook as is widely accepted.

John was an English scholar, diplomat, bishop, author of two influential philosophical works—the *Policraticus* and the *Metalogicon*—and a follower of Cicero. He seems to have been acquainted with the entire Roman rhetorician's available works—*De officiis, De oratore, De inventione* (86 BCE), *De finibus* (45 BCE), and the *Tusculan Disputations* (begun in 45 BCE) (Nederman 2005, 53–54; Smalley 1973, 92–93). The *De officiis* and *De oratore*, major source texts for Cicero's conception of political morality, appear to have been of especial importance to John, as he bequeathed his copies of them, along with a copy of his *Policraticus*, to the cathedral at Chartres (Webb 1941, 128–29).

Like Cicero, John regards politics and rhetoric as moral activities and their practitioners, the prince and the orator, as moral personages. In contrast to the classical republican Cicero, for whom (as we see in chapter 5) the statesman and the orator are ideally the same, for John, living under a medieval monarchy, the orator (or, perhaps more accurately, the eloquent man) is not marked by his political leadership or, even, his public oratory but is characterized by the written counsel and advice he provides to the prince and other members of the governing classes from the solitude of his scriptorium (Liebeschütz 1950, 85, 88–89).

Consistent with Cicero's conception of political morality, John considers morality and utility as sufficiently interdependent to lose their distinct identities. Thus, he writes in the *Policraticus*: "the useful and the honourable [must be] made equivalent. . . . [N]o opinion is more pernicious than the opinion of those who separate the useful from the honourable; and the truest and more useful judgment is that the honourable and the useful may at all times be converted into one another" (John of Salisbury 1990, 4.4, 37).[5] Therefore, the prince and his political activities are moral insofar as they further the *utilitas publica*, the public good. John describes the prince as the "minister of the public utility" (*publicae utilitatis minister*) and "the servant of equity" (*aequitatis servus*)—according to Cicero, equity is a component of the *honestum* (John of Salisbury 1990, 4.2, 31; Cicero 1999e, 1.48). The prince's function is "to seek out and bring about the utility of each and all, and that he may arrange the optimal condition of the human republic" (John of Salisbury 1990, 4.1, 28). But the prince does not effect the public good alone; he is aided by the man of eloquence.

In the *Metalogicon*, John portrays eloquence in language that evokes Cicero's conception of decorum: "Eloquence is the faculty of giving *apt* expression to thoughts which the mind desires to be set forth." And he depicts the eloquent man—"that man, then, who possesses facility in aptly expressing his thoughts in words"—as employing eloquence for utility and morality (John of Salisbury 2013, 1.7.23–24, 139–40; emphasis added).[6] In aptly setting forth the judgment of his mind, according to John, the eloquent man uses a faculty "more beneficial" than can readily be seen" (2013, 1.7.24, 140). Rather than using eloquence solely for his own personal gain, however, John implies that the man of eloquence acts for the welfare of all. Continuing with this praise of eloquence and the eloquent man, John states that "it is because he employs reason and speech that man surpasses in *worth* [*dignitas*]—a synonym for the *honestum*—the rest of animate creation" (2013, 1.7.24, 140; John of Salisbury 1991, 1.7.834d, 24; emphasis added).

While we see the balancing or blending of the *honestum* and *utile* in John's account of eloquence and of the eloquent man, we observe the interrelationship between this balancing or blending, the subordination of means to end, and the obligation to act with decorum in his legitimation of the orator qua advisor's deceit and flattery. The mixing of the moral and the useful *and* its concomitant consequentialism are readily apparent. But decorum is a consistent feature of John's justification of ordinarily immoral speech because the orator qua advisor must (by speaking with decorum) be sensitive to the contexts that morally distinguish apparently identical speech acts. As John contends in the *Policraticus*, echoing Ciceronian decorum, it is a "consideration of place, time, individual, and cause . . . which makes all transactions appear beautiful or condemns them as morally ugly" (Pike 1938, 1.5.37, 28; see also Pike 1938, 7.12.140, 260).

Consideration of place, time, individual, and cause separates immoral flattery and deception from moral flattery and deception. Immoral flattery and deception go hand in hand: "all flattery is accompanied by deception, fraud, betrayal, the infamy of lying" (Pike 1938, 3.5.184, 165). John unequivocally condemns these vices for undermining good government—especially flattery, "by which is understood the use of speech by courtiers to manipulate their superiors in ways that favor the speakers themselves" (Nederman and Dow 2004, 199). But if flattery is *ordinarily* immoral, it is not *always* immoral. John makes this point in the *Policraticus*, where he differentiates between normal and exceptional flattery: "It is not permitted to flatter a friend, but it is permitted to delight the ears of a tyrant" (1990, 3.15, 25). In the case of a tyrant, flattery becomes a morally acceptable means to a higher, more useful end. The orator qua advisor might use it to curb the tyrant's worse impulses or, "when the tyrant could not be otherwise restrained," it could be used to lull him into a false sense of security, so that he may be killed—an act John terms *honestum*, "honorable" or "moral" (1990, 8.18, 205; Webb 1909, 1:364).[7]

Similarly, John distinguishes between regular deception, which he denounces, and useful deception, which he recognizes as moral. In the *Entheticus de Dogmate Philosophorum* (*Entheticus Maior*), an early didactic and satirical poem, John addresses the condition of the virtuous orator qua advisor who to survive among evil courtiers must pretend to be like them, thereby enabling the good counselor to "bring help and advice." John continues: "In order that [the evil courtiers'] savageness may grow more gentle, [the good advisor] usually feigns many things, he simulates that he himself is also savage; he becomes all things to all people; in appearance only he assumes the role of the enemy. . . . That trick is good which yields profit to utility [*utilitas*], when through it joy, life, and salvation are procured" (John of Salisbury 1987, 198–99). Such dissimulation, John explains, is useful. But, as we have seen before, its utility is inseparable from its morality. By "going undercover," the virtuous advisor can better counsel the prince—a beneficial end that justifies conventionally immoral means. John additionally highlights the *honestum* of this dissimulation by linking salvation, the *telos* of all Christians, to *utilitas*. Strictly speaking, as John explains in the *Policraticus*, the moral courtier is not engaged in deceit. John circumscribes "deceit" there as taking place only "when one thing is done and another is pretended; whenever it is performed with the intention of doing harm it is always bad" (1990, 4.12, 62). Because the good advisor does not dissemble with the intention of doing bad—on the contrary, his intentions are good—he only *appears* to be deceitful, while performing a morally justifiable act that is not, by definition, deceit.[8]

In addition to balancing the *honestum* and the *utile*, subordinating means to end, and treating decorum as a moral imperative, John exhibits another characteristic of Ciceronian political morality, argument in *utramque partem*. In the *Metalogicon*, he writes of "the truth of the Pythagorean saying that on every matter it is possible to dispute with probability on both sides of the question [*in utramque partem probabiliter disputari*]" (John of Salisbury 2013, 3.10.139). Although John does not identify this double-sided argument there with Cicero, he employs a form of argumentation used by Academic skeptics both to demonstrate our inability to attain certainty and to determine which position is most probable. John identifies himself in the *Policraticus* and the *Metalogicon* as a devotee of the Academic school "on the authority of Cicero" (John of Salisbury 2013, prologue, 122; Keats-Rohan 1986, 28–29; see also Nelson 1933, 104; Liebeschütz 1950, 88).

We now move backward from the Middle Ages to the age of classical antiquity, from John of Salisbury to Aristotle and Cicero. Despite the significant differences between many of John's fundamental assumptions and those of Aristotle and Cicero—likewise, between Aristotle's and Cicero's basic suppositions—the three share a common rhetorical outlook. This shared rhetorical viewpoint means, at a minimum, that they understand speech as taking place between embodied and situated humans whose rational faculties cannot be cut off from their desires, interests, or historical specificities (Young 2002, 65). In opposition to this outlook is the antirhetorical perspective of those who aspire toward purely rational discourse between disembodied intellects abstracted from their passions, interests, and the particularity of their circumstances. If we embrace the rhetorical approach, we accept that emotional appeals cannot be eliminated from human communication—to many people today, a reasonable opinion. But by vindicating emotional appeals, we run the risk that speakers may use these emotions tendentiously, to confuse their audiences and manipulate them into acting against their convictions and interests. It is to the moral difficulties concerning manipulative emotional appeals that we turn in chapter 1, comparing Aristotle's and Cicero's distinct approaches to these appeals.

Rhetoric, Emotional Manipulation, and Morality: The Contemporary Relevance of Cicero vis-à-vis Aristotle

Responding to the long-standing criticism of political rhetoric as inherently manipulative—used by politicians to control the citizenry through undue emotional appeals—scholars have turned to Aristotle's *Rhetoric* for what they see as a nonmanipulative, morally acceptable conception of political rhetoric. As already stated in the introduction, I look to the less obvious rhetorical thinker, Cicero—so easily portrayed, based on his own words, as a master of emotional manipulation—for a moral conception of rhetoric. In this chapter, I evaluate the two rhetoricians' approaches to morality, rhetoric, and the emotions, specifically emotional manipulation, making use of Nathaniel Klemp's (2011) two conditions of manipulation: first, that it requires the use of hidden or irrational force to affect another's choices; and, second, that it is intentional (62–64). I consider two moral breaches stemming from emotional manipulation. The first moral breach—consequentialist, exemplified by Plato in the introduction—is when politicians, in manipulating an audience's emotions, hinder their listeners from recognizing what is good or beneficial. The second moral breach—nonconsequentialist, represented by Kant in the introduction—is when politicians manipulate their listeners rhetorically, thereby undermining their listeners' autonomy.

DESCRIBING THE RHETORICAL EMOTIONS

Aristotle

Toward the beginning of the *Rhetoric,* Aristotle delineates three *pisteis* (singular: *pistis*) or means of persuasion" that are *entechnic* (i.e., "artful"), that the speaker "invents" to persuade the audience. (*Atechnic* [i.e., "nonartful"] *pisteis* are preexisting proofs not created by the speaker, e.g., witnesses, testimony of slaves taken under torture, contracts.) The three *pisteis* are (1) *ethos,* the means of persuasion that "are in the character of the speaker"; (2) *pathos,* in which there is persuasion "through the hearers when they are led to feel emotion by the speech"; and (3) *logos,* or proof based on rational arguments (Aristotle 1991, 1.2; Wisse 1989, 13–17).

Although *ethos* in Aristotle may superficially resemble a type of emotional appeal that produces in the audience a feeling of trust toward the speaker, it does not evoke emotions. (The emotions in Cicero, as will be seen, are divided between *pathos* and *ethos.*) *Ethos* is the element of speech that presents the speaker as "worthy of credence; for we believe fair-minded people to a greater extent and more quickly [than we do others]." In contrast, *pathos* aims at effecting an emotional response in the audience (Aristotle 1991, 1.2.4; Wisse 1989, 33–34).[1] For Aristotle, orators do not use *ethos* to elicit sympathy or any similar emotion toward themselves; such appeals to sympathy are part of *pathos.*

Ethos affects judgment through the audience's confidence in the speaker's veracity, whereas *pathos,* in Aristotle, influences judgment through variations in the emotions. Thus, in the second book of the *Rhetoric,* where he analyzes the individual emotions most completely,[2] Aristotle (1991) defines the emotions (*pathē*) as "those things which, by undergoing change, people come to differ in their judgments and which are accompanied by pain and pleasure, for example, anger, pity, fear, and other such things and their opposites" (2.1.8). Aristotle discusses twelve emotions in some detail (2.2–11): anger (*orgē*), mildness or calmness (*praotēs*), love or friendly feeling (*philia*), hate (*misos*) or enmity (*ekhthra*), fear (*phobos*), confidence (*tharsos*), shame (*aiskhynē*), kindliness (*kharis*), pity (*eleos*), righteous indignation (*nemesan*), envy (*phthonos*), and emulation or eagerness to match the accomplishments of others (*zēlos*).[3]

Aristotle describes the *pathē* as engendering judgment but does not clearly explain how. The now dominant explanation is that emotions affect judgment through beliefs. If we accept that Aristotle adopts a cognitive approach to emotion, then beliefs elicit emotions, whose variations (caused by these initial beliefs) influence other beliefs or decisions (i.e., judgments) about policies or a defendant's guilt or innocence (Konstan 2006, 37). Aristotle lends support to this explanation in the *Rhetoric* immediately following his definition of the twelve emotions. He tells us that each emotion must be discussed in three ways. Using the example of anger, Aristotle indicates that we must determine: (1) the *state of mind* of people who are angry; (2) "against *whom* are they usually angry"; and (3) "for what sort of *reasons*" (Aristotle 1991, 2.1.8). The mention of objects ("against whom") and grounds ("reasons") is important because "it strongly suggests that Aristotle does not dissociate cognition from emotion" (Fortenbaugh 1970, 54–56). Aristotle does not conceive of emotions as unthinking sensations or feelings; if he did, he could not analyze an emotion's objects and grounds.

Aristotle's discussion of individual emotions supports this interpretation. Before analyzing anger and fear, Aristotle (1991) defines them: "Let anger be [defined as] desire, accompanied by [mental and physical] distress, for conspicuous retaliation because of a conspicuous slight that was directed, without justification, against oneself or those near to one" (2.2.1); "[l]et *fear* be [defined as] a sort of pain or agitation derived from the imagination of a destructive or painful evil" (2.5.1). In both instances, Aristotle implies that a thought or belief is essential to the emotion (Fortenbaugh 1970, 55–56). Anger requires the belief that one has been conspicuously slighted without justification. Fear presupposes the thought of an impending evil. In either case, when the thought is absent, so is the emotion. Therefore, if I am shown that the reasons for my emotion are not relevant, then my emotion should disappear or diminish (Nussbaum 1996, 311). Emotions are "responsive to cognitive modification" and are treated in the *Rhetoric*, especially the second book, as distinct from impulses (Leighton 1996, 223–24).

I have argued that Aristotle primarily assumes a cognitive approach to the emotions. Aristotle does not, however, adopt this approach without exception in the *Rhetoric*. At times, Aristotle advises the speaker to affect the listeners' emotions without basing these emotions on thinking.[4] The most glaring example of such a noncognitive appeal—which is also deceptive—occurs in the third book of the *Rhetoric*, where Aristotle, in discussing style, argues that the listener will be affected by the emotions of the speaker: "and the hearer suffers [literally, "shares the *pathos* of"] along with the pathetic speaker, even if what he says amounts to nothing. As a result, many overwhelm their hearers by making noise" (Aristotle 1991, 3.7.5; Wardy 1996, 79). Aristotle (1991) assumes that the *lexis* (style) the speaker adopts can directly influence the hearer's emotions, if the style is coordinated with the desired emotion (3.7.3). Another instance of eliciting emotions without instilling any prior belief is found in Book 3, in

Aristotle's discussion of delivery. Although Aristotle disparages delivery in oratory as "vulgar" and independent of "facts" and "true justice," he states that one "should pay attention to delivery, not because it is right but because it is necessary." Delivery is "something that has the greatest force" because it can "affect the audience," given "the sad state of governments" and "the corruption of the audience" (3.1.3–6). Unlike the previous example, Aristotle does not explicitly refer to *pathos* in the case of delivery. But it is difficult to explain how delivery affects the audience other than emotionally without prior cognition. (Delivery does not persuade through argument or *ethos*.) And, as Aristotle observes in the same chapter, Thrasymachus discusses delivery in his account of emotional appeals (3.1.7).[5]

Cicero

Although I argue that Aristotle and Cicero approach the emotions in rhetoric differently—and those differences have political and moral implications—Cicero begins his analysis of the emotions much like Aristotle; Cicero also adopts the threefold division of *pisteis* into *ethos, pathos,* and *logos.* In the section of *De oratore* devoted to the invention of arguments, Cicero uses the character Antonius to introduce the three means of persuasion.[6] Antonius explains that, when composing a speech, he initially devotes himself to creating rational arguments and "[a]fter that, I consider very carefully two further elements: the first one recommends us or those for whom we are pleading [*ethos*], the second is aimed at moving the minds of our audience in the direction we want [*pathos*]." Antonius reiterates this point by stating that "the method employed in the art of oratory . . . relies entirely upon three means of persuasion: proving that our contentions are true [argumentation], winning over our audience [*ethos*], and inducing their minds to feel any emotion the case may demand [*pathos*]" (Cicero 2001a, 2.114–116).[7]

In contrast to Aristotle, who categorizes all emotional appeals under *pathos,* Cicero (2001a) divides them between two *pisteis, ethos* and *pathos. Ethos*'s goal is to win over the hearers "to feel goodwill toward the orator as well as toward his client" (2.182).[8] Cicero shows that, like Aristotle, he intends *ethos* to demonstrate the orator's (or the client's) moral character. Cicero has Antonius say: "Well then, the character, the customs, the deeds, and the life, both of those who do the pleading and of those on whose behalf they plead, make a very important contribution to winning a case. . . . Now people's minds are won over by a man's prestige, his accomplishments, and the reputation he has acquired by his way of life" (2.182). Unlike Aristotle, however, for whom *ethos* establishes the speaker's trustworthiness without eliciting emotions, Cicero seeks to effect, through *ethos,* an emotional response in the audience. This difference between Cicero and Aristotle is supported by Cicero's use of *conciliare* (winning over), a verb that "clearly implies a form of acting upon the emotions" (Fantham 1973, 267–68). For example, Cicero (2001a) has Antonius speak of winning goodwill (*benevolentiam conciliare*), to persuade through *ethos,* and of winning esteem (*conciliat caritatem*), an emotion associated with *ethos*; Antonius employs *conciliare* when speaking of the orator winning love (*amor*), an emotion classified under *pathos* (2.115, 2.182, 2.206–207; Gill 1984, 159).[9] Aristotle, however, says nothing of winning the audience's goodwill in relation to *ethos* (Fortenbaugh 1988, 261–62).

Although Cicero uses *conciliare*—a relatively mild verb—when speaking of *ethos* and *pathos,* to describe the orator's appeal to *pathos* he usually employs more forceful verbs, such as *permovere* (excite, affect with violent emotion), *impellere* (compel, constrain), *incitare* (arouse), *capere* (seize), *excitare* (stir up), and *movere* and *commovere* (move and arouse) (2001a, 2.185–87, 2.211–15). This use of powerful verbs suggests the main difference between the types of emotions contained in *ethos* and *pathos.* For Cicero, *pathos* is an appeal to the vehement emotions, whereas *ethos* elicits the more gentle emotions (Cicero 1939b, 128–29). Regarding *ethos,* Cicero (2001a) has Antonius explain that the effect of bolstering a man's character through his "prestige, his accomplishments, and the reputation he has acquired by his way of life" is "enhanced by a gentle tone of voice on the part of the orator" (2.182). In contrast to the orator employing *pathos,* who uses "vigorous oratory" displayed in "some form of sharp and violent emotional arousal to set the juror's hearts aflame," the speaker evoking *ethos* speaks "in a quiet, low-keyed, and gentle manner" (2.183).[10] In discussing proof from *ethos,* however, Cicero has Antonius refrain from specifying which emotions comprise the *leniores affectus* (2.212; May 1988, 10–11). The particular passions contained in *pathos,* that "mode of speaking . . . which stirs the hearts of the jurors quite differently" (Cicero 2001a, 2.185), are similar to those *pathē* Aristotle considers in the *Rhetoric,* but are identified as violent in Cicero and not similarly designated in Aristotle (Cicero 2001a, 2.206–211; Wisse 1989, 34, 242–45): affection (*amor*), hate (*odium*), anger (*iracundia*), envy (*invidia*), pity (*misericordia*), hope (*spes*), joy (*laetitia*), fear (*timor*), and grief (*molestia*).

Although the particular emotions that Cicero lists as relevant to *pathos* are comparable to Aristotle's *pathē* in the *Rhetoric,* Cicero, unlike Aristotle, does not define emotion. And nowhere in *De oratore* does Antonius "offer anything like a clear general statement concerning the nature of emotional response" (Fortenbaugh 1988, 269–70).[11] Rather, Antonius seems to go out of his way to avoid analyzing emotions conceptually. For example, when alluding to debates between Hellenistic philosophers on the emotions, Antonius asserts that it matters not if an orator knows "whether anger was a disturbance of the mind or a desire to avenge pain" (Cicero 2001a, 1.220). Likewise, Cicero has his interlocutors avoid determining whether or not an emotion is the result of beliefs, that is, whether or not to adopt, like Aristotle does, a cognitive approach to emotions.[12]

Although Cicero does not determine the relation between emotion and cognition, *De oratore* is filled with passages that characterize emotional appeals as rhetorical attempts to overpower the audience's rational capacities—passages that imply that emotions are blind impulses detached from cognition. For example, Cicero (2001a) contrasts *ethos* and *pathos* with reasoned argument when Antonius argues that nothing is more important in oratory than for "the orator to be favorably regarded by the audience [*ethos*], and for the audience itself to be moved in such a way as to be ruled by some strong emotional impulse [*pathos*] rather than by reasoned judgment [*logos*]" (2.178). Antonius's point seems to be that the orator can, and should, bypass the hearer's thought processes by appealing to the emotions. Likewise, Cicero has Antonius distinguish between argumentation, on the one hand, and "winning favor" and "stirring emotions," on the other, with Antonius stating about the latter proofs that "I concentrate particularly on the aspect that is most able to move people's hearts" (2.292–93; see also 2.129, 2.214, 2.337).

On closer inspection, however, Cicero does not necessarily oppose reason and emotion. Thus, emotions may be cognitively based without resulting from formal argument. For example, Cicero describes how Antonius established the character of his client, Manius Aquillius, by making him "stand where all could see him," after which he "tore open his shirt, and exposed his breast, that his countrymen might see the scars that he bore on the front of his body," scars from the wounds he received in defense of Rome (Cicero 1953c, 2.5.3; 2001a, 2.124, 2.194–96). Antonius does not establish Aquillius's character here with explicit argumentation. Nevertheless, by "expos[ing] to the jurors the scars on the old general's chest," Antonius instills the thought in his audience that Aquillius is a man of good character because he was willing to sacrifice his life for the Republic.

Not only does Cicero recognize that beliefs create emotions, but, more specifically, he acknowledges that rational argumentation can engender emotions. In *De oratore*, Publius Sulpicius Rufus lauds his legal antagonist, Antonius, for using commonplaces against Quintus Caepio and for filling the proceedings with hatred, indignation, and pity (Cicero 2001a, 2.203; see also 2.108–109).[13] That commonplaces are employed in inventing arguments and that Sulpicius links Antonius's use of commonplaces with overwhelming the audience with emotions shows that Sulpicius does not view argumentation as being opposed to emotional appeals. And Antonius's claim that "I bested your [i.e., Sulpicius's] accusation in the case not so much because the jurors were informed, but because their minds were affected" (2.197–201) is consistent with his eliciting emotions through argumentation. What Antonius means is that he employed arguments to mislead the audience by diverting its attention from the issues relevant to the debate, so that the audience's emotions will be inflamed. His arguments, like many others that Cicero condones, are still rational arguments, even if not germane to the question at hand.

Why does Cicero avoid providing a definitive picture of the relationship between emotion and cognition? I agree with Fortenbaugh (1988) that Cicero purposely refrains from defining emotion because "the nature of emotional response is not easy to pin down" (269–70). As Fortenbaugh explains, anger and fright are grounded on belief; cheerfulness and sadness may be caused by "a physiological condition or an external stimulus like infectious rhythm." Because of such possible differences in the origins of particular emotions, Cicero refrains from generalizing about emotions as a class. Perhaps it would be more correct to say that Cicero refuses to define emotion because he does not want to pin *himself* down on the meaning of emotional response. Reflecting the rhetorical practice of argument *in utramque partem,* where both sides of an issue are presented and debated (Remer 2004, 143–46), Cicero wishes to display the double-sided nature of the emotions in rhetoric—as irrational *and* as consistent with reason. Therefore, he represents the source of emotions ambiguously. For instance, when he finds fault with the absence of *ethos* and *pathos* in the post-Aristotelian rhetorical handbooks, he accentuates the noncognitive character of emotional impulses (Cicero 2001a, 2.201). His concern in this case is to deemphasize reason relative to emotion in order to amplify the need for reintroducing *ethos* and *pathos* into rhetoric. But when discussing *copia* ("expansive richness of utterance"; Lanham 1991, 42) as a strategy for allowing argumentation to affect the hearts and minds of the audience members, Cicero (2001a) roots *pathos* in *logos* (2.109); emotion and cognition, then, are not set in opposition to each other.[14]

MAKING NORMATIVE SENSE OF THE EMOTIONS IN ARISTOTLE

Parallel to Aristotle's cognitive approach to emotion is his conception of the rhetorical means of persuasion as being grounded in argument. In each instance,

Aristotle accepts, even values, emotion as a necessary element of judgment, but roots emotion in reason. Emotion, as already seen, is derived from thought or belief. Analogously, the *pisteis* are founded on rational argumentation: *pathos*, as well as *ethos*, receives its legitimacy as a rhetorical proof through its basis in argument.

The centrality of argument to the *pisteis* and to Aristotle's understanding of rhetoric as an art finds support in his definition of the art of rhetoric: "Let rhetoric be [defined as] an ability, in each [particular] case, to see the available means of persuasion. This is the function of no other art" (Aristotle 1991, 1.2.1). We might assume that Aristotle is adopting here a variant of the commonly used definition of rhetoric as "the art of persuasion" (Plato 1979, 454b5–10). But to define rhetoric as the "art" or "artificer" of persuasion suggests that rhetoric becomes an art when it succeeds at persuasion. Aristotle explicitly avoids making persuasion itself the aim of rhetoric: "[rhetoric's] *function is not to persuade* but to see the available means of persuasion in each case (Aristotle 1991, 1.1.14; emphasis added). For Aristotle, what defines rhetoric as an art is not persuasion per se.

What does it mean to say that, according to Aristotle, the art of rhetoric is not defined by "persuasion" but by "finding the available means of persuasion"? Eugene Garver elucidates the difference between these two definitions by distinguishing between the two ends of an art (*technē*) like rhetoric: first, the external, given end; second, the internal, guiding end.[15] The given end is the purpose of the practice, which in rhetoric is persuading; the speaker achieves the external end when he has successfully persuaded. What defines rhetoric, or any other practice, as an art, however, is its guiding end. In rhetoric, this internal end is finding the available means of persuasion, which means limiting the "means" to argument (Garver 1994, 24–28). Aristotle affirms the centrality of argument in "rhetoric as art" in his introduction to the *Rhetoric*. There he describes rhetoric as based on reasoned argument, especially the enthymeme or rhetorical syllogism, which he terms "the 'body' of persuasion" (Aristotle 1991, 1.1.3). And although Aristotle envisions his own rhetoric as "speaking on the subject," he describes the rhetoric conceived of by the authors of rhetorical handbooks as "say[ing] nothing about enthymemes," that is, ignoring argumentation and focusing mostly on "matters external to the subject," like "verbal attack and pity and anger and such emotions of the soul [that] do not relate to fact but are appeals to the juryman" (1.1.3–4). Aristotle, however, does not delineate what defines a speech as outside the subject. "What is 'outside the subject' is a judgment only the audience can make" (Garver 1994, 39). Aristotle rejects the emotional appeals of the *Arts of Speech*, the technical handbooks, "for it is wrong to warp the jury by leading them into anger or envy or pity: that is the same as if someone made a straightedge rule crooked before using it" (1.1.5).

These excerpts from early in the *Rhetoric* seem to suggest that Aristotle wants to exclude all, or almost all, emotional appeals from rhetoric. Such an understanding of Aristotle would eliminate emotional manipulation as a problem, because emotional appeals would mostly be removed from rhetoric. Purging *pathos* from rhetoric, however, is difficult to harmonize with his detailed analysis of emotional appeals in the second book of the *Rhetoric*. Aristotle's discussion there indicates that emotional appeals are a legitimate part of rhetoric, one of the three *pisteis* that comprise the rhetorical art.[16] The simplest and most persuasive solution to the apparent contradiction between the two parts of the *Rhetoric* is to read Aristotle as recognizing as artistic only those emotional appeals that derive from reasoned argument, that do not digress from the matter in hand. Although Aristotle excludes *some* emotional appeals from the art of rhetoric, he does not reject *all* emotional appeals. The artful appeal to *pisteis* is restricted to those proofs derived from argument. Thus, Aristotle states: "[There is persuasion] through hearers when they are led to feel emotion [*pathos*] by the speech [or argument, *tou logou*]" (Aristotle 1991, 2.1.5). Aristotle accepts that emotional appeals are legitimate rhetorical means of persuasion, "but only provided they are made an integral part of the orderly exposition of and argument for the orator's case" (Cooper 1994, 196–97). Likewise, Aristotle (1991, 2.1.5) maintains that *ethos* as a *pistis* of the rhetorical art "should result from the speech [or argument, *dia tou logou*]" and not from testimonials about the speaker's character (Cooper 1994, 197; Garver 1994, 27).

In limiting emotional appeals to those derived from argument, Aristotle addresses the conditions of rhetoric as an art. In contrast to what we shall find in Cicero, Aristotle is not evaluating *pathos* morally (Garver 2006, 18; Garsten 2006, 118). The *Rhetoric* has norms, but they are artistic norms. The norms regulating emotions, which are grounded in rhetoric's internal (i.e., its artistic) end, require that *pathos* be rooted in argument and that emotional appeals should relate to the subject. In the *Rhetoric*, Aristotle does not ask speakers "to impose external moral rules on themselves." Instead, he restricts "the scope of their competence" by defining the conditions of the art they practice (Garsten 2006, 118).

For emotional appeals to be deemed artistic, they must be consistent with rhetorical norms. Aristotle, however, does not obligate the public speaker to follow these norms. Rhetoric qua art, for Aristotle, does not generate any moral obligations on the speaker because rhetoric qua art does not create moral obligations at all. If the artful rhetorician does not "stoop to winning a case by inflaming the passions of the audience," it is not because doing so is immoral "but because it is not part of the art." The artful rhetorician would refrain from appealing to emotions without argument because doing so would contravene achieving the internal, guiding end of the art (Garver 1994, 210). Nevertheless, as we shall see, Aristotle assumes that the speaker will sometimes pursue the external end of success, not the internal end. Aristotle acknowledges that not all emotional appeals will be, or should be, consistent with the *art* of rhetoric (Garver 1994, 32, 47).

Aristotle does not suggest in the *Rhetoric,* however, that emotional appeals outside artistic norms are, or should be, the rule. The materials for enthymemes from which the *pisteis* are derived are intended to reflect "the structure of ordinary deliberative reasoning." As such, they are meant to approximate the "patterns of reasoning that most people use unconsciously whenever they deliberate" (Garsten 2006, 130–31). Aristotle conceives of emotional appeals that are not based on argument and are external to the subject as out of the ordinary. If he did not, the guiding end of rhetoric would itself be exceptional. But he does not provide any rules or advice as to when the speaker should aim for success at the given end; the speaker must decide for himself or herself when to eschew the guiding end and look to the external end, doing whatever is possible to persuade the audience (Garver 1994, 40, 47–48, 201).

Assuming that emotional appeals are largely controlled by artistic norms, we can then evaluate the conditions created by these norms to determine how problematical emotional manipulation is for Aristotle. In particular, does Aristotle's grounding of emotional appeals in argument diminish emotional manipulation? Because Aristotle does not address the issue directly, we must infer the answer from the implications of his rhetorical norms.

That Aristotle grounds rhetorical emotions in argument means only that the Aristotelian orator does not manipulate emotions directly but does so through argumentation. Emotions, though, can be moved by faulty and false arguments. Nowhere in the *Rhetoric* does Aristotle state that enthymemes must be true. Aristotle not only accepts but also sometimes suggests employing deceptive arguments, offering specific examples of such arguments (Sprute 1994, 125; Wardy 1996, 74–76). For instance, Aristotle advises the speaker, in epideictic oratory, to misrepresent the person being praised as acting "in accordance with deliberate purpose," even when this person's actions are coincidental and chance happenings. Doing so, according to Aristotle (1991), is likelier to win praise because acting "in accordance with deliberate purpose is characteristic of a worthy person" (1.9.32).[17] In addition, Aristotle supports obfuscating the truth when he instructs the *rhetor* "to speak in universal terms of what is not universal," which is "especially suitable in bitter complaint and great indignation" (2.29.10). Further, Aristotle (1991) writes in the *Rhetoric*: "Another [topic], for the accuser, is to find fault with some big thing briefly after praising some little thing at length or, after setting forth many good things [about the opponent], to find fault with the one thing that bears on the case. Such [speakers] are most artful and most unjust; for they seek to harm by saying good things, mingling them with bad" (3.15.10). It would seem that that by approving of erroneous argumentation, Aristotle condones emotional manipulation; listeners are moved deceptively to experience emotions.

When emotions result from false arguments, however, cannot the "incorrect" emotions be changed or eliminated when countered by truthful arguments? And if "misplaced" emotions are likely to be altered by the more truthful speaker's arguments, is Aristotle still responsible (or equally responsible) for condoning emotional manipulation? As Garver (1994) states: "When an emotion is translated into an argument it becomes defeasible." Therefore, the "false" emotion can be diminished or removed by hearers analyzing the speaker's argument itself (134, 119; Nussbaum 1996, 306). Aristotle appears to believe that faulty arguments will likely be defeated, all things being equal, because "the true and just are by nature stronger than their opposites" (Aristotle 1991, 1.1.12). The audience is liable to "detect the fallaciousness of apparent enthymemes not by finding hidden motives but by looking more closely at the argument *qua* argument" (Garver 1994, 162).

For defenders of Aristotle's artistic rhetoric, it seems that Aristotle can be largely shielded from moral culpability in both categories of emotional manipulation, confirming the view that Aristotle eclipses Cicero as an exemplar of the moral use of rhetorical emotions. First, Aristotle can be said to evade the consequentialist critique of rhetoric; appeals to emotions that are largely conformable to reason should not prevent auditors from perceiving their good, whether justice or economic self-interest. Incorrect beliefs that give rise to emotions, even beliefs that are purposefully falsified by the speaker, can be reasoned about, thereby diminishing this threat of manipulation. Second, Aristotle appears less vulnerable to the critique that rhetoric undermines listeners' autonomous decision making. If we assume that the Aristotelian speaker's auditors keep their wits about them, even if emotionally moved, then they retain their freedom of judgment. The audience's consideration of the rhetorical arguments acts as a suitable counterweight to emotional manipulation.

Listeners, though, do not always detect fallacious arguments and will, at times, allow themselves to be manipulated. Garsten, for example, cites

Aristotle's example of judicial oratory, where jurors judge "other people's business," unlike the deliberative genre, where members of the audience vote on laws or policies that affect them. In the rhetoric of the courtroom, jurors, lacking a direct interest in the outcome of the case, seek to be charmed by speakers, "listening merely for their own pleasure [*pros charin*]" and allowing "their own pleasure or pain [*to idio hedu e luperon*]" to distort their judgment (Aristotle 1926, 1.1.10, 1.1.7; Garsten 2006, 122). Thus, Aristotle commends well-run states and institutions, like the Athenian Areopagus, which forbids speech (e.g., emotional appeals) that is "outside the subject" (Aristotle 1991, 1.1.5). The Areopagus was an elite body, composed of the wealthiest Athenian citizens (Allen 2000, 44). For Aristotle, however, Athenian juries' decisions are often influenced by irrelevant emotional appeals.[18] As Garsten (2006, 121–22) relates, in judicial rhetoric, when listeners do not scrutinize the speaker's arguments, Aristotle finds the listeners to be principally responsible for being emotionally manipulated; the audience is complicit in its own manipulation by choosing to listen for its pleasure. That the audience's desire to be charmed minimizes the orator's moral responsibility is plausible.[19] Here we have emotional manipulation, but of a lower order.

Although Aristotle relies on the force of the argument to safeguard hearers from emotional manipulation, emotions instilled by argument cannot always be removed by counterargument, and, therefore, "false" emotions can still manipulate even in artistic rhetoric. As Nancy Sherman (2000, 156) points out, "emotions don't reform at the beck and call of reason." On the contrary, "they cling tenaciously in the face of a considered desire or willing to turn them around" (see also Konstan 2006, 31–32). Personal experience shows the pitfalls of assuming that emotions can be counted on to respond to rational argument. We may continue to feel hatred, anger, love, and other emotions after being shown that the beliefs from which these emotions derived are no longer—or never were—true. As psychoanalytic theory indicates, even if an emotion has cognitive content and may be intentionally modified, the source of the emotion may not be apparent. Surface emotions have roots in the unconscious: "Rage at you may really be about rage at myself, fretful love may be grounded in hidden fears of inferiority, enmity may be a defence against too close an attachment," and so on (Sherman 2000, 157). Therefore, a speaker who incites certain emotions through false or faulty argumentation may tap into preexisting primitive drives that resist factually correct arguments. Although the unconscious sources of some emotions may become intellectually transparent, modifying these emotions is a far more onerous task than can be performed by rhetorical argument. The upshot is that the widespread trust in Aristotle's rationalistic approach to protect against manipulation is misplaced. Emotions do not respond as easily to cognitive modification à la Aristotle's enthymemes as his supporters suggest.

Exemplifying emotional manipulation that was virtually immune to counterargument were the Willie Horton advertisements, which appeared in the George H. W. Bush–Michael Dukakis presidential race of 1998.[20] William "Willie" Horton was an African American man convicted of first-degree murder and sentenced to life imprisonment without the possibility of parole in a Massachusetts state prison. Following a weekend furlough, from which he did not return, Horton raped a woman and assaulted her fiancé, both of whom were white. The pro-Bush camp, through speeches and, most effectively, a series of television advertisements, attacked Dukakis, governor of Massachusetts when Horton was released, for supporting the furlough program that enabled a dangerous criminal to commit rape and assault. These advertisements were highly effective in depicting Dukakis as a liberal who was "soft on crime."

Apropos of the guiding end of rhetoric, the Willie Horton ads present arguments. Taken as a whole, the ads argue that Dukakis opposes the death penalty and supports the furlough program and that the program, during Dukakis's first two terms, furloughed 268 convicts who escaped. The ads contend that Bush, contrary to Dukakis, supports the death penalty for those convicted of first-degree murder, suggesting that, under Bush, Horton would have been executed rather than furloughed. The implications of the commercials' arguments were that Dukakis was soft on crime, Bush was tough on crime, and Dukakis was at least indirectly responsible for the rape and assault committed by Horton after being furloughed.

The Dukakis campaign and the press criticized the ads as false or, at best, misleading. Critics of the ads pointed out that Dukakis inherited the furlough program from his Republican predecessor; that of the 268 escapees from the furlough program, only four had been convicted of first-degree murder; and that Horton was the only one of the escapees who went on to commit rape. In addition, the federal government, during the Reagan-Bush administration, had its own furlough program for convicted felons, and "[u]nder the terms in effect under the Reagan-Bush administration, Horton would have been eligible for furlough" (Jamieson 1992, 40). Despite these and other counterarguments, the public's fear of Dukakis as too liberal on crime continued unabated. A nine-member focus group meeting in Dallas in early September 1988 was split 5–4 in favor of Dukakis. Although this same focus group in November was shown evidence documenting the general success of the Massachusetts furlough program and the exceptionality of the Horton case, its members were now 7–2 in favor of

Bush. The Willie Horton ads had done their damage, and evidence refuting the ads did not sway the focus group members (Jamieson 1992, 31–33). Likewise, Garver (1994) writes: "Many voters reported responding to the Willie Horton advertisements by saying, 'I know that it's an unfair ad, and that it's wrong to blame Dukakis for a program a lot of states use; still, I'm voting for Bush on the strength of that ad'" (161). Artistic rhetoric was by the voters' own accounts insufficient to change minds. The Willie Horton ads elicited emotions in viewers that were not readily responsive to cognitive modification.

The Willie Horton commercials evoke emotions, like fear, that, from a psychoanalytic view, have ideational content, albeit content that is at least partly unconscious. Clearly, the fears evoked by the ads were not only initiated by verbal arguments but also instigated by the first ad's use of a close-up mug shot of Horton that flashes on the screen. (Subsequent commercials, which did not show any pictures of Horton, could rely on viewers having seen the initial commercial or news clips about it.) With the addition of Horton's picture, fears of generic crime were compounded by unconscious drives linked to race, like fears and fantasies about the rape of white women by black men.[21] And belief in psychoanalytic theory is not a prerequisite to accepting that race played a major role in the influence of the ads. Independent of any assumptions about unconscious drives, deeply rooted irrational prejudices about race are generally acknowledged as having played a major role in the ads' influence on the public (Jamieson 1992, 34). In addition, the style and delivery of the Willie Horton ads—we have already seen that Aristotle recognizes that style and delivery may incite emotions without the hearer's initial cognitive appraisal—affected voters' feelings. Consistent with conventional journalistic norms, the commercials are "dramatic, personal, concise, visual, and take the form of narrative" (17). Thus, the Willie Horton ads, independent of content, were vested with the authority of television news.

Rather than presenting factual arguments that voters could consider rationally, the Willie Horton ads were emotionally manipulative when judged by Klemp's conditions of manipulation: the ads appealed to voters' covert or irrational tendencies, and they were intentional. Klemp (2011) himself sees these ads as covert forms of manipulation (66), whereas Garver judges them as overtly manipulative.[22] I believe that there are elements of both types of manipulation, as viewers were aware that some emotional appeals influenced their electoral decisions despite knowing that these appeals were manipulative, but they were also unaware of other manipulative techniques that drove their electoral choices. As for the intentionality of the manipulation, careful analysis of the

Willie Horton commercials leave little doubt that the Bush campaign intended "to employ the race card but to deny that it was doing so" (Mendelberg 2001, 137, 138–44).[23]

The Willie Horton ads are noteworthy as recent examples of effective emotional manipulation. They are not, however, exceptional. Like other instances of emotional manipulation, these commercials (1) impede members of an audience from autonomous decision making and (2) impel them to act against their best interests—both moral wrongs associated with emotional manipulation. Taking the Willie Horton ads, again, as an example, the arguments, imagery, style, and delivery in these commercials unleashed unconscious forces and racial prejudices that hindered voters from choosing freely, even as voters sometimes conceded that they knew they were being manipulated. And the commercials focused voters' attentions on an exceptional instance that had little to no importance for their future well-being and away from other issues that would affect voters, for example, the economy, foreign policy, taxation, social and economic inequalities, and welfare. Once the commercials' producers or, in rhetoric more broadly, the speakers intent on manipulating listeners succeed in their goals, they are morally culpable for this manipulation. Why, given that Aristotle in the *Rhetoric* neither precludes the conditions for emotional manipulation nor morally opposes such manipulation, should not Aristotle share in this culpability? I contend that he does.

Aristotle's artistic norms for rhetoric do not, as I have demonstrated, protect against emotional manipulation. But what if they had? Garver and Garsten, for example, appear satisfied with a rhetorical framework in which the *rhetors* are free of moral obligation in their emotional appeals. I question, however, whether most of us today would be content without any moral obligation. Perhaps we think that politicians who rely on institutional norms without moral obligation are less likely to act morally. Or we may sense that not vesting politicians with moral duties is just wrong. Thus, in the *Discourses on Livy,* Machiavelli approves of institutional arrangements to check corruption, like Rome's balancing of patricians and plebeians (Machiavelli 1996, 1.4). Nevertheless, the absence of personal moral obligation in his politics makes Machiavelli, for many if not most, an ethically dubious character at best.

Aristotle recognizes ethical requirements, and the orator must act ethically if he is to be a virtuous man. These, however, are external moral rules, that is, there is nothing specifically "rhetorical" about the ethical criteria. The ethical standards governing the orator are identical to those governing anyone else. "There is no ethics of rhetoric, there is only an ethics of rhetoricians, and that is just ethics itself" (Garver 1994, 229). Can emotions be virtuous, according to Aristotle? Which emotional appeals does Aristotle find ethical? Does he think the virtuous person is ever justified in manipulating others emotionally? These are interesting questions but are not part of Aristotelian rhetoric. They are questions about Aristotelian virtue and ethics, which Aristotle himself distinguishes from *technē* like rhetoric.

CICERO AND THE MORALITY OF EMOTION

Emotional Appeals in Romulus's Cesspool

If Aristotle's appeals to *pathos,* discussed in the previous section, lend themselves to emotional manipulation, how much more do Cicero's emotional incitements? Unlike Aristotle, Cicero, particularly via Antonius in *De oratore,* explicitly counsels orators to stimulate vehement emotions in order to prevent audience members from thinking rationally. And, Antonius observes, "some pretty clever precepts can be given for *manipulating human feelings* and for capturing people's good will" (Cicero 2001a, 2.32; emphasis added). Despite what seems to be damning evidence against Cicero, however, I will show why his position on the rhetorical emotions is less manipulative than it appears and, most important, how Cicero, in contrast to Aristotle, provides a vision of a moral rhetoric that eschews emotional manipulation.

The exaggerated significance that Cicero attributes to *ethos* and, especially, *pathos* is itself the starting point in extenuating the charge against Cicero's rhetoric as manipulative; his description of the omnipotence of emotional appeals *is* exaggerated. We have already seen that Cicero explicates the emotions antithetically, at times emphasizing their opposition to, at times focusing on their consistency with, reason. Likewise, Cicero offers two contrasting viewpoints on the orator's eliciting of emotions. On the one hand, he presents the orator as wielding *pathos* and *ethos* to overpower his listeners and to lead them to adopt the outlook he wishes. From this perspective, the orator dominates the audience, manipulating it as he sees fit. On the other hand, Cicero also represents the public speaker as evoking emotions sincerely from an audience that can, in general, discern the truth and that elects on its own to be appealed to with vehement emotions. In this scenario, the members of the audience are not controlled by the orator as much as they control the orator themselves. Cicero depicts the two opposing viewpoints by relying on argument *in utramque partem.* He opts for this rhetorical exercise, partly, "because [he] found it gave the best practice in oratory," that is, it allowed the orator to see the strengths and weaknesses of not only his own position but also that of his opponent (Cicero 1971, 2.9). He also selects this type of argumentation because he considers truth to be multiplex, and arguing different sides points up different aspects of the truth (Conley 1990, 37; Sloane 1997, 30–31). Thus, Cicero characterizes the orator as manipulating the audience emotionally *and* as being dominated by the audience because each characterization reflects an element of the rhetorical situation.[24]

To present each position most strongly, Cicero (or his interlocutors) must argue each standpoint robustly, even to the point of exaggeration. For Cicero (2001a, 3.80), "the true, the perfect, the one and only oratory" will be able to "in every case unfold two opposing speeches" with "the vigor that is acquired in the forum," as is "our practice of speaking." It should not be surprising, then, that Cicero argues for the orator's ability to overpower listeners emotionally in the most emphatic terms. The eloquence of the grand style, the most emotional style, Cicero (1939b, 97) writes, "has power to sway men's minds and move them in every possible way" (see also 125, 128). Cicero's hyperbole—Can the orator's use of emotional appeals truly move people in every possible way?—not only uses argument *in utramque partem* effectively but also echoes Gorgias's inflated claims about the power of rhetoric (Plato 1979, 456a–c) and of the orator's words as "bringers-on of pleasure and takers-off of pain" (Gorgias of Leontini 1999, 10). Despite his differences with the sophists, Cicero shares with them, particularly Gorgias, the attribution to rhetoric, especially to emotional appeals, of near magical force.

Against his just-stated view that the orator controls his audience emotionally, Cicero develops the contrary standpoint, beginning with Antonius's explanation of how, when persuading others through *pathos,* he also experiences the same emotions himself. Before describing his own emotionalism, though, Antonius hails Crassus for being stirred by the passions he induces in his listeners: "it seems to me that you are not just setting the jurors on fire, but are ablaze yourself [*ipse ardere*]" (Cicero 2001a, 2.188). Antonius then details his own emotional transformation:

> I swear to you that every time I have ever wanted to arouse grief or pity or envy or hate in the hearts of jurors through my oratory, I was invariably, while working to stir the jurors, thoroughly stirred myself by the same feelings to which I was trying to lead them. . . . For no material is so easy to kindle, that it can catch fire unless fire is actually applied to it; likewise, no mind is so susceptible to an orator's power, that it can be set on fire unless the orator who approaches it is burning and all ablaze himself. (Cicero 2001a, 2.189–90)

Cicero has been read, cynically, as making Antonius into a sort of "method actor," who creates in himself the thoughts and emotions of his public character to successfully move his audience (Zerba 2003, 308). But if winning is part of Cicero's goal in explicating "ipse ardere," so too is characterizing the orator as sincere.

Cicero presents *ipse ardere* as signifying the orator's authenticity. For example, Crassus is said to feel "the self-same emotions" as his hearers because of the sincerity and truth of his thoughts. Similarly, when Antonius reveals his own emotional condition to "great experts" who are his "closest friends," that is, the interlocutors in *De oratore*: "I have no reason to lie about myself," and "I swear to you that every time I ever wanted to arouse [emotions] in the hearts of jurors through my oratory, I was invariably . . . thoroughly stirred myself by the same feelings to which I was trying to lead them" (Cicero 2001a, 2.188–90).

The reasons Antonius offers for why an orator would shun inauthentic emotions minimize, even stand in opposition to, the Gorgianic tradition of rhetoric as magically omnipotent. "Now if, for instance, the grief that we must assume would somehow be unreal and pretended, and if this mode of speaking would involve nothing but deception and imitation and feigning," Antonius explains, "then we would probably require some quite powerful art" (Cicero 2001a, 2.189). The art that Cicero boasted could sway men's minds and move them in every possible way is now not quite up to the task; rhetoric is not sufficiently powerful to succeed when its practitioners are not motivated by genuine emotions.

Cicero highlights the authenticity of the orator's emotions by contrasting the actor and orator. As Antonius observes, actors may, in a certain sense, assume a character's emotions, for example, when they depict "the ancient misfortunes and unreal, fictional griefs of heroes." Actors' emotions, however, are like masks, reflections of others, but not true to themselves. Antonius contraposes his genuineness to the actor's spuriousness: "I am not the actor of another's character, but the author of my own" (Cicero 2001a, 2.193–94). Manipulation, Cicero implies here, cannot coexist with such authenticity. The authentic orator possesses no hidden agenda. The orator here evokes no emotional appeals that conflict with rational arguments: "the power of the thoughts you [the orator] treat and of the commonplaces you handle when you are speaking is great enough to preclude any need for pretence and deception" (2.190). The Ciceronian speaker as presented in *De oratore*'s account of *ipse ardere* does not resemble the crafty emotional manipulator described elsewhere in *De oratore*. Instead, he is a person whose internal self and external persona are identical.

Like Aristotle, Cicero believes that, in general, truth ultimately prevails. He voices this belief most explicitly in the person of Gaius Laelius, the dominant speaker in *De amicitia* (44 BCE), Cicero's dialogue on friendship. There, Laelius affirms that "by the exercise of care . . . , everything pretended and false may be distinguished from what is genuine and true." More specifically, in spite of his intermittently voiced contempt for the lower classes (Wood 1988, 95–97), Cicero, through Laelius, evinces his trust in the *populus*'s ability to discern between manipulative and moral political speakers: "A public assembly [*contio*], though composed of very ignorant men, can, nevertheless, usually see the difference between a demagogue—that is, a smooth-tongued, shallow citizen—and one who has stability, sincerity, and weight" (Cicero 1923a, 95–96).[25] The demagogue—*assentator*—to which Laelius refers, is a flatterer who seeks political advantage by "insinuat[ing] himself into the favour of the assembly" (95). Although Laelius does not expressly speak of the *assentator*'s emotional manipulation, manipulation through flattery typically elicits pleasant emotions. And, as noted earlier, pleasure (or pain) is a concomitant of emotion, at least according to Aristotle's definition of *pathē*. The implication of this discussion in *De amicitia* is that emotional manipulation is usually ineffective in swaying a public audience, *pace* Cicero's own contrary views elsewhere.[26]

We have already seen that Aristotle acknowledges that, in judicial oratory, the jurors' desire for pleasure makes them vulnerable to emotional manipulation, which, as Garsten interprets Aristotle, makes them complicit in their own manipulation. I argued further that this complicity mitigates the orator's moral culpability. Like Aristotle, Cicero recognizes that listeners are not simply passive things manipulated by crafty public speakers. Far more than Aristotle, however, Cicero adverts to the audience's role in impelling the speaker to employ vehement emotional appeals. The people crave the varied emotions the orator can evoke in them: "The listening throng is delighted, is carried along by [the orator's] words, is in a sense bathed deep in delight. . . . They feel now joy now sorrow, are moved to laughter now to tears; they show approbation detestation, scorn aversion; they are drawn to pity to shame to regret; are stirred to anger wonder, hope fear" (Cicero 1939a, 188). And the grand style, which I previously described as the most emotional, is the style "which all look up to and admire" (Cicero 1939b, 97). Its antithesis, the Stoic style of speech, is "unsuitable for the orator" because it is "meager, dry, cramped, and disjointed." Ciceronian oratory, however, "must be adapted to the ears of the crowd," which, contra the Stoic's way of talking, includes pleasing the public and stirring its emotions (Cicero 2001a, 2.159). Because the audience expected, even respected, "loud ostentations of emotion," it was possible, in Cicero's day, for the orator to "get very close to, or even past, the edge of what we would consider plain manipulation, without losing one's credibility" (Wisse 1989, 263–64).

Thus, Cicero concludes his case for the audience's control of the orator, which he offers in opposition to his alternate view of the orator manipulating the audience emotionally.[27] How persuasive, however, is his defense of orators as not emotionally manipulative? His characterization of the authentic orator, who experiences the emotions he elicits in others, may be a useful corrective to the stereotype of the politician who employs emotions as expediency dictates. Nevertheless, although not all politicians cynically exploit emotions, enough do. Therefore, Cicero has not eliminated the problem of emotional manipulation by banking on the emotional authenticity of politicians. As for Cicero's faith in the people's capacity to distinguish between a demagogue and a trustworthy politician, we too, as democrats, trust that the electorate can generally differentiate between politicians who habitually manipulate us and those who do not. But the citizenry is confounded enough by emotional manipulation— witness again the effectiveness of the Willie Horton advertisements—that the problem of emotional manipulation in politics remains.

Cicero's observation that the people want the orator to excite them emotionally, however, is of greater relevance. The audience members' wish for vehement emotional appeals mitigates the orator's moral culpability because they are partners in, and arguably initiators of, their own manipulation. The people's involvement in their manipulation, though, does not free the manipulating orator from moral responsibility. Even if Cicero, in one side of his argument, overstates the orator's power to sway listeners with *pathos,* public speakers can *and* do emotionally coerce audiences. Public speakers engage in such manipulation not only covertly but even overtly, such as when listeners know they are being moved emotionally, yet are still exploited because of their irrational tendencies (Klemp 2011, 63). That audiences desire to be stimulated with strong emotions does point up their power over the orator and opens up the possibility of the people restricting emotionally manipulative appeals. Orators must comply with their audience's wishes: "The eloquence of orators has always been controlled by the good sense of the audience, since all who desire to win approval have regard to the goodwill of their auditors, and shape and adapt themselves completely according to this and to their opinion and approval" (Cicero 1939b, 24). The strength of Cicero's argument here for popular control of the orator reflects a truth about the rhetorical situation: public speakers influence audiences, but, in the final analysis, orators cannot succeed without their audience's approval. This power of audience over speaker, as will be seen, is embodied in the principle of decorum.

Like Aristotle's discussion of the rhetorical emotions, Cicero's account lacks moral obligation. But Cicero transmutes the orators' need to adapt their speech to circumstance from a pragmatic precept into a moral virtue. This change is embodied in "decorum," which denotes that for speech to be effective it must fit in with (*decet*) "the characteristic features of the speaker, subject, audience, occasion, or medium" (Hariman 2001, 199). Cicero summarizes this concept when he writes, "I shall begin by approving of one who can observe what is fitting [*deceat*]. This, indeed, is the form of wisdom that the orator must especially employ—to adapt himself to occasions and persons" (Cicero 1939b, 123). Decorum determines which emotional appeals are legitimate or appropriate according to the situation.

Although decorum is a marginal concern for Aristotle compared to Cicero (Garver 1994, 48), the Stagirite anticipates Cicero's use of decorum, in the *Rhetoric,* prescribing there that style should be "neither flat nor above the dignity of the subject, but appropriate [*prepon*]"; it must fit the speaker and subject consistent with the proper mean (Aristotle 1991, 3.2.1–3). (Cicero translates the Greek "*to prepon*" as "decorum" [1939b, 70].) But although Ciceronian decorum includes the need to adapt one's speech to the dignity of subject and speaker, it (unlike the Aristotelian concept) also entails conforming one's speech both to the demands of context, that is, the audience, *and* of place and time (Kaster 1982, 2–3). Accordingly, Cicero accommodates emotional appeals to the requirements of the situation, as decorum dictates; Aristotle does not.[28] Perhaps most important for our present purposes, however, is that *to prepon* in the *Rhetoric* is not a moral concept.

For Cicero, decorum imposes a moral duty on the orator to accommodate his thought and language, including his emotional appeals, to propriety. Cicero, in his rhetorical works, does not explicitly delineate decorum as a moral concept. Rather, he develops decorum as an obligation more ambiguously rooted in aesthetic sensibilities and the practical necessities of persuasion. Nevertheless, even in his rhetorical writings, Cicero alludes to the ethical character of decorum. For example, Cicero (1939b) links decorum in rhetoric to the moral duty of propriety (72). Cicero also grounds decorum in the sense of community (*communis sensus*), which he vests with moral force (Remer 2010, 1070–71; Kapust 2011a, 95–100). It is in *De officiis* (written in 44 BCE), however, that Cicero most fully develops decorum as a moral virtue and duty.[29] As Cicero (1991a) argues there, decorum "cannot be separated from what is honourable: for what is seemly [*decet*] is honourable [*honestum*], and what is honourable is seemly" (1.93–94). And Cicero applies decorum specifically to oratory, in *De officiis,* when discussing the roles "we assume for ourselves by our own decision," that is, our vocations (Cicero 1991a, 1.115; Gill 1988, 173–74).

For Cicero, decorum is the primary moral standard for emotional appeals in political speech. In the Roman Republic, the two main arenas for deliberative or political oratory are the *contio* and the Senate. Each body has its own decorum controlling emotional appeals. In the *contio*, most appeals are to the vehement emotions (Cicero 2001a, 2.337). In *De oratore*, Cicero associates the passionate speech called for in the *contio* with "some grander, some more brilliant mode of oratory," which is required by "the passionate emotions of the crowd" (2.337). The audience at a public meeting, which ranged as high as fifteen thousand to twenty thousand listeners (Ramsey 2007, 124), provided the orator with his "greatest stage" (Cicero 2001a, 2.338), a setting that naturally stirs orators "to employ a more distinguished mode of oratory" (*ornatius dicendi genus*). As previously discussed, the orator's use of *ethos* and *pathos* before public assemblies is required by the audience, which delights in experiencing a spectrum of emotions. The propriety of which emotions to elicit and when they should be incited, Cicero suggests, is ultimately settled on by the "assent of the multitude and the approbation of the people"; their verdict, not the opinions of the experts or even of the orator himself, is determinative (Cicero 1939a, 185–86, 188–89).

This contional mode of oratory anticipates what Cicero (1939b, 20, 69) would come to term in the *Orator* (46 BCE) the "grandiloquent" ("grand") or "vigorous style," the most vehement of the three styles of oratory (plain, middle, and grandiloquent). The connection between, if not the identity of, contional oratory and the high style is implied by Cicero's use of the same terms to describe them: *ornatus* (ornate) and *gravis* (stately) (Cicero 2001a, 2.338, 2.337, 2.333; 1939b, 97, 99). Like the orator speaking at a *contio*, the orator employing the grand style must be "trained and equipped to arouse and sway the emotions" (1939b, 20). In both forms of oratory, the speaker should aspire to attain the heights of eloquence.

The other setting for political oratory is the Senate. Because the Senate was a smaller deliberative institution, with two hundred to slightly more than four hundred members of the political elite typically attending (Ramsey 2007, 124),[30] different emotional appeals were considered appropriate for speeches to this body. In theory, at least, rhetoric in the Senate was more restrained. As Antonius observes, a speaker's advice in the Senate was to be handled "with less display, for this is a wise council, and many others must be given the opportunity to speak" (Cicero 2001a, 2.333); speech in the Senate was to be free, or largely free, of *pathos* and affect (Mack 1937, 17). Based on Cicero's published speeches to the Senate, however, *pathos* was in fact used. Invective, with its goal of turning the audience's emotions against the orator's opponent, was a common feature of senatorial oratory (Mack 1937, 82; Cicero 1942c, 74). And even under optimal conditions, Cicero observes that "when the topic [being discussed] is so important," then copiousness (*copia*), the "nonrational" use of stylistic abundance, is needed either to win over the Senate or to supply it with information (Cicero 1999e, 3.40; 1928, 3.40).

The emotional appeals Cicero deems appropriate in the *contio* and Senate reflect the decorum of these bodies in his own day. But Cicero is well aware of the corrupt condition of the late Roman Republic. In a letter to Atticus, in which he criticizes "our friend Cato," he writes of the rigid Stoic: "He speaks in the Senate as though he were living in Plato's Republic instead of Romulus' cesspool" (Cicero 1999a, letter 21). Cicero completed *De oratore* in 55 BCE, during a period of political crisis, just three years after his banishment by the tribune Publius Clodius Pulcher. Emphasizing his awareness of the Republic's precariousness, Cicero sets *De oratore* in 91 BCE, during another period of political crisis, when the Roman Senate was divided over the enfranchisement of Rome's Italian allies. (The Social War between Rome and the Italians began just slightly after the dialogue was supposed to have taken place.) Because Cicero sees himself as speaking to an audience, even in the Senate, that is often poorly informed, insufficiently public spirited, too willing to be entertained, and sometimes downright dishonest, he does not hesitate to overwhelm the audience with strong emotions in lieu of approaching them with more judicious speech.

But even if the audience participates in its own emotional manipulation, as I noted above, the orator, as well as the rhetorician who promotes manipulative tactics, cannot elude moral responsibility. From Cicero's perspective, the orator's moral obligations are determined by decorum. (As already seen, Aristotle does not concern himself, in the *Rhetoric*, with the public speaker's moral obligations; the bounds of legitimate emotional appeals are determined by artistic norms, which the orator may or may not choose to follow.) For Cicero, the audience's acceptance of vehement emotional appeals *and* the propriety of such appeals in his political context morally justify the kinds of appeals he recommends in *De oratore*. Cicero is especially willing to yield on ethical norms when the welfare of the *res publica* is threatened. Thus, he contends in *De officiis* that assisting "one's country . . . [takes] precedence in all duties." Cicero not only gives priority to the obligation to one's country, he believes that serving the interests of the country is honorable by definition (Cicero 1991a, 3.90, 3.40). As an orator himself, Cicero viewed many of his public words and actions as dictated, and justified, by the good of the Republic.

As a general proposition, Cicero's evaluation of the morality of emotional manipulation according to context seems reasonable. "Moral evaluations of manipulation depend on context. . . . [T]he circumstances of politics are complex, and situations will inevitably arise where manipulation is morally permissible" (Klemp 2011, 79). Perhaps Cicero's circumstances sometimes demanded emotional manipulation. Still, the willingness of orators, including Cicero, to use *pathos,* in its most excessive forms, to achieve their ends should give us pause. When moving an audience through violent emotions becomes the norm—as it did for Cicero—rather than something exceptional, we are descending into uncomfortable moral territory. Cicero, however, does not limit himself to his own political conditions but envisions a future political and legal community where political speech is not inclined to lapse into emotional manipulation. I turn now to Cicero's vision of a different, better political reality and the shift in emotional appeals that accompanies this vision.

A Better Decorum

Because the *communis sensus* changes over time, rhetorical proofs, such as appeals to the *pathē,* must change too. In *De oratore,* Antonius asserts that "the fundamental requirement for speaking persuasively is to know the character of the community [*mores civitatis*]. *Since [it] frequently changes, our mode of speaking should often change as well*" (Cicero 2001a, 2.337; emphasis added). As seen earlier, *to prepon* in Aristotle excludes the orator's need to adapt to different audiences. Aristotle does not direct *rhetors* to alter their pathetic appeals consistent with changes within political communities.[31]

Cicero not only acknowledges the mutability of emotional appeals in deliberative oratory, he also advocates change. We find Cicero's call for improved political speech in *De legibus,* the dialogue in which he presents a superior version of the Roman legal system. In line with Stoic thought of the first and second centuries BCE, Cicero's laws in *De legibus* refer to human legislation that prescribes intermediate appropriate actions (*media officia*), that is, duties that can be followed by imperfect humans—all humans who are not wise men. In contrast to intermediate actions, perfectly appropriate actions, termed "right actions," are commanded by natural law, which is only attainable by the wise man (Asmis 2008, 2, 11–12, 15–16, 22). This distinction between perfect and imperfect duties is reiterated in *De officiis,* where Cicero confirms that the duties he discusses in this book are "those that the Stoics call 'middle' [*media*]. They are shared and widely accessible" (Cicero 1991a, 3.14–16). Thus, the laws of *De legibus,* which include rules about political speech, and the ethical decorum of *De officiis,* which undergirds the moral nature of emotional appeals, are both connected to intermediate duties, relevant, as is rhetoric, for real, that is, imperfect humans.

Cicero proposes a law in *De legibus* that departs significantly from the guidelines for emotional appeals in *De oratore.* Cicero's initial submission of this law is concise: "Let those things which are brought before the people or the senate be moderate [*modica*]" (Cicero 1999e, 3.10). Cicero's further excursus on this "important" and "excellent law" explains that by "moderate" he means "decent [*modesta*] and calm [*sedata*]," terms that connote speech quite different from the political oratory of *De oratore.* Although contional oratory in *De oratore* is intended to excite and incite the audience's emotions, the political oratory of *De legibus* is designed to calm the audience. Take the term "*modica,*" which describes the milieu of the Senate and *contio* in *De legibus.* In the *Orator,* Cicero uses a form of *modica* repeatedly to denominate or characterize the middle style (1939b, 21, 69, 95, 98, 101), which he distinguishes from the grand style by its eschewing "the fiery force" of the high style and by the "even tenor of its way" (21). In this discussion of the middle style, Cicero pairs *modica* at least four times with some form of *temperatum,* which denotes self-restraint, the antithesis of both the "grand, impetuous, and fiery" high style (99) and its antecedent, the oratory of the *contio.* And like the speech proposed in *De legibus,* which is calm [*sedata*], the middle style "proceeds in calm and peaceful [*sedate placideque*] flow" (92). Cicero's goal of calmer political speech in *De legibus,* however, is not tantamount to the extirpation of emotional appeals from deliberative oratory. Like the middle style, the political speech of *De legibus* is designed to be "moderate and tempered" (95), in language *and* in the eliciting of passions.

Unlike the orator of Cicero's rhetorical works, who generally controls the audience to maneuver them as he sees fit—"to win over their inclinations, to drive them at will in one direction, and to draw them at will from another" (Cicero 2001a, 1.30)—the orator (*actor*) presiding over political meetings in *De legibus* is not driven to incite the audience members' emotions or manipulate their wills. Although Cicero (1999e) describes *De legibus*'s orator in similar language, as directing and shaping "not only the minds and wishes of his hearers, but almost their expressions as well" (3.40), the orator's intention here is to calm emotions. As J. G. F. Powell interprets this passage, the orator directs the audience in the Senate and "in the popular assembly too. Now this is an excellent law because it keeps unruly demagogues under control. The preservation of moderate proceedings depends on the *actor*" (Dyck 2004, 538).[32] In arguing that Cicero's goal here is to maintain moderation, I am not asserting that he is concerned with fostering individual autonomy. More likely than not, he is primarily interested in ensuring the state's welfare.[33] Regardless of his motivations, Cicero supports moderate political speech, which is contrary to emotional manipulation.

The decorum mandated in *De legibus,* like the decorum of Cicero's rhetorical works, is grounded in the *communis sensus.* The "sense of community" in *De legibus,* however, is less transitory than that of the rhetorical works. Although Cicero describes the character of the community in *De oratore* as changing frequently, in *De legibus* the *communis sensus* derives from the deeply rooted values of the community, which are stable, if not immutable.[34] Both *De legibus,* which treats near-ideal laws, and *De republica* (begun in 54, circulated in 51 BCE, though available to us today with significant gaps), which discusses the ideal state, represent the sense of community as originating in the wisdom of the ancients, which is confirmed through long-standing communal acceptance. For example, Cicero explains that the *mos maiorum* (the custom of the forefathers) was—until the widespread corruption of his own day—respected by all, and preserved by the "great men" over the generations (Cicero 1999d, 5.1; Brunt 1988, 56–58; Roloff 1938). According to Cicero, the community's acceptance of the Roman Constitution, like the *mos maiorum,* is grounded in enduring tradition. For Cicero, the Roman Constitution is "the organization of the State so wisely instituted by our ancestors"; it is the best constitution ever because it represents the Romans' "practical, collective wisdom," its principles having been tested over a long period of time (Cicero 1958a, 137; Asmis 2008, 31). Cicero bolsters the moral force of the Roman Constitution by associating it with the Stoic natural law. For example, he has his close friend Atticus state, when referring to the Roman Constitution, that "our laws are in accordance with nature; the wisdom of our ancestors" (Cicero 1999e, 2.62).[35] According to Cicero, the Roman Constitution *and* the decorum of the ancient traditions, if not perfect, are still naturally just.

Cicero considers the emotionally restrained oratory of *De legibus* to be superior to the passionate oratory of his rhetorical works. The code of laws Cicero presents in *De legibus,* including his law for political speech, is intended to be as ideal a set of laws as attainable by those who are not wise men. The decorum that controls the political speaker in this dialogue is based on the sense of community derived from ancestral values, which is morally superior to the short-lived decorum of the orator speaking during the Republic's last days. Not only did Cicero believe in this more enduring decorum's moral superiority, but we today—living during a period of intense political partisanship—are likely to consider it morally preferable to the decorum of Cicero's time and, within limits, the standards of political speech today. The political speech enshrined in Cicero's *De legibus* avoids the immorality of emotional manipulation by toning down emotions intended to overwhelm reasoned thought. It promotes good consequences—at least it does not hinder them—and it allows hearers to make their own decisions freely.

Cicero's dream of restrained political speech anticipates the current calls for political civility. But like many current proponents of civility, Cicero has no clear plan for effecting the change of heart necessary to implement his legislative proposal.[36] Cicero's revised decorum, implicit in his law, must be accepted by the people. Because the auditors are the ultimate authority of decorum in rhetoric, Cicero is unwilling to impose his revised law on the audience. Accordingly, in *De legibus,* Cicero (1999e) responds to his friend Atticus, who questions the feasibility of gaining support for his proposed legislation: "What I say does not refer to this senate or to men of the present, but to *those of the future who may wish to obey these laws*" (3.29; emphasis added). If we turn to Cicero's specific law regulating deliberative oratory, his contemporaries may not have supported its passage because they largely delighted in emotional appeals. Likewise, and despite protestations to the contrary, today's electorate is attracted to vehement emotional appeals, or at least it is moved by them—consider, for example, the effectiveness of negative campaigning.

CONCLUSION

I conclude by revisiting the question of emotional manipulation in Aristotle and Cicero, adverting to those elements of the "Ciceronian response" that make it more relevant today than Aristotle's. I took as my point of departure Klemp's two essential conditions of emotional manipulation: (1) as a form of force and, (2) as intentional. I also highlighted two moral faults of manipulation: (1) manipulation's bad consequences for hearers and (2) its denial of autonomous decision making. Based on the scholarly literature and a superficial reading of both rhetoricians, I conceded that Cicero appears far more open to charges of emotional manipulation than Aristotle. It has been my aim to demonstrate otherwise.

Emotional manipulation is a greater problem in Aristotle than initially appears. His rationalist approach to rhetoric, which largely roots emotional appeals in argumentation, does not safeguard the audience from false or irrational manipulative emotions. In addition, Aristotle suggests that *pathos* can be elicited by nonargumentative sources (e.g., style and delivery), which can themselves give rise to manipulation. Further, Aristotle's rhetorical norms are not moral but are derived from the art's internal ends. The Aristotelian orator qua orator is not morally bound to follow or avoid any specific practices, including the avoidance of excessive emotional appeals. True, the Aristotelian orator qua freeborn, adult, male citizen *should* be virtuous, but Aristotelian virtue stands apart from Aristotelian rhetoric. For Aristotle, what makes a person virtuous relative to emotion differs from what characterizes a good orator relative to emotion.

In contrast to Aristotle, Cicero condones emotional manipulation less than he initially appears. As I demonstrated, Cicero presents a double-sided view of rhetoric, each side containing a portion of a more complex truth. He counters one claim—that the orator can almost magically manipulate audiences—with another in which the audience is seen as controlling the orator. By acknowledging the audience as the ultimate decision maker, bolstered by its ability—even in *contiones*—to discern the truth, Cicero downplays what appears, in much of his rhetorical writings, as the near ubiquity of emotional manipulation. Moreover, the audience's penchant for emotional stimulation diminishes the orator's— and Cicero's—moral responsibility for seeking to overwhelm the audience emotionally. Thus, although I, by and large, accept Klemp's two conditions of manipulation, because he states them categorically (i.e., manipulation either does or does not exist), he ignores the presence of degrees of manipulation. The further emotional appeals approach pure manipulation, the greater the manipulator's culpability.[37]

Unlike Aristotle, Cicero grounds rhetoric in a morality based on decorum. Because Cicero vests the orator with moral obligation, he speaks to us in a way that Aristotle cannot. We do not compartmentalize politicians' speech and actions into a separate sphere with its own amoral norms, as does Aristotle. We— even the cynical among us—expect that politicians are bound by, and should heed, their moral duties. Like Cicero, we want politicians to be restrained by moral rules, even if we grant, like Cicero, that politicians' moral duties sometimes differ from those of the citizenry at large (Cicero 1991a, 1.113).[38] Part of what we find troubling about Machiavelli, as I contend in chapter 3, is that his political actors are governed by the *utile* (the useful or expedient), but not also by the *honestum* (the moral). For us, as for Cicero, politicians must balance the two.

Because Cicero's rhetorical morality is based on decorum, how the orator *should* employ emotion will vary with context. Thus, Cicero suggests that moral standards are more permissive when the state's existence is threatened and stricter under healthier political conditions. His claim that vehement emotional appeals (that overshadow rational thinking) are sometimes morally justifiable is worth careful consideration today, when a black and white approach to political ethics seems insufficient. For example, in war, when the enemy uses propaganda to unify its population against us, is it morally correct to forego all use of propaganda? Are otherwise objectionable emotional appeals—overwhelming the audience with extreme patriotic feelings, temporarily eliciting friendly feelings toward former (and future) enemies to advance military ends, even deepening hatred for the enemy by emphasizing their atrocities and minimizing their positive actions—necessarily to be condemned in just wars, like the fight against the Nazis? Although I am not delineating the particulars of when and where such appeals may be justified, or even whether these particular appeals *can* be justified, I think it reasonable to concede that emotional manipulation is to be accepted begrudgingly under some political conditions.

Finally, Cicero's vision of an explicitly moderate rhetoric distinguishes him from Aristotle. This vision, for Cicero, is grounded in the traditional values of the people, and, if it is to be realized, must be accepted by the people once more. This vision is also not utopian, not the ideal of the Stoic wise man, but a practically achievable improvement on Cicero's own status quo. Thus, in *De legibus,* Cicero (1999e) tells his brother, Quintus, that the latter's conservative idealism—which Cicero largely shares—must be tempered by political realities even in the framing of a superior legal code (3.26, 3.33). Cicero's proposal for more moderate and restrained political discourse anticipates current demands for political civility today. We still face the same question, however, of how to move from our decorum, which countenances emotional manipulation in politics, to one that does not.

CHAPTER 2

Political Morality, Conventional Morality, and Decorum in Cicero

Over the past several decades, especially since September 11 and the beginning of the War on Terror, the political execution of normally immoral actions once considered exceptional has become almost routine. "In various meaningful ways, the exception has merged with the rule. 'Emergency government has become the norm'" (Gross 2003, 1022; Special Senate Committee on National Emergencies and Delegated Emergency Powers, 93rd Cong., cited in Gross, 1022). I do not argue that recognizing a discrete political morality justifies all or most of these recent departures from ordinary morality and constitutionality. I maintain, however, that the proliferation of such politically directed deeds highlights the timeliness of Cicero's two-tiered theory of morality. The danger of holding politicians to a universal, unvarying moral standard, that is, "to identify morality with innocence . . . would ultimately set the politicians free to disregard morality altogether" (Hampshire 1989, 12). Cicero eschews the fantasy of a morally pure politics for the reality of a politics that is moral yet tempered by political realities. By proposing a politically pragmatic morality rather than a philosophically untainted one, Cicero begins to reverse the process begun in antiquity in which the unity of eloquence and philosophy, politics and morality were split *between* politics and eloquence "unaccompanied by any consideration of moral duty," on the one hand, *and* philosophy and wisdom "prosecuted vigorously in quiet seclusion by the men of highest virtue," on the other (Cicero 1949, 1.1–1.5; 2001a, 3.56–62). How Cicero seeks to effect a conceptual reconciliation between the practical and the moral is a fundamental question of this chapter.

According to conventional wisdom, "politicians are a good deal worse, morally worse, than the rest of us" (Walzer 1973, 162). In the previous chapter, we focused on a contextually dependent moral wrongdoing, emotional manipulation, which is more prevalent among politicians than the rest of us. But the moral vagaries of politicians extend beyond emotional manipulation. Setting aside the unjustifiable self-serving immoralities of politicians, like the taking of bribes or the use of political power to obtain sex, there are behaviors that violate ordinary moral standards but that politicians sometimes justify as moral because they are necessary for the public interest. For example, seemingly motivated by the greater good, politicians lie to their constituents; they spy on fellow citizens and on friendly leaders abroad; they torture suspects to obtain information; and they kill extrajudicially the innocent, the guilty, and those in between.

These apparently immoral practices characterize the dilemma faced, especially by politicians, in which "a particular act of government (in a political party or in the state) may be exactly the right thing to do in utilitarian terms and yet leave the man who does it guilty of a moral wrong" (Walzer 1973, 161). Michael Walzer defends the political necessity and moral justifiability of "dirty hands," although he also argues that because the choice is between two evils, the political actor, even in choosing the lesser evil, has committed a moral wrong. And because he has committed a moral crime, he will, if he is a moral politician, "acknowledge and bear (and perhaps . . . repent and do penance for) his guilt" (1973, 167–68).[1] Walzer, however, is not alone in justifying ordinarily or conventionally immoral actions on the grounds of the greater good. An impressive list of contemporary political theorists, philosophers, and social thinkers (e.g., Max Weber 2009, 121–23; Thomas Nagel 1978, 75–90; Bernard Williams 1978, 55–73; 1981, 60; 1987, 115–37; and Stuart Hampshire 1978b, 23–53[2]) defend the proposition that political actors are at times morally enjoined to act contrary to ordinary morality.

Does the dilemma of "dirty hands" presuppose two different moralities, one ordinary and the other political?[3] Cicero contends that it does.[4] In this chapter, we examine the origins of this distinction between moralities as developed by Cicero, the first political thinker—at least the first whose writings are extant—to differentiate between general moral standards and moral standards specifically applicable to politicians. Cicero grounds his conception of political morality in his theory of *personae* (roles), in which each role (including the role of political actor) possesses its own moral duties. As we shall see, Cicero's theory of *personae* is based on decorum, the moral-rhetorical concept discussed in the previous chapter.

Machiavelli, however, not Cicero, is the historical thinker most often linked to the idea of a "two-tiered" morality, ordinary and political (Berlin 1972; Hampshire 1989, 162–68). Isaiah Berlin, for example, finds two moralities in

Machiavelli: the political (Roman or classical) morality that Machiavelli him-self adopts and the Christian (conventional) morality, which he rejects (1972). But Cicero defended his two-tiered morality more than fifteen hundred years before Machiavelli, and, as discussed in the next chapter, Cicero argues for the *morality* of necessary but unsavory political actions, whereas Machiavelli defends bad actions *not as moral* but as *useful*.

Cicero's two-tiered morality deserves attention for its originality, but, in ad-dition, it merits investigation for its contemporary relevance. The *personae* theory on which it is grounded anticipates the work of recent scholars who speak of "role-based morality" or "role-based redescription" in which persons acting in certain roles are insulated from some standards of ordinary morality because of the principles and rules that define their roles.[5] Like other accounts of role moralities, Cicero's *personae* theory has the advantage of regarding at least some role-based departures from conventional morality as nevertheless moral (Applbaum 1999, 51–52). Role moralities, including Cicero's, allow us to evade the dilemma faced by Walzer, who describes the conventionally im-moral acts of politicians as both "doing what it is wrong to do" (1973, 164) and doing what it is "often right to do" (174). Explicating this apparent paradox, Kai Nielsen criticizes what he sees as Walzer's "mistaken way" of conceptual-izing things: "In doing things we ought to do, we cannot (*pace* Walzer *et al.*) do wrong. We may do things that in normal circumstances would be horribly wrong, but in these circumstances of dirty hands, they are not, *everything con-sidered*, wrong" (Nielsen 2000, 140–41). Although Nielsen does not respond to Walzer by turning to role-based morality, role morality theory replies to Walz-er's apparent paradox by classifying the normally immoral actions of politi-cians as moral, reflecting the discrete morality of the politician's role.

Decorum distinguishes Cicero's *personae* theory from other accounts of role morality, which provides Cicero's account with a greater consistency than most other versions of role morality. Advocates of role morality generally ground the morality of the role in a source distinct from that of ordinary or "impartial" morality (Markovits 2008, 158–63).[6] As we shall see later in this chapter, Cicero, in his *personae* theory, despite differentiating the morality of the role from general morality, nonetheless identifies role and ordinary mo-rality as rooted in a comprehensive decorum-based moral framework. Thus, most other accounts of role morality must contend with the difficulty of recon-ciling two conflicting moralities, the role morality of, for example, lawyers or politicians *and* ordinary, non-role-specific morality—a problem engendered, in part, by the discrete underpinnings of these two moralities. Cicero's ac-counts of ordinary and role-specific morality, however, share a common source in decorum, which means that moral actors (e.g., lawyers or politicians *and* ordinary citizens) are required to comport themselves according to a single fundamental standard, that is, what is appropriate to the context.

Further, because Cicero's *personae* theory is based on decorum, it can— indeed, must—be adaptable to situations other than Cicero's own and be sensitive to the particular circumstances in which political actors find themselves, for example, whether they operate in political conditions that are largely tranquil or unstable. The foundation of Cicero's moral theory in decorum enables morality, including political morality, to change over time. For instance, Cicero's morality, which subordinates the well-being of the individual to the welfare of the political community, does not accord well with modern morality's usual, if not dispositive, emphasis on the individual over the community. Cicero's decorum-based morality, however, can accommodate the shift from the subordination of the individual to the community, characteristic of Cicero and other classical thinkers, to the greater focus on the individual in relation to the community, which generally characterizes modern moral theory.[7]

Given the centrality of decorum to Cicero, it seems reasonable to ask, "Does Cicero's distinction between political and ordinary morality make sense within our own context?" Do we accept, not simply expect, a different set of moral standards for political leaders? That politicians worldwide are commonly condemned as hypocrites and liars, if not worse, would seem to indicate the absence of tolerance for, let alone agreement with, the idea of a distinct political morality. Nevertheless, although scholarly opinion is divided, a significant number of respected academics, as we have seen, defend the position that what is generally immoral may, depending on the context, be considered morally necessary for the political actor. Further, American constitutional theory and practice, interpreted through what Ronald Dworkin terms a "*moral* reading" of the Constitution, are sources of insight into the moral principles of the nation. As Dworkin argues: "The moral reading proposes that we all—judges, lawyers, citizens—interpret and apply [the] abstract clauses of [the Constitution] on the understanding that they invoke moral principles about political decency and justice" (Dworkin 1996, 2).[8] By examining constitutional theory and practice for their underlying moral assumptions, we can detect the long-standing recognition of a political morality distinct from ordinary morality.

Especially during threats to national security, politicians have been typically held, constitutionally, to different standards than private citizens.[9] Thus, the US Supreme Court concedes that "while the Constitution protects against invasions of individual rights, it is not a suicide pact," suggesting that Congress may enact legislation that subordinates individual rights to the moral duty of national self-preservation (*Kennedy* v. *Mendoza-Martinez*, 372 U.S. 144, 160 [1963]). Likewise, Thomas Jefferson argues that "[t]he laws of necessity, of self-preservation, of saving our country when in danger, are of a *higher obligation*" than a "strict observance of the written laws" (1984; emphasis added). Echoing Cicero's maxim *salus populi suprema lex esto* (let the safety of the people be the highest law), Jefferson writes: "To lose our country by a scrupulous adherence to written law, would be to lose the law itself, with life, liberty, property and all those who are enjoying them with us; thus absurdly sacrificing the ends to the means" (1231).[10] Much like Jefferson before him, Abraham Lincoln too (in upholding his suspension of the writ of *habeas corpus* against Chief Justice Roger Taney's decision [*Ex parte Merryman*, 1861] that Lincoln acted unconstitutionally [Basler 1953, 4:430][11]) maintains that the welfare of the Union trumps ordinary morality or legality.[12]

CICERO AND THE DISTINCTIVE NATURE OF POLITICAL MORALITY

Cicero recognizes a morality for humankind in general and additional moralities for particular persons or vocations, including a morality for politicians. Of Cicero's three main works on moral philosophy, *De finibus bonorum et malorum*, *Tusculan Disputations*, and *De officiis*, the first two investigate morality largely unrelated to politics, whereas the third emphasizes practical social and political morality (Cicero 1991a, xxiii). Although Cicero composes *De officiis* in the form of a letter to his son Marcus, he intends the work as a plea to the younger generation to devote itself to a life of public service (Colish 1990, 143–44; Cicero 1991a, xviii). But even though *De officiis* devotes most of its discussion to the practical morality of public life, Cicero introduces the work by affirming that the moral duties discussed in this treatise encompass both the public *and* the private spheres: "For no part of life, neither public affairs nor private, neither in the forum nor at home, neither when acting on your own nor in dealings with another, can be free from duty" (1991a, 1.4).[13]

The basis for Cicero's distinction between moralities is a fourfold division of *personae*, which Cicero proposes in *De officiis*.[14] Cicero's four *personae* are (1) the role common to all humans as rational beings, (2) the *persona* nature assigns to persons individually, (3) the role dictated by chance or circumstance, and (4) the *persona* we choose for ourselves in deciding "who and what we wish to be, and what kind of life we want" (1991a, 1.107–17). Among the professions identified by Cicero as part of the fourth *persona* are politicians—orators,[15] magistrates, and the elected public officials who held executive power in the Roman Republic (1991a, 1.115, 1.124; Lintott 1999b, 94–104; Vishnia 2012, 64–65).

The *officia* (moral duties) that are incumbent on all persons derive from the first *persona* (Cicero 1991a, 1.107). Thus, the moral duties that derive from the four moral virtues common to humanity—wisdom, social virtue (divided between justice and kindness or liberality), greatness of spirit, and seemliness—are obligations of the first *persona*. These virtues make up the *honestum* (the moral or honorable; 1991a, 1.15).

For Cicero, the morality of the first *persona* must be set against the distinct *officia* of the remaining *personae*. Rather than requiring us to subordinate the duties of the other three *personae* whenever they conflict with any of the virtues of everyday morality, Cicero instructs us not to act viciously when undertaking our individual duties. When arguing that the pursuit of our own nature should not clash with universal nature, Cicero explains: "Each person should hold on to what is his as far as it is not vicious [*vitiosa*], but is peculiar to him" (1991a, 1.110). Likewise, he counsels that we should maintain constancy when we adopt a plan of life entirely consistent with our nature, as long as our nature "is not a vicious one" (1991a, 1.120). Cicero voices a similar sentiment, using "cruelty" (*crudelitas*) rather than viciousness as the moral limit: "cruelty is extremely hostile to the nature of man [the basis of ordinary morality], which we ought to follow" (1991a, 3.46). Unless we interpret Cicero as excluding viciousness (or cruelty) but not the particular requirements of ordinary morality, then actions that Cicero deems morally acceptable for the fourth *persona* would conflict with the *officia* of our common human rationality. For example, Cicero excuses lawyers for playing fast and loose with the truth, which, unless we understand the moral demands of the first *persona* to be of a general nature (e.g., avoiding viciousness or cruelty), would leave us (and Cicero) with an inconsistency between the moral obligation of the first *persona* (required by justice) not to deceive (Cicero 1991a, 1.110, 1.115) and the moral laxity of the fourth *persona*. Likewise, Cicero maintains that the *honestum* normally obligates us to follow the established customs and conventions of a community—"these are themselves rules" (1913a, 1.148). But philosophers like Socrates and Aristippus, Cicero observes, acted contrary to societal convention because of their idiosyncratic natures. If Cicero maintained that the specific obligations of the first *persona* prevail over the *officia* of the individual (or second) *personae*—a proposition I reject—he could not justify Socrates's and Aristippus's departures from universal nature, while still denying the rest of us the same prerogative (Cicero 1991a, 1.148).

When discussing the professions, Cicero (1991a) is most candid about the moral justifiability of the lawyer's divergence from everyday norms: "scruples should not prevent us from occasionally defending a guilty man, provided he is not wicked and impious. The masses want it; custom permits it; humanity tolerates it. In lawsuits, a judge should always strive for the truth, but an advocate may sometimes defend what looks like the truth, even if it is less true" (2.51). Immediately preceding his exculpation of lying for the defense, Cicero even refuses to condemn all prosecutorial lying, denouncing only deceiving a jury to endanger an innocent person's status as a citizen (2.51). He implies here that prosecutorial dishonesty in lesser crimes may be acceptable. And, in fact, Cicero concedes in *Pro Cluentio* that prosecutors, including himself, mislead their audiences: "In my capacity as prosecutor I had made it my first object to work upon the feelings both of the public and of the jurors, and I was quoting, not from my own opinion, but from current rumour" (2000a, 139). He further upholds the acceptability of prosecutorial misrepresentation, at least in the sense of presenting ill-considered and inauthentic arguments. Cicero justifies lawyerly deception, in part, by adopting the assumption that underlies our adversarial legal system, that is, "the truth will emerge from the clash of opposing opinions" (Dyck 1996, 435). Lawyers, among them prosecutors, are employed to plead for their client. They are hired to offer the best possible arguments, which do not necessarily reflect their personal opinions. In the end, though, truth will out.

Let us use another example with which, perhaps, more people can identify today: the heroic soldier fighting a just war. We may characterize this soldier—suppose him a soldier in the Second World War fighting valiantly against the Nazis—as most conspicuously virtuous. Nevertheless, this soldier stands outside the moral standards appropriate for ordinary persons. In wars, even just wars, soldiers, even virtuous soldiers, kill enemies who are denied the benefit of legal trials. Such virtuous soldiers are also responsible for "collateral damage" in which innocents are unintentionally injured or killed. However heroic we consider these soldiers to be, they cannot be our moral paragons in daily life. Their morality must, to some degree, differ from our everyday morality.

Cicero not only identifies the politician as a distinct role but also identifies the political actor as occupied in the most important of activities.[16] In distinguishing the politician from others, Cicero also distinguishes the politician's morality from that of others. Cicero understands that the rules of politics are sufficiently different from the rules of everyday life that the virtuous statesman is not always to be emulated by regular citizens. Cicero forgives statesmen, especially founders of states, many of their sins, even transforming their vices into virtues. He does so because their actions benefit the state. Thus, in *De officiis*, Cicero finds that Lucius Junius Brutus, consul and founder of the Republic, committed no injustice when he deposed his innocent colleague Lucius Tarquinius Collatinus from his consulship for the sin of sharing his family name with Rome's last king, the despised Lucius Tarquinius Superbus (1991a, 3.40). Likewise, in *De republica*, Cicero overlooks Romulus's murder of his brother, Remus, because of the former's success as founder of Rome (1999d, 2.4–21).[17] As politicians, they were beholden to the *officia* of their role, which required them to act for the public good with impartiality, fixing their gaze on what benefits citizens, forgetful of their own advantage, and caring "for the whole body of the republic" (1991a, 1.85). Their political duties even outweighed the particular precepts of ordinary morality, so long as they avoided viciousness or cruelty.[18]

In addition to Brutus and Romulus, Cicero offers another statesman, the Athenian lawgiver Solon, as justifiably following his individual *persona* over the requirements of conventional morality. To evade the Athenian law that forbade, on pain of death, advocating the retaking of the island of Salamis from the Megarians, Solon feigned madness. This "outstandingly cunning and crafty" deception enabled Solon to recite a poem urging the Athenians to recover Salamis, with the impunity vouchsafed a madman, after which the Athenians not only repealed the restraining law on advocating recapture of the island but also soon recovered the island. Although such deceit would have been dishonorable for the run-of-the-mill citizen, Cicero sanctions Solon's simulation of insanity; the Athenian statesman was motivated "both to make his own life safer" (an insufficient justification) and "the more to assist the republic" (a statesman's obligation; 1991a, 1.108). Although Cicero's discussion of Solon appears in a section discussing exceptional behavior linked to the second *persona*, the line between the three "individualistic" *personae* is often unclear, and Cicero justifies Solon's action by referring to the Republic's welfare, which is the duty of a statesman.

If Cicero argues for a distinct role morality for politicians, what is a politician in the Roman Republic? The *Oxford English Dictionary* (3rd ed.) defines a politician as "one who is professionally involved in politics as the holder of or a candidate for an elected office." Applying this definition to the Roman Republic is complicated by the differences between the political structures and offices of the Republic and those of present-day states; the Ciceronian politician is not the same as the politician in modern representative democracies. For example, legislative representatives, today, comprise a significant proportion of those we would identify as politicians, but the Roman Republic did not have legislative representatives. Instead, lawmaking was the prerogative of the citizens, who constituted the popular assemblies, specifically the *comitia centuriata*, the *concilium plebis*, and the *comitia tributa* of the late Republic (Vishnia 2012, 90–97; Lintott 1999b, 50–64).

Roman senators were members of what was, arguably, the most powerful political body in the Republic (Lintott 1999b, 66); for Cicero, the Senate was *the* fundamental political body of the state.[19] The Senate, however, was not a legislature but, nominally, "a council summoned by magistrates to tender advice, and its decrees took the form of recommendations" (Brunt 1988, 14). And although its members, former magistrates, wielded effective political power, they were nevertheless considered *privati*, private persons who held no public office (Botsford 1909, 102). Therefore, they were not officially politicians, although they should be considered de facto politicians.

Political orators in the Republic devoted themselves to politics, arguing for or against the passing of laws and policies, most famously at *contiones*. And public speakers at *contiones* were either magistrates or senators (Morstein-Marx 2004, 163), meaning that, at a minimum, they were de facto politicians. In addition, Cicero emphasizes the deliberative orator's status as politician by identifying this orator with the statesman, as I demonstrate in chapter 5. And even though political orators qua orators were not elected to office—election to office is a component of the *OED*'s definition of politician—they were confirmed or rejected by the people, as I show in chapter 5. But as orators per se, they did not exercise the exceptional political powers that are the focus of this chapter.[20]

For purposes of this chapter, which concentrates on the morality of extraordinary political actions, magistrates—foremost among them, the consuls—are the model politicians of the Roman Republic. In line with the *OED* definition, magistrates in the Republic are professionally involved in politics as holders of elected office. Magistrates, who formed the executive power of the Roman government, were generally elected annually and possessed *potestas*, power or capability legitimated by statute or custom. The two consuls, who were also elected annually, held the supreme form of *potestas* entitled *imperium*, command—which Cicero termed *regium imperium*, the "royal power of command" (1999e, 3.8)[21]—the ultimate authority to lead, judge, and advise (Vishnia 2012, 60, 64–69; Lintott 1999b, 95–96).[22] For Cicero, the executive power of the consuls was supreme (2000b, 3).

Cicero differentiates, in *De officiis*, between the duties of the politician and others in his tripartite division between magistrate, ordinary citizen, and foreigner. Concerning magistrates he writes: "It is, then, the particular function of a magistrate to realize that he assumes the role of the city [*se gerere personam civitatis*] and ought to sustain its standing and seemliness, to preserve the laws, to administer justice, and to be mindful of the things that have been entrusted to his good faith" (1991a, 1.124). Cicero next outlines the *officia* of the ordinary citizen: "A private person, on the other hand, ought first to live on fair and equal terms with the other citizens . . . ; and secondly to want public affairs to be peaceful and honourable. For we are accustomed to think and say that such a man is a good citizen [*bonum civem*]." As for the foreigner or resident alien, Cicero denies him any function in the Republic: his duty is "to do nothing except his own business . . . , and never to meddle in public affairs, which are not his own" (1.124).

In distinguishing between the politician and the ordinary citizen, Cicero emphasizes the magistrate's moral obligation to be active in serving the public. In contrast to politicians, private citizens are expected to desire the public good, but, Cicero implies, their involvement in public affairs is more passive than active.[23] As private persons who did not choose the political life, they did not commit themselves to undertaking the *officia* distinctive of the politician.

From among the magistrates, the consuls are vested with an especial moral responsibility to care for the safety of the people, particularly during periods of crisis. Thus, Cicero begins his dictum "let the safety of the people be the highest law [*salus populi suprema lex esto*]" (which he states in *De legibus*) with the words "*for them* [*ollis*]," referring to the consuls (1999e, 3.8; emphasis added). Although Cicero intends this dictum for the consuls, the duty of ordinary citizens to the Republic also supersedes all other responsibilities: "Our country [gave us birth or rearing] . . . with the understanding that she has a claim on the largest and best part of our minds, talents, and judgment for her own use, and leaves for our private use only so much as is beyond her requirements" (1999d, 1.8). As we shall see, according to Cicero, even private citizens must sometimes violate conventional moral and legal norms to protect the state. Nevertheless, their obligation to act for the state differs from that of politicians. When possible, ordinary citizens are "to strengthen the bulwarks of the republic" not by acting independently but by supporting the political authorities (Cicero 2000b, 3). In *Pro Rabirio perduellionis*, Cicero explicitly charges the consuls to intercede on behalf of the Republic during domestic emergencies: "[I]t is the duty of a good consul, when he sees everything on which the state depends being shaken and uprooted, to come to the rescue of the country" (2000b, 3). Although Cicero uttered these words (or something like them) in a speech defending Gaius Rabirius against a charge of high treason almost twenty years before he presented the system of *personae* in *De officiis*, his support here of the political leadership's unique duty to defend the Republic is consistent with the role morality he would eventually vindicate. When framed in the language of *personae* theory, the morality of the politicians' *persona* affords them the opportunity, even requires them, to depart from the ordinary morality of private citizens.

When the Republic prospers in peace, Cicero follows a path of demanding that politicians follow both the law and ordinary morality to the utmost. As danger to the Republic increases, however, he permits politicians greater latitude in departing from set law and morality. The leeway Cicero affords politicians during emergency conditions is exemplified in his defense of the politician's obligation to defy the right of *provocatio*, when conditions demand it. As Andrew Lintott explains, "[n]ormally, the person of a citizen . . . was protected from physical harm or manhandling on a magistrate's orders by the right of *provocatio*, which was "a citizen's right of appeal to the Roman people against a magistrate's summary use of power." When an appellant petitioned for the right of appeal, "a magistrate had to gain approval from a popular assembly before exercising his jurisdiction" (Lintott 1999b, 89; *Encylopedia of Ancient History*, s.v. "provocatio."). The politician's duty to flout *provocatio* is not without moral significance because, as Cicero suggests, it is not only a legal right per se but a right vested with moral import. For Cicero *provocatio* is the "protector of the community," which fulfills the highest moral duty, that is, safeguarding the welfare of the state (Cicero 2001a, 2.199; Colish 1990, 148). Moreover, Cicero calls *provocatio* the "champion of liberty"—*libertas* being a core value of the Republic, the possession of which distinguishes citizens, who lack any master, from slaves, who are subject to the arbitrary domination of others (Cicero 2001a, 2.199; 1999d, 2.43).[24]

Cicero justifies the politician's violation of the right of appeal in the context of the *senatus consultum ultimum* (the Senate's ultimate decree)—a decree in which the Senate exhorts the consuls or other magistrates to do whatever is necessary to defend against what it deems a violent threat to the Republic's security. The *senatus consultum ultimum* was first legitimated during the late Republic after Lucius Opimius, consul of 121 BCE, was acquitted of killing citizens without a proper trial, therefore in defiance of the *provocatio* laws. Opimius sought and received the Senate's support, in the form of the *senatus consultum ultimum*, in suppressing Gaius Gracchus, Marcus Fulvius Flaccus, and their followers, who attempted to enact far-ranging social reforms to (from the Senate's perspective) the detriment of the state. According to Cicero, the Senate approved Opimius's use of force against the Gracchans in the following terms: "Whereas Lucius Opimius the consul has spoken on a matter touching the State, the Senate on that matter has decreed that Lucius Opimius the consul should defend the State" (1926, 8.14). Bolstered by the Senate's decree, Opimius mustered a force of senators and *equites* to overpower the Gracchans, killing many of them, contrary to the right of appeal. Although Opimius was later prosecuted before the people for executing Roman citizens who had not been legally condemned, he was acquitted in a trial before the people in the Centuriate Assembly, which, in effect, authorized the *senatus consultum ultimum* as an institution of last resort (Drummond 1995, 90–93; Lintott 1994, 84–85).

Cicero himself, as consul, obtained the Senate's support in the form of a *senatus consultum ultimum*, which, according to Cicero, vindicated his extrajudicial killing of the Catilinarian conspirators. The Catiline conspiracy (or, more correctly, the second Catilinarian conspiracy) refers to a plan, hatched by the Roman senator Catiline (Lucius Sergius Catilina) with the aid of some aristocrats and disaffected veterans, to overthrow the Roman Republic. In 63 BCE, Cicero exposed the plot, forcing Catiline to flee Rome, after which he was killed in battle. Five of Catiline's leading conspirators, however, remained in Rome and, after their role in the conspiracy was discovered, were incarcerated and put to death—Cicero had them strangled—without benefit of the Roman citizen's right to a formal trial.

Cicero did not order the killing of the conspirators unilaterally. Rather, his actions found support from the Senate, which issued a *senatus consultum ultimum* stating "that the consuls would take heed that the commonwealth suffer no harm" (Sallust 1931, 29). The execution of Roman citizens without a trial, just for their intentions and not for overt acts of hostility against the state, was an extraordinary action that had never been undertaken previously, even under the authority of the ultimate decree. Nevertheless, Cicero believed that, given the danger to the state, he was required to disobey ordinary norms and laws. And although Cicero typically supported the subordination of magistrates to the Senate's authority, he recognized magistrates as having an independent duty to protect the Republic in any way they could; Cicero regarded the *senatus consultum ultimum* only as additional backing for the magistrates' extraordinary actions (Lintott 1999b, 91–93). As seen earlier, Cicero, in *De legibus* and *Pro Rabirio perduellionis*, vests magistrates—consuls in particular—with their own obligation to save their country when endangered, suggesting that the Senate did not grant powers to the magistrate (via the *senatus consultum ultimum*) that they did not already possess. Thus, Hugh Last maintains: "the *ultimum consultum* of the Senate was in essence only an attempt to strengthen the resolution of the magistrates in the face of a danger which might call for action of peculiar vigour and determination. It implied a promise of senatorial support; but neither in theory nor in fact did it add to the legal powers which they already held. It conferred on them no new authority nor did it even purport to remove any of the restrictions which were imposed by statute on the use of their *imperium*" (Last 1932, 84–85).[25]

In *Pro Murena*, Cicero justifies his actions in the Catilinarian affair—he obliquely characterizes them as his "use of force and severity"—by asserting that "the part of sternness and severity" was "thrust upon me by the State . . . as the majesty of this realm demanded in her citizens' supreme peril" (1977a). With no mention of the Senate here as empowering his "consular edict" against Catiline, Cicero suggests that the *imperium* of his office, what in *De officiis* he would term the *officium* of the fourth *persona*, compelled him to defend the *res publica*. Foreshadowing his *personae theory*, he contrasts "his leniency and mercy which I learned from Mother Nature," which he would associate with the *officia* of the second *persona*, with the punitive measures imposed upon him by the state. Attacking Catiline and his coconspirators called for Cicero to "overcome [his] natural inclination," his "temperament and usual practice," which he could indulge in less threatening situations.

Cicero indicates that private citizens are also sometimes permitted to transgress conventional norms in defense of the state. But he implies that the right of private citizens to contravene the law is a *pis aller*, acceptable only when politicians do not fulfill their roles. For example, Publius Scipio chose "extreme lawlessness," the unsanctioned killing of Tiberius Gracchus, because the consul Publius Mucius "was considered somewhat lacking in energy when the deed was in contemplation" (Cicero 1923b, 91). Cicero uses Scipio's example to present an a fortiori argument calling on the Senate to take action against Catiline—an argument based on the assumption that consuls have a greater responsibility than private citizens for the extralegal killing of treasonous citizens: if Scipio, a private citizen, killed Tiberius Gracchus, "even though [Gracchus] was not seriously undermining the Constitution of the Republic, [s]hall we, the consuls, then tolerate Catiline whose aim it is to carry fire and the sword throughout the whole world?" (1977b, 1.2–3).[26] Nevertheless, Cicero's support for private citizens' breaking accepted law and custom suggests that he does not anchor political morality solely in the *officia* of the fourth *persona*; the well-being of the state, according to Cicero, must be protected by all, even regular citizens who lack an explicitly political role.[27] Pursuing the *honestum*, an obligation on every human as part of the first *persona*, requires all citizens to pursue the common good, as the honorable is involved "with [the] conservation of organized society" (1913a, 1.15; Dyck 1996, 100–101).[28] Thus, Cicero justifies Marcus Junius Brutus's assassination of Julius Caesar on the grounds of tyrannicide, even though Brutus lacked public authority (1991a, 3.19, 3.23,

3.84; Wiseman 2009, 201–7). Likewise, Cicero applauds Cornelius Publius Scipio's killing of Tiberius Gracchus for political reasons, even though Scipio was a private citizen (1977b, 1.3; 1923b, 91; 1971, 4.51).

Cicero's examples, however, suggest that some *privati* have priority over other *privati* in breaching ordinary law and morality for the safety of the Republic. The distinct natural *personae* of zealous citizens may justify their normally improper actions, in contrast to the like actions of most private citizens—Cicero describes Scipio, for example, as *fortissimus* (most courageous; 1923b, 91; 1991a, 3.16). Moreover, the lines between political and nonpolitical roles are sometimes unclear. Scipio and Brutus are *boni* (good men), who, though not officially politicians, are the *optimates* from which the political class is derived. Presumably, it is of these *boni* that Cicero writes: "we ought to respect and revere those whose life has been conspicuous for its great and honourable deeds . . . just as if they had achieved a specific honour or command" (1991a, 1.149). Perhaps the great men of the Republic, even when private citizens, rightfully assume prerogatives denied lesser citizens. Nevertheless, although Cicero endorses the ordinarily unacceptable deeds of private citizens, he recognizes that magistrates, principally consuls, have a unique and preeminent role in doing whatever is necessary (including the use of disagreeable means) to ensure the safety of the state, in line with the duties of the fourth *persona*. In the next section, we see how Cicero bases his moral theory, specifically his role-centered morality, on the rhetorical concept of decorum, which demarcates Cicero's *officia* as contextual and variable, changing among—and evolving within—communities.

Cicero's Rhetorical Ethics, *Personae*, and Decorum

Cicero's morality, as manifested in his theory of *personae*, includes moral obligations incumbent on all persons (the first *persona*) and moral obligations applicable to smaller subdivisions of humanity (the second, third, and fourth *personae*), such as the distinct set of *officia* binding politicians. In De officiis, Cicero embeds the obligations of the *personae* in his rhetorical conception of decorum (1991a, 1.100–21).

Decorum, as we saw in the previous chapter, is the rhetorical concept that speech must be adapted to fit "the characteristic features of the speaker, subject, audience, occasion, or medium" (Hariman 2001, 199), which Cicero transforms from the pragmatic perception that orators must accommodate their oratory to prevail into a moral virtue. Like the orator whose speech must be appropriate (or decorous) to the subject matter and *personae* ("the roles or characters of speaker and audience"), we must conduct our lives appropriate to our generic natures as rational human beings, our specific natures as individual persons, our roles assigned by chance or circumstance, and our chosen vocations (Schofield 2012, 46). Decorum for us qua rational humans requires that we follow the *honestum*, that which distinguishes our nature from that of the beasts (Cicero 1991a, 1.96).[29] In contrast to our generic decorum, our decorum as unique persons or as members of particular groups focuses on difference within the human family, "for what is most seemly [decet] for a man is the thing that is most his own" (Cicero 1991a, 1.13).

Because Cicero's decorum is rooted in rhetoric, it makes little sense to speak in Ciceronian terms of a universal, decontextualized decorum. For Cicero (1991a, 93), decorum and the *honestum*—which are inseparable and almost indistinguishable—must always originate in one's particular society. Decorum expresses this idea in linking moral behavior to the deeply rooted values of one's community. Cicero writes that "in oratory, the very cardinal sin is to depart from the language of everyday life, and the usage approved by the sense of the community" (1942a, 1.12). The "sense of the community," which delimits the boundaries of what the orator can say or do, corresponds to "the established customs and conventions of a community," which ought to control what all members of the community do (1913a, 1.148), which Cicero commonly equates with Rome's ancient traditions.

Dean Hammer captures Cicero's perception of ethical obligations as communally embedded when he writes: "We may be citizens of the world, but for Cicero we are born for our country (*De off.* I.7.22), our closest connection is citizenship (*De off.* I.17.53, 57, 58; *De leg.* 2.2.5), [and] we have a greater obligation to those nearest us (*De off.* I.14.45; I.17.54–55; I.17.57)" (2014, 88). But there is another side to Cicero's morality that is in tension with my claim that Cicero's decorum and *honestum* are rooted in a specific context. This other approach to morality is not particularistic but cosmopolitan: the morality derived from natural law.[30] For a significant number of thinkers, past and present (Nussbaum 1997; Nussbaum 2000b, 184–85), Cicero's main contribution to the tradition of Western political thought is his theory of natural law. Why then, as will become even clearer through the rest of the book, do I look to the norms of individual communities rather than a universal conception of justice, that is, natural law, for Cicero's political morality? As discussed in chapter 1, Cicero distinguishes between two types of moral duties—(1) perfect and (2) middle or intermediate. The first sort of duties, he asserts in *De officiis*, is demanded only of the wise man, the Stoic moral ideal unattainable by real-life human beings. The second group of duties, however, is "shared and widely accessible" (1991a, 3.14), which is why Cicero expects actual persons to fulfill only these duties. Accordingly, Cicero writes "[t]he duties I discuss in these books [the three books of *De officiis*, which concern practical ethics] are . . . those that the Stoics call 'middle'" (1991a, 3.14). These middle duties are not universal but evolve within specific communities, in line with Cicero's belief that the superior code of law he proposes in *De legibus*—a code that itself re-flects Roman practice and custom—must be fit to the ancestral Roman Consti-tution (Asmis 2008, 25–31). In contrast, natural law commands "right actions," that is, perfect duties, which are applicable only to wise men. Therefore, the universal law, with its perfect duties, does not direct the actions of politicians or the rest of humanity.[31]

Moreover, the morality of politicians derives from the decorum of the fourth *persona*, the role or profession, "which we assume for ourselves by our own de-cision" (1991a, 1.115). As I shall now explain, the duties of this *persona* are espe-cially linked to particular, not universal norms—the vocations Cicero envisions when delineating the fourth *persona*, for example, lawyers and politicians, be-ing the creations of particular communities. Thus, when Cicero discusses the morality specific to legal advocates, his examples are specific to the Roman Republic. More important for purposes of this book, the duties of politicians, according to Cicero, are also embedded in the same distinct political commu-nity, the Roman Republic.

When Cicero grounds the duties of the fourth *persona* (i.e., of one's chosen vocation) in decorum, he implies that this decorum is determined not only by the particular profession but by the wider Roman political community. Thus, in conceding that the advocate may occasionally use eloquence to defend a guilty client, Cicero (1991a) suggests that the relevant decorum (to which the advocate must adapt) is the decorum not only of fellow advocates but also of the broader society: "the masses want it; custom permits it; humanity tolerates it" (2.51). In contrast, the decorum of individual persons, that is, the duties of the second *persona*, is linked to their idiosyncratic natures. The Homeric heroes Ulysses and Ajax differed in how they reacted to their abominable circumstances: Ulysses accommodated himself to them; "[Ajax] would have preferred to seek death a thousand times than to endure" Ulysses's indignities (1.113). Yet Cicero approves of both their behaviors because "[r]eflecting on such matters, everyone ought to weigh the characteristics that are his own and to regulate them, not wanting to see how someone else's might become him" (1.113). Why, then, are the advocate's departures from general norms, like truth telling, linked to the desires and consent of the wider community? The answer, I believe, lies in how professions like legal advocacy involve the public (and the public's values) in a way that the choices of individual heroes do not. Unlike the heroic warriors of Homer's *Iliad* and *Odyssey*, who were not beholden to the decisions of a larger group, Roman advocates present their cases before juries, who ultimately decide their clients' guilt or innocence. The legitimacy of Roman advocates, it may be said, depends on the willingness of Roman citizens to vest them with authority. Because legal advocates owe their existence as lawyers to communal recognition, the community's sense of decorum is dispositive for this profession.[32]

Like legal advocates, who are fabricated by society, politicians are created and legitimated by the political community, the members of which vest politicians with their authority.[33] The status of politicians is "constituted by its collective acceptance," and, in order to perform their functions, there must be continued community acceptance of their status (Searle 1995, 117).[34] The politician's dependent status is supported by Cicero's references to the orator-statesman as a procurator, a manager, beholden to his master, the citizenry (Remer 2010, 1067–69). Like the procurator, who has no position without the landowner who "creates" him, the politician has no vocation without the *populus* that creates him.

Again, like legal advocates, politicians affect the community, for good or ill, and, therefore, the decorum of the community, not the idiosyncratic decorum of individual politicians or of politicians as a distinct class, should direct their speech and behavior. Cicero (1949) acknowledges both the beneficial and the baneful effects of politicians in *De inventione,* where he praises the orator-statesman for civilizing humans and schooling them in justice but also condemns eloquent leaders for lacking a sense of moral duty in corrupting cities and undermining the lives of men (1.3). Thus, with an eye to communal values, Cicero interprets the manipulative speech of the orator-statesman not as harming the audience but as accepted, even desired, by the audience—words and deeds that accord with the *sensus communis* and the community's sense of decorum (1939a, 187–88; Wisse 1989, 263–64).

The duties of all four *personae* reflect a particular context—late republican Rome. Although Cicero does not directly address the dispositive force of foreign mores on their native peoples—he evinces little interest in non-Roman values—the logic of his decorum-based theory of *personae* impels us (and him) to recognize different moralities for different communities. Duties, including political duties, change from society to society. For example, in recognizing

Socrates and Aristippus as exceptions to the general principle that citizens must follow established custom and practice, he suggests that other Greeks should conform to the enduring traditions of their own *poleis*.

If Cicero moves us to acknowledge differences between communities, does he also accept moral change within a community? Cicero is commonly criticized for upholding the moral values of the Roman elite. For example, he has been taken to task for asserting that the duties of his particular *personae* affirm conventional social roles and the styles associated with them, rendering these roles and styles "invulnerable to the criticisms of those who attack them in the name of our common humanity, that is, of the first persona" (Gill 1988, 193–94). Even if we understand the common humanity of the first *persona* as also grounded in communal mores, Cicero's *personae* theory can be attacked, in toto, as unyielding and inflexible.

Despite his conservatism, however, Cicero accepts, even legitimates, moral change within societies, including Rome. True, he calls for a return to ancestral values, so that acting decorously refers to adapting oneself to the genuine (i.e., ancient, not transitory) moral values of the Republic. Nevertheless, Cicero demonstrates his own ambivalence to such a reactionary response. In *De oratore*, Antonius asserts that "the fundamental requirement for speaking persuasively is to know the character of the community [*mores civitatis*]. Since [it] frequently changes, our mode of speaking should often change as well" (Cicero 2001a, 2.337). Cicero implicitly approves of evolving morality in Rome in designating *ius gentium* (the law of nations) as one of three categories of law, along with *ius civile* (civil law) and *lex or ius naturae* (natural law). As most Roman legal scholars agree, *ius gentium* was drawn from the actual laws of particular peoples, which included the laws of foreigners (Remer 2011, 233–38). Given his belief in the indivisibility of law and morality, Cicero seems to acknowledge that Roman morality may come to include principles derived from other peoples, so long as these principles are eventually Romanized. Cicero also envisions salutary changes to Rome's existing laws in his *De legibus*, where he intends his repair of Roman law to go hand in hand with moral change (Asmis 2008, 1–33). And although this moral change is to be based on a return to what he characterizes as the true ancestral virtues, and therefore his call *ad fontes* appears contrary to progressive change in morality, Cicero reinterprets traditional Roman moral principles to permit forward movement in moral theory—not only a retrenchment to the conservative status quo or a reversion to a putative golden age when even more elitist values reigned.

The evolution of political morality in Cicero derives from his Academic skepticism, which, like his rhetoric, uses argument *in utramque partem* to arrive at that which is most probable (Michel 1960, 158–73; Cicero 1971, 2.9; 1999d, 3.8; 2001a, 3.80). For Cicero, the skeptic's rule of "discussing both sides of every question" promotes the probable truth ("in no other way did I think it possible for the probable truth to be discovered in each particular problem" [1971, 2.9]), and according to Academic skeptics probability is the best truth available (Cicero 1942b, 3.80). Cicero's probable truth—arrived at through two-sided argumentation—however, is not a philosophical truth detached from practicality (Dyck 1996, 37–38). Rather, Cicero decides which moral positions are most probable, in large part, by evaluating their utility. Probability itself connotes for skeptics and, in particular, Cicero that which is useful: "*probare* [from which *probabile*, 'the probable,' is derived] can mean 'to test and to acknowledge as useful'" (Görler 1992, 162).

By appropriating elements of different Hellenistic philosophies based on how they contribute to the well-being of the state, Cicero adapts his conception of political morality to changing conditions, as decorum requires. He affirms his right to select philosophies eclectically as an Academic skeptic: "our Academy grants us great freedom, so that we may be justified in defending whatever seems most persuasive" (Cicero 1991a, 3.20). In accordance with this, Cicero incorporates Stoic values into his political and moral theory when he finds them most persuasive. As an alternative, he adopts Peripatetic values when he deems them most "probable."[35] And he defends the Roman character of these Hellenistic philosophies, despite their Greek provenance, by Romanizing them: "In *de Oratore*, as later in *de Re publica*, Cicero gave a considered argument for the position . . . that Greek learning . . . could only be rescued, or even understood, by anchoring it . . . in a social and moral context—in the service of Roman tradition and Roman values" (Zetzel 2003, 137).[36]

Rather than providing a single moral theory, Cicero's argument *in utramque partem* offers partial, tentative responses to moral dilemmas. Like modern political morality, which is composed of several sometimes contradictory philosophical strains—for example, deontological and utilitarian (Walzer 1973, 161–62; Nagel 1978, 75–91)—Cicero's political morality is also derived from various philosophical camps, whose ideas he reinterprets and reconstitutes into a distinct complex morality.

Despite his criticism of Stoic beliefs as overly rigid, imprudent, inconsistent with Roman tradition, and unsuited for the masses (Cicero 1977a, 60–67, 74; Stem 2006, 210–22; Leff 1998, 79–80; Cicero 2001a, 2.159), Cicero justifies his decision, in *De officiis*, to follow the Stoics, or more correctly the modified Stoicism of Panaetius, "not as an expositor, but, as is my custom, drawing from their fountains when and as it seems best, using my own judgement and discretion" (1991a, 1.6). He sides with the Stoics, in *De officiis*, because he finds their conception of the *honestum* to be the most appealing morally. But Cicero also adopts Stoic perspectives, in *De officiis*, *De republica*, and *De legibus*, because of the Stoic account of universal human equality and law (Colish 1990, 95–104; Cicero 1991a, 3.23–31), thereby enabling him to transcend conservative Roman moral practice, while maintaining that he is defending traditional Roman virtues. For example, he upholds a conception of justice common to all humanity that requires a morality in warfare that is highly protective of enemy combatants.[37] It is even argued that Cicero's Stoic-influenced duties of justice foreshadow Kant's dictum that human beings should be treated as ends rather than means (Nussbaum 2000b, 182–85). But although Cicero extols Stoic ideals of cosmopolitan justice, he subordinates these values to Rome's native morality. For Cicero, the utopian aspirations implicit in Stoicism do not prevail over the Roman Constitution and the morality inherent in it, which are themselves naturally just and independent of Stoic influence (Asmis 2008, 26–28).[38] The gap between the ideal universal law and existing Roman law leaves room for Cicero to modify Roman law in a way that is progressive but still consistent with Roman tradition rather than alien values.[39]

Although he turns to the Stoics for his ideas about justice and our common humanity, Cicero looks to Aristotle's followers, the Peripatetics, for a broader notion of liberty defined as political participation. Cicero was never a champion of an expansive political role for the *populus*. Nevertheless, he defended, on practical and moral grounds, an "appropriate" political involvement for the people against ultraconservatives, like his brother Quintus, who were committed to reducing "the force of the mob" vis-à-vis the *optimates* (Cicero 1999e, 3.15–26).[40] In *De republica*, Cicero (1999d) criticizes aristocracies for denying the common people almost all liberty insofar as the people in an aristocracy "lack any role in common deliberation and power" (1.43).[41] This defense of modest popular political participation has been shown to have its roots in the Peripatetics. Likewise, Cicero's support of the mixed constitution—which guarantees a political role for the one, the few, and the many—as the best constitutional form can be traced back to the Peripatetic school (Frede 1989, 86–94; Cicero 1999d, xv).

Conclusion: Popular Authorization of the Politician's Morality

Cicero grants politicians latitude in determining when it is necessary for them to adopt the unconventional standards of political morality, that is, the decorum of their *persona*. Nevertheless, for Cicero, the decorum of political morality is not based on the politician's personal opinion but (like generic morality) is rooted in the values of the political community, which the politician must apply. Does Cicero require the politician when acting during political crises to obtain the support of the people? Although Cicero does not identify the people as the arbiter of community values, he acknowledges (as we saw in the previous section) the political orator's need to adapt his speech to the current character of the community (*mores civitatis*), suggesting that the people influence, if not determine, the community's values. Does Cicero present a means by which the public may authorize the conduct of politicians acting under extraordinary circumstances? We shall consider two possibilities for such public authorization, focusing on the second possibility: (1) *ex ante* approval, where the people authorize the politically mandated actions in question before being carried out; and (2) *ex post* approval, where the people condone the politician's actions after the fact. We shall examine Cicero's own standpoints on these two possibilities and reflect on how viable these options are for politics today. (We shall not, however, consider here the potential legal penalties of not receiving approval; our concern is with the morality, not the legality, of political actions, although the line between the two is often blurred. We shall assume for our purposes here that the most likely penalty for a political actor whose morally dubious actions are not popularly ratified is the loss of political office.[42])

Strictly speaking, Cicero does not *oblige* politicians to gain popular authorization—either prior or subsequent to acting—for their departures from ordinary norms. Regarding *ex ante* approval, we find that although magistrates possess executive power to act autonomously, Cicero believes it prudent for them—and for himself as consul during the Catilinarian affair—to gain the backing of the Senate, in the form of the *senatus consultum ultimum*, when breaking with accepted law and ordinary morality. But senatorial authorization *is not* popular authorization. The Senate did not represent the people; it was not a representative institution of any kind (Millar 1998, 7).

Shifting the question of prior authorization to our own time, *ex ante* public approval is typically unsuited to present-day politics.[43] The people (or their representatives) cannot be expected to approve of decisions before the fact. Often there is no time for such authorization. And, in contemporary politics, the most morally problematical actions are usually formulated (and often carried out) in secrecy, without public awareness—political assassinations and drone strikes, for example. In addition, given the political actor's need to make quick decisions, he or she will be hindered from pursuing the common good if limited by the restrictions of *ex ante* approval. Moreover, *ex ante* approval can only be granted for proposed actions. But neither the politician nor the approving body is able to predict the future with much accuracy; political actions as actually performed often differ from the proposed actions in morally significant ways. For example, although a political actor may intend (and receive approval) to kill the leadership of a terrorist organization, the political actor may receive information prior to an attack (but after receiving *ex ante* approval) that the terrorist leadership cannot be isolated from innocent civilians. The political actor, therefore, may nevertheless decide to eliminate his or her targets, accepting the death of innocents as necessary "collateral damage."

Cicero seeks *ex post* popular approval in his extrajudicial killing of the five Catilinarian conspirators, though he never argues that such authorization is necessary. He neither questions the legality of the Senate's *consultum ultimum* nor believes that, in principle, there is any need to revisit or defend his actions against the Catilinarian conspirators. Nevertheless, while he was in exile, Cicero's allies ensured that his previous actions were, de facto, approved not only by the Senate but also by the Roman citizenry more generally.

The Senate's *ex ante* approval of the Catilinarian executions did not settle the matter of Cicero's extrajudicial actions. Publius Clodius Pulcher, who entered the *tribunate* in 58 BCE, was driven by a desire for revenge—Cicero provided damaging testimony against Clodius in his trial for sacrilege in 61 BCE—to bring about Cicero's downfall. Thus, supported by Julius Caesar and Pompey the Great, Clodius proposed a bill, approved as law, that anyone who had a Roman citizen put to death without trial (read: Cicero) should be denied access to fire and water (the elementary means to sustain life). On the day that Clodius's bill was voted on, Cicero left Rome. Immediately following his departure, Cicero's house and properties were destroyed. This destruction was followed, in turn, by the passage of another set of laws proposed by Clodius; the laws declared Cicero an outlaw, set four hundred miles from Italy as the distance within which his outlawry would apply, established a penalty for anyone who sheltered him within this prescribed limit, authorized the confiscation of his property, and prohibited any proposal to invalidate or repeal these laws from being brought before the Senate or people. Although Cicero's *ex ante* approval from the Senate might have sufficed under more auspicious political conditions, the *consultum ultimum* did not function for Cicero as it was intended. Final approval of Cicero's extrajudicial executions (as well as his public rehabilitation) would be the result of *ex post* actions, not of *ex ante* senatorial approval. Until his recall in 57, Cicero spent sixteen months in exile.

In Cicero's accounts of his allies' efforts to recall him, he emphasizes the participation of citizens from across Italy.[44] The Senate supported Cicero's restoration (Kelly 2006, 122–24), but Cicero—or at least his allies—desired broader support. Cicero (1958a) maintained that a vote of the people was unnecessary to recall him, only a resolution of the Senate (73). But although Pompey—who became Cicero's defender after falling out with Clodius—agreed that a popular vote was not legally required to secure Cicero's position "and to be rid of all popular excitement against [him], . . . [he] thought it advisable that a resolution of the Senate should be accompanied by a favourable vote of the Roman People" (75). Cicero describes, in exaggerated language, how "[t]here is no guild in this city, no community, whether of the villages or the high-lands . . . which did not register most complimentary decrees dealing not only with my restoration but also with my merits. Why should I enlarge upon the heaven-inspired and never-to-be-forgotten decrees of the municipalities and colonies, and indeed of the whole of Italy" (1923b, 74–75; see also 31; 1953a, 39). Cicero recounts the vote by the citizens of Capua for his return (1953b, 25; see also 1953a, 39). He takes note of the "resolutions of the tax-farmers, the guilds, and every section and order of society as I could never have imagined, let alone dared to dream of" on his behalf (1953b, 41). Cicero boasts that the Senate, the forum, and the courts have never endorsed another's restoration as vociferously as his own (1958a, 128). Cicero, however, recognizes the vote for his recall in the *comitia centuriata*, "which above all other assemblies our ancestors wished to be called and considered most authoritative" (1923e, 27), as the most decisive. In Cicero's depiction, this vote of the most conservative of the assemblies—its vote was weighted toward the wealthier classes—was not a second choice decided upon by Cicero's allies only after Clodius violently prevented a vote months earlier in the more popular *concilium plebis*. Rather, he styles the *comitia centuriata*, when it unanimously called for Cicero's restoration, as a synecdoche for "the whole of Italy," which "flocked on one day to Rome" (1953b, 34); it was "that unexampled throng, Italy in person one might almost say" (1991c, 25).

Although Cicero (1923b) acknowledges the widespread acclaim accorded his "eminent merits" in general (75), he takes special effort to point up the near universal ratification of his extrajudicial executions. The pursuit of Cicero's recall to Rome inevitably required the justification of his earlier deeds against the Catilinarians, and Cicero describes these actions, euphemistically but with consistency of language, as his saving the Republic. Thus, in his "Third Catilinarian" addressed to the people, Cicero terms his destruction of Catiline and his conspirators as "*hav[ing] secured the salvation of you all*" (1977b, 3.25; emphasis added).

Cicero's recall effort suggests two stages to his *ex post* approval: first, his associates defend his actions to the public, and, second, the people endorse them. For example, he reminds the people in a *contio* that Pompey "*demonstrated to you that it had been by my measures that the republic had been preserved,*" and the people took heed, recalling Cicero through their vote in the *comitia centuriata* (Cicero 1923d, 16–17; emphasis added).[45] Cicero describes in similar terms how the people, in *contiones*, "heard men of the highest standing and consequence, leaders of the community, all our Consulars, all our Ex-Praetors, speak with one voice, *bearing unanimous witness that I alone had saved the Commonwealth,*" "that *if I had not been Consul when I was, the Commonwealth would have perished root and branch,*" after which the people recalled Cicero in the *comitia centuriata* (1991b, 17; emphasis added; also see 1923e, 26; 1923d, 16). Cicero underscores the people's ratification of the Catilinarian killings by juxtaposing the accusation of his enemy, the former consul Lucius Calpurnius Piso, with the people's reaction. Piso attacked Cicero for having acted against the Catilinarians with cruelty (*crudelitas*; 1953b, 14), which, as we have already seen, is contrary to the *officia* of the first *persona*, even for politicians. Against Piso's charge, Cicero responds that "[t]he malignant imputations of cruelty have by now been hushed, because it is seen that I have been yearned for, demanded, and appealed to by the ardent longing of all citizens, not as a cruel tyrant, but as a tender parent" (1923b, 94–95).

Although Cicero never concedes that popular authorization was legally necessary for his recall, his conviction that the people are ultimately sovereign (see chapter 5) and his belief, noted above, that political morality is rooted in the community provide a principled (and not simply pragmatic) basis for the people's ratification of his morally questionable actions, consistent with the process that Cicero's associates followed to effect his restoration. But the explicit turn toward popular *ex post* approval, directly or through the people's representatives (and not, for example, an aristocratic senate), is an artifact of modern republicanism or democracy. Thus, Thomas Jefferson writes that "on great occasions every good officer must be ready to risk himself in going beyond the strict lines of law, when the public preservation requires it." Like Cicero, Jefferson believes that it is permissible, in "extreme cases" and when the good of the country requires it, for politicians to depart from normally acceptable behavior. But, Jefferson adds, these actions must be approved, after the fact, by the American people or their representatives in Congress (cited in Gross 2003, 1107–8).[46]

Likewise, Oren Gross (2003) argues that the people, as sovereign, must determine "whether the values, principles, rules, and norms" that were violated by politicians during national emergencies are too basic to be abandoned (1118). Gross suggests that because the political actor must gain public ratification for ordinarily unacceptable actions (i.e., normally improper, even for political leaders), the possibility of public rejection (and the sanctions that may follow) will likely restrain politicians from pursuing such options, impelling them to seriously question their morally questionable plans (1100–1101). Although Gross, like Jefferson, is primarily interested in the people's *ex post* ratification of public officials' extra*legal*, not extra*moral*, decisions, the people are the final arbiters of both the legality and the morality of politicians' emergency actions. Gross merges the evaluation of politicians' moral and political behavior, contending that the general public must determine, after the fact, whether or not counter-emergency actions should be considered justifiable or excusable "from a moral or legal perspective," that is, whether or not politicians "run afoul of a community's fundamental principles and values" (1100; see also 1110).

Gross envisions a twofold process of *ex post* approval akin to that followed by Cicero's allies. First, the politician must give reasons after the fact to justify his or her actions before the people. The need to offer reasons after the fact (i.e., to defend one's actions before the people) "adds another layer of limitations on governmental action" (2003, 1123–25). Gross adds: "The task of giving reasons requires the actor to present publicly various types of arguments—prudential, pragmatic, and moral. This, again, serves to check a possible rush to use extralegal powers" (1125). Second, after hearing the political actor's justifications, the public evaluates the political actor's deeds to determine whether to ratify them, in toto or in part, after the fact. As Gross explains, in *ex post* approval, not only are public officials forced to make "both a pragmatic analysis of and moral assessment of their illegal actions" but also the people are required to take a stand on the matter, so that both political actors and the public are "politically, legally, and morally responsible" for the decisions made (1128). For Gross, the people can only judge (and share responsibility in) the morality of political actors if they are made aware of the previous questionable actions.

Although both Gross and Cicero describe a process of *ex post* approval by the people, their criteria for ratification are not identical; Gross's standards for popular approval are more ambiguous than Cicero's. Gross appears to leave it up to the public to determine for itself the grounds for approving or rejecting the legality or morality of an official's *prima facie* extralegal measures. Cicero, however, identifies the basis of the *populus*'s endorsement on his saving the Republic; for Cicero and, he implies, the people, protection of the Republic is the ultimate moral good. But ensuring the well-being of the state is most obviously a matter of utility—less obviously of morality. What is the relationship in Cicero, then, between the *honestum*, the moral, and the *utile*, the advantageous? For much of this chapter, Cicero appears to argue that political morality is indistinguishable from what is most beneficial to the state—a position if not identical to Machiavelli's at least sufficiently close to the Florentine's to make us ask whether Cicero's political morality merely anticipates Machiavelli's conviction that political expediency trumps all moral concerns. In the next chapter, I argue that Cicero, in contrast to Machiavelli, does not abandon the *honestum* for the *utile*. Rather, he believes that morality and utility must both be maintained. But, as we shall see, Cicero keeps hold of both by placing them in an uneasy state of equipoise—a feat that Machiavelli shows no interest in attempting. Machiavelli, as I shall soon show, rejects the possibility of retaining both morality and utility in politics.

CHAPTER 3

Rhetoric as a Balancing of Ends: Cicero and Machiavelli

In his youthful work on rhetoric, *De inventione* (published about 86 BCE), Cicero lists the ends for deliberative (political) oratory as *honestas* and *utilitas*, (the good or honorable and the useful or expedient). In more mature writings, like *De oratore* (55 BCE) and *De officiis* (44 BCE), Cicero maintains a similar position: that the morally good and the beneficial are reconcilable. For example, Cicero assumes in *De officiis* the identity of the *honestum* and the *utile*. He states there that "there is one rule for all cases; . . . either the thing that seems beneficial must not be dishonorable, or if it is dishonorable, it must not seem beneficial" (1991a, 3.81).[1] In recent years, Victoria Kahn (1994) and J. Jackson Barlow (1999) have offered Machiavelli's "rhetorical politics"—a politics "attuned to the rhetorical concerns of effective political action" (Kahn 1994, 24)—as a more coherent and intellectually honest alternative to Cicero's attempt to reconcile irreconcilables.[2] They contend that, unlike Cicero, Machiavelli accepts the impossibility of simultaneously upholding the morally good and the useful. For Machiavelli, the successful political actor must choose the *utile* over the *honestum* (Kahn 1994, 32; Barlow 1999, 640)—a reading of Machiavelli that I too accept.[3] Thus, Machiavelli suggests in chapter 18 of *The Prince* that "to be good is often useful not to oneself but to one's enemies, while to be bad is often the prerequisite of doing good" (Hulliung 1983, 195).

Cicero, however, is not alone in his internal tensions. As Kahn demonstrates, Machiavelli's account of *virtù* is itself variable. For example, he sometimes includes morality as an element of excellence (*virtù*), at other times not. I contend in this chapter, however, that Kahn's interpretation of Machiavelli's contradictoriness as only "apparent," a variability that is rhetorically inspired rather than logically deficient, applies not only to Machiavelli, as Kahn would have it, but also to Cicero. I argue that both Machiavelli *and* Cicero eschew "clear-cut or permanent distinctions" within *virtù* and between the *honestum* and the *utile*, respectively, because they wish to signal the political actor's need for flexibility (Kahn 1994, 30). Insofar as Cicero's internal contradictions, like Machiavelli's, are apparent, but not real, I hold that Machiavelli does not offer a political approach that is superior to Cicero's, at least not in the sense of greater intellectual coherence.

Despite their similarities, however, Cicero and Machiavelli differ from each other in that Cicero, in contrast to Machiavelli, openly affirms that politics is incomplete without a dual commitment to the good and the beneficial. I examine Machiavelli's focus on the useful and public as opposed to Cicero's additional commitment to the honorable and to the private. I analyze, in particular, the pursuit of glory in Machiavelli as it derives from early classical culture, which was preoccupied with appearances and the search for immortality. I argue that Cicero, while not abandoning the quest for glory, also vests this concept (under Stoic influence) with a private, moral character. In doing so, Cicero adheres to the rhetorical principle of decorum, which obliges orators to adapt themselves to context. This principle, I maintain, is not only a matter of expediency for Cicero but also a moral duty. While Cicero accommodates himself tõ a Roman world in which private morality was already an important part of one's life, Machiavelli violates decorum, attempting to resurrect a heroic ideal that disappeared long ago.

I concentrate, in particular, on Cicero's *De officiis* because, as other commentators have noted, it is probable that Machiavelli read this work and was affected by it. Thus, it is likely that Machiavelli derived from it the metaphor of the fox and the lion in chapter 18 of *The Prince*, as well as his antitheses between generosity and parsimony in chapter 16 and between love and fear in chapter 17. More important, current scholars have recognized that Machiavelli identifies his relationship to Cicero—whether as follower, critic, or something in between—by making use of the ideas and structure of *De officiis*, the work in which Cicero explicates the connection between the *honestum* and the *utile* (Barlow 1999; Kahn 1994; Colish 1978).

APPARENT CONTRADICTIONS IN MACHIAVELLI AND CICERO

Niccolò Machiavelli's relationship to his Renaissance contemporaries has long been the subject of debate: some portray him as breaking completely with

Renaissance humanism, while others depict him as a true, if not typical, Renaissance humanist.[4] Because Cicero was the dominant classical influence on the Renaissance humanists, Machiavelli's relationship to his contemporaries is based, in large part, on his position relative to Cicero.[5] Accordingly, Machiavelli's connection to Cicero has itself been a matter of controversy. Although Machiavelli has been presented both as emulating Cicero as well as rejecting him entirely, the most plausible position, I believe, is taken by Victoria Kahn and J. Jackson Barlow, who maintain that Machiavelli's relationship to Cicero is more ambiguous.[6]

For Kahn and Barlow, Machiavelli begins with Cicero's assumptions as his starting point only, largely, to reject them for a more radical position.[7] Kahn, who devotes *Machiavellian Rhetoric: From the Counter-Reformation to Milton* (1994) to Machiavelli's reception in the Renaissance, observes Machiavelli's "complicated relationship to the humanist tradition"—his "debt, as well as his criticism of, the humanist rhetorical tradition." She analyzes this ambivalence by focusing on the rhetorical character of both the humanists' and Machiavelli's arguments.[8] Kahn identifies the humanist tradition with "the Ciceronian ideal of harmony between the *honestum* and the *utile*" (1994, 9, 58). Barlow concentrates specifically on Machiavelli's relationship to Cicero in *De officiis*. Although he does not address the rhetorical character of these thinkers, his analysis is consistent with Kahn's rhetorically based approach; he attends to the role of circumstance, political success, and the useful—all elements of what Kahn terms "rhetorical politics" (1994, 8–9)—in Cicero and Machiavelli.

Both Kahn and Barlow suggest that Machiavelli's flexible (or rhetorical) politics is more coherent than Cicero's moralistic politics. Although rhetoric by its nature can be employed for good or ill, Cicero, later emulated by the humanists, denied the two-sidedness of rhetoric. In the Ciceronian tradition, the rhetor is bound by the *honestum*. Kahn explains that Machiavelli rejects this idealization of rhetoric (and of politics). In its place, he substitutes a view of politics that is "more deeply rhetorical" than it had been in the humanist tradition in the sense that he, unlike the humanists, is not bound, a priori, to any specific ideology or set of values (Kahn 1994, 8, 59);[9] his political actor can respond more flexibly to situations based solely on the needs of the case. Machiavelli is unencumbered by the Ciceronian legacy that locked the orator/ statesman into pursuing both the good and the useful, as if the two were always identical. According to Barlow, Machiavelli does not remain, as does Cicero, "within a classical framework in which the objectives of success are limited by nature," in which force and fraud are precluded. Recognizing that moral goodness and political effectiveness often conflict, Machiavelli abandons this untenable balance between the two in favor of the useful (Kahn 1994, 9, 32);[10] "Machiavelli sees politics as unlimited by considerations outside politics itself" (Barlow 1999, 637). In Barlow's terms, Machiavelli shows us how Cicero "tries to find a middle way in *De Officiis*" between unrestrained politics and excessive moralizing. Ultimately, however, "Cicero himself is not successful in reconciling them" (Barlow 1999, 644).

Machiavelli's solution to the tensions within Ciceronian rhetoric, however, is itself problematic. Although Cicero, as Kahn and Barlow suggest, faces the difficulty of reconciling the honorable and the expedient, Machiavelli also faces internal contradictions. One such contradiction is Machiavelli's inconstant use of *virtù*.[11] Machiavelli's variable usage is seen in his accounts of Cesare Borgia and Agathocles of Sicily in *The Prince*. At first glance, the two rulers, respectively, represent a contrast between the presence and absence of *virtù*. In chapter 7, Machiavelli presents Cesare Borgia as a prince who achieved power by fortune. Although he "attained his position through the favor and help of his father, and lost it when these disappeared," Machiavelli insists that Borgia was a man of *virtù*: he did "all those things that a far-seeing [*prudente*] and able [*virtuoso*] man should do, in order to put down his roots in territories that he had acquired thanks to the power and favor of others." He possessed "so much ability [*virtù*] . . . that he would have overcome all the difficulties if he had not had those armies on top of him, or if he had been in good health." Machiavelli finds Borgia's example sufficiently compelling to declare: "I do not know what better precepts to offer to a new ruler than to cite his actions as a pattern" (1988, 23, 28).

In chapter 8, Machiavelli presents Agathocles, in opposition to Borgia, as a man who rose to power by crime, not fortune. But despite the political success that Agathocles (unlike Borgia) attained, Machiavelli denies Agathocles's *virtù* and glory. He acknowledges Agathocles's political accomplishments. "[T]hrough overcoming countless difficulties and dangers," Machiavelli writes, "he rose up through the ranks of the militia, and gained power, which he afterwards maintained by undertaking many courageous and dangerous courses of action." But after praising Agathocles's determination, Machiavelli states: "Yet it cannot be called virtue [*virtù*] to kill one's fellow-citizens, to betray one's friends, to be treacherous, merciless and irreligious; power may be gained by acting in such ways, but not glory. . . . [H]is appallingly cruel and inhumane conduct, and countless wicked deeds, preclude his being numbered among the finest men. One cannot, then, attribute either to luck or favor or to ability [*virtù*] what he achieved without either" (1988, 31). These comments lead Quentin Skinner to conclude that Machiavelli disapproves of tyrants, like

Agathocles, "who never make the least attempt to behave virtuously even in favourable circumstances." Skinner tells us that "for Machiavelli a man of completely vicious character, like Agathocles, can never be considered a man of true *virtù*" (1978, 1:137–38).

Skinner's reading of Machiavelli distinguishes clearly enough between men of *virtù*, like Borgia, and men lacking *virtù*, like Agathocles—though Skinner never explains what a "completely vicious character" means to Machiavelli. But, as Nathan Tarcov notes, Skinner ignores Machiavelli's concomitant depiction of Agathocles as virtuous, a man of "such energy [*virtù*] of mind and body" that he rose to become military governor of Syracuse. For Machiavelli, because of "the *virtù* displayed by Agathocles" in confronting danger and adversity, "there is no reason for judging him inferior to even the ablest general" (Tarcov 1988, 201–2). And despite Agathocles's "appallingly cruel and inhumane conduct, and countless wicked deeds," Machiavelli even cites Agathocles as a model of someone who committed cruel deeds well and who remedied his standing, in some measure, "both with God and with men" (1988, 30–31, 33).

Machiavelli's account of Agathocles suggests an uncertainty about the Sicilian's status, unnoticed by Skinner. Machiavelli's indecisiveness, however, appears to extend beyond Agathocles's character, implying a contradiction or incoherence in Machiavelli's understanding of *virtù*. Machiavelli's refusal to call Agathocles virtuous seems to indicate a moral dimension to *virtù*. His attribution of *virtù* to Agathocles, however, implies that *virtù* is an amoral, if not immoral, concept. This conflicting notion of *virtù* within Machiavelli's account of Agathocles is further complicated by the portrayal of Borgia in *The Prince* as resorting to trickery and violence to further his power (Kahn 1994, 29). Thus, the original division between Borgia's *virtù* and Agathocles's absence of *virtù* now looks baseless. Kahn's and Barlow's initial claims that Machiavelli is more consistent than Cicero would appear to be undermined.

Kahn, however, convincingly makes sense of what she describes as "the apparently contradictory reiteration of *virtù*" in *The Prince* by denying that any "clear-cut or permanent distinctions" in defining *virtù* can be made. For Kahn, Machiavelli's *virtù* is not incoherent or contradictory inasmuch as he does not commit himself to any single definition of *virtù*: "Given Machiavelli's dramatic and rhetorical view of the world of politics, it is not surprising that he offers us no substantive or thematic definition of *virtù*. This is not simply a failing of analytical skill but a sophisticated rhetorical strategy, the aim of which is to destabilize or dehypostatize our conception of political virtue, for only a destabilized *virtù* can be effective in the destabilized world of political reality." Kahn sees Machiavelli as staging or dramatizing "this lack of conceptual stability" with the examples of Cesare Borgia and Agathocles. "Neither in the case of Borgia nor in the case of Agathocles can crime be called *virtù*, because *virtù* cannot be *called* any one thing. In short, once the temporal dimension of circumstance is introduced, the fact that crime cannot necessarily be called *virtù* means also that it can be called *virtù*." Kahn believes that, by refusing to specify what *virtù* is or is not, Machiavelli assumes a more rhetorically profound position than Cicero. In Machiavelli, "the criterion of correct action is not moral goodness or the intrinsically moral judgment of prudence but the functional excellence or effectiveness of *virtù*" (Kahn 1994, 30, 25, 32).[12]

But Kahn fails to recognize that Cicero's "irreconcilable" distinction between the *honestum* and the *utile* parallels Machiavelli's own irreconcilable distinctions within the concept *virtù*. Kahn and Barlow treat Cicero's adherence to contradictory ends as a failure to confront political reality. But Kahn does not allow that Cicero might harmonize ends that cannot always be harmonized because he, like Machiavelli, approaches politics rhetorically. *Pace* Kahn, Cicero's own "conceptual confusion" should be viewed as permitting greater freedom for orators/political actors to accommodate themselves to circumstance.

In *De officiis*, Cicero maintains that the two ends, the *honestum* and the *utile*, do not conflict and that the *utile* is subordinate to the *honestum*, which should either be sought alone (the early Stoic Zeno's position) or "at least should be thought entirely to outweigh everything else (as was Aristotle's view)" (1991a, 3.34–35). On closer inspection, though, the pursuit of the honorable and the useful, under the domination of the honorable, is not always the guiding principle that Cicero declares it to be. Marcia Colish (1978, 86–90) points up how Cicero, in *De officiis*, frequently defines the honorable in terms of the useful, even when the useful is viewed in terms of self-interest. When discussing liberality, an element of justice, and therefore the honorable, Cicero states: "We should look both at the conduct of the man on whom we are conferring a kindness, and at the spirit in which he views us, at the association and fellowship of our lives together, and at the dutiful services that he has previously carried out *for our benefit* [*ad nostras utilitates*]" (1991a, 1.45; emphasis added). Cicero thus delineates liberality, at least in part, by usefulness. Similarly, the three virtues of justice, courage, and temperance are designed to allow "excellence and greatness of spirit to shine out," which includes "increasing influence" and "*acquiring benefits for oneself and those dear to one*" (1991a, 1.17; emphasis added). And in discussing temperance, Cicero advises that professions that "either require good sense or else *procure substantial benefit* (*non mediocris utilitas*) . . . are honorable for those who belong to the class they befit" (1991a, 1.151; emphasis added).

Sometimes Cicero seems to betray those principles that most clearly distinguish him from Machiavelli, like Cicero's criticism of force and deceit, exemplified by the lion and the fox (Barlow 1999, 636–37).[13] In chapter 18 of *The Prince*, Machiavelli advises that the ruler must frequently eschew justice: "a ruler must know how to act like a beast," able to "imitate both fox and lion," especially the fox. The metaphor of the fox and the lion, however, appears over fifteen hundred years earlier in *De officiis*, where Cicero condemns the methods of both animals as "most alien to a human being." He adds that "deceit deserves a greater hatred" (1991a, 1.41). Consistent with his condemnation of the fox, Cicero commits himself to the standard "that what is true, simple and pure is most fitted to the nature of man." Yet this rule conflicts with his concession, later in *De officiis*, that "scruples should not prevent us from occasionally defending a guilty man," because "an advocate may sometimes defend what looks like the truth, even if it is less true" (1991a, 1.13, 2.51).

Besides expanding the honorable to include the useful as it relates to benefitting oneself, Cicero raises the common good or utility above all else, so that the honorable comes to include social utility (Remer 2004, 147–48). Colish (1978, 89–90) and Giorgio Jossa (1964) even argue that it is social utility that ultimately dominates. For Cicero, "it is certain that it is not the *honestas* that makes the *utilitas*, but the *utilitas* that makes the *honestas*, because the *honestas* . . . consists exactly in the realization of the *communis utilitas*, the advantage of the community" (Jossa 1964, 276). Accordingly, in discussing social utility, Cicero allows that "occasions often arise when the actions that seem most worthy of a just man, of him we call good, undergo a change, and the opposite becomes the case." These include setting aside such requirements as "telling the truth, returning a deposit, carrying out a promise" because adhering to the normally honorable would not "serve the common advantage" (1991a, 1.31).

But Colish's claim that the useful dominates all oversimplifies Cicero in *De officiis*. Cicero does not assimilate the honorable to the useful any more than he fulfills his own claim to subordinate the useful to the honorable. Cicero's intermingling of the categories "honorable" and "useful" (and of exceptions to these categories) produces the same effect as Machiavelli's inability to commit himself to any one version of *virtù*: to suggest that words and actions must be decided by circumstance. The consequence of Cicero's definitional variability is to make Cicero more rhetorical. Without either the honorable or the useful—individual or social—determining the outcome a priori, rhetors must decide for themselves. Unlike Machiavelli, who limits himself to deciding actions according to the principle of utility, Cicero is committed to balancing the honorable and the useful, not only against each other but from within each standard. The upshot is that the absolute categories become more liquid, with the rhetor having to decide contextually. Cicero writes in *De inventione*: "There are then certain matters that must be considered with reference to time and intention and not merely by their absolute qualities. In all these matters one must think what the occasion demands and what is worthy of the persons concerned, and one must consider not what is being done but with what spirit anything is done, with what associates, at what time, and how long it has been going on" (1949, 2.173–76; see also Leff 1998, 69, 75–76).

The Elements of Glory

The effect of the discussion in the previous section was to diminish the differences between Cicero and Machiavelli. In contrast to Kahn and Barlow, who view the flexible or rhetorical Machiavelli as superior to the morality-bound Cicero, I have argued that Cicero's own variable treatments of the honorable and the beneficial suggest an adaptability in Cicero similar to that which Barlow and Kahn find in Machiavelli. Cicero distinguishes himself from Machiavelli by adhering to the honorable. But Cicero's idealistic defense of the honorable, as just argued, is not without its own accommodation of the truth to the audience's values. And if Colish is correct, "that Machiavelli, like Cicero, thinks that, in the long run, the best way to achieve the appearance of virtue is actually to be what one appears to be," then the gap between Cicero and Machiavelli shrinks to insignificance (1978, 91).

What Colish misses in blurring the line between appearance and actuality is that Machiavelli's concern with appearances is not tantamount to an obligation to be virtuous. In contrast to Colish's view, Machiavelli does *not think* that in the long run the best way to achieve the appearance of virtue is actually to be what one appears to be. Machiavelli believes that the prince must do more than depart from virtue occasionally. He sees the ruler's need to act with cunning, trickery, and violence as a permanent condition (see Wolin 2004, 197–98, on Machiavelli's novel openness in asserting that violence is a permanent characteristic of political life): "A ruler . . . should seem to be exceptionally merciful, trustworthy, upright, humane and devout," but he must also "be capable of entering upon the path of wrongdoing when this becomes necessary" (Machiavelli 1988, 62).

And Machiavelli believes that immoral methods will always be necessary in politics, to one degree or another, because human nature is vicious and unchanging. He writes in *The Prince*: "For this may be said of men generally: they are ungrateful, fickle, feigners and dissemblers, avoiders of danger, eager for gain." He states this view even more powerfully in the *Discourses*: "[A]ll men are bad, and . . . they always have to use the malignity of their spirit whenever they have a free opportunity for it." These characteristics of human nature, like human nature more generally, are as permanent as the movement, order, and capacities of the "heaven, [the] sun, and [the] elements" (1996, 1.3, preface). Instead of devoting himself to virtue consistently, Machiavelli's prince adopts a code of behavior similar to that presented by Glaucon in the *Republic*, where justice is pursued out of self-interest, as beneficial but not as a moral obligation (Plato 1961b, 357b–67e).

I have shown in the previous section that Cicero and Machiavelli's "internal contradictions" lend a greater fluidity to their concepts of the *honestum* and the *utile* (Cicero) and *virtù* (Machiavelli), which, in turn, provides them with greater liberty of action in adapting themselves to circumstance. But while their explications of specific concepts (or relations between concepts) may be mutable, they are more fixed about the ideals they value: Machiavelli's choice of the beneficial alone as opposed to Cicero's fidelity to the honorable *and* the beneficial. (As seen earlier, because of this difference, Kahn and Barlow argue that Machiavelli is more intellectually honest than Cicero.) The difference between Cicero and Machiavelli in relation to the *honestum* and the *utile*, however, is characteristic of a more general difference between the two. Cicero seeks to reconcile disparate ideals by balancing them. Machiavelli, in contrast, chooses between ideals, rather than balancing them. Balance pervades Cicero's writings and life. In his *Letters to Atticus*, for example, Cicero himself describes his "whole line of conduct [as] nicely balanced"—"avoiding treading on [his political enemies'] toes, though without currying popularity or sacrificing principle (1999b, letter 119)." Likewise, Robert Hariman writes that within Cicero's republican style, "both influence and integrity will come from balancing the tensions between assertion and deference, virtue and virtuosity, or similar elements of the art of persuasion" (1995, 106). As for Machiavelli, Isaiah Berlin, in his classic essay "The Originality of Machiavelli," argues that Machiavelli forces us to choose between a Christian or humanist morality, which he rejects, and a pagan, political morality, which the Florentine adopts, "taking little interest in the values that this choice ignored or flouted." There is for Machiavelli no balancing act or compromise that will guarantee us "justice and mercy, humility and *virtù*, happiness and knowledge, glory and liberty, magnificence and sanctity" (Berlin 1972, 196, 198). The *honestum* and the *utile* are incompatible, and so, too, are a host of other ideals that we would like to believe can coexist but cannot.

An example of how Cicero and Machiavelli differ in their stands on holding multiple ideals can be seen in their treatments of glory; in his conception of glory, Cicero balances different ideals—the honorable and the beneficial, the public and the private—while Machiavelli maintains a conception of glory that is consistent with the beneficial and the public. In *The Prince*, Machiavelli is preoccupied with the useful as it concerns the ruler. And Machiavelli defines what is beneficial to the ruler primarily by what will bring him the greatest glory. Hannah Arendt writes: "Machiavelli's criterion for political action was glory" (1958, 77). Likewise, Eugene Garver notes that "while action that is its own end was interpreted by Aristotle to mean acting for the sake of the noble, in Machiavelli it will mean acting for the sake of glory" (1987, 83–84; see also 128, 152–53).[14] In the *Discourses*, Machiavelli emphasizes the common benefit and glory of the people in a republic. In both *The Prince* and the *Discourses*, glory is achieved through great public performances. As Russell Price writes in his account of *gloria* in Machiavelli: "For Machiavelli, glory seems to consist essentially in the external recognition of outstanding deeds or achievements" (1977, 591). The greatest deeds that earn the praise of other men, according to Machiavelli, are those achieved in diplomacy, war, or politics—but especially politics. Second only to the authors of religions, Machiavelli praises most the founders of political regimes. "Among all men praised, the most praised are those who have been heads and orderers of religions. Next come such as have established republics or kingdoms" (1996, 1.10). But even Machiavelli's founders of religions should be understood politically, as Machiavelli does Moses, a founder of a religion *and* a principality, whose actions and methods are comparable to other political founders like Cyrus, Romulus, and Theseus (1988, 20).[15]

In *The Prince*, Machiavelli explains how acting nobly and gloriously benefits the prince by securing his rule. Using King Ferdinand of Spain, an example from his own time, Machiavelli writes that Ferdinand "has always plotted and achieved great things, which have never failed to keep his subjects in a state of suspense and amazement, as they await their outcome." And because these glorious deeds "have followed one another so quickly" Machiavelli concludes that "nobody has had enough time to be able to initiate a revolt against him." The upshot of performing glorious acts is that the people "want to be on your side . . . want to become followers." Therefore, Machiavelli counsels the prince to try "in every action to obtain fame for being great and excellent" (1988, 77; 1999, 111). If he succeeds in gaining this reputation, he will enhance his stability (Garver 1987, 42).

Besides this concrete benefit, glory brings with it a more amorphous but, for Machiavelli, no less important advantage in the immortality it bestows on its possessors. In resurrecting the ancient Greek and perhaps especially the ancient Roman view of worldly glory, Machiavelli revives a significant component of the classical worldview: that immortality is pursued through the "works and deeds and words" performed in the *polis*. The classical Weltanschauung that Machiavelli recovers, however, is not that of Plato, Aristotle, the Stoics, or other ancient philosophers and philosophies. Machiavelli revives the heroic ideal of the *vita activa* and the public life. It is Machiavelli whom Arendt singles out as "the only postclassical political theorist who, in an extraordinary effort to restore its old dignity to politics, perceived the gulf [between the sheltered life in the household and the merciless exposure of the polis] and understood something of the courage needed to cross it" (1958, 35; see also 17–21; Price 1977, 629).[16] Those outstanding individuals sufficiently courageous to cross the gulf and to succeed could make a name for themselves that would transcend their own deaths. Glory, not Christian salvation, might provide a life beyond the grave. This possibility was open not only to individuals, however, but to states too. The glory that ancient Rome attained, for example, survived well beyond the demise of the Republic. And though the Roman Republic may have been shorter lived than Venice, *la Serenissima Repubblica*, Machiavelli prefers the glory of Rome, with its "tumults and universal dissensions" to the tranquility and stability of Venice, a "weak republic" lacking glory. Rome's instabilities, Machiavelli argues, are but "an inconvenience necessary to arrive at Roman greatness" (1996, 1.6).

But this public space that Machiavelli tries to recapture is one of appearances. Carlin Barton, another writer nostalgic for ancient glory, describes the Roman *persona* and the role expressed by it as "the very boundary and definition of one's being, the *sine qua non* of existence." In contrast to our notion "that you can save your soul even if you have lost your face," the Romans believed that they "lost their souls when they lost their faces"; a Roman, "relieved of the burden or mask, removed from the endless challenges of the context, . . . was not the authentic, genuine, original self as we imagine it, but a void" (Barton 2001, 57, 64). Machiavelli reflects this anxiety over appearances by equating popular acclaim with political success. Unlike Cicero, who (as will be seen) has a more complex and ambivalent attitude toward glory, Machiavelli scarcely shows any concern about how fleeting glory can be. Neither does he look into the souls of the men pursuing glory. As Price explains, "he neglects what might be called the psychology of the search for glory" (1977, 629).

In contrast to Machiavelli, Cicero's views on glory make room for both the *honestum* and the *utile*. Further, they contain elements of both the public and the private. Cicero's concept of glory, however, evolves over time, from his youthful position, where glory is defined solely by its useful and public elements, to his more mature standpoint, where glory comes to include the honorable and the private. What is perhaps most striking about Cicero's discussions of glory is that Cicero mixes the elements of glory so that neither he nor his audience are forced, as Machiavelli would have us, to choose between some elements as opposed to others. As Hariman points out, Cicero advises Atticus to have regard "to my honor, reputation, and interest." In this letter, Cicero places reputation "on rightly equal terms with ethical principle and self-interest, and its artful composition provides the means for joining the other, often contrary impulses" (1999b, letter 101; Hariman 1995, 139). Yet Cicero recognizes that these competing values must ultimately be balanced so that a decision can be made. As he writes in another letter to Atticus: "There is no chance for evasion" (1913b, 7.1). Cicero, when rising before the Senate chamber, must compress into a "single, dramatic moment" a position derived from "the complex considerations of honor, expediency, principle, loyalty, character, circumstance, and more" (Hariman 1995, 108).

Although I do not attempt here to explain in any detail the sources of Cicero's intellectual evolution, Stoicism played a part. The Stoics believed that virtue was the only thing that was good. Cicero echoes this doctrine in the *Parodoxa stoicorum* (completed in 46 BCE) where he states: "I deem good only what is right and honorable and virtuous" (1942, 9). They also turned toward the private by making the condition of the soul the ultimate criterion of a person's well-being: "Speaking strictly, the Stoics said that nothing good or bad can affect the body of a human being; good or bad in the strict sense, can only be predicated of states of the soul and actions which are defined by the state of the soul" (Long 1996, 248).[17] (The Roman Stoics emphasized social responsibility and ethics in action, thus they, like Cicero, argue that virtue or the *honestum* manifests itself in action [Reydams-Schils 2005, 3].) As such, goodness was not to be determined by public approbation but by the well-being of the *psychē*. Cicero too eventually asserts that moral actions are to be carried out and judged independently of public acclaim, though he does not maintain this position consistently. To his death, Cicero often links honorable deeds with glory understood as public praise.[18]

In *De inventione*, the young Cicero defines glory as "a person's having a widespread reputation accompanied by praise" (1949, 2.166). And in his early speeches, he betrayed no self-consciousness about his own ambitions for glory and appears to perceive glory as unquestionably desirable. Cicero sees glory as a means of advancing his career: "[t]o rise in the world and carve out a career for himself a *novus homo* like Cicero needed above all to have his name well known at Rome" (Sullivan 1941, 383; see also Long 1995b, 216). After Cicero reaches the rank of consul, though, he moves beyond a short-term view of glory. He now speaks of glory, in the classical terms Machiavelli would resurrect, as a way of gaining immortality. Defending Gaius Rabirius against a charge of high treason (63 BCE), Cicero speaks "of a glory more lasting than . . . mortal life" (1927b, 29). One year later, in his defense of Archias the Poet, Cicero even more emphatically connects glory to immortality: "Deep in every noble heart dwells a power which plies night and day the goad of glory, and bids us see to it that the remembrance of our names should not pass away with life, but should endure coeval with all the ages of the future" (1923f, 29; Sullivan 1941, 383–84).

In later writings, Cicero distinguishes between vulgar popularity (*fama popularis*) and true glory (*vera gloria*), which is often tantamount, for him, to the distinction between the popularly based glory and the glory bestowed by the *boni*, the good persons. In the *Tusculan Disputations*, Cicero speaks of "popular acclaim, which offers a perverted caricature of the beauty that belongs to true distinction"; its pursuers "spend their lives in great emptiness, chasing not a solid figure but only a shallow-shape glory." He contrasts this specious glory with "real glory," which is "a solid thing, clearly modeled and not shadowy at all: it is the unanimous praise of good persons, approval sounded without bias by those who know how to judge excellence of character" (1971, 3.3–4; see also 3.61). In describing genuine glory, Cicero adverts to both the public and private aspects of glory. True glory is based on virtue, a person's "excellence in character." But it also represents "the unanimous praise of good persons," perhaps a more discerning group than the *populus* but a group whose approval the honorable person seeks, nevertheless. Elsewhere in the *Tusculan Disputations*, Cicero defends his disparaging of the common people's praise by way of a question: "Can anything be more foolish than to suppose that those, whom individually one despises as illiterate mechanics, are worth anything collectively?" Based on his view of the lower classes, Cicero asserts that the wise man will "reject the distinctions bestowed by the people [*populus*] even if they come unsought" (1927c, 5.104). In book 2 of *De officiis*, however, Cicero tempers his apparent rejection of popular acclaim. As in the *Tusculan Disputations*, he depicts a normative concept of glory, which he describes here as the "peak and perfection of glory [*summa . . . et perfecta gloria*]." Unlike the *Tusculan Disputations*, however, Cicero in *De officiis* recognizes this highest glory as the praise of the common people. The highest, truest glory consists in the love, faith, and admiration of the masses (1991a, 2.31).

In his mature writings, Cicero points up the usefulness *and* the moral character of glory. He defends glory in *De officiis* as part of the *utile*. As A. A. Long writes: "Cicero does not approach glory in *Off.* II as a necessary or *per se value*, but as something instrumental to securing friends and to engaging in public life. He treats glory not as a self-sufficient objective of the just man, but as something he should seek to acquire because of its utility to his role in the life of the community" (1995b, 231). He also concedes that while glory is often opposed to "justice and genuine courage," it spurs men of distinction to "right actions and great service to the state." The community, therefore, "benefits from the actions that justify the attribution of true glory"; the pursuit of glory produces social utility (Long 1995b, 224–33).[19] As seen earlier, Cicero maintains in *De officiis* that the useful cannot be isolated from the honorable. Thus, glory too cannot be separated from the honorable. For Cicero, true glory cannot conflict with the *honestum* (Long 1995b, 229–333).

He rejects an important part of the *utile*, the belief that public glory can make one immortal, in "Scipio's Dream" in book 6 of *De republica*, where Scipio related a dream in which his grandfather, the war hero Africanus, speaks to him as follows:

> What fame can you achieve in what men say, or what glory can you achieve that is worth seeking? . . . And you surely don't believe that from the lands which you know and cultivate, your name or the name of any of us can cross the Caucasus which you see there, or swim the Ganges over there? Who is there in the rest of the earth, at the extremes of east, west, north, or south, who will hear your name? And if you remove those, you of course see the narrow bounds set on the expansion of your glory. And even the people who talk about us—how long will they do that? (1999d, 6.20–21)

Cicero has Scipio continue (quoting Africanus) to deny the immortality of glory. Even if our offspring should desire to pass on our glory, natural disasters prevent us from achieving long-lasting glory. Africanus asks Scipio, "What is that human glory really worth which can last scarcely a fraction of a single year?" His grandfather counsels Scipio to look to the heavens, the dwelling place for all eternity: "[D]o not place your hopes in human rewards: virtue itself by its own allurements should draw you towards true honor" (1999d, 6.25).

But Cicero, until the very end, never abandons the belief—the belief he disparages in the *Somnium Scipionis*—that true glory can generate immortality. In the *Tusculan Disputations* Cicero writes: "in this commonwealth of ours, with what thought in their minds do we suppose such an army of illustrious men have lost their lives for the commonwealth? Was it that their name should be restricted to the narrow limits of their life? No one would ever have exposed himself to death for his country without good hope of immortality" (1927c, 1.32–33; see also 1.109–10). Likewise, in *Phillipics* 14 (43 BCE), in a funeral tribute to the soldiers killed fighting Antony's forces—delivered about six months before Cicero's murder—he observes: "Brief is the life given us by nature; but the memory of life nobly resigned is everlasting. And if that memory had been no longer than this life of ours, who would be so mad as, by the greatest labor and peril, to strive for the utmost height of honor and glory? . . . Thus, in exchange for life's mortal state, you will have gained for yourselves immortality" (1926, 14.31–33; see also 9.10). These statements that Cicero made not long before he died evince a consistent linking of glory to immortality, notwithstanding Cicero's condemnation of this linkage, most notably in "Scipio's Dream."

The public character of glory, which Cicero, like Machiavelli, embraces in his view on immortality, finds its opposite in his stand that our obligation to pursue the honorable does not depend on public response: "Even if [the honorableness we seek] is not accorded acclaim, it is still honorable, and as we truly claim, even if no one praises it, it is by nature worthy of praise" (1926, 1.14).[20] And in book 1 of *De officiis*, Cicero states: "A true and wise greatness of spirit judges that deeds and not glory are the basis of the honorableness that nature most seeks" (1991a, 1.65; see also Long 1995b, 227). Barton refers to a change in *virtus* that appears in Cicero and in the Roman thought of his contemporaries. "*Virtus*, the active principle par excellence, congeals into patience, endurance, passive resistance; it began to be used of internal qualities, even those unseen or unacknowledged." As opposed to the heroic Roman focus on public virtue, Barton (2001, 124) explains that *virtus* looked increasingly like our modern sense of "virtue" (see also Barton 2001, 125–26; Long 1995b).

As with the honorable, Cicero never commits himself to a single definition of glory. In part, Cicero's conceptualization of glory evolves over time. But, even in his maturity, Cicero does not adopt a consistent understanding of glory. Rather, in embracing a rhetorical approach to language, he delineates glory contextually, as best fits his purposes at the time—sometimes valuing the praise of the masses, sometimes belittling it, at times emphasizing the external character of glory, at other times restricting glory to an internal condition of virtue. Cicero's different positions on glory, however, are not departures from the values of his society, but reflections of the complexity (and transitional nature) of those values. Thus, both his pursuit *and* rejection of public glory are authentically Roman. How he balances between the diverse uses of the term, though, are particular to Cicero.

Decorum: The Appropriate and the Moral

As I argued earlier, Machiavelli's view of glory is derived from heroic antiquity. But in his attempt to resurrect a spirit long gone—alien to Western society, at least since the victory of Christianity—Machiavelli ignores a central tenet of the rhetorical tradition: decorum. Because ideas once spoken are indissolubly linked to the conditions of their transmission, that is, to language, tone, organization, time, place, and the like, the classical rhetoricians taught that the successful orator must be mindful of propriety or decorum. Cicero pursues the appropriate in adhering to the complex ideas of his audience. For example, it would have been a breach of decorum for a Roman orator, in Cicero's time, to ignore appeals to the *honestum*, while appealing to his audience only on the grounds of the *utile*.

The Renaissance humanist Desiderius Erasmus underscores the centrality of decorum to Cicero in the *Ciceronianus* (1528), his critique of those Italian humanists who singled out Cicero as the only model of correct and stylish Latinity. These "Ciceronians," Erasmus argued, imitate the words and style of Cicero but reject the essence of Cicero, his decorum. "Cicero spoke in the best possible way in the age he lived in. Would he still have spoken in the best possible way if he had adopted the same style in the age of Cato the Censor, Scipio, or Ennius?" Erasmus contends that the true Ciceronian speaks appositely, "partly according to the subject-matter, partly according to the persons involved, including both speakers and audience, partly according to place, time, and other circumstances" (1986, 28:73, 380–81; see also 396, 399–401, 448).

In contrast to Cicero, Machiavelli upholds a vision of glory that is out of touch with his own time and is inconsistent with decorum. Thus, although Skinner emphasizes the significance of honor and glory to both Machiavelli and his contemporaries—the Renaissance humanists—he distinguishes between the belief of Machiavelli's contemporaries "that if a ruler wishes to . . . achieve the goals of honor, glory and fame, he needs above all to cultivate the full range of Christian as well as moral virtues" and Machiavelli's rejection of Christian (and conventional) morality as a prerequisite of true glory (1978,

1:131–32; see also 100–101, 118–19, 121). Machiavelli's dismissal of the *honestum* as an element of glory is out of step with his peers' acceptance of the necessary connection between glory and morality. In addition, whereas eternal salvation was, at a minimum, a (stated) concern for the Renaissance humanists as a whole, for Machiavelli the immortality of public fame was the ultimate goal.

It can be argued, however, that Machiavelli does not ignore the *honestum*, that while he believes that the political actor must choose the beneficial above the honorable, he is aware that the common people desire their rulers to be honorable. Therefore, Machiavelli emphasizes the need for rulers to *appear* honorable, even when not. Thus Machiavelli maintains in chapter 18 of *The Prince* that though his prince "need not actually possess"—or often *should not* actually possess—the traditional virtues, "he must certainly seem to" have them: "Having and always cultivating them is harmful, whereas seeming to have them is useful; for instance to seem merciful, trustworthy, humane, upright and devout, and also to be so. But if it becomes necessary to refrain, you must be prepared to act in the opposite way, and be capable of doing it" (1988, 62). Machiavelli, however, minimizes the need for the prince to appear moral when he argues that regarding "all human actions, and especially those of rulers . . . , men pay attention to the outcome." The means used by a ruler who schemes to conquer and preserve the state, "will always be judged to be honorable and be praised by everyone. For the common people are impressed by appearances and results." For Machiavelli, then, decorum may not even require that the prince appear honorable, at least in the long run, as the example of Agathocles's ultimate acceptance by his people would suggest.

There is another dimension of decorum, however, that Machiavelli ignores: decorum as an ethical ideal, not only a matter of expediency.[21] The boundaries decorum places on the orator's range of actions are moral, not merely expediential. Because decorum requires speech (or action) appropriate to the situation, Cicero's decorum-based morality demands different responses depending on circumstance, including different duties determined by one's position in society, as we saw in the previous chapter's discussion of *personae*. To fulfill our moral duty, we must ascertain the other character of nature, which is "that assigned specifically to individuals" (1991a, 1.107). For Cicero, however, individual "seemliness" is always judged in a social context, so the moral requirements of following our individual nature must include the "proper dispositions for each period of life and the rules of propriety defining a class society" (Hariman 2001, 204).

Decorum depends on context, but contexts vary both within one's society and between societies. For Cicero, the *honestum* must always originate in the particular, including one's particular society. Decorum expresses this idea in linking moral behavior to the deeply rooted values of one's community. By grounding his speech and actions in his community's values, Cicero delineates a concept of glory—one that includes the honorable—more complex than Machiavelli's. As discussed earlier, Cicero, more generally, blurs the lines between morality and usefulness. The political actor, for Cicero, must not only balance between the *honestum* and the *utile*, but must also consider what to do in a world in which the lines between (and within) the *honestum* and *utile* are unclear.

Kahn and Barlow prefer Machiavelli's consistency to Cicero's attempts to reconcile irreconcilable norms. Isaiah Berlin takes a similar approach, though his focus is on Machiavelli. Berlin states that Machiavelli is "transparently honest and clear" because he refuses to harmonize that which cannot be harmonized; he will not "compromise with current morality." Berlin argues that, while virtually all political thinkers—though he does not, we could well include Cicero here—accept a world in which ideals are ultimately compatible, Machiavelli forces us to see that they are not: "Machiavelli calls the bluff . . . of one of the foundations of the central Western philosophical tradition, the belief in the ultimate compatibility of all genuine values" (1972, 189–90).[22]

But while Machiavelli's apparent forthrightness may be more attractive than Cicero's ambiguities, in sundering *virtù* from the deeply rooted values of his society, Machiavelli offers us a rootless theory. Embracing the useful without the honorable and proposing that immortality can be attained through glory do not reflect his community's ideals. Rather, as I maintained earlier, Machiavelli turns to the classical heroic period for his inspiration. Perhaps Garver is even more precise than I have been when he argues that Machiavelli does not revert to the classical world of paganism, per se, but to neopaganism—a type of morality that pays lip service to ancient paganism but is, in reality, a new moral system in confrontation with Christian morality: "Ancient pagan morality could not see Christian morality as a real possibility, but neopagan morality is a permanent argument against a competitor it cannot refute but must continue to argue against" (2003, 72–73). Garver sees Machiavelli's neopaganism as a plausible attempt to conjure up the spirit of an irrecoverable past—classical paganism—to destroy the appeal of Christian morality. But Garver recognizes that the values of neopaganism are not derived from Machiavelli's own community. Furthermore, Machiavelli's values, as Garver points up, are not the values of *any* society, present or past. Rather, his resurrection of ancient glories subsists in the "realm of appearances" (Garver 2003, 81).

Conclusion

Cicero, particularly Cicero's rhetoric, influenced Machiavelli. Machiavelli, however, broke with Cicero on the political role of the *honestum*. In contrast to Cicero, who embraced the *honestum and* the *utile* (with the *honestum* as the ultimate end), Machiavelli rejected the possibility of adhering to both. Instead, he argued that leaders must be guided by the useful; successful rulers cannot permit themselves to be hamstrung by moral considerations. I maintain, however, that Cicero's adherence to the moral sense of his community is consistent with the rhetorical principle of decorum. Unlike Cicero, Machiavelli's abandonment of the *honestum* and his apotheosis of ancient heroic ideals set him at odds with the values of his own day, and, thus, he rejects decorum's obligation to follow the established customs and conventions of one's community.

But what of Machiavelli's and Cicero's relevance for today? The views I present below cannot be demonstrated by texts, and I do not try to prove their scientific truth. Nonetheless, I believe that despite the common view (held by much of the general public and many academics) that Machiavelli speaks to us more directly than does Cicero, Machiavelli's devotion to the *utile* alone is as problematic for moderns as for earlier generations. I think there is little question that Machiavelli's attempt to resurrect an antiquated view of glory, including the promise of immortality, is a still more fanciful goal in our times than in the days of the Renaissance. Even modern-day votaries of the heroic culture, like Arendt, accept that archaic glory cannot be revived from the dead: "not even the rise of the secular in the modern age . . . sufficed to save from oblivion the striving for immortality which originally had been the spring and center of the *vita activa*" (1958, 21).

Yet we live in a world in which our actions—whether as individuals acting politically or as states pursuing foreign policies—often seem more consistent with Machiavellian self-interest than with the high-minded goals that Cicero often touts. However, I believe that by limiting his concern for the *honestum* to its appearances, Machiavelli eliminates an important part of what it means to be a human being. Thus, both Machiavelli *and* Cicero acknowledge the importance of the *utile*. But Cicero goes further and intermingles the ethical and the useful. I suggest that in doing so he reflects the fullness of our humanity, which is not restricted to either the ethical or the beneficial. Just as it would be hard to imagine a society that is oblivious to the useful, so too I find it difficult to conceive of a society that would disregard—that would be unmotivated by— ethical ideals. Machiavelli, however, counsels princes and republics to govern sans such ideals, with political expediency as the guiding principle instead.

Cicero manifests his belief that a concern with the *honestum* is not limited to Romans—that right and wrong are transcultural—in his Stoic-inspired understanding of natural law as "right reason, consonant with nature, spread through all the people." He concedes that the specific legislation of this law varies among polities. Nevertheless, he maintains that its basic principles are universal: "There will not be one law at Rome and another at Athens, one now and another later; but all nations at all times will be bound by this one eternal and unchangeable law" (1999d, 3.33).[23]

I do not go so far as Cicero in arguing that there exists a universal law with a specific content. I only offer the weaker claim that a moral sense is basic to our species, regardless of the community in which we live. The ways in which we balance that moral sense with our private interests—or the interests of the political community—are diverse. Cicero does not offer, nor does he claim to offer, a simple solution to this balancing. For Cicero, the relationship between the *honestum* and the *utile* is determined by context. And because he recognizes that human beings in all societies must grapple with these (sometimes) competing ideas, he continues to be pertinent to us today in at least this way that Machiavelli is not.

Justus Lipsius, Morally Acceptable Deceit, and Prudence in the Ciceronian Tradition

Machiavelli's rejection of Ciceronian morality is often paired, in the scholarly literature, with the presumed break from Cicero of another sixteenth-century political thinker, Justus Lipsius. The once-famous South Netherlandish humanist (1547–1606), author of the *Politicorum sive Civilis Doctrinae libri sex*, or *Politica* (1589), Lipsius is now, like his formerly celebrated work of political theory, mostly renowned among a limited number of scholars (Morford 1991; Brooke 2012, 12, 14). As a political theorist, he is most commonly viewed today—particularly among Anglophone historians of political thought—as an erstwhile Ciceronian who comes to reject the traditional moralism of the Roman orator for the moral realism of the ancient Roman historian Tacitus (Waszink 2004; Tuck 1993, 40, 48, 44; Peltonen 1995, 125; Burke 1991, 485).[1] As Jan Waszink (2004) contends, Lipsius in the *Politica* parts company with Cicero "most importantly, on the use of deception and fraud," adopting Tacitus's position that "politics are not about what should be done, . . . but about the much less presentable, and often cynical question what the realities of power and necessity demand" (91, 96–97).[2] Even J. H. M. Salmon, who questions the dominant interpretation of Lipsius in which the late humanist rejects Cicero for Tacitus, presents a similar although less polarized account of Lipsius's intellectual development, which acknowledges Lipsius's Tacitist turn, albeit without claiming that his embrace of Tacitus involves a concurrent abandonment of Ciceronian political morality. Thus, Salmon (1980) explains that Lipsius began as a traditional Ciceronian moralist and, "after changing the focus of [his] attention to Tacitus, returned to Cicero with new insight" (322).[3]

I argue, however, that Cicero, not Tacitus, is the primary and consistent source of Lipsius's political morality, specifically his belief that the ruler is morally justified, when political necessity demands, in dissimulating and deceiving. Lipsius (2004) bases his political morality, which he terms "mixed prudence"— "*the Prudence which uses deceit*"—on Cicero's rhetorical perspective, notwithstanding the mature Lipsius's abandonment of the practice of popular oratory (507; unless otherwise indicated, italicized quotations from the *Politica* appear as such in the original). From his earliest political writings through the *Politica*,[4] Lipsius adopts prudence, whose meaning he derives from Cicero's decorum, as his political touchstone. (Although I argue that Cicero is the dominant influence on Lipsius's conception of prudence, particularly his mixed prudence, I acknowledge the influence of Aristotle's *phronesis* on Lipsian prudence—as established by Diana Stanciu [2011], who also concedes Cicero as another possible source of Lipsius's prudence.[5]) Like Ciceronian decorum, Lipsian prudence is unstable and variable because of the inherent instability of politics. Again like Cicero's decorum, Lipsius's prudence is inseparable from virtue and morality. The standard of political morality for Lipsius as for his intellectual forebear Cicero must, like the orator's speech, be contextually determined. Therefore, under some circumstances, as when the welfare of the state is at stake, Lipsius sanctions the prudent use of dissimulation and deception. Although I acknowledge that Lipsius allies himself with Tacitus in many of his political ideas, the focus in this chapter is on his ideas concerning the relationship between politics and morality. And Cicero, not Tacitus, is the dominant lifelong influence on Lipsius's conception of political morality.

Settling whether Lipsius remains committed to or rejects Cicero's political morality has important implications for the continuity and meaning of a Ciceronian tradition of political morality. It has become intellectually fashionable to divide the Renaissance (or early modernity) between an early Ciceronian and a late Tacitean period. Richard Tuck (1993, 5–6, 39–40, 62–63) expresses the idea of this division by distinguishing between two humanisms: an "'old' humanism [that] was dominated by the ideas and the style of Cicero," which flourished during the Quattrocento and the first two-thirds of the sixteenth century; and a "new" humanism dominated by the ideas and style of Tacitus, which predominated beginning in the 1570s. Similarly, Maurizio Viroli (1992, 257–61) argues that in the early seventeenth century, Tacitus was portrayed as the "symbol of the new 'politicians'"—a thinker guided by reason of state free from the constraints of Ciceronian moralism. This presumed shift in humanism is exemplified most often by Lipsius (Tuck 1993, 45–64).[6] If, however, Lipsius does not abandon Cicero for Tacitus but remains, as I argue, committed to Cicero's political morality, then the reigning assumption that the late sixteenth (or early seventeenth) century witnessed the end of Ciceronian political morality, if not disproved, is at least considerably weakened. The continuation of Ciceronian political morality into the seventeenth century and beyond allows for the evolution of Ciceronian political thinking into modernity. This political morality presents early modern political actors with a middle road situated between the path of moral purism, in which politics is governed by conventional norms, and Machiavelli's path, which rejects the *honestum* in favor of the *utile* alone.[7]

The Case for Lipsius's Realignment

The Dominant Account: Shift to Tacitus from Cicero

Lipsius adopts Tacitus's prudence to instruct princes and their counselors in how to deal with the world of hardboiled politics. He finds in Tacitus's studies of the Roman emperors practical examples, insights, and advice that are relevant for the monarchical politics of the late sixteenth century. In dedications to two editions of Tacitus, which he published before the *Politica*, Lipsius highlights Tacitus's prudence and the contemporary relevance of his writing because of *similitudo temporum*, the similarity of Tacitus's period to Lipsius's own. First, in his dedication to the Emperor Maximilian of his 1574 edition of Tacitus's works, Lipsius describes Tacitus as "[a] sharp writer, my God, and a *prudent one*," especially relevant to "this time and circumstances. . . . [H]ere everyone can be informed about the courts, the princes, their inner lives, their plans, commands, and deeds, *and, in most things the similarity with our own time being evident, his mind can grasp the truth that similar causes lead to similar outcomes*" (Waszink 2004, 94–95; emphasis added). Second, in his dedication to the States of Holland of the 1581 edition of his commentary on Tacitus's *Annals*, Lipsius describes Tacitus as illustrating a range of political dangers characteristic of both imperial Rome and the late Renaissance, from the excesses of tyranny to "the evils of liberty restored." Tacitus's revelations of how politics is actually conducted offer princes ("those in whose hands are the rudder and tiller of the state") lessons on how to manage their own political affairs (Morford 1993, 138). Eight years after publishing this dedication, Lipsius (2004) suggests in the *Politica* that Tacitus is pertinent not only to the prince but even more so to the prince's advisors, who should use him *"as their guide for his Wisdom and Prudence"* (733).

Lipsius's interest in Tacitus as a source of political wisdom reaches its high point in 1589 with the appearance of the *Politica* (Morford 1993, 139). He composes the *Politica* as a cento, that is, a composition created by joining citations from different authors. We can gain some sense of the importance of Tacitus in the *Politica* by comparing the frequency of quotations from him to that of other authors quoted in the work. Tacitus is cited on nearly every page, 528 quotations out of a total of 2,069, including the first and last quotations (Morford 1993, 142). Of the more than one hundred authors whom Lipsius (2004) cites, Tacitus takes pride of place: "CORNELIUS TACITUS *stands out among them, who must be especially mentioned, because on his own he contributed more than all the others together. The reason for this is the man's Prudence, and the fact that this text is very full of pithy formulations*" (255). As in the two previous dedications, Lipsius calls attention here to Tacitus's prudence.

Tacitus's prudence appears elsewhere in the *Politica*. For example, in the *nota* to *Politica* 1.9, Lipsius (2004) applauds Tacitus "[n]ot with respect to eloquence or other [stylistic] virtues, but with respect to those things which we are dealing with now, that is, *the marks of Prudence and good judgement. Who tells more truthfully than he, or more briefly? Who teaches more in telling? Which moral topic* [moribus] *is there which he does not touch upon?*" (96–97; emphasis added). Here, in addition to hailing Tacitus's prudence for its usefulness, Lipsius ties it to morality, taking note of how the Roman historian addressed the breadth of moral matters.

Although Lipsius deems Tacitus a political realist, Lipsius's Tacitus, as Waszink (2004, 97) in particular explains, does not eschew moral judgment. Thus, according to Waszink, Lipsius employs Tacitus's *Annals* in the *Politica* to educate future monarchs "because of the moral judgement displayed in the text" (97). For example, Lipsius quotes Tacitus's *Agricola* approvingly for his "*mix[ing] the honourable* [honestum] *and the useful* [utile]" (Tacitus, *Agricola* 8.1, cited in Lipsius 2004, 509)[8]—in apparent contrast to Machiavelli, who abandons the *honestum* for the *utile*. Thus, though Lipsius commends Machiavelli as a thinker who "impresses me," he pairs this respect with the recognition that he "sometimes goes against morality" (231).[9] (Seven years later, to avoid continued placement on the Roman Catholic Church's *Index Librorum Prohibitorum*, Lipsius further distances himself from Machiavelli, substituting his previous, more restrained description of the Florentine with the new terms "shrewd" and "often immoral.") Similarly, Lipsius portrays Machiavelli as unique among contemporary political theorists—his "genius I do not despise, sharp, subtle, and fiery as it is"—but is distressed by Machiavelli's not having "directed his Prince on the straight path towards that great temple of Virtue and Honour! But all too often, he strays from that road, and while he intently follows the footpaths of advantage, he wanders from this royal road" (231).

Lipsius, however, never disparages Tacitus for being immoral. His accolades for Tacitus, as opposed to his endorsement of Machiavelli, are unqualified. But, as Waszink suggests, Lipsius looks to Tacitus for his subordination of morality to political reality rather than for his moral outlook. In other words, Tacitus provides Lipsius with a vision of politics as more concerned with "what the realities of power and necessity demand" than with "what should be done," that is, "the politics of justice" (Waszink 2004, 97). Such realities include Tacitus's Machiavelli-like observation, cited by Lipsius, that although "*it is more desirable to protect one's majesty through justice,*" the prince may not always be able to follow this more desirable path: "*with lawlessness and strength on either side of you, you will find peacefulness vanity; where might is right, self-control and righteousness are reserved for the stronger*" (Tacitus, *Germania* 35.4 and 36.1, cited in Lipsius 2004, 434; Tacitus 1970c, 35.4, 36.1). Similarly, Lipsius cites Tacitus who again anticipates Machiavelli by speaking of "*spectacular qualities resembling virtues, species virtutibus similis,*" which Lipsius implicitly (and Tacitus explicitly) sets over against actual virtues (Tacitus, *Annals* 15.48, cited in Lipsius 2004, 442; Tacitus 1937, 15.48). By citing the *exempla* of prudence with which Tacitus furnishes him, Lipsius seeks to confirm "his view that the ruler should not be afraid of using his power, but that he should do this *effectively*, the end (public peace and safety) always being more important than the details of moral or constitutional justice" (Waszink 2004, 149).

The consensus among today's scholars is that in using Tacitus to emphasize political efficiency over morality, Lipsius necessarily parts ways with Cicero, who subjugates the politically useful to the moral. That Lipsius came to distance himself from several of Cicero's positions—including his rhetorical style, republicanism, patriotism, and commitment to the *vita activa* (Croll 1969; Waszink 2004, 138, 139, 140–42; Burke 1969, 151–53)—is not being questioned here. What is open to doubt—what I argue is an erroneous opinion—however, is that Lipsius broke with Ciceronian morality, which is perceived as his most fundamental departure from Cicero (Waszink 2004, 91). What proof is there of this split? Waszink, who, among Lipsian scholars, seeks to demonstrate this split most assiduously, provides two main proofs for the break. First, he offers the argument that because Lipsius justifies princely deception he, perforce, splits from Cicero. This argument is based on an understanding of Cicero as defining the *utile* in terms of the *honestum*. As Waszink explains, "Their respective ideas on the conflict of expediency (utility) and moral rectitude brings us to the core of the differences between Lipsius' and Cicero's moral and political thought. . . . [As Cicero states in *De officiis* 3.64:] 'it is never expedient to do wrong, because it is always immoral; and it is always expedient to be good, because goodness is always moral.' In other words, the conflict between right and expedient can only be apparent" (Waszink 2004, 142–43). Lipsius's defense of *prudentia mixta*, Waszink concludes, is at odds with the "'Ciceronian' position of the sixteenth century," which was itself based on Cicero's own standpoint.

This conflict of principles between Cicero and Lipsius manifests itself in Waszink's second argument, that Lipsius, in citing and commenting on Cicero primarily in his discussion of mixed prudence, attacks Cicero directly (Waszink 2004, 143–44). Waszink finds proof of this attack in Lipsius's critique of Cicero's apparent moralism. After introducing his defense of mixed prudence, Lipsius disparages (in his later 1589 edition of the *Politica*) those who object to mixed prudence as "pure hearts" and "childish"—that is, Cicero, whom Lipsius cites as indiscriminately condemning all ambushes, simulations, and treachery (*De officiis* 3.68). Lipsius (2004) addresses those who reject all political fraud and deceit—again, Cicero—by asserting: "You definitely err" (507; Waszink 2004, 143–44).[10]

The Dominant Account Questioned

The widely accepted account of Lipsius's embrace of Tacitus over Cicero, as supported most forcefully and clearly by Waszink, is flawed. Although Lipsius incorporates many citations of Tacitus into his *Politica*, he does not use Tacitus to develop his conceptual defense of mixed prudence or, for that matter, the conceptual basis of his political theory more generally. Thus, Lipsius identifies Tacitus as central to his understanding of prudence, but Tacitus's "*prudentia* is to be found in his narrative," not in theoretical explications: "The prudence of Tacitus is to be found in his knowledge of the realities of power, his psychological insights, his brilliant accounts of the nobility and meanness of human character, his perception of the subtle relationship between the ruler and those closest to him" (Morford 1993, 150), not in any formally stated theory of *prudentia*. (As Mark Morford notes of "Tacitean *prudentia*," "Tacitus himself seldom used the word" [150].[11]) Lipsius, however, is concerned with more than finding relevant *exempla*; he also wishes to delineate the concept. Similarly, Tacitus does not provide Lipsius with a theoretical defense of mixed prudence, which Lipsius himself offers. For Lipsius, princely deceit is permissible under some conditions because such deceit promotes the common good, which is a moral imperative. What Tacitus furnishes Lipsius, instead, is a wealth of historical examples of how deceit has been conducted in the Roman imperial period, examples that may be useful in instructing a late Renaissance prince and his counselors in determining what is prudent deceit (or how to react to others' deceit).

That Tacitus does not offer Lipsius a theoretical grounding for political morality is implied by the near absence of Tacitus from Lipsius's conceptual explication of mixed prudence in book 4, chapter 13 of the *Politica*. Paradoxically for Waszink et al., Cicero, not Tacitus, is the central character of 4.13, the chapter in which Lipsius ostensibly formulates his most essential break with Cicero. True, Cicero is cited less frequently than Tacitus in the *Politica* as a whole, 198 times versus Tacitus's 528 (Waszink 2004, 138).[12] In 4.13, however, Cicero is cited 11 times to Tacitus's 1. Acknowledging "the considerable number of Cicero-quotations used in IV.13 as material to construct Lipsius' point of view," Waszink suggests enigmatically, but not enlighteningly, that "one might perceive [in chapter 13] a strategy to defeat Ciceronianism with quotations from Cicero" (91). Even in 4.14, where Lipsius demarcates the practice, not the theory, of legitimate deceit—where one would expect Tacitus to appear more prominently—Cicero is cited 18 times to Tacitus's 11.

Waszink's two arguments with which he supports his claim that Lipsius abandons Cicero on matters of political morality will be refuted in the next section, when I address Cicero's influence on the *Politica*. Suffice it to say, for now, that Waszink's first argument, based on his interpretation of the relationship between the honorable and the useful in Cicero, is not self-evident, as Marcia Colish and Giorgio Jossa among others have shown. As seen in the previous chapter, Colish (1978) argues, and Jossa agrees, that rather than defining expediency in terms of morality, Cicero instead assimilates "the *honestum* to the *utile* by recasting the traditional meaning of the terms" (89). Nor is Waszink's second argument demonstrative. Waszink correctly states that Lipsius cites Cicero disapprovingly—suggesting Cicero's moralism and naiveté—but Waszink does not reconcile these rare unfavorable quotations of Cicero with the overwhelming number of quotations in which Lipsius cites the Roman orator approvingly. Lipsius citing Cicero both pro and contra mixed prudence—especially as he is cited much more frequently pro—does not diminish Cicero's importance for Lipsius; it only raises questions about Lipsius's ambiguous use of Cicero, which must be addressed.

The Consistent Lipsius

The Early Lipsius: Variae Lectiones *and* Orationes

The presumed shift between an early Ciceronian and a later Tacitean Lipsius is belied by Lipsius's lifelong commitment to Cicero's conception of political morality. In his youthful *Variae Lectiones*, published in 1569, and *Orationes*

Octo, published in 1572, Lipsius evinces a flexible political morality that he identifies with Cicero, not Tacitus.[13] A comparison of Lipsius's views on political morality in these works with those in the *Politica*, published over twenty-five years later, demonstrates a consistency of themes and opinions: prudence, the primary political faculty, directs the political actor in how to adapt his opinions and principles to changing circumstance; the metaphor of the ship of state is used to delineate this accommodation to context; the common good legitimates a political actor's flexibility in opinion or principle; and the morality of the political deed is evaluated, in part, by the motive or aim of the actor.

Throughout his preface to the *Variae Lectiones*, dedicated to Cardinal Granvelle, a man "born with prudence" and "among few [prudent] men in our memory," Lipsius (1585) deems prudence a most necessary ability in defense of the *patria*. Those who ruled and steered the Republic by prudence, according to Lipsius, were wiser and far rarer than the military men who enlarged or defended their homeland (preface). And Lipsius refers to "our Cicero" as one of the few "from all antiquity whom we ought to place into that class of prudent and best men" (preface). What Lipsius considers praiseworthy about prudence, especially as a political faculty or virtue, is that it enables the political actor to adapt himself to changing circumstances. Lipsius adumbrates this characteristic of prudence in his fifth oration, where he finds in Cicero the model of the prudent à la flexible politician. Lipsius links Cicero's prudence to his capacity for change as the situation demands. Thus, Cicero, "the most prudent man [*prudentissimus*], felt [that] with changing times the logic of his plans must vary" (Lipsius 1726, 76).

Lipsius elucidates this prudent flexibility with the "ship of state" metaphor, which Cicero frequently employs (May 1980; Vasaly 2013, 155), in which political rule is symbolized as command of a naval vessel. Centuries before Cicero, Plato disseminates this metaphor, in the *Republic*, and uses it to liken democratic politicians to sailors "wrangling with one another for control of the helm, each claiming that it is his right to steer though he has never learned the art [of navigation]." These unruly sailors seek authority from the shipmaster— Plato's metaphor for the masses—who is "slightly deaf," visually impaired, and lacking knowledge of navigation. Ultimately, the successful sailors gain command of the ship by "binding and stupefying" the shipmaster with drugs and drink. In contrast to these ignorant sailors stands "the true pilot," the philosopher, who has, metaphorically, mastered the science of navigation, who gives his "attention to the time of the year, the seasons, the sky, the winds, the stars, and all that pertains to his art" (Plato 1961a, 488a–89a). Like the philosopher ruler in the *Republic*, Plato's philosopher qua pilot applies abstract, unwavering knowledge, implied by the pilot's expertise in navigating by the stars. (With the philosopher at the helm, the influence of the masses can be ignored, eliminating the disorders attendant on trying to win them over.) As opposed to the seasons, sky, and winds—especially the latter two—which vary considerably, the stars appear as a consistent beacon. Because of the philosopher's proficiency in following the guiding stars, the useless sailors mockingly call the true pilot a "stargazer" (Plato 1961a, 489a).

Before we turn to Lipsius's handling of the metaphor, compare Plato's depiction of the philosopher as pilot with Cicero's representation of the statesman as steersman. In a letter to his friend Publius Cornelius Lentulus Spinther, Cicero defends his changing views about political leaders—leaders whose own character did not change significantly but whose public standing changed—by denying that he is committed to "sticking fast to one set of opinions, when circumstances have changed and the sentiments of honest men are no longer the same." He explains his commitment to "moving with the times" by adverting to the ship of state metaphor. Like Plato, Cicero portrays the steersman as the most appropriate leader. But unlike Plato's pilot, whose knowledge presumably leads to smooth sailing, Cicero's helmsman is noted not for his capacity to navigate through calm waters but for his skill in avoiding disaster by altering the ship's course when necessary. Although it is best to avoid the storm (*tempestas*) at sea when possible, Cicero (2001b) observes, when the storm cannot be circumvented, the ship should "make harbour by changing tack, [as] only a fool [*stultum*] would risk shipwreck by holding to the original course rather than change and still reach his destination."[14] Applying the ship of state metaphor to politics, Cicero concludes: "Unchanging consistency of standpoint has never been considered a virtue in great statesmen." Statesmen maintain their political morality by adhering to their goals ("the harbor") even if they shift opinions ("tacking") in the process: "it is our aim [*spectare*], not our language, which must always be the same" (letter 20.21).

Now compare Lipsius's use of the ship of state metaphor in the fifth oration to Cicero's. Like Cicero, Lipsius (1726) eschews the simplicity of Platonic steersmanship. He briefly considers the possibility of "steady conditions and favorable winds" that the pilot can easily navigate (78). He immediately abandons this possibility, however, to focus instead on stormy weather (the same term *tempestas* that Cicero refers to in his letter to Spinther) and on the helmsman "who must respond to the storm" (78). Again, like Cicero, Lipsius describes as foolish or stupid (*stultum*) anyone who holds to "one particular rule" or "single standard," rather than relying "on personal judgment" in the face of "such a wide variety of circumstances and human opinions" (78). And, quoting almost verbatim from Cicero's letter to Spinther, Lipsius states: "We always have to keep one purpose in mind. Just as sailors often have to make a change of course in order to reach the port, so too those who govern the republic need not always judge situations the same, but they must always keep their eyes on the same aim [*spectandum*]" (78).

What of the moral implications of changing course based on which way the wind blows? In the fifth oration, Lipsius considers, only to reject, the claims that Cicero's political "flip-flopping" is a moral flaw. Lipsius (1726) repudiates the common accusation that Cicero was an unprincipled politician who attacked senators only to defend them later "when they were taken back into favor" (73). And he forcefully defends Cicero against what he terms the "slanders," "lies," and "mockeries" of "spiteful men" who accuse Cicero of turning "from his former virtue at every point . . . [and of] directing the Republic toward the will of Pompey or the pleasure of Caesar" (75). Lipsius finds Cicero's variableness to be morally justified because it was dictated by the common interest (*communis utilitas*), which reflects Cicero's own view in the *De officiis* that the common good or utility cannot be separated from morality (Remer 2009, 6–9; Colish 1978, 89–90; Jossa 1964, 274–76; Miller 1994, 25–27).[15] For Cicero (1991a), assisting "one's country . . . take[s] precedence in all duties" (3.90). In line with Cicero, Lipsius (1585) couples the "advantage of the Republic" (*reipublicae utilitas*) and the "standard of morality" (*honestatis regula*) (preface). Accordingly, Lipsius concedes Cicero's inconstancy of opinion but denies its immorality. "There are times during which you would scarcely be able to be constant without harming yourself or *the Republic*. . . . For [Cicero] changed his opinion, I admit it. But he changed it not by whim . . . or any inconstancy of the mind; rather, he was compelled by a certain necessity of the times and by the unfairness of men" (Lipsius 1726, 76; emphasis added). Similarly, Lipsius avers that despite being condemned, Cicero's "fickleness *provided more fully for the Republic* than the constant stubbornness and the stubborn constancy whether of Cato or of others" (78–79; emphasis added). Lipsius repairs to the ship of state metaphor again, explaining that Cicero understood that "when the storm has reversed and the minds of the people have changed," then the *communis utilitas* required that "the sails must be directed to that man [whether Caesar or Pompey] to whom the wishes and the upheavals of the time incline" (77–78).

Lipsius further justifies Cicero's variability of opinion by adopting Cicero's position that the moral status of an action is determined by taking into account the actor's motivations.[16] In his *De inventione*, the young Cicero contends that "[t]here are . . . certain matters that must be considered with reference to time and *intention* and not merely by their absolute qualities" (1949, 2.176; emphasis added). Because he generally adopts a modified version of Stoic morality, Cic-ero agrees with the Stoics that "whether our actions are good or evil depends on our intentions" (Schinkel 2007, 158). Similarly, in his fifth oration, Lipsius (1726) contends that Cicero's inconsistency is morally justified by the Roman orator's proper motivation: "For . . . in all matters . . . you must consider not just the deeds but also the very actions, their causes and reasons, and from these judge the deeds themselves as either disgraceful or morally right" (76).

In his oration defending Cicero, Lipsius presents Cicero's variableness of speech and action as thoroughly moral. This position is consistent with Cicero's characterization, in *De officiis*, of morally questionable behavior per-formed in the service of the state as unquestionably moral. For example, Cic-ero maintains—contrary to common opinion today—that stealing another's food to save one's own life is, in general, morally objectionable. Cicero argues, however, that the common interest trumps the injustice of depriving persons of their individual goods: "If, however, you are the kind of person who, if you were to remain alive, could bring great benefit to the political community and to human fellowship, and if *for that reason* you deprive someone else of some-thing, that is not a matter of rebuke." Cicero terms such questions as "very easy to decide" because "the neglect of the common benefit [*communis utilitatis*] is . . . contrary to nature; for it is unjust" (1991a, 3.29–30; emphasis in original).

In the *Variae Lectiones*, however, Lipsius concedes Cicero's "dirty hands" (Walzer 1973, 161), that is, he acknowledges the moral taint that inevitably at-taches itself to some of Cicero's political actions, notwithstanding Cicero's having made the right political choice. (As we shall see, Lipsius accepts in the *Politica* that politics inevitably involves dirty hands.) Lipsius attributes this judgment to Cicero, who admits to choosing the lesser of two evils in a letter to his friend Atticus (Cicero 1984, 7.18). According to Lipsius's preferred read-ing of a passage in the letter, Cicero describes his decision to follow Pompey to Spain with the terms *Haec optima in malis* (This is the best in evil cir-cumstances), not *Haec opto malis* (I chose this in evil circumstances). Lipsius (1585) paraphrases Cicero's sentiment as follows: "I will go, Cicero says, with Pompey into Spain, not because it is safest or most entirely morally right [*hon-estissimum*], but out of the two evils that present themselves, let us well select the best one" (52).

Lipsius's emendation here is consistent with Cicero's admission in other letters that his actions, although necessary for the good of the state, are less than fully moral. For example, in another letter to Atticus, Cicero contrasts his own belief in moral compromise with the moral inflexibility of the Stoic Cato, whom Cicero designates "sometimes a political liability." Cicero refers in his letter, specifically, to the state's private tax collectors, who after negotiating their contract—a contract that usually resulted in their being paid handsomely for their services—demanded that their contract be renegotiated. In this instance, in 60 BCE, the tax collectors saw that they would lose money on their contract. Cato took the moral high ground: "contracts were meant to be lived by and, if need be, suffered under" (Goodman and Soni 2011). Cicero agreed that Cato's position was the more principled, complaining to Atticus: "Could anything be more shameless than tax farmers repudiating their contract?" But Cicero, nevertheless, sided with the tax farmers, who, as part of the equestrian order, joined with the senatorial order to form the *concordia ordinum*, the harmony of the orders. For Cicero, moral perfectionism had to be sacrificed for the well-being of the state, which he saw as endangered by the possible split between the Republic's leading orders. Cato maintained his integrity, but only by blinding himself to the squalid realities of his political context.[17]

The Mature Lipsius: The Politica

Even more than his early writings, Lipsius's *Politica* is replete with the praise of prudence as the supreme political faculty. Lipsius (2004) describes prudence, in his political *magnum opus*, as "the proper ruler of Civil Life" (261) and as the ruler's leader, even the leader of "Virtue itself, or at least the guide" (283). Lipsius (2004) captures the spirit of prudence as the capacity to accommodate oneself to circumstance when he describes prudence as "tak[ing] time, place, and people [*tempora, loca, homines*] into consideration, and chang[ing] with the slightest change in them; and [as] different in every place to such an extent, that it is not even the same with respect to one thing" (383–84). Although he does not cite the source of this description, Lipsius derives it from Cicero's (1939b) definition, in the *Orator*, of decorum, which Cicero relates to oratory but also, as with prudence, to life: "In an oration, as in life, nothing is harder than to determine what is appropriate. The Greeks call it *prepon*; let us call it *decorum* or 'propriety'" (70–72). Prudence, as Lipsius points out, requires flexibility according to time, place, and person; and decorum, as Cicero characterizes it, calls on the orator to differentiate, in speech, "in respect of place, time, and audience" (*locus aut tempus aut auditor*). That Lipsius delineates prudence by restating Cicero's account of decorum underscores the similarity between the two concepts. Both presuppose propriety, what Cicero terms "[t]he universal rule, in oratory [and] in life" (1939b, 71). Victoria Kahn (1985), paraphrasing Cicero's discussion in the *Orator*, states: "Just as the orator is guided by decorum in adapting his speech to the exigencies of the moment, so the prudent man enacts decorum in the moral sphere by responding to the particular and contingent in human affairs" (35). Cicero "defines decorum in the political realm as prudence" (Kahn 1985, 35), and Lipsius, in turn, procures his understanding of prudence from Ciceronian decorum.[18]

In the *Politica*, Lipsius resurrects the ship of state metaphor to use Cicero's authority to support not only variableness but also the limited use of deceit in politics. Before quoting Cicero, however, Lipsius (in his own words) makes an analogy between prudence, the political virtue that demands variableness, and the capacity and means to steer the ship of state. Prudence, Lipsius (2004) begins by stating, "is useful . . . most of all in government. Which is not only vulnerable without Prudence, but even I dare say, nothing at all." After initially comparing prudence to a magnet's needle without which it is impossible to navigate a ship, Lipsius then compares prudence to a goddess without whose inspiration "no one can navigate a commonwealth" (347). As he defended Cicero in the fifth oration against claims of moral defect, Lipsius champions a counselor's right to advise the ruler to change policies in line with changing conditions. In his *Pro Balbo*,[19] Cicero justifies his own rapprochement with Caesar against criticisms of inconsistency by arguing that, despite past disagreements with Caesar, he must now "adapt [himself] to the present needs of the State and . . . promote concord." Cicero expresses this conviction with the ship of state metaphor, which Lipsius now adopts: "*To regulate the course of the state, as if it were a ship, according to the difficulty of the circumstances, I cannot see as an expression of inconstancy*" (Cicero, *Pro Balbo* 61, as cited in Lipsius 2004, 359). Lipsius, however, breaks no new ground in the sort of morally dubious behavior he sanctions here. As in the *Orationes*, Lipsius permits political inconstancy when it benefits the public. But Lipsius confines his circumspect remarks here to counselors, who, as political subordinates, must comport themselves more closely with the demands of conventional morality.

Lipsius (2004), however, accords rulers much greater latitude than their subordinates to engage in what is normally considered immoral political action.[20] Thus, Lipsius later extends the ship of state metaphor to argue "that it is lawful and permitted [for the prince to deceive] now and then" (509). He finds support for his contention in Cicero's above-cited letter to Spinther, in which Cicero vindicates inconsistency of standpoint (and which Lipsius paraphrases, in the fifth oration, to do much the same): "And that if *you cannot reach the harbour* by *sailing* straight, *you do it by a different course*" (Cicero, *Letters to Friends* 1.9.21, as cited in Lipsius 2004, 509). In the *Politica*, Lipsius (2004) interprets "reaching the harbor sailing by a *different course*" not, as Cicero intended it, to validate some degree of political flip-flopping but, as Lipsius terms it, to justify mixing prudence "with a little drop of deceit" (509).[21] Consistent with his early reading of Cicero's (1984, 7.18) letter to Atticus in which Cicero acknowledges opting for the lesser of two evils, Lipsius recognizes the political necessity of dirty hands.[22] Mixed prudence, in which "good and pure liquid" is combined with "the sediment of deceit," not only is inevitable but, Lipsius (2004) maintains, "is allowed" (507). Citing again another of Cicero's letters to Atticus to criticize moral perfectionists in politics, Lipsius states: "They seem not to know this age and its *men, and to speak their opinion as if in Plato's Republic instead of in the dregs of Romulus*" (Cicero, *Letters to Atticus* 2.1.8, as cited in Lipsius 2004, 507).

Reflecting Cicero's (and his own early) belief that motivation affects, if not decides, the morality of one's actions, Lipsius (2004) qualifies his legitimation of a prince's use of deceit: "so long as it is done moderately and with good aims" (509). And what constitutes "good aims" for Lipsius? Again, Lipsius relies on Cicero's words to argue his case: "*the advantage and well-being [utilitas salusque] of the state*" (Cicero, *Pro Plancio* 93, as cited in Lipsius 2004, 509). Lipsius continues his argument with another quotation from Cicero, beginning with his own words emphasizing the political actor's motivation: "For with this *aim* [emphasis added], *that which is often considered disgraceful, will not be disgraceful*" (Cicero, *De officiis* 3.19, as cited in Lipsius 2004, 509).

Following Cicero's position in *De officiis*, Lipsius maintains, as he did in the fifth oration, that the advantage of the state is an essential element of the moral. "*Fraud and deceit*," "*play*[ing] *the fox when dealing with a fox*" are permissible "for the Prince now and then . . . if it serves public profit and well-being [*publicus Usus Salusque*]" (Lipsius 2004, 507).[23] Once more, Lipsius makes use of Cicero's words: "*To forsake the common good is against nature*, not only against reason" (*Communis utilitatis derelictio contra naturam est, non solum rationem*) (Cicero, *De officiis* 3.30, as cited in Lipsius 2004, 507). Because he accepts the Stoic principle that nature is moral, Cicero (1991a) contends that the *communis utilitas* is included in the *honestum*: "The honourableness [or 'moral goodness' (*honestum*)] that we seek is created from and accomplished by [nature and reason]" (1.14).[24] Based on Cicero's identifying the public interest with morality, Lipsius (2004) contends that "there is place for Mixed Prudence with the Prince" (507).

The *Politica* is a more complicated work than the two earlier writings already discussed. And contrary to those who argue that the *Politica* marks a clear break with Cicero, it instead incorporates a more sophisticated use of Cicero's methodology. Thus, in addition to adopting the substance of Cicero's views on political morality, which he did in the *Variae Lectiones* and the

Orationes, Lipsius in the *Politica* also embraces Cicero's method of destabilizing concepts, which allows the political actor greater flexibility in speaking and acting as circumstances require. As discussed in chapter 3, Cicero destabilizes the distinction between the *honestum* and the *utile*, in *De officiis*, through his inconsistent use of these concepts. The result of Cicero's destabilizing of the *honestum* and the *utile* is that he prevents these concepts from being defined a priori. By denying them a single, specific meaning, he intends for the *honestum* and the *utile* to be applied rhetorically, that is, contextually. Therefore, when required by the common advantage, actions normally unjust, like lying, can themselves be deemed honorable (Remer 2009, 5–9).

Like Cicero, Lipsius subverts the univocality of political and moral concepts. We have already seen that Lipsius (deriving his conception of prudence from Cicero's definition of decorum) depicts prudence as unstable and changeable, and as "not even the same with respect to one thing." He recognizes, to paraphrase Victoria Kahn's (1994, 25) comment on Machiavellian *virtù*, that only a destabilized prudence can function in the destabilized realm of politics. Paradoxically, Lipsius further deprives prudence of any stable meaning by also characterizing it, in the *Politica*, as "a principle of stability" (Patrick 2007, 12). In contrast to his description of prudence as "chang[ing] with the slightest change in [time, place, and people]," Lipsius (2004) offers another version of prudence as a capacity that directs us predictably and exactly to correct actions, a tool that Lipsius compares (in the hands of the political leader) to an architect's "level and plumb line" (283), tools that perform their task of ensuring that structural lines are straight, reliably and with precision.[25] Here Lipsius defines prudence, the "leading principle," as "THE UNDERSTANDING AND CHOOSING [*INTELLECTUM ET DILECTUM RERUM*] OF WHAT IS TO BE SOUGHT OR AVOIDED" (283), suggesting, by virtue of its generalized language, a single, universal rule applicable in all conditions. By introducing competing conceptions of prudence, Lipsius undermines the constancy of the term. Thus, Lipsius does for prudence what Cicero does for morality in *De officiis*: by divesting the concept of any single sense, he expands the range of meanings open to the political actor, which can be selected according to necessity. For Lipsius, like Cicero, the more flexible the concept—for Lipsius prudence and for Cicero the *honestum*—the greater the freedom accorded the political actor to depart from the constraints of conventional morality.

More specifically, as Cicero extends political morality beyond the bounds of conventional morality by intermixing the honorable and the useful, Lipsius moves beyond the limitations of traditional morality by inconsistently representing the relationship between virtue and prudence. Like Cicero's *honestum* and *utile*, Lipsius's virtue and prudence are portrayed as inseparable: "Civil Life I define as the life WHICH WE ENJOY IN COMMUNITY WITH OTHER PEOPLE, TO THE MUTUAL BENEFIT OR PROFIT. To this life I assign two Leaders, Prudence and Virtue. . . . For I do not consider anyone a truly good citizen, unless he is also virtuous. Without Virtue, the other guide is mere cunning and malice, and anything rather than Prudence. And the rudder of Prudence may be the proper ruler of Civil Life, it cannot dispense with the use and assistance of that other compass" (Lipsius 2004, 261).[26] But Lipsius is at odds with himself over the connection between virtue and prudence in politics. At times, Lipsius distances virtue from political action. For example, concerning goodness, a branch of virtue, he writes: "I shall only work [it] with a light tool, *as it does not strictly speaking belong to this structure of politics, but to one of morality*" (281; emphasis added). Lipsius, however, immediately reverses himself from what seems to be a Machiavelli-like exclusion of morality from politics, asserting that he "must, however, discuss [goodness] here, in order that you realise its indispensability" (281). Consequently, Lipsius distinguishes himself from Machiavelli, who retains prudence but abandons virtue.[27]

In discussing the acceptability of deceit, Lipsius again wavers regarding the necessity of prudence *and* virtue in politics—or, perhaps more accurately, regarding the meaning of virtue relative to prudence in politics. Initially, Lipsius contends that deceit is illegitimate in politics. Thus, he maintains that "[t]here are two things which make a prince legitimate and independent by his own means: Prudence and Virtue." Virtue, according to Lipsius (2004), "must . . . be adopted by the King . . . because it is fitting, that he who excels in status, excels also in virtue" (311–13). Shortly thereafter, Lipsius once more emphasizes the appropriateness of virtue in politics: "the possession of Virtue is useful and becoming for the Prince" (317). Although Lipsius suggests that every kind of virtue is useful and becoming in politics, he singles out justice as especially necessary. Comparing justice to the sun, he explains that "if this Sun does not illuminate the entire process of government, there is only darkness, storm, and rain in it" (317–19). Then, quoting Cicero's *De officiis* (1.23), Lipsius affirms: "*Faithfulness is the basis of Justice*" (331). Therefore, kings must not employ deceit as a political means. So dishonorable is deceit that "*faith must be kept even towards the perfidious*" (335).

When considering mixed prudence, however, Lipsius (2004) concedes that "it is lawful and permitted now and then" (509) to discard virtue, that is, virtue qua honesty, which is how Lipsius just interpreted virtue. Of the two inseparable "Leaders" of civil life, Lipsius appears willing to grant that only prudence is indispensable, as "Prudence does [not] stop being Prudence when it is mixed with a little drop of deceit." But rather than admit to abandoning virtue when political necessity requires, Lipsius instead reinterprets virtue so that it sometimes permits deception. "[W]hy does it mean I depart from Virtue?" Lipsius asks, when referring to his sanctioning the limited use of dishonesty (509). Yet only one chapter following his reconciliation of virtue and deceit, Lipsius defines *all* deceit, including "light deceit," which he recommends without reservation, as "CLEVER PLANNING *WHICH DEPARTS FROM VIRTUE* OR THE LAWS, IN THE INTEREST OF THE KING AND THE KINGDOM" (513; emphasis added).

How, then, does Lipsius view the roles of prudence and virtue in politics? Based on what we have seen, he provides at least six—sometimes consistent, sometimes inconsistent—responses: (1) both virtue and prudence play necessary roles; (2) unlike prudence, virtue or goodness is a matter of morality not politics; (3) a political ruler must be not only prudent but virtuous, especially just, and, therefore, he must eschew deceit; (4) a ruler must sometimes employ deceit, which is to say that he must be prudent; (5) employing deceit *can be* consistent with virtue; and (6) deceit may be a necessary tactic but, by definition, is contrary to virtue. Lipsius leaves us no reason to identify any specific answer as more authentically his own. He does not privilege one response over the other. Instead, he presents us with several viewpoints, all of them plausible, from which to choose. In doing so, Lipsius emulates Cicero's skeptical and rhetorical use of argument *in utramque partem*, in which each (or every) side of a question is considered in order to attain the most probable truth available (Michel 1960, 158–73; Cicero 1971, 2.9; 1999d, 3.8). For Lipsius, as for Cicero, this truth is not static but depends on what best fits the context. And as Cicero speaks of decorum to express that which is most fitting or appropriate, Lipsius most often speaks of prudence, one meaning of which, as we have seen, Lipsius appropriates from Cicero's definition of decorum. Lipsius also speaks not only of prudence qua decorum but of decorum directly to indicate that the ruler must be virtuous in the sense of avoiding deceit because that is what is most appropriate to the situation at hand. Thus, we have seen that Lipsius writes of the king, "it is fitting [*decorum est*], that he who excels in status, excels also in virtue." Similarly, he observes that "the possession of Virtue is useful and becoming [*decora*] for the Prince" (Lipsius 2004, 316–17). But Lipsius's statement, in one section of the *Politica*, that decorum requires "virtue defined as honesty" from the ruler is not tantamount to the claim that decorum *always* requires the ruler to abjure deception. Decorum necessitates different things at different times, so that under exigent circumstances decorum may require the prince to deceive. From Lipsius's perspective, living in a time of moral degeneracy—as he believed he and Cicero did—filled with "Cunning men, bad men" (507) justifies a different moral standard for statesmen and princes.

Because Lipsius (2004, 231–33) structures the *Politica* as a cento, he applies the same kind of multisided argument to the words and phrases of ancient authors (which he selects and arranges to reflect his own opinions) as he does to his own words, which he describes as the cement connecting the ancients' maxims. I turn my attention now to how Lipsius uses Cicero two-sidedly on matters of political morality. In discussing mixed prudence, Lipsius arranges quotations from Cicero as arguments *in utramque partem*, so that Cicero is positioned on either side of the debate over the moral legitimacy of deception in politics. Like Cicero the orator, who sets forth antithetical, albeit plausible, arguments in preparing a speech, Lipsius structures Cicero's statements on the morality of deceit *in utramque partem*. In defending mixed prudence, however, Lipsius himself backs only one side of Cicero's arguments, that is, his defense of political morality as embracing social utility. Here Lipsius implies, as Cicero argues, that the case for conventionally immoral speech and action is the most probable truth.

Lipsius uses Cicero as exemplary of both support for and opposition to mixed prudence, with the pro-Lipsian Cicero trumping the anti-Lipsian Cicero. Thus, in book 4, chapter 13, where Lipsius introduces us to mixed prudence, he cites Cicero eleven times, eight in favor of mixed prudence and three against it. The first two citations from Cicero portray him as adopting conventional morality, followed by two quotations from Cicero pointing up the impracticality of inflexible moralism in politics. Lipsius's fifth quotation from Cicero calls for unadulterated honesty; the subsequent six quotations are all adduced to bolster Lipsian mixed prudence.[28] Both the greater number and the positioning of pro-Lipsian quotations to refute the preceding quotations serve to undermine the Ciceronian argument against Lipsius. In the ensuing chapter 14, in which Lipsius further expounds on mixed prudence, he cites Cicero eighteen times, only once in disagreement and the remaining seventeen times either fully or largely in agreement with his point of view.

Despite his frequent positive use of Cicero to justify mixed prudence—more frequent than his use of any other classical author to support a morality adapted to politics—Lipsius sometimes, if not often, cites Cicero inaccurately. Even Lipsius readily admits to having "quoted certain things incorrectly, and not in accordance with the spirit of the writer in question." For Lipsius (2004), "weaving a *Cento* . . . [indicates that] these departures from the original meanings are always allowed and even praised" (237).[29] Like the other thinkers Lipsius cites in the *Politica*, Cicero is sometimes quoted out of context.[30] Lipsius's mixing together of accurate and inaccurate citations of Cicero, however, raises questions about how authentic the link is between Cicero's pragmatic political morality and Lipsius's mixed prudence.[31] How reliable an authority for mixed prudence can Cicero be, when Lipsius presents us, not infrequently, with only a simulation of Cicero?[32] That Lipsius's defense of mixed prudence is influenced by Cicero, however, is corroborated by the following: first, Lipsius often supports Cicero's position with contextually accurate citations of the Roman orator; second, Lipsius's contextually correct citations of Cicero may be further elucidated (and the Ciceronian influence on mixed prudence pointed up) by viewing Lipsius's citation in its broader context;[33] and third, in *Politica* 3.13, Lipsius's quotations of Cicero, even when cited out of context, correctly reflect Cicero's opinion, if not from the specific text cited, then from others parts of Cicero's corpus.

Let us turn again to *Politica* 4.13, Lipsius's discussion of mixed prudence. Lipsius begins by setting two versions of Cicero against each other, seriatim. Lipsius (2004) describes the first version, in his marginal notes,[34] as the position of "some strict men" who deny "[c]unning may be used by a king" (507). And he supports this portrayal of Cicero with two quotations that, when read in context, do not fully confirm Cicero as the rigid moralist Lipsius seeks to portray. In the first quotation, Lipsius misquotes Cicero as defending the Stoic position, which "only approve[s] of that straight road which leads with virtue to honour" (507); Cicero actually states that *toil* is the only straightforward path to glory (1958b, 41). Although, strictly speaking, Lipsius misquotes Cicero, he captures Cicero's view of the Stoics as prizing unadulterated virtue, which is equated here with "toil."[35] In the second citation, Lipsius presents Cicero as advocating the Stoic view of reason as inimical to deceit and malice. The words cited, however, are actually spoken in the dialogue *De natura deorum* (begun in 45 BCE) by Cotta, an Academic skeptic critical of the Stoics, who argues, in context, that "if men abuse the reason which the immortal gods have bestowed with good intentions, and exploit it for deceit and malice, it would have been better for such reason to be withheld [from] . . . the human race" (Cicero 1997, 3.78). Notwithstanding these inaccuracies, Cicero, in fact, unconditionally rejects the use of deception, primarily in *De officiis*, in a series of statements that Lipsius (2004, 331–35) himself accurately cites and concurs with, earlier in the *Politica*.

Lipsius's (2004, 507) second version of Cicero is that of a realist who recognizes that "men and habits dictate the opposite" of political moralism. Lipsius delineates this version, as he did his first version, with two citations from Cicero. In the first of these citations, Lipsius accurately quotes Cicero's criticism of those who operate in his day as if they were in Plato's ideal state, not in the dregs of Rome. (In Cicero's full text, Cato the Younger is the object of guarded criticism.) The second citation seemingly exposes the times as "consist[ing] entirely of fraud, deceit, and laws," although Cicero, in the original context, is actually condemning not his generation but the plaintiff, Gaius Fannius Charea, whom Cicero attacks in his defense of Quintus Roscius (Lipsius 2004, 507). Although this second quotation is cited out of context, it reflects Cicero's actual pessimism about the late republican period in which he lived. Cicero (1991a) exhibits a similar perception of the age when he writes in *De officiis*: "I only wish that the republic had remained in its original condition, rather than fall into the hands of men greedy not merely for change, but for revolution" (2.3).[36]

After presenting the opposing opinions of mixed prudence (both sides appropriated from Cicero), Lipsius asserts a moral principle, derived from Cicero, that condemns mixed prudence. As Lipsius submits, "[the Prince] *may lay no ambushes, may not simulate, may do nothing treacherously*" (Cicero, *De officiis* 3.68, as cited in Lipsius 2004, 507). Lipsius does not cite Cicero altogether in context here: the subject of the sentence in Cicero's text is not "the prince," but "reason," and the statement regards not political deception but deception in the sale of property.[37] Nevertheless, the maxim is consistent with Cicero's general opposition to deceit. For example, Cicero (1991a) commends the actions of the Roman consul Marcus Atilius Regulus, who kept his word even though he knew "that he was going to a very cruel enemy [the Carthaginians] and most sophisticated torture. For all that, he thought that his oath should be kept" (3.99–100). Thus, even Lipsius's out-of-context citations of Cicero are consistent with standpoints Cicero adopts in another place.

Lipsius's rejoinder to Cicero's Stoic-based prohibition against dissimulation and deceit is the distinctly Ciceronian argument that the *utile*, which in its true form cannot be separated from the *honestum*, is best exemplified by the advantage and well-being of the state. Therefore, Cicero maintains, activities that are normally deemed immoral (and thus impermissible) become moral (and thus obligatory) when they benefit the state in times of need, as decorum or prudence mandates.[38] Lipsius emphasizes the Ciceronian provenance of this argument with six citations from Cicero, five cited in context. These statements and the broader context from which they are cited demonstrate that the duty toward the Republic's common good is fundamental to Cicero's conception of the moral.

Lipsius uses Cicero's language, from *De officiis*, to express the transformation of the normally immoral to the moral: "*that which is often considered disgraceful* [or 'morally wrong'], *will not be disgraceful* [or 'morally wrong']" (*De officiis* 3.19, as cited in Lipsius 2004, 509). What kind of ordinarily immoral act does Lipsius have in mind, that is, what type of act does Lipsius describe as "seem[ing] to contain a disgraceful element"—but "[o]nly seemingly" (509)? He selects his example from Cicero's speech on behalf of Gnaeus Plancius, where Cicero justifies the switching of factional allegiances—a practice he engaged in—so long as *"we choose to stand upon that part* [i.e., with that party] *to which the advantage and the well-being of the state direct us"* (*Pro Plancio* 93, as cited in Lipsius 2004, 509).

What Lipsius singles out (from *Pro Plancio*) as morally wrong under normal circumstances, however, is not what Cicero himself exemplifies as ordinarily immoral in *De officiis*. The generally immoral act that Cicero (1991a) "suggest[s] as an example . . . that can be more widely applied," in *De officiis*, is a far more compelling example than the changing of political allegiances; it is to "kill not merely another man, but [a tyrant who is] . . . a close friend" (3.19). As he explains, the Roman *populus* does not deem the killing of a tyrant (even when a close friend) a crime; rather, it "deems that deed the fairest of all splendid deeds." Is the act justified because *utilitas* has prevailed over *honestas*? Cicero responds: "No indeed; for honourableness [*honestas*] followed upon what benefitted [*utilitas*]" (3.19). Why, if Lipsius agrees with Cicero that morality must be determined contextually, does he ignore Cicero's example of the tyrannicide? Lipsius counsels the ruler's subjects to adopt a Stoic attitude of constancy toward the abuses of tyrants—accepting tyrants as divine punishments, similar to other natural disasters like earthquakes, pestilence, and war—which suggests that Lipsius was more comfortable omitting Cicero's glorification of the tyrannicide (Young 2011, 2.7, 127). Unlike Cicero, Lipsius (2004), in maturity, had a "distinct preference for Monarchy" because of its antiquity and its harmony with nature and reason—a form of government antithetical to "the government of the many," which brings *"fragmentation"* and "Chaos" (297–301).

And now we arrive at the core of Lipsius's justification for mixed prudence: Cicero's argument that the benefit of the Republic is an essential element of the *honestum*. Lipsius presents this argument in two maxims he incorporates from *De officiis* 3.30–31; both extol the morality of the common good. The first maxim states: *"To forsake the common good is against nature,* not only against reason" (*De officiis* 3.30, as cited in Lipsius 2004, 507).[39] The second maxim declares: *"He is always performing his duty by acting in the interest of the people and the community"* (*De officiis* 3.31, as cited in Lipsius 2004, 509). Both quotations are imbued with the language of morality. The first links the common welfare to nature, which, as we have seen earlier, Cicero equates with the moral. The second identifies social benefit with the duties or *officia*, about which Cicero (1913a) writes: "on the discharge of such duties depends all that is morally right, and on their neglect all that is morally wrong in life" (1.4). In addition, the second maxim underscores the comprehensiveness of Cicero's claim about those who serve the community, that is, that they *always* discharge their moral duty, which suggests the broad range of ordinarily objectionable behavior that, when such behavior promotes the common welfare, is rendered morally sound.[40]

In contrast to chapter 13, where Lipsius defends the general concept of mixed prudence, chapter 14 is devoted, primarily, to Lipsius's delineation of the types of deceit and their degrees of acceptability. Lipsius (2004) distinguishes between three levels of deceit: light deceit, "which departs only slightly from virtue, and contains not more than a little drop of malice, which category I take to contain distrust and dissimulation"; middle deceit, "which departs further from virtue, and comes very close to sin," for example, bribery and deception; and, finally, grave deceit, "which deviates not only from virtue but even from the laws and represents a solid and full-fledged malice, such as breach of faith and injustice" (513). Lipsius recommends the first kind, tolerates the second, and condemns the third. In this chapter, as in the preceding one but to an even greater degree, Lipsius cites Cicero approvingly. In chapter 14, however, unlike the previous chapter, Cicero is more often cited out of context. Of the eighteen citations from Cicero, eight are patently inconsistent with Cicero's original context; two more are cited in context but are written by Cicero's friend Plancius to Cicero and not by Cicero himself; and another two citations, which Lipsius puts forward to demonstrate the ruler's need to suspect all others, sufficiently exaggerates Cicero's distrust of everyone as to distort his basic viewpoint.[41] In further contrast to chapter 13, in chapter 14 not only does Lipsius cite Cicero out of context but Lipsius imputes viewpoints to Cicero (in the maxims Lipsius derives from him) that Cicero does not adopt elsewhere.

Employing his trifold categorization of deceit, Lipsius presents Cicero, in chapter 14, as most often legitimating light deceit, while saying little about middle and grave deceit. In his own writings, however, Cicero rarely addresses light deceit, more often discussing and recommending, in appropriate conditions, the political use of middle and, in more restricted situations, grave deceit. Although Cicero does not emphasize light deceit—distrust and dissimulation—as often as Lipsius suggests, Cicero most clearly recognizes the need for dissimulation in oratory. Lipsius, however, omits this most common instance of dissimulation in Cicero. For example, in *Orator* 49, Cicero (1939b) notes that the effective orator must "conceal what cannot be explained away, and even suppress it entirely, if feasible, or distract the attention of the audience."

Lipsius's omission of *Orator* 49 reflects his general disregard of Cicero's rhetoric in the *Politica*. Thus, as noted above, Lipsius derives his conception of prudence as ever variable from Cicero's *Orator*, but he neglects to cite the *Orator* as his source. This is in contrast to Lipsius's use of the work in his youthful writings. In the *Politica* he cites Cicero's *De oratore* twice, almost side by side, for its acclaim of history as the *"life of Remembrance"* and as *"the light of truth, the mistress of life"* (*De oratore* 2.38, as cited in Lipsius 2004, 289), but not for its rhetorical significance. In context, however, Cicero subordinates this commendation of history to his broader praise of eloquence and the ideal orator; Cicero (2001a) concludes his statement on history by asking, "what other voice but the orator's invests [history] with immortality?" (2.36). Lipsius (2004, 521–23) not only ignores Cicero's rhetorically based statements on light deceit but takes no notice of what Cicero the rhetorician writes about deception—a component of middle deceit and a commonly used oratorical device. For example, Cicero (1991a) justifies forensic orators' lying to protect the guilty: "scruples should not prevent us from occasionally defending a guilty man"; and "an advocate may sometimes defend what looks like the truth, even if it is less true" (2.51).[42] But Lipsius does not cite Cicero's defense of deception. Instead, Lipsius (2004, 521) cites Plato, the archenemy of rhetoric, as mandating deception in his *Republic*.

Lipsius evinces his lack of interest in—better, his disdain for—public rhetoric when, in his discussion of middle deceit, he distorts the Ciceronian understanding of "win[ning] over the hearts of men, *conciliare sibi animos hominum*" (*De officiis* 2.17, as cited in Lipsius 2004, 519). For Cicero, the phrase connotes persuasion and rhetoric.[43] Lipsius, however, reinterprets the Ciceronian understanding of the phrase to signify princely corruption. As Lipsius explains, the prince seeking to win over the hearts of men has two means available: "Persuasion and Gifts. The first way is used rarely, but the other very often, given '*the corruption and depravity the admiration of riches has caused to the morals*' of today" (*De officiis* 2.71, as cited in Lipsius 2004, 519). Cicero himself, however, neither associates the winning of hearts with corruption nor, as far as I am aware, justifies corruption per se, although as a forensic orator he defends Lucius Licinius Murena (in *Pro Murena*) against charges of *ambitus*, electoral corruption.

If Lipsius grounds his conception of prudence and political flexibility in Ciceronian rhetoric, why does he refuse, in the *Politica*, to explicitly acknowledge his debt to this rhetorical tradition? Although the mature Lipsius does not break with Cicero's political morality, he declines to identify himself with Ciceronian rhetoric—even though he embraces Cicero's rhetorical perspective—because he sees public oratory as irrelevant in, or even dangerous to, a monarchy: he scorns (and fears) the masses, to whom public oratory is directed; and politics, in a monarchy, is conducted among a small elite, where mass oratory is absent. Thus, Lipsius observes in one of his letters that, in his day, "the trend is [not] to make speeches," and he confirms his aversion to engaging in the oratory of antiquity (cited in Nisard 1852, 8). As already seen, by the time he writes the *Politica*, Lipsius is a fervent monarchist. And although Lipsius rejects Tacitus's authorship of the *Dialogus*, he accepts the critique of public oratory presented by Curiatus Maternus, one of the interlocutors in the *Dialogus*.[44] Under the Republic, Maternus argues, the freedom associated with public oratory presented "the opportunity of launching characteristically spiteful tirades against the leading men of the state": "The art [of rhetoric] which is the subject of our discourse is *not a quiet and peaceable art*, or one that finds satisfaction in moral worth and good behaviour: no, really great and famous oratory is a *foster-child of licence*, which foolish men called liberty, *an associate of sedition, a goad for the unbridled populace*. It owes no allegiance to any. Devoid of discipline, it is insulting, off-hand, and overbearing. It is a plant that does not grow under a well-regulated constitution" (Tacitus 1970b, 40; emphasis added). In addition, public oratory serves no purpose under one-man rule: "What is the use of one harangue after another on public platforms, when it is not the ignorant multitude that decides a political issue, but a monarch who is the incarnation of wisdom?" (41; emphasis added).

Lipsius displays his antipathy to the masses with forty-three antipopular citations, most from Tacitus, but a not insignificant number (six quotations) from Cicero. He summarizes his view of the *populus* in his marginal notes, where he "lists" his "knowledge of [the] people's sentiments": "It [i.e., the multitude] is given to emotions. It is without judgement. It follows the crowd. It is jealous. It is suspicious. It believes anything. It magnifies of its own accord. It discusses what it is forbidden to discuss. It is prone to chaos. Especially if someone stirs them up. It loves hot-headedness. It disregards the commonwealth. But they are concerned for their own interests. It is courageous with words: But nothing more. [And i]t never keeps the right measure" (Lipsius 2004, 403-9). In his quotations of classical authorities opposed to popular political control, Lipsius generally cites Cicero's remarks on the *populus* in their original context, sometimes overstating but not fabricating the Roman orator's occasionally displayed hostility toward the masses. Nevertheless, the republican Cicero, unlike the monarchist Lipsius, recognizes that, as an orator, he is ultimately beholden to the people. Fergus Millar (1998, 173–74), though exaggerating the Roman Republic's status as a democracy, correctly observes that the Roman people are sovereign in the Republic and that Cicero acknowledges this state of affairs. Therefore, Lipsius considers Tacitus, for whom the emperor not the Roman *populus* was sovereign, a better source of *exempla* than Cicero. Lipsius, however, retains Cicero's political morality, although he tries in the *Politica* to efface any hints of the republicanism and its concomitant, mass oratory, with which this morality was intimately linked.

Conclusion

I have argued that Lipsius's mixed prudence, the prudent use of deceit he grants rulers, derives from Cicero's conception of political morality and not from Tacitus's historical accounts, as is commonly maintained. Lipsius values Tacitus's historical *exempla* for the insights they offer on monarchical rule in corrupt times. He mines Tacitus's writings for their contemporary relevance in instructing rulers and their counselors on how to handle political situations that require morally ambiguous or even immoral responses. Tacitus, however, does not provide Lipsius with a theoretical basis for the moral practice of politics; Cicero does.

Lipsius finds in Cicero an understanding of political morality shaped by a presumed obligation to advance the common interest. For Lipsius, as for Cicero, what is defined as immoral in everyday life is not always immoral in politics, when the common welfare is at stake. Lipsius identifies prudence as the faculty that enables political actors to determine how to accommodate their deeds to their contexts—a conception of prudence that has its roots in Cicero's rhetorically based decorum. Unlike Machiavelli's prudence, Lipsius's is tied to the *honestum*, the moral.

Lipsius's defense of a flexible morality in politics can be found in his earliest writings, the *Variae Lectiones* and the *Orationes*, and is manifest in his discussion of mixed prudence in his political masterpiece, the *Politica*. Rather than personifying the end of Ciceronian humanism and the beginning of Tacitist humanism, as current scholars have typically suggested, Lipsius remains a committed Ciceronian, at least in matters of political morality. But while he persists in his dedication to Ciceronian political morality, he adapts this morality to his own context. Ciceronian decorum, which calls on orators to adapt themselves to different contexts, bids Lipsius to pay heed to how societal assumptions differ between late republican Rome and late Renaissance Europe. Accordingly, Lipsius's political morality focuses on the actions of the ruler and not, as Cicero's does, on the leading statesmen of the Republic.

Although Lipsius's accommodation of Cicero's political morality to conditions of one-man rule makes Cicero more relevant to Lipsius's society, it makes him less relevant for today's mass representative democracies. Lipsius, however, also fits Cicero to a Christian or postclassical context—an adaptation that renders Cicero's political morality more pertinent to our own political situation. The accommodation that I have in mind is Lipsius's tempering of the classical political world's subordination of the well-being of the individual to the well-being of the political community—his modifying a morality that was social, not individual, to a morality that values the individual. Although Cicero balances both the common good and individual interests to a greater extent than either of his Greek predecessors, Plato or Aristotle, his balance is weighted more toward the welfare of the community than to that of the individual. For Cicero (1991a), the good of the *res publica* is regarded most highly: "let the safety of the people be the highest law" (*salus populi suprema lex esto*) (3.8). For example, we saw earlier that Cicero condemns stealing food, even to keep someone alive, if the person is not politically significant, but justifies stealing to keep someone alive if that person "could bring great benefit to the political community and to human fellowship." But Lipsius lives in a Christian world in which, normatively, obedience to God trumps one's obligation to the state and in which God is believed to demand respect for, and defense of, the individual soul independent of social or political context (Berlin 1972). What is appropriate for Cicero and what is appropriate for Lipsius, then, by Cicero's own rhetorical perspective, differ. Lipsius therefore departs from Cicero's practice in matters of grave deceit.

When introducing grave deceit, Lipsius (2004, 513) condemns the practice categorically, including the breaking of oaths, which Lipsius categorizes as a form of grave deceit. In rejecting breach of faith out of hand, Lipsius dissents from the real Cicero (1991a), who in *De officiis* defends breaking one's oath when such breach of faith is necessary for the common good: "from time to time it becomes just to set aside such requirements as . . . the carrying out of a promise" because it is a fundamental of justice "that one serve the common advantage" (1.31).[45] (Although Lipsius [2004, 525] finds support for his position in Cicero's account of Regulus, Regulus's decision to keep his oath and suffer a cruel death was motivated by concern for the Republic's interest.) In opposing breach of faith and injustice (i.e., furthering your "interests in wicked rather than cunning ways" [525]) regardless of the consequences, Lipsius introduces the precepts of Christian morality, as decorum bids him. Thus, he cites Saint

Isidore of Seville as condemning breach of faith (525) and Deuteronomy as denouncing injustice as *"an abomination to the Lord"* (531).

Despite the demands of decorum, however, Lipsius retreats from his unqualified repudiation of grave deceit. After citing Aristotle and Democritus as conceding the need for princes to act unjustly, Lipsius (2004) states, "I will concede that a Prince, in very troubled and difficult cases, must do not what is beautiful to say but what is necessary in practice" (531). Deviating from absolutist Christian morality, Lipsius accepts that "it is right [for the prince] to depart slightly from human laws; but only in order to preserve his position, never to extend it" (531). Perhaps Lipsius believes that decorum for the ruler is neither fully Christian nor classical, that is, not determined wholly by the common good. Rather, like his prudence, the morality of a ruler's actions can never be specified a priori but is forever unsteady and wavering, dependent on context.

Because Lipsius lived under and supported monarchical rule, he revised Cicero's ideas on deceit and dissimulation from a republican to a monarchical context, in line with the rhetorical principle of decorum. Similarly, Edmund Burke, the authors of *The Federalist*, and John Stuart Mill, who participated in, and were committed to the political necessity of, representative legislative assemblies, accommodated Cicero's conception of political representation (derived from the orator-statesman's functions as representative) to their own eighteenth- and nineteenth-century political settings. Like Lipsius, these later political thinkers found Cicero's rhetorically based morality relevant to their own polities—in the case of the modern theorists, Cicero's belief in the political representative's moral obligation to adhere to the community's deeply rooted values. Although political deception may be a more obvious moral concern than communal control of the political representative, the moral significance of the community's values did not elude Cicero's notice; nor did it escape the attention of Burke or the authors of *The Federalist*. In the following chapter, we shall examine Cicero's conception of political representation, his account of the proper role of the representative in relation to the sense of community (*communis sensus*), along with exploring how Burke, the authors of *The Federalist*, and J. S. Mill retain the core of Cicero's political representation, while adapting it to their own contexts.

The Classical Orator as Political Representative: Cicero and the Modern Concept of Representation

Contemporary scholars largely agree that political representation is a modern phenomenon. Hannah Pitkin (1967) states: "The concept of representation, particularly of human beings representing other human beings, is essentially a modern one." Although Pitkin acknowledges that "representation" as "human beings acting for others," or as a concept relevant to political institutions, has its roots in the Middle Ages, one can infer that the ancient Greeks and Romans had no such conceptions. Pitkin maintains that the concept of representation does not develop into what we understand it to mean politically until much later: "Initially, neither the concept nor the institutions to which it was applied were linked with elections or democracy, nor was representation considered a matter of right" (2-3).[1] I argue in this chapter, however, that Cicero, the classical Roman rhetorician and political thinker, envisions his ideal orator-statesman as a representative of the Roman people. And although Pitkin accurately observes that the ancient Romans did not vest their own word *repraesentare*—from which we derive our modern English "representation"—with its current meaning, she does not consider the possibility that the ancients may have used other words to connote "political representation" (3).[2] I contend that Cicero uses terms, including *procurator, auctor, tutor, dispensator*, and *vilicus*, to describe the ideal orator-statesman, particularly in *De oratore* and in *De republica*, in ways that suggest representation.

But my case for Cicero's orator as political representative is not limited to word usage. Pitkin and subsequent writers on political representation have developed what Andrew Rehfeld calls the "standard account" of political representation, which involves a set of procedural criteria, primarily "*authorization and accountability* usually by way of *free and fair* elections" and the representative's duty to act independently on behalf of the constituents' interests (Rehfeld 2006, 2–3; emphases in original; Pitkin 1967, 235). Cicero, I argue, anticipates this account of political representation by applying the same criteria to his orator-statesman. Thus, Cicero's account of the orator-statesman contains both the conceptual and procedural elements of representation that Pitkin and like-minded scholars delineate.

Moreover, the characteristics of political representation that Pitkin limits to modernity are not only found in Cicero; it is possible to speak of a Ciceronian outlook on representation that is present in the writings of Edmund Burke, the authors of *The Federalist* (James Madison, Alexander Hamilton, and John Jay, who wrote collectively under the pseudonym Publius), and John Stuart Mill, especially in his *Considerations on Representative Government*. I have chosen these three Anglo-American political thinkers because, as a whole, the French, the other great source of modern theories of political representation, consciously separated themselves from the classical tradition (Urbinati 2006, 231n23). By contrast, early British and American theorists of representative government, for example, Burke, Publius, and Mill, generally recognized the classical antecedents of their theories. This awareness stands at odds with current authors on representative government, who generally deny or overlook the ancient roots of political representation.

Let me be clear about what I mean and, perhaps more important, what I do not mean when speaking of a Ciceronian outlook on, or approach to, representation adopted by these eighteenth- and nineteenth-century writers. There is good reason to believe that the accounts of representation in Burke, Publius, and Mill were influenced directly by Cicero's works and that these authors were conscious of this influence. They studied Cicero and refer to him in their writings. They make use of the same arguments in discussing the representative that Cicero employs regarding the orator: for example, that this person derives his authority from the people, that he should consider their views in making decisions, and that he is responsible for upholding their interests based on his own judgment of what that requires. These positions, however, are fairly generic, basic to the standard account of representation. The three writers evince a more clearly Ciceronian stance in identifying representation with a natural aristocracy acting for the common good. Here, too, however, these ideas are arguably found elsewhere, for example, Plato's *Republic* and Aristotle's *Politics*, although the natural *aristoi* of these Greeks are neither authorized by nor accountable to the people as they are in Cicero. Examining the three later theorists with an eye to Cicero, however, brings to the fore certain ideas that are specifically Ciceronian, in that Cicero introduced them into the Western political tradition: the role of the *sensus communis* (i.e., sense of the community in guiding the statesman); the importance of prudence in political decision making, but particularly in managing the tension between the representative's subordination to *and* independence from the people (often termed the "trustee-delegate dichotomy"); the moral, as opposed to simply expediential, character of these ideas; and the basis of these ideas in the rhetorical situation, in which orator and audience, representative and represented, are interdependent.

Although I maintain that the above concepts are Ciceronian and that Burke, Publius, and Mill *may* have been—even were *likely*—aware of their Ciceronian provenance, I do not claim that they were necessarily conscious of acquiring these quintessentially Ciceronian concepts, or the different parts of the standard account, from Cicero. Because of the long interval between Cicero and the modern thinkers, Ciceronian concepts were picked up and adapted by other writers, and it is possible that Burke, Publius, and Mill were directly influenced by these transmitters of Cicero's concepts. I do claim, however, that I may legitimately characterize Burke, Publius, and Mill as heirs to the Ciceronian account of the ideal orator-statesman qua representative. They are heirs, regardless of whether they were cognizant of their intellectual debt to Cicero, because he is the source of certain prominent ideas about representation, and they structure their arguments about representation along Ciceronian lines.

My argument that Cicero's works contain an account of representation and that later thinkers adopted this account has implications for the current debate about representative theory. Rehfeld criticizes the reigning view of political representation on two grounds. First, he finds fault with the standard account of representation for confusing political representation per se with normative legitimacy (Rehfeld 2006, 2–4). According to Rehfeld, Pitkin and like-minded writers have injected norms—for example, authorization and accountability through free and fair elections—into what should be a morally neutral theory of representation. The introduction of largely democratic norms of legitimacy into the meaning of representation, Rehfeld believes, renders the standard account unable to examine the global phenomenon of representation in nondemocratic entities such as dictatorships and nongovernmental organizations (NGOs); they are by definition excluded from consideration (1–2).

Although Rehfeld affirms, contra the standard account, that political representation is ancient, having "been extensively used and discussed for over two millennia" (2006, 2), he suggests that the addition of a moral dimension to representation is more recent and its presence superficial. For example, "political representation in, say, the early modern period in England, was less about legitimizing practices as about a practical way for the monarchy to extract taxes from the people" (3–4).[3] Toward the beginning of his article, Rehfeld appears to blame the confusion between normative and empirical representation on Pitkin's almost inexplicable domination of the field: "Pitkin's work quickly became the point of departure for anyone writing on the topic [of representation], whether in political theory or elsewhere in the field, and has shaped the debate ever since it was published" (3n6). Later, Rehfeld explains the intermingling of the normative and empirical because "the study of political representation has been done within the context of democratic (or increasingly democratic) regimes" (18).

Regardless of the precise reasons that political representation has been closely linked to normative concerns, Rehfeld does not view this link as profound. But if, as I argue, the normative character of representation dates back to Cicero, and his moral assumptions were taken up by some of the most prominent founders of modern representative theory—not only Pitkin and her followers—to form a coherent account of representation, then perhaps there is a deeper link between morality and representation than Rehfeld acknowledges, and the alacrity with which he tries to detach one from the other should give us pause.

Second, Rehfeld finds troubling the traditional "trustee-delegate" dichotomy, which denotes whether political representatives "act as they believe is best for the nation versus acting as their electoral constituents desire" (2009, 214–15).[4] Rehfeld believes that this binary, which has long been accepted as a central characteristic of political representation, collapses (and obscures) what he identifies as three fundamental aspects of representation: aim of legislation, source of judgment, and responsiveness. Each distinction, Rehfeld continues, presents two possibilities (223). The aim of legislation may be either republican (promoting the greater good) or pluralist (promoting the good of a part, e.g., the electoral constituency). The source of judgment may be self-reliant (i.e., relying on one's own judgment) or dependent (i.e., depending on the judgment of others). And responsiveness can be divided between the "gyroscopic" (i.e., "those who are less responsive to sanctions") and induced (i.e., "those who are more responsive to sanctions"). Rehfeld notes that the representative as trustee is usually assumed to possess the first characteristic in each of the three distinctions, and the representative as delegate is typically associated with the latter characteristics. Nevertheless, Rehfeld states, "[b]ecause 'aims,' 'judgment,' and 'responsiveness' may vary independently, creating eight possible combinations (2 x 2 x 2), collapsing them into two types ('trustee' or 'delegate') obscures these other possibilities" (215). He calls, therefore, for replacing the traditional "trustee-delegate" distinction with the tripartite set of distinctions, which, he concludes, neither oversimplifies the representative's (or the decision maker's) possibilities, as the dominant binary does, nor provides an overly complex set of choices, as would a "hundred- or thousand-celled table" that offers yet more options (225).

In contrast to the standard account of representation, whose historical roots, he implies, are comparatively shallow, Rehfeld initially confirms the "historical longevity" of the distinction between "trustees" and "delegates," which he "traces back at least to . . . the early 13th century." He, however, undermines this initial assessment in his ensuing historical summary: medieval representatives, he continues, had little independent authority to act and "were merely to give their constituency's . . . assent to the king's demand for money" (Rehfeld 2009, 215, 217); Burke, who is viewed by scholars as the model of the trustee position, "never uses the term in his *Speech to the Electors at Bristol*, keeping the parts more clearly separate"; it is only "two centuries later [that] those views have been conflated into the designation 'trustee'" (218). In the end, for Rehfeld, the trustee-delegate distinction appears to be of latter-day vintage, less a consistent conception than a repository for more carefully crafted distinctions that the trustee-delegate binary jumbles together into one or the other category.

By demonstrating that a coherent account of representation starts with Cicero and is then revived by later theorists, I challenge Rehfeld's goal of dispensing with the division between the representative as trustee and as delegate.[5] Although the trustee-delegate dichotomy may not apply to all instances of representation, its significance for representation as envisioned by Cicero and the Anglo-American theorists should prevent us from discarding it as irrelevant. The eight categories that Rehfeld's distinctions yield are superfluous when applied to Cicero, Burke, Publius, and Mill. They all agree that the dominant aim of their representative is the good of the whole. As for source of judgment, their ideal representative is primarily self-reliant, although the representative's judgment is determined by the values of the community and may shift to dependent, that is, contingent on prudential considerations. For the theorists analyzed here, being dependent on the judgment of others is tied to the representative's responsiveness to sanctions. In Cicero and Publius, the representative alternates between less or more responsive based on prudence; even Burke does not clearly reject responsiveness to sanctions in all cases. (Only Mill, as I show, expects his ideal representative to ignore sanctions, and in this matter Mill departs from the Ciceronian account of representation.) This alternating between categories is explicable in Cicero's orator-statesman and in the representative of the Anglo-American thinkers because of the Ciceronian commitment to a conception of prudence based in rhetoric.[6] We shall begin our inquiry into the Ciceronian account of representation by examining the meaning of representation and the terms Cicero employs that connote this concept.

What's in a Name? That Which We Call a Representative

The current scholarly agreement that the idea of representative government is modern does not indicate that all theorists recognized as originators of modern representative government viewed political representation as of recent origin. For example, Madison, in *Federalist* 63, observes "that the position concerning the ignorance of the antient [*sic*] government on the subject of representation is by no means precisely true in the latitude commonly given to it." He cites the Roman tribunes to support his claim. They and the Spartan *ephori*, though "small indeed in number . . . [were] annually *elected by the whole body of the people*, and considered as the *representatives* of the people, almost in their *plenipotentiary* capacity" (Hamilton, Madison, and Jay 2003, 308–9; emphases in original). Cicero himself, however, does not explicitly identify the tribunes as popular representatives but rather acknowledges them as protecting the plebeians by "curtailing the power and influence of the senate," which had restricted their liberty, or by checking the power of the consuls (Cicero 1928b, 2.59; 1928a, 3.14–16; 1995, 217). Cicero implies more strongly that the consul is a kind of representative, referring to him with a term I later discuss in greater detail, *tutor* (1942b, 3.3).

Pitkin (1967, 8–12) argues that there is no ancient term for "representation" as it is understood today. In its modern meaning, "representation means, as the word's etymological origins indicate, *re-presentation*, a making present again. . . . [R]epresentation, taken generally, means the making present *in some sense* of something which is nevertheless *not* present literally or in fact." Because "the single, basic meaning of representation will have very different applications depending on what is being made present or considered present, and in what circumstances," Pitkin also argues that this "single, basic definition is not much help." To do "justice to the various more detailed applications of representation in various contexts," Pitkin analyzes different theorists' understandings of representation and the relationship between "representation" and other seemingly similar terms.

A complete account of Pitkin's different conceptions of representation and related ideas is beyond the scope of this chapter. Nevertheless, I consider now one aspect of her review: the "array of analogies" intended to illuminate the activity of representing. Pitkin observes: "The representative has been variously likened to or defined as an actor, an agent, an ambassador, an attorney, a commissioner, a delegate, a deputy, an emissary, an envoy, a factor, a guardian, a lieutenant, a proctor, a procurator, a proxy, a steward, a substitute, a trustee, a tutor, and a vicar" (167, 119). Pitkin explains that "[a]lthough each of the suggested analogies is in some contexts or in certain ways like a representative, none of them is synonymous in meaning with 'representative'" (120–21). Pitkin classifies "these rival terms in a few major groups on the basis of similarity of meanings." Most relevant for Cicero is her category of "terms centering on the idea of taking care of another or acting in his interest: 'trustee,' 'guardian,' and the various words deriving from 'procurator.'" Although Pitkin acknowledges that there are analogies to be drawn to "representative," she concludes that this category of terms is not equivalent to "representative" because it does not suggest an independent role for the "someone else" who is taken care of or whose interests are acted for (131).

Contrary to Pitkin, I argue that in Cicero's case such terms entail a role for those whose interests are protected. In this section, I support my argument by examining Cicero's use of these terms in two works: *De oratore*, in which Cicero develops his conception of the ideal orator, and *De republica*, in which Cicero expounds his view of the best commonwealth and its statesman. To better understand Cicero's intentions, I analyze the Roman legal context for one of these terms, *procurator*.

Rather than seeing these two dialogues as explicating distinct roles for its protagonists, I treat the two works as delineating a common ideal—the model orator-statesman. In contending that *De oratore* and *De republica* are both concerned with portraying the ideal orator-statesman, I see my position as consistent with the recent work of Elaine Fantham in which she examines how Cicero idealizes the leadership of the orator-statesman in the two dialogues. For Fantham (2004, 311–19), these works—in varying degrees—highlight "the importance of eloquence in wise government" and the need for a man possessing the proper virtues to advise and serve the state. My goal here, unlike Fantham's, is to analyze the orator-statesman as a type of representative. The representative character of this ideal is partly borne out by the terms employed to describe him.

Both dialogues share a common set of terms to describe the ideal figure of these works, the orator-statesman. Among the jointly used names used are *rector*, *princeps*, *procurator*, and *tutor*. *Rector* and *princeps* concern political leadership, which underscores the significance of the statesman, not only in an obviously political work such as *De republica* but also in *De oratore*. Along with *rector* and *princeps*, another term of political authority is employed in *De oratore*—*auctor*. *Procurator* and *tutor* denote guardianship or agency, which is basic to Cicero's views on representation.

In *De oratore*, Antonius says of the statesman, "he who knows and uses everything by which the advantage of a State is secured and advanced should be regarded as the *rector*, helmsman, of the state, and the *auctor*, author, of public policy" (Cicero 1942a, 1.211). Antonius later describes the statesman as "the *auctor*, author, of public policy" (1.215) and *procuratione civitatis egregius*, an "outstanding manager of public affairs." Antonius (1.216) then speaks of Pericles, "the most eloquent man in Athens" as the *princeps* (leader) in that community. Until this point in the discussion (i.e., prior to the beginning of the second book), Antonius still differentiates between ideal orator and statesman, a position he later abandons in favor of the unity of orator and statesman—thereby linking terms signifying statesmanship with the more ambitious ideal of the orator-statesman.[7] In *De oratore* (3.63), Crassus, who defends the ideal of the orator-statesman from the beginning of the dialogue, refers to the ideal statesman again as "the *auctor* [author] of public policy . . . who employs his eloquence in formulating his thoughts in the Senate, before the people, and in public court cases." *Procurator* appears again in *De oratore* (3.131), when Q. Lutatius Catulus describes Crassus, whom Cicero appears to conceive as an approximation of the ideal orator-statesman, as being engrossed in "*orbis terrae procuratione*, the government of the entire world, and the administration of a vast empire, [having] succeeded in acquiring and grasping so vast a range of facts, and having coupled with all this the knowledge and the practical activity of one whose wisdom and oratory gave him influence in the state."[8]

Cicero introduces the third book of *De oratore* (1942b, 3.3) with a description of Crassus's final speech before his death. In this defense of the Senate against the consul L. Marcius Phillipus, Crassus is said to have "lamented the Senate's misfortune of being reduced to orphanhood" by a "consul, who ought to be like . . . a faithful *tutor*" (guardian). Although Crassus does not equate a consul with an orator-statesman here, "a consul's duty," like an orator-statesman's, is "to consult the interests of his native land" (1.165). The best example of the consul as a synthesis of statesman and orator is found in Cicero's speech *Pro Murena*. There, Cicero does not explicitly portray the eloquent consul as the ideal of *De oratore* or *De republica* but depicts him as capable of bringing men to the highest point (Cicero 1977a, 24; Fox 2007, 117; Millar 1998, 100).

As already noted, in *De republica*, Cicero designates the orator-statesman with four of the same terms found in *De oratore*. He introduces *tutor, procurator,* and *rector* in a single section of the dialogue in which Scipio Aemilianus contrasts the tyrant with the ideal statesman: The tyrant Tarquinius Superbus "by the unjust use of power that he already had, entirely overturned monarchic government." Scipio sets over and against this tyrant another type of man, the orator-statesman "who is good and wise and knowledgeable about the interests and the reputation of the state, almost a *tutor* [guardian] and *procurator* [manager] of the commonwealth; that, in fact, is the name for whoever is the *rector* [guide] and *gubernator* [helmsman] of the state. Make sure you recognize this man; he is the one who can protect the state by his wisdom and efforts" (Cicero 1928b, 2.51). The fourth term appears when Gaius Laelius (1.34) addresses Scipio (who, like Crassus in *De oratore*, is portrayed as a possible model for the orator-statesman) as a "*princeps*, leader of the commonwealth" (Cicero 1999d, 1.34).

Rector and *princeps*, common to the two dialogues, establish the political leadership of the orator. In *De oratore*, *rector* is used to define the ideal statesman. In *De republica*, *rector* is paired with *gubernator*, frequently used by Cicero to designate leadership (Cicero 1928b, 205–6).[9] *Princeps* is a pivotal word of authority in a Roman context, along with "*auctor*, which, as seen, is found in *De oratore*, but not *De republica*" (Wisse, Winterbottom, and Fantham 2008, 97).[10]

Procurator and *tutor*, likewise found in *De oratore* and *De republica*, characterize the nature of the orator-statesman, who cares for the well-being of others. This watching out for the interests of others is fundamental to the ideal orator's role as representative. The *procurator* in *De oratore* 1.215 is sometimes translated as a "representative of interests"—literally, the word means agent (Greenridge 1971, 237–38; Leeman, Pinkster, and Nelson 1985, 2:138). But as James Zetzel explains, when Scipio refers to the orator-statesman as *quasi tutor et procurator rei publicae*, "almost a guardian and manager of the commonwealth," he is speaking metaphorically: "*tutor* is a legal term for a guardian, *procurator* the administrator of an estate" (Cicero 1995, 205). Cicero again draws a parallel between the statesman and caretakers in *De republica* 5.5, where Scipio speaks of the statesman as the *vilicus* (overseer) and *dispensator* (manager). These metaphors convey a sense of the orator-statesman speaking for, and defending, the common good. This ideal figure represents the people in the sense that he acts for them. The orator-statesman represents the public as if he were protecting its legal interests and property. Pitkin (1967, 125) argues, however, that "acting for" is insufficient. The true representative stands "as a miniature or embodiment of the whole." Cicero, though, does view the orator-statesman as an embodiment of the whole state.

According to Robert Hariman, Cicero views the Roman Republic as constituted in discourse. Public oratory defines and sustains the Republic, and conversely it is endangered by silence: "for without the continuing discussion of public duties, virtue could wane, citizens become distracted, forces of change gather strength as political energies dissipate" (Hariman 1995, 110–11). As oratory sustains the Republic, the ideal orator personifies the Republic by distinguishing himself from all other citizens to such an extent that he uniquely possesses the virtues of the commonwealth. Crassus's description of the ideal orator in *De oratore* 1.30–34 suggests this role for the public speaker. He emerges alone, "out of an infinite crowd," who with only his words is able to lend aid to those in distress, raise up the afflicted, offer people safety, free them from danger, and save them from exile. "[T]he leadership and wisdom of the perfect orator," Crassus asserts, "provide the chief basis, not only for his own dignity, but also for the safety of countless individuals and of the State at large."[11]

Cicero, in his speeches, presents himself as the embodiment of the Republic. Cicero not only identifies harm to the state as harm to himself, but harm to himself as harm to the state. Cicero's identification of himself with the state, for example, runs through *Pro Sestio*, a speech on behalf of the tribune Publius Sestius, in which Cicero links Sestius to himself and himself to the state. In one passage, Cicero, for example, speaks of the wound of his own exile as the "greatest possible wound to the State" (Cicero 1958a, 31; May 1981, 308–15). Thus, in Christian Habicht's words: "Cicero had, in fact, become the idea of the Roman Republic" (Habicht 1990, 99).[12] Cicero's identification of the state with himself suggests his distinct lack of humility. His conflation of state and self, however, addresses more than Cicero's healthy ego. His words derive, at least in part, from Cicero's belief that no one better embodies the commonwealth than a public orator who acts for the Republic's good.

If the representative stands for the whole, then what room is there for the represented? This question implicitly underlies Pitkin's willingness to concede an analogy between "procurator" (along with similar terms of guardianship) and "representative," although denying an identity between them. For her, "procurator" and similar words leave no role for the guarded to act on their own, which is essential to representation. A brief analysis of "procurator" in Roman law, however, demonstrates that this representative does not monopolize all activity without a place for the represented to be involved. The *procurator* was an informal representative who administered the estate or estates of his *dominus* (master). His "less perfect mandate" is often contrasted with the *cognitor*, who possessed a "more perfect mode of representation." The difference has been outlined as follows: "When the *cognitor* has been appointed and has represented, the right of action is entirely lost by the *dominus*. . . . On the other hand, when representation takes the less perfect and specific form of that exercised by the procurator, the right of action by the *dominus* is not held to be consumed" (Greenridge 1971, 237-40).

Notwithstanding Pitkin's intepretation of *procurator*, Romans of Cicero's time would have viewed the *procurator* as a kind of representative with restricted freedom of activity (consequently leaving greater room of action for the master) vis-à-vis the *cognitor* (Greenridge 1971, 237-40).[13] The upshot of this examination of alternate words for "representation" is that by using the *procurator* as the metaphor for the orator-statesman, Cicero suggests that like the *dominus*, who has power to act, the people—the true master of the Roman orator—play a significant role independent of their representative.[14]

The Elements of Ciceronian Representation

Pitkin includes authorization and accountability through elections in her explication of representation: "We would be reluctant to consider any system a representative government unless it held regular elections, which were 'genuine' or 'free.'" She contends that representing "means acting in the interest of the represented, in a manner responsive to them." But she also depicts representation as requiring that the "representative must act independently; he must be the one who acts," although the "represented must also be [conceived of] as capable of independent action and judgment, not merely being taken care of." Pitkin believes that, ultimately, the representative and the represented should not be at odds with each other. "[D]espite the resulting potential for conflict between representative and represented about what is to be done," she states, "that conflict must not normally take place" (Pitkin 1967, 235, 209-10).

Bernard Manin, whom Rehfeld (2006, 3) describes as "animated by the norms Pitkin described," encapsulates the criteria of representation in "[f]our principles [that] have invariably been observed in representative regimes, ever since this form of government was invented: (1) [t]hose who govern are appointed by election at regular intervals; (2) [t]he decision-making of those who govern retains a degree of independence from the wishes of the electorate; (3) [t]hose who are governed may give expression to their opinions and political wishes without these being subject to the control of those who govern; [and] (4) [p]ublic decisions undergo the trial of debate" (Manin 1997, 6). Likewise, Urbinati (2006, 20-25), despite distinguishing between three theories of representation—the first two (judicial and institutional), which she criticizes, and the third (political), which she supports—implies that elections are common to all theories of representation and that the represented and their representatives are interdependent, each possessing a degree of independence.

Authorization and accountability by way of elections, which Pitkin and similar theorists posit as prerequisites of representation, is found in Cicero's elucidation of the theory and practice of rhetoric in republican Rome. For Cicero, the subordination of the orator to the people (implicit in his referring to the orator-statesman as *procurator*) derives from the *contio* (i.e., the nonvoting informal assembly), in which the orator spoke before the people, who could variously approve or reject him. The *contio* met before formal voting political assemblies were convened or at any time a presiding magistrate decided to convene such a meeting (Morstein-Marx 2004, 7–12). Even more than the voting assemblies, the *contiones* were viewed as the expression of the will of the *populus Romanus*, par excellence (120–21, 127). Although the *contiones* were open to all citizens, only a small part of the Roman citizenry, primarily urban dwellers, actually attended these informal assemblies (Morstein-Marx 2004, 128; Mouritsen 2001, 38–45). Nevertheless, Roman convention equated the *contio*'s audience, regardless of its size, with the Roman people. As Morstein-Marx points out, Cicero addresses the *contio* with the "second-person plural pronoun, or its adjectival form *vester*, as the equivalent of *populus Romanus*" (2004, 120–21; Cicero 1927a, 1–6, 26). Thus, the *contio* stood in for the people-as-a-whole, and, as such, the *contio*'s audience approved the orator as its representative.

Ancient orators, per se, were not elected in the manner that modern-day representatives are selected. The people, however, were still afforded a clear opportunity to confirm or deny orators as their spokesmen. (In addition, Cicero appears to envision his ideal orator-statesman as elected to office like the consuls of his own day.) To begin with, even before an orator appeared at a *contio*, the people exercised their influence by, in effect, only permitting those speakers they viewed as sufficiently acceptable—for example, possessing authority—to address them. Accordingly, only senators were seriously considered as orators (Morstein-Marx 2004, 163n10). Thus, potential speakers who anticipated a hostile audience, most likely opponents invited by the presiding magistrate who intended to put their adversaries' "feet to the fire of public outrage," often bowed out beforehand, with the opposition relying instead on "constitutional obstruction" and "symbolic resistance" to influence legislation (Morstein-Marx 2004, 164–67, 174–75). Once the orator stood before the *contio*, the audience exercised its franchise either by supporting the speaker—remaining silent, thereby permitting him to speak, or applauding—or by voting against him through shouting him down, drifting away from the audience, hurling objects, even threatening his life (Cicero 1999a, letter 38; 1958a, 77; Millar 1998, 47; Morstein-Marx 2004, 123; Mouritsen 2001, 44, 47–48, 53; Wallace 2006, 107–28).

By the time of the vote, after the *contiones* preceding the political assemblies, citizens had the opportunity to deliberate on matters and were afforded, theoretically at least, some distance from the "force" of the orator's speech and a chance to assess the orator and his arguments.[15] In addition, even citizens not present at the *contio* could see the text of the law before the vote. "The principle of publicity both in the posting up of a text of the law and in the recitation of its complete text on the day of voting was fundamental." Cicero, for example, discusses proclamations that were posted and the impossibility of clearing these posted *edicta* because the crowd delighted in reading them (Millar 1998, 83–84, 130–31).[16]

Thus, Cicero's view of the orator-statesman as beholden to the people rests on the orator's ongoing need for the audience's approval—less of a concern for the modern representative, who is elected only at intervals. Cicero emphasizes the orator's reliance on the audience when he writes in the *Orator*: "The eloquence of orators has always been controlled by the good sense of the audience, since all who desire to win approval have regard to the goodwill of their auditors, and shape and adapt themselves completely according to this and to their opinion and approval" (Cicero 1939b, 24).

Cicero, however, transforms the orator's need for public approbation from mere necessity to ethical principle: the orator is morally bound to obey the deeply rooted values of the community. Cicero writes that "in oratory, the very cardinal sin is to depart from the language of everyday life, and the usage approved by the sense of community [*communis sensus*]" (Cicero 1942a, 1.12). Included in the "sense of community" are what P. A. Brunt (1988) calls the "stock of ideals which commanded almost universal assent, though they could be interpreted in widely divergent ways and brought forward to justify the most diverse policies" (49). And the right of common people to participate in politics was such an ideal, accepted not only by *populares* but by optimates like Cicero. In its most straightforward rhetorical sense, *sensus communis* refers to "the whole set of unstated assumptions, prejudices, and values that an orator can take for granted when addressing the audience" (Schaeffer 2004, 278), a meaning distinct from how the term was used by Aristotle before Cicero and by other classical Roman thinkers after Cicero.

Aristotle is credited with introducing the concept *sensus communis*, the Latin translation of the Greek term *aesthesis koine*, which he uses in *De anima*.

Unlike the meaning of *sensus communis* in Cicero's *De oratore* (i.e., as a set of notions common to the community), Aristotle's *aesthesis koine* is a faculty of the psyche that perceives, combines, and interprets those aspects of the external world that are delivered by the five senses. As opposed to his *sensus communis*, which is used as a cognitive faculty, Aristotle employs *endoxa* rhetorically in his *Topics* to denote "opinions and values that were held in common by most or all" (Bayer 2008, 1137; Van Holthoon and Olson 1987, 3; Bugter 1987, 94–95; Schaeffer 2004, 280). This separate term, although closer to what Cicero would come to mean by *sensus communis*, is not the one adopted by modern theorists of representation. Aristotle's willingness to admit *endoxa* as premises in rhetorical argumentation contrasts with his refusal to "allow them to figure as epistemologically legitimate articulations of social and ethical ends" (Haskins 2004a, 14).[17] Aristotle, unlike Cicero, does not vest rhetorical concepts—including *endoxa*—with moral significance. As we saw in the first chapter, Aristotle's orator is governed, qua orator, by the artistic (not ethical) rules of rhetoric. His orator (like others citizens) must act ethically to be virtuous, but his ethical rules are derived from outside rhetoric, not, like Cicero, from within rhetoric itself. As for post-Ciceronian Roman thinkers (e.g., Seneca, Juvenal, and Marcus Aurelius), they shared an understanding of *sensus communis* as a common social sensibility (Bayer 2008, 1137–39), which also differed from Cicero's use of the phrase.

The *sensus communis*, as Cicero understands it, originates in the wisdom of the ancients and is confirmed through long-standing communal acceptance. For example, Cicero explains that the *mos maiorum* (the custom of the forefathers) was—until the widespread corruption of his own day—respected by all and preserved by the "great men" over the generations (Cicero 1999d, 5.1; Brunt 1988, 56–58; Roloff 1938). Like the *mos maiorum*, the community's acceptance of the Roman Constitution, according to Cicero, is grounded in enduring tradition. For Cicero, the Roman Constitution is "the organization of the State so wisely instituted by our ancestors" and is the best constitution ever because it represents the Romans' "practical, collective wisdom," its principles having been tested over a long period of time (Cicero 1958a, 137; Asmis 2008, 31). Cicero reinforces the moral force of the Roman Constitution by associating it with the Stoic "natural law." For example, he has his close friend Atticus state, referring to the Roman Constitution, that "our laws are in accordance with nature; the wisdom of our ancestors" (Cicero 1999e, 2.62). And he himself cites the Stoic definition of law as rational, *natural*, eternal, and unchanging to demonstrate that the Roman Constitution is just by nature, not a product of convention (Cicero 1999d, 3.33; Asmis 2008, 27).

Because Cicero morally obliges the orator (along with other citizens) to abide by the "sense of community," Ciceronian rhetoric mandates that the orator's obligation to communal ideals—true ideals rooted in ancestral morality—is more than expediential. Cicero affirms that one such ideal, popular liberty, is a principle of the Constitution. As Cicero explains in *De republica*, the Roman Constitution as a mixed constitution ("this combined and moderately blended form of commonwealth") is superior to others in its selecting the best traits of the three "pure" types of commonwealth—monarchy, aristocracy, and democracy—in a fashion that avoids the particular faults of each simple type (Cicero 1999d, 1.44, 1.69). Democracy in its unadulterated form may become extreme, giving rise to excessive license, resulting in extreme slavery and tyranny (1.68). But Cicero, through the character of Scipio, approves setting aside some things "for the judgment and wishes of the people" (1.69). And Cicero has Scipio extol the Roman Republic for the liberty it grants its citizens (1.47). Even for the conservative Cicero, the people, as the sovereign, have ultimate power.[18]

Besides the normative criteria of accountability, authorization, and elections, the standard account of representation emphasizes the representative's obligation to act for the people using his or her own judgment. Hence, Pitkin (1967, 209) requires the representative to act independently, to use discretion and judgment when acting, and to be the one who acts. The ethical responsibilities of the orator toward the public that Pitkin and others describe are anticipated by Cicero. Using several metaphors of caretaking and guardianship for the orator-statesman (e.g., *procurator*), he indicates that his paragon functions, within limits, independently of the people. The source of the orator's obligation to do right as *he* sees fit derives from Cicero's conception of rhetoric, specifically his view of the orator-statesman as a moral exemplar. Cicero's orator, as delineated in *De oratore*, is both moral and wise (Cicero 1942b, 3.55). He is part of a "natural aristocracy" that ought to rule and whom the people should recognize as their proper rulers. Cicero envisions leaders who stand above the common citizenry in their ability to discern the good of all, willing to stand their ground in the face of the "most insistent clamours" and "all other storms and tempests . . . that are met with upon the troubled waters of popular meetings" (Cicero 1953a, 3–5; Morstein-Marx 2004, 168–70). These men in charge of public affairs are entrusted with "the management of the republic" (*procuratio rei publica*), duty bound to neglect their own personal interests or the interests of only part of the citizenry in favor of the "care of the whole body of the republic" (Cicero 1991a, 1.85). As "good" or "right-thinking men" (*boni*), they will be supported by the "true people" (*verus populus*), as opposed to the hostile crowd, who are an unrepresentative mass (*peculiaris popularis*), contradicting the true will of the Roman people (Cicero 1958a, 103–27; Morstein-Marx 2004, 148–49).[19]

Controversially, the independence Cicero grants his ideal orator in relation to the people extends (as explicated in chapter 1) to emotionally manipulating them, at least under some circumstances, for the common good. As Antonius says in *De oratore*, "nothing in oratory, Catulus, is more important than . . . for the audience itself to be moved in such a way as to be ruled by some strong emotional impulse rather than reasoned judgment" (2001a, 2.178). Cicero justifies such methods in *De officiis* with his claim that "things that relate to truth and to keeping faith" must sometimes be set aside for the sake of the common advantage (Cicero 1991a, 1.31; Remer 2004, 146–48). Cicero also manifests his independence as an orator in criminal cases, which are political by nature, when he speaks in his own name, independent of the client's instructions, as he does in his defense of Roscio Amerino (Cicero 1930b, 129).[20]

The two-sided nature of representation that characterizes the standard account of representation—the ultimate power of the represented *and* the independence of the representative—is most commonly referred to in today's literature as the tension between the trustee and delegate models of representation. Cicero alludes to this tension within the duties of the orator-statesman when speaking of the "mere handful" of "men excelling in oratory . . . who by their counsel and wisdom [*consilio et sapientia*] could control and direct [*regere et gubernare*] the helm of state" (Cicero 1942a, 1.7–8). Although the first set of terms, "counsel and wisdom," connotes an ideal orator subordinate to the citizens, the second set, "control and direct," alludes to an orator who acts with a greater degree of independence from the citizen body. This double-sided nature of the orator-statesman—as independent *and* dependent or, in modern terms, as trustee *and* delegate—is characteristic of Cicero's rhetorical approach, in which the orator seeks flexibility in speech and action according to context.[21] Rather than committing himself to any single option, the Ciceronian orator often balances the two sides in question, shifting between one and the other. Cicero writes in *De inventione*: "There are certain matters that must be considered with reference to time and intention and not merely by their absolute qualities. In all these matters one must think what the occasion demands" (Cicero 1949, 2.176; see also Leff 1998, 69, 75–76).

The mode of reasoning about contingent matters that determines the best course of action between the two models of representation is prudence. In Hariman's (2003, 5, 11) words, "prudence is a mentality dedicated to balancing the contradictory tendencies in any complex situation." And prudential reasoning is essentially rhetorical (Kahn 1985, 35). Prudence is linked to decorum, a universal characteristic of classical rhetoric, in which speakers accommodate themselves to circumstance. And like decorum, which Cicero maintains is "inseparable from moral goodness," prudence is defined ethically, designated by Cicero as one of the four cardinal virtues (Cicero 1913a, 1.93–94, 96; Cape 2003, 35–65).

The distinctiveness of Cicero's conception of prudence is pointed up by contrasting it with the creator of the other main classical model of prudence, Aristotle. This difference is important for the Ciceronian orator's ability to navigate between his roles as trustee and delegate. Prudence (*phronesis*) for Aristotle requires that when confronted with making a decision about how to act in a particular situation, the person of practical wisdom (the *phronimos*) must pursue the intrinsically good over the instrumentally good (Depew 2004a, 166–77; 2004b, 167–75). For Aristotle, then, if the statesman is deciding whether to act according to the people's wishes or his own sense of what is right, and if the statesman is also making this decision as a *phronimos*, then his decision must accord with noble values (*ta kala*). The line between intrinsic good and instrumental good, between the moral (*honestum*) and the beneficial (*utile*), however, is less clear for Cicero, as it is for any practical politician. The Ciceronian orator must consider whether if, in taking a principled position, he might sufficiently antagonize the public (or important individuals) so that in the future the orator's good policy proposals will be rejected. For example, to placate a popular audience, Cicero presents himself to a *contio* as sympathetic to agrarian laws, although in philosophical writings and a private letter, he condemns agrarian laws and the common people supporting such laws (Cicero 1930a, 2.7–10; 1991a, 2.78; 1999a, letter 16.11). In presenting himself as a popularist supporter of agrarian reform, the Ciceronian orator (unlike the Aristotelian *phronimos*) is compromising between intrinsic and instrumental goods. This prudent compromise, from Cicero's perspective, can itself be moral because his conception of the moral includes within it elements of the expedient. The prudence adopted by later theorists of representation discussed in this chapter is Ciceronian, not Aristotelian.

Ciceronian Representation Revived

Having shown how the criteria of the "standard account" are found in Cicero and how Cicero grounds these standards in rhetoric, I now turn to "representation" as explicated in the works of Burke, Publius, and Mill. Examining their theories in relation to Cicero highlights the similarities between the eighteenth- and nineteenth-century authors and the Roman rhetorician, including those similarities that point toward the source of their ideas in Ciceronian rhetoric.

Edmund Burke and Ciceronian Representation

Of the three authors discussed here, Edmund Burke most appears to endorse the representative's independence from the people, without leaving room for the influence of the represented. Nevertheless, Burke (1996, 69) grants some role for the public when he writes that a representative ought "to live in the strictest union, the closest correspondence, and the most unreserved communication with his constituents. Their wishes ought to have great weight with him; their opinion high respect; their business unremitted attention." Burke is aware of the importance of elections for what he and most of his fellow citizens commonly mean by "political representatives," that is, members of the House of Commons. He interprets elections as a means for the people to control non-elected governmental institutions and their own electors: "[T]he setting up any claims adverse to the right of free election . . . tends to subvert the legal authority by which the House of Commons sits." And the attempt in Burke's own time to "*alter the right of elections itself*" would, according to Burke, only have reinforced the already ongoing silent progress of the "separation of the representatives from their constituents" (Hoffman and Levack 1967, 29–30; emphasis in original). Even for Burke, the representative does not act independently of the people at all times. Although Burke's representative does not seek—in contrast to Cicero's orator before the *contiones*—the popular audience's approval after each speech, he must conform over the long run to the people's feelings.

Like Cicero, Burke vests popular consent with moral authority. But consent for Burke is determined by the longstanding values of the community. These tradition-based ideals express themselves simply as "prejudices" but also manifest themselves, with greater complexity, in the "constitution." Prejudice, for Burke, refers to a notion that finds its source in "the general bank and capital of nations, and of ages" rather than originating in individual reason (Burke 1989, 138), and Burke uses prejudice in the same way as Cicero's *sensus communis* (Schaeffer 2004, 278). For example, Burke condemns revolutionary France's rejection of "the great influencing prejudices of mankind" with their contempt for "the antient permanent sense of mankind" (1989, 212–13).[22] Like Burke's use of prejudice, he utilizes *mos maiorum* to uphold the moral authority of ancestral values. The terminology is analogous to Cicero's. Burke describes the *mos maiorum* as "the principal rule of polity to guide . . . judgment in whatever regards our laws" (1962, 68).

More formal than prejudices, but still grounded in tradition, is the constitution, which, "working after the pattern of nature," is the foundation of government and privileges. The constitution's character is both particular and universal. Burke (1989, 84) maintains that its roots in the principles of the forefathers binds up the constitution of our country "with our dearest domestic ties; adopting our fundamental laws into the bosom of our family affections"; and tying together "our state, our hearths, our sepulchers, and our altars." Consistent with Cicero's Roman Constitution, Burke's English Constitution finds legitimacy through natural law. For Burke, the English Constitution does not always meet the full standards of natural law. But, overall, he maintains that the British Constitution is based on traditional natural law, standing in "the hierarchy of moral and legal values" just beneath the natural law (Stanlis 1991, 25–26).

Burke, like Cicero, justifies a popular role in politics as constitutionally supported. In a speech to the House of Commons attacking that body's overturning of John Wilkes's election as MP for Middlesex, Burke states: "That the people should not choose their own representative is a saying that *Shakes* the constitution. That this House should name the representative—is a saying which followed by practice subverts the constitution" (1981, 228–30; emphasis in original). The electors' freedom of choice is "a right prior" to the House of Common's right of judging.

For Burke, political leaders must begin, as did Cicero's ideal orator, from the basic assumptions of the people: "I cannot conceive how any man can have brought himself to that pitch of presumption, to consider his country as nothing but *carte blanche*, upon which he may scribble whatever he pleases . . . ; a good patriot and a true politician, always considers how he shall make the most of the existing materials of his country. A disposition to preserve, and an ability to improve, taken together, would be my standard of a statesman" (Burke 1989, 206).

In his own political practice, Burke attempts to follow this rhetorical standard of a statesman, that is, to argue your position from within the basic values of your audience, even if you suggest "improvements" to the current status quo. For example, in his "Speech on Conciliation with America" before Parliament, Burke appeals to his listeners' deep-seated principles, distinguishing these principles (e.g., respect for self-taxation as an element of liberty) from their recently acquired feelings (e.g., a tyrannical and violent spirit), which do not reflect their community's traditions (Browne 1993, 48–59).

The representative's freedom of decision making vis-à-vis his electors is an idea most closely associated with Burke. The Burkean member of the House of Commons is not a representative because he derives his power from the people. According to Burke, the role of representative is not intrinsically based on popular elections; unelected leaders and magistrates are representatives, too: "The king is the representative of the people; so are the lords; so are the judges." They *and* the member of the Commons "all are trustees for the people" (Hoffman and Levack 1967, 28). All are the people's representatives because they act for the good of the nation, not because they are popularly endorsed. (His emphasis on elections, however, implies that he sees the elected representative as the norm.)

Like Cicero, Burke argues that the people's representatives should come from a natural aristocracy. In *Reflections on the Revolution in France*, Burke writes that people recognize that when they elect their representative, they do so not "to the exercise of authority as to a pitiful job, but as to a holy function; . . . they will confer that power (which any man may well tremble to give or to receive) on those only in whom they may discern that predominant proportion of active virtue and wisdom, taken together and fitted to the charge" (Hoffman and Levack 1967, 316).

This elite, distinguished from the "common sort of men" by its superiority in intelligence, wisdom, and character, has the good of the nation as a whole as its goal. "A true natural aristocracy is not a separate interest in the state or separable from it. It is an essential integrant part of any large body rightly constituted" (397–99). To the extent a representative, emerging from this natural aristocracy, has his own set of cares and concerns, "[i]t is his duty to sacrifice his repose, his pleasures, his satisfactions [to his constituents]; and, above all, ever, and in all cases, to prefer their interest to his own" (Burke 1996, 69).

In arriving at a decision, the representative acts as the trustee of the people who must decide what *he* thinks is in their interest, not as a delegate beholden to the constituents' wishes. Burke affirms this position in his "Speech to the Electors of Bristol," where he acknowledges that representatives "ought always most seriously to consider" their constituents' opinions but asserts that members of Parliament cannot be "bound blindly and implicitly to obey, to vote, and to argue for [their constituents' views], though contrary to the clearest conviction of his judgement and conscience" (1996, 69). The representative is bound to follow "his unbiased opinion, his mature judgement, his enlightened conscience" as a "trust from Providence." And if he sacrifices his judgment to their opinion, "he betrays" them, instead of serving them (69). Burke requires the representative to avail himself of the people's sentiments, but not to take orders from them.

The representative's judgment, for Burke, is based on more than personal opinion or sectional interests. The representative defends the common interest of the people, which is unitary: "Parliament is a *deliberative* Assembly of *one* Nation, with *one* Interest, that of the whole; where, not local Purposes, not local Prejudices ought to guide, but the general Good" (Burke 1996, 69; emphases in original). When his electors choose a representative for their district, Burke explains, they choose a member of Parliament, not a member of Bristol.

Although Burke emphasizes the representative's duties as trustee over his role as delegate, I have shown that he also recognizes that the representative is ultimately subordinate to the people; representatives stand for election and obligate themselves to the community's deeply rooted values. Like Cicero concerning the orator, Burke avoids defining exactly when the representative is more trustee and when he is more delegate. Because of the variability, Pitkin (1967, 168) describes Burke as "seldom systematic and not always even consistent." Burke's "inconsistencies" become comprehensible, though, when he is viewed rhetorically, that is, when he is understood as relying on the rhetorical virtue of prudence to determine the representative's place in the balance between trustee and delegate.

Burke's commitment to prudence and the connection between Burkean and Ciceronian prudence is widely acknowledged (Browning 1984, 63). Like the orator, who must adapt his words to particular contexts, Burke and Cicero assert that statesmen must accommodate their policies—and words—to the needs of the moment. In line with Cicero's attitudes toward prudence, Burke condemns the rejection of prudence by some of his own contemporaries: "Prudence (constituted as the God of this lower world) . . . and conformity to circumstances [have been] wholly set at naught in our late controversies, and treated as if they were the most contemptible and irrational of all things" (1996, 316).

Prudence over abstract principle permeates all Burke's political theory: "All government, indeed every human benefit and enjoyment, every virtue, and every prudent act, is founded on compromise and barter" (Burke 1996, 157). Although he aligns himself most one-sidedly with the view of representative as trustee, he balances between the two models of representation, sometimes leaning in favor of greater citizen participation. Thus, Burke respects the legitimacy of both unelected and elected representatives, terming the first type of representation "virtual" and the second type "actual." Concerning the franchise for Catholics in Ireland, who are widely accepted as "virtually" represented, Burke designates "[t]he whole question a matter for prudence. I do not put the thing on a question of right." Burke responds to those who oppose offering "actual" representation to the Irish Catholics by asserting that continuing to deny them the suffrage will create a seditious multitude that will endanger the stability of the state (Hoffman and Levack 1967, 494–96). Political prudence, not sympathy toward their plight—or claims of natural right—is how Burke sustains his defense of voting privileges for Irish Catholics. Because Burke grounds his argument on prudence, he does not generalize from the Irish example. Rather, he sees himself as "taking up this business singly and by an arrangement for the single object" (498).

The Burkean representative who prudently accommodates his position on the question of the Irish Catholic franchise would appear to be acting justifiably in accommodating his parliamentary vote, at times, to his electors. But Burke's "Speech to the Electors of Bristol," with its rejection of authoritative instructions and its commitment to the representative's considered judgment over the people's sentiments, suggests otherwise. Burke's own history of supporting policies despite their unpopularity with his constituency further appears to confirm Burke's principled, but imprudent, stance in relation to his electors. Nevertheless, Burke himself refrains from explicitly stating that representatives may *never* reasonably adapt themselves to the represented. What Burke repudiates are mandates from the electors, "obeying [their] instructions, and having no opinion but [the electors']" or "implicitly" obeying the opinion of the people (Burke 1996, 632, 661–62). Burke justifies to his constituents, in the "Speech at Bristol Previous to the Election," his independence from their opinions—his support for free trade with Ireland and Catholic emancipation, his defense of the American colonists, his backing of a legislative bill to prevent the perpetual imprisonment of insolvent debtors, and so on (620–64). His unwillingness to apologize to them for his "impolitic stubbornness," however, must be weighed against his conceding that "their wishes ought to have great weight" (662). Burke may himself never have found a policy whose immediate circumstances legitimized compromising with the public, but he leaves open the possibility that conditions could warrant such a concession.

The Federalist and Ciceronian Representation

As with Burke, the authors of *The Federalist* see elections as intended to limit how far representatives can stray from their constituents' opinions. Madison, in *Federalist* 57, however, maintains that rather than elections per se, it is elections of representatives limited by "the term of appointment . . . [that] will maintain a proper responsibility to the people" (Hamilton, Madison, and Jay 2004, 277). Particularly, in the House of Representatives, "the restraint of frequent elections" will elicit "in the members an habitual recollection of their dependence on the people" (279). Madison also believes that the electoral system "cannot fail to produce a temporary affection at least to their constituents" (278). It is only natural, according to Madison, that representatives will feel gratitude and benevolence toward those who elected them, and the affection that representatives will feel for their electors makes it more probable that the representatives will seriously consider their constituents' viewpoints, a position Hamilton maintains in *Federalist* 35, where he writes that a representative "dependent on the suffrages of his fellow-citizens . . . should take care to inform himself of their dispositions and inclinations and should be willing to allow them their proper degree of influence upon his conduct" (161).

In *Federalist* 39, Madison contends that a republic should be defined as "a government which derives all its powers directly or indirectly from the great body of the people" and that "[i]t is *sufficient* for such a [republican] government" for its officers to be appointed "either directly or indirectly, by the people" (Hamilton, Madison, and Jay 2004, 182). But *The Federalist* also makes clear that the consent of the people, on which the US government rests, includes more than its representatives being elected by the people, but that its representatives must reflect the values of the people. Madison and Hamilton even point to the uniquely Ciceronian provenance of this principle by speaking of the "sense of the community," Cicero's *sensus communis*, when referring to the community's essential values. In *Federalist* 63, Madison asserts that in all free governments, the *sense of the community* will "ultimately prevail over the views of its rulers" (307). Likewise, in *Federalist* 71 Hamilton affirms that "[t]he republican principle demands" that the *sense of the community* "should govern the conduct of those to whom they trust the management of their affairs" (349). In these passages, Madison and Hamilton echo Cicero in grounding representation in the community's values and ideals. In *Federalist* 49, Madison reflects, more particularly, on the rhetorical benefits that accrue to the government when it is supported by public sentiment. Like the ancient orator, whose reputation depends on aligning himself with public opinion, Madison recognizes that "the most rational government will not find it a superfluous advantage, to have the prejudices of the community on its side" (246).

The quotations from *The Federalist*, however, have been selective. Madison and Hamilton modify the "sense of the community" by "cool and deliberate" (in *Federalist* 63) and "deliberate" (in *Federalist* 71). The authors of *The Federalist* speak of "the deliberate sense of the community" to distinguish it from nonauthoritative, less genuine opinions of the people. Thus, Madison contrasts the "cool and deliberate sense of the community" with popular opinions "stimulated by some irregular passion or some illicit advantage." There are "particular moments in public affairs" when the people are "misled by some artful misrepresentations of interested men" that the represented will "afterwards be most ready to lament and condemn" (Hamilton, Madison, and Jay 2004, 307). Hamilton differentiates between the "deliberate sense of the community" and "every sudden breese of passion" or "every transient impulse" (349). These distinctions between genuine and merely apparent senses of the community parallel the lines drawn by Cicero and Burke between the *sensus communis* founded on ancestral morality, which is the true sense of the community, and the people's superficial values, which are detached from their longstanding ideals. Writing for a nation establishing a *novus ordo seclorum*, that is, without an ancient past from which to derive its values, the authors of *The Federalist* discover a substitute for antiquity in the citizenry's reasoned, as opposed to superficial, opinions.

Despite the United States' lack of ancestral traditions, Madison recognizes the need "to suspend the blow meditated by the people against themselves, until reason, justice and truth can regain their authority over the public mind" (Hamilton, Madison, and Jay 2004, 307). Madison identifies these representatives with a "temperate and respectable body of citizens," who ought to act independently while concomitantly being responsive to the electorate. They are the "chosen body of citizens" in a republic who, Madison writes in *Federalist* 10, "refine and enlarge the public views, . . . whose wisdom may best discern the true interest of their country, and whose patriotism and love of justice, will be least likely to sacrifice it to temporal or partial considerations" (44). As Manin (1997, 117) observes, Madison's use of "chosen body" to describe the new country's representatives has a twofold meaning: first, as elected; second, as constituting a "chosen Few," who are the wisest and most virtuous.

The *Federalist* upholds (wittingly or not) Cicero's ideal of the orator-statesman standing distinct from, and above, the people, while defending the Republic's common good. The authors of *The Federalist* intend the representative, as do Cicero and Burke, to rise from the natural aristocracy. Although Madison does not use this term in *Federalist* 57, he vests political leaders with the qualities of mind and character with which Cicero endows the ideal orator-statesman in *De oratore* and *De republica* and with characteristics similar to those Burke provides his representatives in his writings. Rulers ought to be "men who possess most wisdom to discern, and most virtue to pursue the common good of society" (Hamilton, Madison, and Jay 2004, 277). Likewise,

Madison in *Federalist* 10 writes of "the suffrages of the people . . . more likely to center on men who possess the most attractive merit and the most diffusive and established characters" in large republics, where "each representative will be chosen by a greater number of citizens" (45). Publius's emphasis on representatives as natural aristocrats implies a limited role for the constituents, albeit balanced against the conception of a participating citizenry.

Publius solves—more accurately, manages or balances—the tension between the representative as trustee versus delegate, as did Cicero, prudentially. Most of Publius's references to "prudence" in *The Federalist*, however, appear far removed from the orator's prudence à la Cicero. Instead of Cicero's attention to *human* prudence, Publius most commonly speaks of the *institutional* prudence of the Constitution—checks and balances, separation of powers, federalism, and so on. These "inventions of prudence," as Madison terms them in *Federalist* 51 (253), are noteworthy for limiting the powers of self-interested and passionate citizens *and* politicians. Although the authors of *The Federalist* may limit human prudence, they far from eliminate it. The prudence of the orator, now vested in the representative, is present in *The Federalist*, albeit not as explicitly as in Cicero or Burke. Prudence remains the means to navigate between the representative's "subordination to" and "independence from" the represented.

The Federalist's discussion of the political representative is largely abstract (e.g., discussing how the new constitutional structure is likely to engender good representatives) rather than specific (e.g., representatives are not advised on how to act in particular circumstances, such as when to defer to the electors or act independently). But Ciceronian prudence, grounded in the rhetorical situation, is characterized by its specificity, seeking the best way to speak or act according to the occasion. Such rhetorical prudence, however, is evinced in Publius's accounts of the Constitutional Convention (especially Jay's *Federalist* 2 and Madison's *Federalist* 37–40). In these accounts, the authors address the prudent actions of representatives in a particular situation: the deliberations surrounding the writing of the US Constitution. In praising the convention's delegates for their practical wisdom, Publius in effect presents these delegates as exemplars of prudence for future legislative representatives after the Constitution's approval.

The Federalist's descriptions of the delegates at the convention and of future congressional representatives do not differ appreciably, except for attributing to the delegates qualities more directly related to their actual deliberating, qualities that are linked to prudence. For example, as seen above, the anticipated representative is depicted as wise, virtuous, and acting for the common good. The representative is also portrayed as patriotic and a lover of justice (Hamilton, Madison, and Jay 2004, 44). Likewise, in *Federalist 2*, Jay writes of the convention delegates as men, "many of whom had become highly distinguished by their patriotism, virtue and wisdom" (7). But Jay also lauds them in language suited to past decision making. In the same article, he writes that they recommended "only such measures, as after the most mature deliberation they really thought *prudent* and adviseable" (8; emphasis added). For Madison and Hamilton, prudence was manifested in the delegates' willingness to compromise their ideal theory to circumstance. The Connecticut Compromise between large and small states becomes the primary venue for prudence. In *Federalist 37*, Madison states that due to circumstances "the Convention must have been compelled to sacrifice theoretical propriety to the force of extraneous considerations. . . . [U]nder the pressure of all these difficulties, the Convention [was] forced into some deviations from that artificial structure and regular symmetry, which an abstract view of the subject might lead an ingenious theorist to bestow on a Constitution planned in his closet or in his imagination" (173). Hamilton, in *Federalist 62*, speaks to the same conflict between large and small states, and like Madison he identifies compromise as the only possible solution. Again, like Madison, he contrasts theory, which cannot always be adopted, with phrases redolent of prudence—"mutual deference and concession," "the peculiarity of our political situation," "advantageous consequences which may qualify the sacrifice"—and even "the advice of *prudence*" itself, by which Hamilton justifies the convention's departures from unrealizable ideals (emphasis added).

Returning to prudence in determining the balance between trustee and delegate, the example of the convention suggests how representatives must adapt their decisions to circumstance, including compromising ideals to political necessities. When, then, do representatives need to reflect the current opinions of the represented, and when should they depart from the views of the represented? The answer is based on the two conceptions of the people presented in *Federalist 63*: first, as reflecting the common good in their current opinion (i.e., when popular opinion is the same as "the cool and deliberate sense of the community"); second, when the people support partial interests, a temporary condition "which they themselves will afterwards be the most ready to lament and condemn." In the first instance, Publius expects the representative to transmit the represented's views as they are. In the second case, Publius expects the representative to substitute his considered opinions for the "temporary or partial considerations" that have gripped the represented, which he writes of in *Federalist 10*. The description of decision making in the convention, however, implies that representatives should, or at least may, sometimes prudently adapt ideals, like the general interest, to political exigencies. Partial interests at the convention were acceded to so long as these concessions did not thwart the public good as the final result. Publius implies that the need to curry favor with the public is most critical when treating the pursuit of reelection to office by members of the House of Representatives. These representatives are restrained by frequent elections, and in *Federalist* 57, Madison expects that "they will be compelled to anticipate the moment when power is to cease, when their exercise of it is to be reviewed, and when they must descend to the level from which they were raised" (Hamilton, Madison, and Jay 2004, 279). Unlike the members of the Senate, who are elected for six-year terms, the members of the House must prudently attend to their electors' desires.

Like Cicero, who publicly endorsed popular positions he personally opposed to garner support for future political ventures, *The Federalist* does not demand that representatives turn a blind eye to their political ambitions—quite the opposite—so long as the common good emerges in the end. Thus, in *Federalist* 35 Hamilton assumes that citizens will vote for representatives who defend their partial interests—merchants representing commercial and manufacturing interests and landholders representing the interests of landed property—and he maintains, with no moral disapproval, that candidates for the favor of the people "should be willing to allow them their proper degree of influence upon his conduct" (Hamilton, Madison, and Jay 2004, 161). In *Federalist* 35, granting the people their "proper degree of influence"—even when their interest is partial—is acceptable because their factionalism is negated by representatives whose origins are in "the learned professions." These representatives, according to Hamilton, are the likeliest impartial arbiters, who will side with either of the partial interests "so far as it shall appear to [them] conducive to the general interests of the society" (161). Prudence, it would seem, does not demand the same actions of representatives, given that they must satisfy different electorates.

John Stuart Mill and Ciceronian Representation

Of the three modern theorists discussed in this chapter, John Stuart Mill devotes himself most to the popular role in government. Mill maintains that "it is evident, that the only government which can fully satisfy all the exigencies of the social state, is one in which the whole people participate," and popular "participation should everywhere be as great as the general degree of improvement of the community will allow" (1977a, 412). Nevertheless, Mill acknowledges, "since all cannot, in a community exceeding a single small town, participate personally in any but some very minor portions of the public business, it follows that the ideal type of a perfect government must be representative" (412).

Like Burke and Publius, Mill seeks to ensure that electoral safeguards are in place so that representatives do not stray *too* far from their electors. Even more than the other thinkers, the nineteenth-century advocate of representative government emphasizes that the representative's "obligation of a frequent return to [his constituents] for a renewal of his commission, is indispensable to keeping his temper and character up to the right mark" (Mill 1977a, 501). Mill, however, differs from Burke and Madison, and Cicero before them, in rejecting the inherently moral character of the "sense of the community," whether this sense is defined as current public opinion or as ancestral ideals. Mill argues that opinions around which a consensus has formed are not necessarily true. Every age has held opinions "which subsequent ages have deemed not only false but absurd; and it is as certain that many opinions, now general, will be rejected by future ages, as it is that many, once general, are rejected in by the present" (Mill 1977b, 230). Rather than standing in reverence of the wisdom of the ages, like Cicero and Burke, Mill (1977b, 272) rails against the "despotism of custom [that] is everywhere the standing hindrance to human advancement."

Although the community values, "may be in some points erroneous," Mill (1977a) defends the significance—even the obligatory nature—of these ideals on prudential grounds: "Such convictions, when they exist in a people, or in any appreciable portion of one, are entitled to influence in virtue of their mere existence, and not solely in that of the probability of their being grounded in truth." Mill recognizes the political fact that "[a] people cannot be well governed in opposition to their primary notions of right." The proper relationship between governors and governed, representatives and represented, "does not require the electors to consent to be represented by one who intends to govern them in opposition to their fundamental convictions" (510–11). Mill goes so far as to contend that electors are "not only entitled, but often bound, to reject one who differs from themselves on the few articles which are the foundation of their political belief" (511). Any representative who refuses to submit to the basic values of the electorate can justifiably be dismissed by the voters.

Consistent with the "standard account of representation," Mill (1977a) retains the balance between the responsiveness of the politician to the electors and the independence of the politician from the voters: "We have from the first affirmed . . . the coequal importance of two great requisites of government: responsibility to those, for whose benefit political power ought to be, and always professes to be, employed; and jointly therewith, to obtain, in the greatest measure possible, for the function of government, the benefits of superior intellect" (506). And, he writes: "It is important that [the representative] have the greatest latitude of individual opinion and discretion, compatible with the popular control essential to free government" (501).

When viewing the representative as a trustee acting for the common good, Mill also upholds the tradition dating back to Cicero, which Burke and Publius preserve, of the orator-statesman qua natural aristocrat: "Like Cicero, Mill believed that a law is good when it 'considers the welfare of the people rather than their wishes' . . . : citizens have to be persuaded that what they perceive to be a short-term loss would, in fact, be a long-term gain" (Urbinati 2002, 114).[23] Accordingly, their representatives aim at the "common good" or "general interest," which is morally superior to "private partialities" (Mill 1977a, 412).

Mill's description of the Roman Senate, ideally composed of the members of the natural aristocracy, parallels Cicero's own words. Cicero describes the Roman Senate as "a wise deliberative body" (1942a, 2.33) that would act "as the guardian, the president, the defender of the State" (1958a, 137); Mill (1977a, 516) hails the same body as "the most consistently prudent and sagacious body that ever administered public affairs." To Mill, a contemporary English council analogous to the Roman Senate would be composed "of those most competent, . . . most inclined to lead [the people] forward in any right course." This council "to whom the task would be entrusted of rectifying the people's mistakes, would not represent a class believed to be opposed to their interest, but would consist of their own natural leaders in the path of progress" (516; see also 478). This belief in progress, however, distinguishes Mill's natural aristocracy from Cicero's and Burke's. Although Mill, like these predecessors, supports the common people's "deference to mental superiority" in the form of their representatives, Mill's (1977b, 267–68) "persons of genius" are dedicated to originality, the discovery of new truths, the commencing of new practices, and setting the example of "more enlightened conduct," not custom or reverence for the *mos maiores* because of their antiquity.

Although Mill values prudence as the primary faculty in political decision making, in line with the Ciceronian outlook on representation, he differs from Cicero, Burke, and Publius in vesting the electors, *not* the representative, with the duty to determine the prudent balancing between trustee and delegate. For Mill, successful statesmen were prudent statesmen. Hence, in praising the Roman Senate, he terms it "the most prudent and sagacious body" ever. And in enumerating those qualities that make persons most fit for public service, Mill singles out those characteristics that are related to prudence: *actual* public service; manifesting wisdom that "has been justified by the results"; and having given advice that "has been followed by good consequences" (Mill 1977a, 508–9). But when discussing whether the representative should act independently or remain faithful to the electorate's opinions, Mill confers the power of determining this balance on the electors. *They* are to judge the matter prudently.

Mill emphatically refuses representatives the right to act prudently in responding to voters' reactions, even though these representatives formulate their political positions by prudently accommodating themselves to—that is, making compromises based on—other particularities. Mill charges the representative who compromises on the points of difference with the electors with "treason against his especial office [and] abdication of the peculiar duties of mental superiority, of which it is one of the most sacred not to desert the cause which has the clamour against it" (Mill 1977a, 510). Mill's demand here that the representative remain "a man of conscience" who insists "on full freedom to act as he in his own judgment deems best" parallels his account of the person of genius in *On Liberty*, whose individuality is a bulwark against the tyranny of prevailing opinion. In exacting such moral purity of the representative, Mill sacrifices this public servant's political efficacy, a goal important not only to Cicero, Burke, and Publius but to Mill himself in his broader treatment of the representative.

CONCLUSION: IMPLICATIONS OF CICERONIAN REPRESENTATION

Against the scholarly consensus that political representation is a modern phenomenon, I have argued in this chapter that Cicero develops an outlook on representation tied to his idealization of the orator-statesman, which is consistent with what Rehfeld calls the "standard account" of political representation. I have further argued that Cicero's rhetorically based view of representation is taken up, consciously or not, by Edmund Burke, the authors of *The Federalist* (a.k.a. "Publius"), and John Stuart Mill in their versions of political representation. I have supported this argument by showing that these modern authors understand *sensus communis* and prudence in a specifically Ciceronian sense and make use of these concepts in explaining their views on representation. If these arguments are correct, then Rehfeld's "general theory of political representation" is more problematic than initially appears. Because the moral values of the standard account are more deeply rooted than he suggests, dating back to Cicero and revived by the Anglo-American founders of modern representation, separating out the empirical from the normative deeply damages representation as we have come to know it.

Rehfeld's other significant departure from the reigning view of representation is his call for supplanting the trustee-delegate distinction with a tripartite set of distinctions based on the decision maker's aim of legislation, source of judgment, and responsiveness to sanctions. He maintains that the traditional binary conceals the more complex possibilities inherent in representation (and decision making more broadly). I have established, however, that the trustee-delegate distinction is an important part of the account of representation beginning with Cicero and later adapted by Burke, Publius, and Mill. Substituting Rehfeld's newly minted distinctions for the trustee-delegate debate, with its "historical longevity," obscures how the links between characteristics in the conventional dichotomy are not arbitrary but part of a cohesive whole. Cicero and the three Anglo-American thinkers agree that the aim of the representative is the common good. Again, all concur that the representative's source of judgment is this representative's own perception of what the common good requires. These thinkers manifest this view in their support of a representative who is part of a natural aristocracy and whose judgment is superior to that of the common people. But the modern writers see formal elections (and Cicero views popular support in general) as ensuring that the representative is ultimately accountable to the people. This viewpoint is based in the rhetorical situation in which orators *and* representatives find themselves, standing separate from—even above—the people in a certain way but, in the end, subordinate to the people on whom they depend for their power and legitimacy. This subordination to the people also enjoins representatives to base their judgment on the community's assumptions, the *sensus communis.* The writers examined in this chapter acknowledge that prudence, as Cicero conceives it, shapes the representative's judgment. Prudence is, at least for Cicero and Publius, what determines a representative's responsiveness to sanctions. Even Burke does not exclude the possibility, in all cases, of a representative rightfully taking sanctions into account when arriving at a judgment. For these theorists, "dependent" judgment and "induced" responsiveness meld into a single category when prudent concern for one's future opportunities influences the representative's policy position. Only Mill explicitly condemns an induced representative, notwithstanding Mill's overall commitment to prudence in representatives' decision making.

CHAPTER 6

Deliberative Democracy and Rhetoric: Cicero, Oratory, and Conversation

In the previous chapter we saw that Cicero's conception of representation presupposes that the people are ultimately sovereign, as manifested by the people's right to vote in the assemblies (Millar 1998, 172–74). In addition, Ciceronian representation posits that the orator is a kind of representative, who, although retaining a degree of independence from the people, must ground his arguments on the deeply rooted values of the community. For Cicero, the orator is given his authority (or has it removed) by his audience, the people. Although Cicero acknowledges the principle of popular sovereignty, he does not concern himself with the people's need to discuss political issues with each other (prior to their voting) as part of their sovereign powers. Rather, he accepts the Roman practice of the *contio*, in which political issues are debated in front of the *populus*, but only by persons whom the presiding magistrate selects (Morstein-Marx 2004, 7–12). Popular conversation ensues in the period—usually about three weeks—between the authorized public speeches of the *contiones* and voting, but neither Cicero nor other writers of the period promote such speech, presumably out of fear of encouraging an overly participatory *populus*, who might threaten the prerogatives of the *optimates*.

By contrast, in modern representative democracies, there is common acceptance of the practical need for, and the normative importance of, political discussion among citizens. By the eighteenth century, the French philosopher le Marquis de Condorcet defends the idea of popular conversation where citizens meet and exchange views, "to allow the people to understand an issue and clarify their views" and to arrive at a judgment that they "will then express in the act of voting" (Urbinati 2006, 202–3).

The dominant model of popular discussion today is deliberative democracy, whose proponents maintain that democracy requires not only voting per se but also a process of deliberation among citizens: "It is a necessary condition for attaining legitimacy and rationality with regard to collective decision making processes in a polity, that the institutions of this polity are so arranged that what is considered in the common interest of all results from processes of collective deliberation conducted rationally and fairly among free and equal individuals" (Benhabib 1996b, 69).[1] Seyla Benhabib, like most deliberative democrats, values deliberation on practical grounds, that is, improving decision making through collective rationality, but also argues that deliberation morally legitimates the coercive powers of democratic institutions. Thus, Benhabib explains: "only those norms (i.e., general rules of action and institutional arrangements) can be said to be valid (i.e., *morally binding*) . . . , if such agreement were reached as a consequence of a process of *deliberation*" (Benhabib 1996b, 70; emphases added). Likewise, Bernard Manin et al. argue that the majority principle in democracies, which requires the minority to follow the decisions of the majority, receives its legitimacy from "the deliberative process in which everyone was able to take part, choose among several solutions, and remain free to approve or refuse the conclusions developed from the argument" (Manin et al. 1987, 359). Although the minority is forced to follow a decision that they had opposed, the minority was included in the decision making process—"a process in which the minority point of view was also taken into consideration" (359).[2]

Common to most contemporary proponents of deliberative democracy is the assumption that deliberation is manifested in conversation, which is the preferred model of political communication.[3] For such political theorists as Amy Gutmann, Dennis Thompson, Seyla Benhabib, Joshua Cohen, John Dryzek, Cass Sunstein, and James Fishkin, deliberative democracy is an ideal of reasoned political discourse,[4] in which political deliberation takes the form of "public conversation" (or "discourse" or "dialogue") (Gutmann and Thompson 1996, 131). Simone Chambers summarizes the consensus among nearly all deliberative democrats: "Contemporary theory almost always understands this process [of deliberation] as ideally undertaken in dialogue and conversation with others" (Chambers 2009, 332). She further acknowledges the "obvious affinities between the critical role of dialogue in forcing interlocutors to give an account, and the ideals of deliberative democracy" (329).[5]

Unlike proponents of deliberative democracy, Cicero, like other classical rhetoricians, identifies deliberative oratory, not conversation, as the dominant genre of political speech. Cicero, however, also identifies conversation (*sermo*) as another kind of rhetoric that was not much discussed by other ancient rhetoricians. His conception of conversation anticipates the ideal of conversation upheld by today's advocates of deliberative democracy. (This similarity between conversational models, however, has not been recognized by most theorists of deliberative democracy, who largely identify their discursive ideal with more recent figures, like Jürgen Habermas or Immanuel Kant.)[6] By comparing both Ciceronian oratory and conversation with deliberative democratic discourse, we shall see why Cicero chooses political oratory over conversation as the primary mode of political communication. And in analyzing Cicero's rationale for selecting oratory over conversation, we shall see the relevance of his arguments to contemporary politics. I argue later in this chapter that Cicero's choice of deliberative oratory over deliberation qua conversation better reflects the reality of politics not only in his time but in our own, and that deliberative democracy's moral requirements do not sufficiently take into account the actual practice of politics. Ideals are morally useful. The deliberative democrats' ideal of a deliberative society, however, is sufficiently out-of-touch with politics as practiced (or even possible) that it undermines the value of their deliberative ideal.

DELIBERATIVE ORATORY AND CONVERSATION IN CICERO

The Deliberative Genre

Beginning with Aristotle, the principal exponents of classical rhetoric, including Cicero, have identified three basic categories of speech: deliberative, judicial or forensic, and epideictic or demonstrative (Aristotle 1991, 1.3; Cicero 1949, 1.7; Quintilian 2001b, 3.4.12–15). The deliberative genus has its origins in the political assembly, where the deliberative orator seeks to persuade or dissuade his audience from taking action, like going to war. Judicial oratory is used in the courtroom, where the speaker tries to persuade the jury of his (or his client's) innocence or guilt. And epideictic oratory is the genre concerned with praise and blame, intended, most often, for ceremonial occasions like funerals.

Although I am specifically concerned here with the deliberative genre, not public oratory in general, the three oratorical genera, or at least the deliberative and the judicial, which are discussed most by Cicero (and in the major texts of classical rhetoric), possess five common characteristics: they are directed to the concrete; they are delivered in popular arenas; they structure the relationship between participants unequally; they appeal to emotions; and they are agonis-tic.[7] Because of these common characteristics, I examine deliberative oratory in the broader context of the chief oratorical genres.

That the main tendency of classical rhetoric is directed to the concrete means, first, that the orator attempts to lead his audience to action. This rela-tionship between rhetoric and action is explicit in the traditional three *officia oratoris*, or duties of an orator: to prove (*probare*) or instruct (*docere*), to please (*delectare*), and to stir (*movere*). Of the three *officia*, it is the last duty, which is focused on action, that receives Cicero's highest praise: "it is the one thing of all that avails most in winning verdicts," and in it "is summed up the entire virtue of the orator" (1939b, 69–70). Cicero gives voice to the orator's goal of persuad-ing to action by arguing that action surpasses speculative knowledge because "study and knowledge of the universe would somehow be lame and defective, were no practical results to follow" (Cicero 1913a, 1.153).

To say that rhetoric is concrete indicates, second, that orators concern them-selves with specific and immediate matters, not abstract questions (O'Malley 1979, 41). The distinction between the specific and immediate on the one hand and the abstract on the other is captured by the rhetorical division between *the-ses* and *hypotheses*, *definite* and *indefinite* questions: "*Definite* questions involve facts, persons, time and the like"; "*indefinite* questions are those which may be maintained or impugned without reference to persons, time or place and the like."[8] The rhetorician has traditionally involved himself with the *definite* question, the philosopher with the *indefinite* question. Thus, the young Cicero excludes the latter from oratory: "I think that everyone understands perfectly," he writes, "that these [abstract] questions are far removed from the business of an orator" (Cicero 1949, 1.8). And although Cicero in his mature writings even-tually includes the *indefinite* question in the orator's repertoire—at least in the "outstanding orator's"—abstract arguments in the main genera are still subordi-nated to the specific and immediate issues (1939b, 45–46; 2001a, 3.120–121).[9] As James May and Jakob Wisse observe, despite Cicero's later claim that rhetoric deals with *theses*, "all rhetoricians in their actual systems, restricted themselves to their traditional material, the rhetorical *hypotheses*" (May and Wisse 2001, 25).

Deliberative rhetoric and the other two chief types of oratory are also char-acterized by a popular audience: political meetings (*contiones*), juries, and crowds gathered for special occasions.[10] Rhetoricians note this fact by counsel-ing the orator to accommodate himself to the language and assumptions of the masses. Thus, Cicero observes that "all the procedures of oratory," as opposed to the arcane subject matter of other arts, "lie within everyone's reach, and are concerned with everyday experience. . . . [I]n the other arts the highest achievement is precisely that which is most remote from what the uninitiated can understand and perceive, whereas in oratory it is the worst possible fault to deviate from the ordinary mode of speaking and the generally accepted way of looking at things" (2001a, 1.12–13).

Oratory is hierarchical. In politics, for example, Cicero thought that while all male adult citizens, regardless of status, may have some voice in the government, the elite of good birth and wealth should be granted more power than the masses (Wood 1988, 92, 127, 165–68). Roman practice largely reflected Cicero's perspective. A few are speakers, the majority are listeners. This distinction between speaker and audience, assumed by classical rhetoricians, was the normal pattern of deliberation in the world of classical oratory. In republican Rome, deliberation in the Senate was closed to the common citizens, and in the *contiones*, as noted earlier, speakers had to be invited by the presiding magistrate (Taylor 1966, 15–19). As a classicist observes in a recent study, "the distinction between speaker and listener was also characterized by socio-political differentiation and a hierarchical relationship—with negligible exceptions, those who spoke were members of the political elite drawn from the higher echelons of society" (Morstein-Marx 2004, 16).

Cicero views emotional appeals as necessary in oratory. Cicero follows Aristotle's division among three modes of persuasion: *ethos* (character), *pathos* (emotion), and *logos* (argumentation). In oratory, Cicero emphasizes emotional appeals—the least rational—above the others; he depicts *pathos* as the quintessential oratorical talent. Thus, he writes that "everyone must acknowledge that of all the resources of an orator far the greatest is his ability to inflame the minds of his hearers and turn them in whatever direction the case demands. If the orator lacks that ability, he lacks the one thing most essential" (Cicero 1939a, 279). For Cicero, the masses do not decide on reason alone. The average person's nature necessitates extrarational appeals.

The manner in which the orator appeals to passions alludes to rhetoric's agonistic or "fighting" nature. The orator uses passions purposefully. He excites the audience's passions both to persuade them of his position and, in deliberative and judicial oratory, to defeat his opponent: "to prove one's own case and demolish the adversary's" (Cicero 1939b, 122).[11] The contentious character of political speech is suggested by the fact that the Greek word *agon* not only means "contest" or "struggle" but also denotes the "public assembly" and "assembly place" (Rahe 1992, 43) Consistent with the conception of oratory as agonistic, Cicero adopts the metaphor of the orator as soldier, vanquishing his enemies on the battlefield (2001a, 1.157, 2. 84; 1939b, 42), and rhetoric is represented as a struggle in which one side wins, and the other side loses.

Conversation

In addition to the three main oratorical genres, there exists another kind of rhetoric, conversation, which Cicero delineates in *De officiis*. There, he contrasts conversation, *sermo*, with oratory, *contentio*: "Speech also has great power, and that in two areas: in oratory and in conversation. Oratory [*contentio*] should be employed for speeches in lawcourts, to public assemblies or in the senate, while conversation [*sermo*] should be found in social groups, in philosophical discussions and among gatherings of friends—and may also attend dinners" (Cicero 1991a, 1.132, 2.48–49).[12] Although Cicero acknowledges that conversation is a distinct type of rhetoric, he admits that it is not adequately treated by the rhetoricians: "Guidance about oratory is available, provided by the rhetoricians, but none about conversation, although I do not see why that could not also exist" (1991a, 1.132). Not systematically analyzed by the ancient rhetoricians, conversation's rhetorical status has been easy to overlook.

Nevertheless, as a genre of rhetoric, conversation must be guided by rhetorical precepts: "such advice as there is about words and opinions will be relevant also to conversation" (Cicero 1991a, 1.132). And like all rhetoric, Cicero contends that conversation is governed by the principle of decorum, according to which speakers must accommodate themselves to circumstance (Ijsselling 1976, 35). Cicero's belief that conversation should be treated rhetorically would suggest that he formulated an appropriate decorum for his own conversational writings, that is, his dialogues, which include most of his rhetorical and philosophical works.[13] Cicero attests to his use of rhetoric in the dialogues, when he differentiates in *De finibus* between the rhetoric he employs there, "the rhetoric of the philosophers," and "the sort which we use in the law-courts" (1914, 2.17; 1927c, 1.112).

Sermo embraces the gamut of conversations, but I focus in this chapter on a subset of *sermo*: the philosophical dialogue. In his *De officiis*, Cicero delineates what appears to be a single conception of conversation. When examined in the broader context of his works, however, Ciceronian conversation is not a single category but encompasses several subcategories. (Even in *De officiis*, Cicero distinguishes between "philosophical discussions" and "conversations among gatherings of friends" [1991a, 1.132].) As will be seen, Cicero's philosophical conversation most closely anticipates deliberative democracy.[14]

What are the relevant differences between oratory and conversation? We can distinguish five characteristics of conversation that, when contrasted with the five characteristics of oratory seen previously, highlight the differences between the two rhetorical categories: conversation's philosophical orientation; its elitism; its social equality among interlocutors; *sermo*'s emphasis on rational argumentation as the sole (or at least predominant) legitimate mode of persuasion; and its nonadversarial character.

As already seen, oratory is characterized by its concreteness. Inasmuch as concreteness implies a concern with action, then conversation must also be characterized as concrete. So Cicero states: "Conversations are for the most part about domestic business or public affairs or else the study and teaching of the arts" (1991a, 1.135). These subjects are to be treated, in conversation, with an eye to how they will eventually be put into practice. Thus, concerning a dialogue about the Supreme Good, Cicero writes that "the argument ought to amend our lives, purposes and wills, not just correct our terminology" (1914, 4.52).

But even though conversation is action oriented, it is not directed toward a specific action, as is oratory. Conversation, then, is not concrete in the sense that it is directed toward specific and immediate matters. Instead of the *definite* question, conversation examines the *indefinite* question. Another way to describe this difference is to say that conversation is philosophical, and oratory is not. Conversation's philosophical subject matter is illustrated by Cicero's list of *indefinite* questions, or "propositions of an abstract character." The "indeterminate, unrestricted and far-extending sort of investigation" includes discussions of the following: "good and evil, things to be preferred and things to be shunned, fair repute and infamy, the useful and the unuseful, besides moral perfection, righteousness, self-control, discretion, greatness of soul, generosity, loyalty, friendship, good faith, sense of duty and the rest of the virtues and their corresponding vices, as well as the State, sovereignty, warlike operations, political science and the ways of mankind" (1942a, 2.65–68). These are the sorts of questions, Cicero explains, that fall outside the three main kinds of oratory, and although they are "spoken of by nearly every writer, [they are] explained by none." True, the orator may want to "weave [these questions] skillfully into his discourse, and moreover to speak of these very things in the same way as founders of rules of law, statutes, and civil communities spoke," but it is not his duty "to advise on these matters one by one, as the philosophers do" (1942a, 2.65–68).[15] In other words, the orator can use abstract questions to support his arguments, but such issues are not the focus of his speeches.

The affinity between conversation and philosophical issues is apparent from Cicero's own conversational writings. Cicero's philosophical works are mostly composed in the form of conversation, and even those dialogues that are not, strictly speaking, philosophical, reflect a philosophical tendency.[16] For example, Cicero's most important rhetorical work, *De oratore*, is a philosophical treatment of rhetoric, not a technical manual for orators. His goal, there, is to heal the breach between philosophy and rhetoric, for which he blames Socrates: "the source of the rupture, so to speak, between the tongue and the brain, which is quite absurd, harmful, and reprehensible" (2001a, 3.50–61). To philosophers who maintain that the *indefinite question* and philosophy are the concern of dialectic, not rhetoric, Cicero replies that such matters can be addressed rhetorically by conversation. Thus, Cicero speaks of the "rhetoric of the philosophers," an oxymoron to those who accept an unbridgeable gap between philosophy and rhetoric (1914, 2.17).

Conversation is well suited to philosophy because of the unhurried fashion with which its interlocutors and readers can consider the subject. They can mull over the issues and are under no pressure to make an immediate decision. In contrast to oratory, which addresses the world of *negotium* (the fact of being occupied), conversation is tied to the condition of *otium* (leisure) (Cicero 1933b, 2.3; 1991a, 1.13; 2001a, 2.19; Tinkler 1987, 287–88; Michel 1960, 365; Ruch 1958, 83–85). It is not that conversation eschews matters of business or public affairs, but that it approaches them with greater detachment. For example, rather than deciding on a specific question of war and peace, conversation considers the preliminary question of when is war justified. Cicero's own period of philosophical activity, when he composed most of his dialogues, took place during his period of *otium*, the years 45 and 44.[17] So long as he "was held entangled and fettered by the multifarious duties of ambition, office, litigation, political interests and even some political responsibility," he did not have the leisure to engage in philosophical reflection, the kind portrayed in his dialogues.[18]

The differences between conversation and the dominant genres of oratory in subject matter point to their distinct forums. The deliberative, judicial, and epideictic genres are addressed to a popular audience because they concern matters that the public at large can understand and decide: political issues that touch the people directly, the innocence or guilt of the accused, and personal character. Conversation, however, deals with philosophical questions that Cicero considered beyond the grasp of the common man. The appropriate context for conversation, therefore, is not the large audience but the smaller, elite group. As Cicero puts it, "the precision of speech we employ, when abstract truth is critically investigated in philosophical discussion, is one thing; and that employed, when we are adapting our language entirely to popular thinking, is another" (1913a, 2.35; 1914, 2.17, 2.80–81). Echoing Plato of the *Republic*, Cicero contends that it is not simply that the masses are intellectually incapable of being philosophical but that the masses are naturally antiphilosophical: "For philosophy is content with few judges, and of set purpose on her side avoids the multitude and is in her turn an object of suspicion and dislike to them, with the result that if anyone should be disposed to revile all philosophy he could count on popular support" (1927c, 2.4; Plato 1961b, 494a). The people's bias against abstract thinking absolutely precludes a popular setting for philosophical discussion.

Although elitist in whom he deems fit for intellectual conversation, Cicero is egalitarian among those considered competent, encouraging the participation of potential interlocutors. In politics, Cicero thought that while all male adult citizens, regardless of status, should have a say, the elite of good birth and wealth should have a disproportionate share of power relative to their number (Wood 1988, 92, 127, 165–68). But in conversation, once you are admitted to the group, no such barriers are erected to the expression of opinion. Cicero writes that in conversation no speaker should "exclude all others as if he were taking over occupancy of his own estate. He should think it fair in shared conversation, just as in other things, for everyone to have a turn." Thus, one of Cicero's interlocutors states: "Let anyone, who will, state the subject he wishes discussed" (1991a, 1.134; 1927c, 4.8). And as speakers are free in Ciceronian conversation to voice their opinions, they are also free to arrive at their own judgments (1927c, 4.7, 2.63, 5.83; 1933b, 1.17, 3.95; 1914, 5.76).

Unlike oratory, where Cicero counsels use of the most intense passions, conversation, for Cicero, ought to be "gentle," "calm and restrained" (Cicero 1991a, 1.134, 1.3). Classical rhetoric's two nonrational proofs, *ethos* and *pathos*, are excluded from conversation. *Ethos*, when understood as the appeal to the speaker's authority, is eliminated because, as Cicero argues, relying on someone else's opinion—Cicero includes himself—substitutes blind faith for reason (1933b, 1.10; see also 1927c, 2.63). *Pathos*, the eliciting of the audience's passions, is rejected in conversation because the passions, whether "distress and fear" on one extreme or "extravagant joy and lust" on the other, "conflict with deliberation and reason" (1927c, 5.43). In the interests of rational discourse and greater truth, Cicero advises the speaker to shun the passions and to avoid those actions that will excite them. Of all the passions, it is anger, in particular, that Cicero singles out for opprobrium. He does so because anger, more than any other emotion, undermines rational reflection: "nothing can be done rightly or thoughtfully when done in anger" (1991a, 1.136).[19] That anger is inappropriate to conversation, however, does not exclude it from conventional oratory. Anger and allied "negative" emotions like hatred, ill will, fear, and so on, are acceptable tools for the orator in persuading his mass audience (2001a, 2.185, 189–90).[20] Their exclusion from conversation, like the ban on appeals to authority, is the result of conversation's separate rules of *decorum*.

Cicero, however, wants to rid conversation of only those passions that are deemed destructive, what he terms "excessive movements of the spirit that do not obey reason" (1991a, 1.136). Not included in these prohibited passions are constructive emotions, like devotion, the desire for truth, or the impulse toward fellowship (1927c, 4.55; 1991a, 1.13). Cicero distinguishes between such well-reasoned affects (*eupatheiai*) and emotions in general (Graver 2002, 43, 135–38). The inclination for fellowship is the impetus for friendship, and it is friendship that is the paradigmatic association for *sermo* (Cicero 1991a, 1.50–56).

Conversations, Cicero writes, "flourish most of all in friendships" (1991a, 1.58). The relationship between interlocutors should resemble a community of friends. This conversational model stands in stark contrast to oratory's agonistic ideal, where fellow orators confront each other as adversaries. Where the orator aims in the dominant rhetorical genres to beat his opponent, the speaker's purpose in conversation is to seek out the truth, collectively, with the other interlocutors. Cicero, therefore, explains his own mission in *De finibus*, a dialogue on ethics, as follows: "For our object is to discover the truth, not to refute someone as an opponent" (1914, 1.13; see also 1927c, 4.47). Like Ciceronian conversation, the Socratic *elenchus*, "the method of scrutiny-by-cross-examination," presupposes friendship, or at least good will, between interlocutors. The inquiry, Plato writes in letter VII, must be conducted with "benevolent disputation" and "without jealousy (Plato 1961a, 344b). Both Socrates and Cicero use the dialogic method toward the same end of finding the truth. For them, the search for philosophical truth is better enhanced by the interlocutors' common bonds than by their antagonistic posturing.

Ciceronian Foreshadowings of Deliberative Democracy

Not surprisingly, Cicero's conception of conversation and the discursive model suggested by theorists of deliberative democracy are distinct. Ciceronian conversation is private, philosophical, and elitist; deliberative democratic discourse is public, political, and equal for all citizens. These differences, however, are not as great as would first appear. For deliberative democrats, the distinctions between public and private, political and philosophical are weak. Within deliberative democracy, Benhabib contends, "the lines between the public and the private . . . can be renegotiated, rethought, challenged, and reformulated," so that we might "reconsider and rethink very controversial [and traditionally non-public] issues about privacy, sexuality, and intimacy" (Benhabib 1996b, 83–84). In like manner, proponents of deliberative democracy emphasize the need for conversation on values. Gutmann and Thompson champion the advantages of deliberative democracy over "the standard theories of democracy" for fulfilling "the need for ongoing discussion of moral disagreement in everyday political life," and Chambers maintains that "highly contested notions of moral truth" should not be excluded from the public deliberation (Gutmann and Thompson 1996, 12; Chambers 1996, 76). Unlike those liberals who want to exclude such quasiphilosophical issues as abortion and euthanasia from public debate (Ackerman 1980), deliberative democrats eschew prior restraints on which matters may be publicly deliberated. And although Jane Mansbridge along with seven other prominent deliberative democrats (James Bohman, Simone Chambers, Thomas Christiano, Archon Fung, John Parkinson, Dennis F. Thompson, and Mark Warren) state that a deliberative system—a system that "encompasses a talk-based approach to political conflict and problem-solving"—engages in discussion in matters that "have a practical orientation," they write that by "practical orientation" they "mean the discussion is *not purely theoretical* but involves an element of the question 'what is to be done?'" (Mansbridge et al. 2012, 9; emphasis added), thereby leaving substantial room for philosophically inclined conversation.

Besides their common focus on values/philosophical matters, the two conceptions of conversation—Ciceronian and deliberative democratic—exhibit four other areas (paralleling the differences between oratory and conversation) with clear similarities: the forum of speech, the equality of speakers, the legitimate mode of persuasion, and the speakers' attitudes toward each other. The appropriate forums for conversation, for both Cicero and most theorists of deliberative democracy, are largely not public assemblies but nonofficial social gatherings. Cicero distinguishes between oratory, which was practiced in the public spaces of the Roman state, and conversation, which was used in informal, social settings.

Similarly, deliberative democrats seek to expand political discourse beyond the traditional forums of political deliberation. For some, like Gutmann and Thompson, the goal is not to reject the deliberations of official political bodies but to supplement the discourse of "legislative sessions, court proceedings, and administrative hearings" with conversations held in "meetings of grass roots organizations, professional associations, shareholder meetings, and citizens' committees in hospitals and other similar institutions" (Gutmann and Thompson 1996, 12; see also 40). Seeking to further expand the occasions for informal citizen discussions, Mansbridge identifies "the everyday talk of homes, work-places, and places where a few friends meet" as crucial parts of the full delibera-tive system (Mansbridge 1999, 212, 211).

The desire to move beyond state institutions is especially manifest in Haber-mas and in deliberative democrats most influenced by him, like Benhabib and Dryzek. Habermas's distrust of deliberation in governmental bodies can already be found in his historical analysis of the emerging public sphere. The bourgeois public sphere was the "sphere of private people come together as a public." Because the public sphere developed outside the state, its members could engage in rational-critical debate with each other and with public officials (Habermas 1989, 27–31). Criticism of the state was freer when voiced outside state institutions, in the coffee houses, salons, and political journals (31–73). When addressing critical political discourse in advanced Western democra-cies, Habermas also locates discursive democracy outside state institutions. Using the image of a "*decentered society*," in which "democracy no longer needs to operate with the notion of a social whole centered in the state," he looks to conversation in nonofficial associations—"the peripheral networks of the politi-cal public sphere." The deliberations Habermas envisions "find a basis in the associations of a civil society quite distinct from both state and economy alike" (Habermas 1996, 27, 29–30). Echoing Habermas, Dryzek is "profoundly suspi-cious of the contemporary state." For him and other critical theorists, "the ideal is a separate public sphere"; "the proper location for any discursive designs is the public space between individuals and the state" (Dryzek 1994, 40). Benhabib, like Habermas, defends the model of a decentered public sphere (Benhabib 1996a, 7). She rejects as outmoded the idea that legislative bodies are the locus of discursive democracy: "no modern society can organize its affairs along the fiction of a mass assembly carrying out its deliberations in public and collec-tively"; this fiction "belongs to the early history of democratic theory." Instead, Benhabib argues that "[*i*]*t is central to the model of deliberative democracy that it privileges*" less-formal, nongovernmental groups—"a *plurality of modes of association* in which all affected can have the right to articulate their point of view." These modes of association "can range from political parties, to citizens' initiatives, to social movements, to voluntary associations, to consciousness-raising groups, and the like" (Benhabib 1996b, 73–74; emphasis in original).

Cicero and advocates of deliberative democracy agree that the participants in conversation must be treated equally. In contrast to Ciceronian delibera-tive oratory, where most citizens are at best spectators, Ciceronian conversa-tion is egalitarian within the group: the characters in his dialogues encourage each other to speak and to decide individually about the issues discussed. The demand for equality is even clearer in deliberative democracy, where supporters of the theory list equality as essential to political discourse. Joshua Cohen includes equality—both formal and substantive—as one of four conditions for deliberative decision making (Cohen 1989, 22–23), and equality dominates James Bohman's list of the "basic normative requirements and constraints on deliberation" (Bohman 1996, 16).[21] For Benhabib, a moral principle that undergirds deliberative democracy is "egalitarian reciprocity," which maintains that "each individual has the same symmetrical rights to various speech acts, to initiate new topics, to ask for reflection about the presuppositions of the conversations" (Benhabib 1996b, 78; see also 69–70). This equality, which is at the core of deliberative democracy, is more than a right accorded all potential participants, more than the "absence of exclusionary barriers." It is a belief that, for deliberative democracy to work, "it is essential that as many voices as possible are heard in the debate . . . , that a high level of participation be maintained" (Chambers 1996, 197–98). While Cicero believed that political deliberation must be restricted to the few, deliberative democrats promote "extensive deliberation" (Gutmann and Thompson 1996, 37). Although in recent years some deliberative democrats have come to accept that oratory is a necessary part of political communication, that is, that political speech is structured hierarchically between speaker and audience, they do not abandon dialogue as the paradigm of political speech. For example, Chambers concedes that deliberation in a mass democracy must, realistically, include oratory—"monological speech"—which is asymmetrical (2009, 334). Nevertheless, she defends deliberative rhetoric (or oratory) because, she argues, it can ultimately involve participation by ordinary citizens: "Hearers must be engaged by the speech"; "[i]t ought to spark active reasoning and thoughtfulness" (2009, 335). Likewise, she maintains that although "face-to-face democracy can never replace mediated democracy," we can still hope that "first, face-to-face democracy supplements mediated democracy and second, that the process of mediation does not adversely effect [*sic*] the quality of democracy" (Chambers 2009, 341). What Chambers apparently envisions is a deliberative system that contains many forms of popular communication, including oratory, dialogue, and other less formal conversations, in which deliberation à la dialogue emerges from the interaction between the system's different parts (Mansbridge et al. 2012).

Cicero and theorists of deliberative democracy agree that rational argument, as opposed to emotional appeals, is the distinctive mode of persuasion in conversation. Unlike deliberative oratory, where Cicero often emphasizes the passions above reason, in conversation Cicero maintains that rational argument is the only acceptable proof. Likewise, deliberative democrats identify deliberation with rational discourse. Thus, Benhabib writes that collective deliberation must be conducted "rationally and fairly" (1996b, 69). For Habermas, deliberation legitimates public discourse and decision making because it is based on communicative rationality, "the force of the better argument," which "neutralizes all motives other than that of the cooperative search for truth" (Habermas 1995, 88–89). (Habermas contrasts communicative rationality or "communicative action" with "strategic action," in which actors are not interested in mutual understanding but in attaining their individual goals.) Because only the "force of the better argument" should persuade participants, Habermas and other theorists of deliberative democracy seek to "set conditions such that only rational, that is, argumentative, convincing is allowed to take place" (Chambers 1996, 99). He excludes "all those maneuvers by which a speaker engages with the emotions and subjective states of her listener. In conventional parlance, this means avoiding rhetoric, which has a bad name precisely because it engages not only with reason but also with emotions" (Allen 2004, 55). Echoing Habermas's opposition to the strategic use of emotions, in which the speaker advances personal, not common ends, Benhabib rejects "affective" and "situated" modes of communication. Such rhetoric, she contends, "*moves* people and achieves results without having to render an account of the bases upon which it induces people to engage in certain courses of action rather than others" (1996b, 83; emphasis added).

Because rational conversation is unlikely in mass democracies—for example, "the deliberative competence of mass publics is suspect" (Fishkin 1991, 21)—a growing number of deliberative democrats now champion minipublics as forums for rational, nonemotional deliberation. Minipublics are mini because they are small in size, and they are publics because "there is usually some claim that deliberation mirrors, represents, or speaks for some larger public" (Chambers 2009, 329–30). James Fishkin, perhaps the most renowned proponent of minipublics, describes his version of a minipublic—a "deliberative opinion poll"—as modeling "what the electorate *would* think, if it had a more adequate chance to think about the questions at issue" (Fishkin 1991, 1). In mass publics, emotions intrude where they do not belong, undermining deliberative abilities (Marcus 2010, 5). Fishkin voices his fear that emotions may sufficiently silence reason so that "aroused publics might, on occasion, be vulnerable to demagoguery. They might be stirred up to invade the rights or trample on the essential interests of minorities" (Fishkin 1991, 21). Fishkin believes that deliberative opinion polls, because they are designed to facilitate deliberation, can escape the irrationalism and emotionalism to which mass publics are prone.

Many deliberative democrats, however, have backed away from excluding emotional appeals from political discourse (Chambers 2009; Dryzek 2000,

5-55; Dryzek 2010; Bohman 1996, 7; Mansbridge 1999, 225-26; Gutmann and Thompson 1996, 134-37; Rehg 1997, 358-77). Notwithstanding this change, even these deliberative democrats define deliberation by its rationality, not its use of emotions. For example, Gutmann and Thompson acknowledge that "passionate," even "extremist" rhetoric may be necessary, but they categorize "impassioned and immoderate speech" as " 'nondeliberative" albeit acceptable because such speech serves as "necessary steps to deliberation" (Gutmann and Thompson 1996, 135; Garsten 2011, 163). Gutmann and Thompson even concede that "deliberation does not always have to take the form of a reasoned argument" because listeners "could respond with their own [rational] arguments" (1996, 136). Nevertheless, they legitimize impassioned speech as deliberative only insofar as the use of emotions ultimately leads to rational argumentation (in the form of rational responses).

Another rhetorically inclined deliberative democrat, John Dryzek, validates emotional appeals when such appeals enable the transmission of rational argumentation. Thus, Martin Luther King Jr. was able to move a white audience initially opposed to the civil rights movement "through frequent invocation of the language of the Declaration of Independence and the United States Constitution." Because of the place of these documents "in the hearts of white Americans," many whites were able to rethink their previous assumptions. By utilizing emotions, King could "lead adherents of the established discourse of liberalism to question and ultimately redefine some key terms of that discourse." Without emotional appeals, King's arguments supporting civil rights "would have fallen on deaf ears." Therefore, transmission of King's rational argumentation "was aided, perhaps even made possible, by the accompanying rhetoric" (2000, 52). For Dryzek, although emotions are an acceptable, even necessary part of political speech, they are only a means (and, therefore, subordinate) to rational argument.[22]

Cicero's view of the speakers' proper attitude toward each other in conversation is closer to that adopted by supporters of deliberative democracy than to the speakers' attitude to one another in deliberative oratory. In contrast to Ciceronian deliberative oratory, which is agonistic, Ciceronian and deliberative democratic conversation is cooperative; the speakers are linked "in a search for common ground" (Chambers 1996, 162). According to Benhabib, this cooperative-agonistic dichotomy underlies the distinction between two different political visions, between deliberative democracy (the "proceduralist-deliberative model of democracy") and the "agonistic model of democratic politics," advanced by political theorists like Hannah Arendt, Sheldon Wolin, and Chantal Mouffe (Benhabib 1992, 90-95; Benhabib 1996a, 7). Particularly in the deliberative democratic version of conversation, the common ground sought is not, however, always clear: truth? the best answer for the particular circumstances? or a modus vivendi? In addition, whether common ground means, in deliberative democracy, agreement or agreement to disagree is sometimes ambiguous. Cicero, for example, did not expect agreement between interlocutors in his dialogues, although consensus is sometimes reached between them (1933a, 2.147–48). Some deliberative democrats, however, aspire to consensus more clearly than Cicero did in his dialogues (Habermas 1979, 1; Chambers 1996, 156–57). Nevertheless, they concede that consensus is an ideal that cannot be realized in practice (Chambers 1996, 158). Like Cicero, theorists of deliberative democracy counsel civility, not confrontation, in conversation, even on those matters in which the interlocutors are destined for moral disagreement (Gutmann and Thompson 1996, 73–91).

A Ciceronian Critique of Deliberative Democracy

Why did Cicero view deliberative oratory, and not conversation, as the main genre for politics? Cicero's choice of deliberative oratory is based, partly, on the elitist assumption that the common people cannot be appealed to through reason. Because political speech is public and directed primarily toward the masses, Cicero believed that emotional appeals were necessary, and deliberative oratory made use of such appeals. Cicero held that conversation, because it is conducted among a smaller, more select group, could rely on rational argument alone. His distinction between the rational best class of citizens and the passion-driven common people, however, is a distinction that most would not find acceptable today.

Cicero's choice of oratory over conversation, though, is not based solely on an antiquated classist assumption. Rather, as I contend in this section, he also considers deliberative oratory to be the dominant means of political communication for nonclassist reasons—reasons that relate to the differences between oratory and conversation already delineated. I further maintain in this section that his reasons are still relevant today and can form part of a critique of deliberative democracy. Although Cicero's reasoning is substantiated by much current empirical research into politics, this research does not *prove* Cicero's position vis-à-vis that of the deliberative democrats; conclusions based on social-scientific evidence are suggestive, not definitive. Normative political theory, however, cannot ignore empirical political science lest it engender lofty ideals that are inconsistent with actual political practice—a point developed in this chapter's conclusion.

Before beginning the Ciceronian critique of deliberative democracy, I think it only fair to mention that deliberative democracy, by emphasizing the importance of expanding the forums of political speech (à la conversation), enlarges the possibilities of free speech well beyond those that Cicero imagined. As seen in the previous chapter, Roman citizens had opportunities to discuss political matters outside *contiones* (where they had no right to speak), but such informal speech was not legally guaranteed let alone promoted. In contrast, deliberative democrats encourage greater opportunities for popular political discourse. We must distinguish, however, between deliberative democracy's extending the boundaries of political speech by promoting popular conversation and its identifying political speech with conversation. Although the former is a good that few would deny, the latter is problematical for reasons Cicero suggests in his account of deliberative oratory.

Oratory is better suited to politics than conversation, according to Cicero, because of oratory's focus on action. As we have seen, conversation—Ciceronian and deliberative democratic—is more philosophically oriented and less directed toward action. Thus, while deliberative oratory is structured so that it initiates a formal decision to act, that is, voting—magistrates promulgated legislative bills in a *contio* between seventeen and twenty-five days prior to any vote on legislation (Morstein-Marx 2004, 8)—conversation does not lead in any direct way (or often in any way at all) to action. And action, for Cicero, is superior to "mere theoretical knowledge" because "learning about and reflecting upon nature is *somewhat truncated and incomplete if it results in no action*" (Cicero 1913a, 1.153; emphasis added; 1991a, 1.153). In contrast to Aristotle, who ultimately chooses the philosophical life as superior to the political, Cicero argues that the political life surpasses the contemplative: "For there is no principle enunciated by the philosophers—at least none that is honorable—that has not been discovered and established by those who have drawn up codes of law for States" (Aristotle 1984b, 1325b14–33; Cicero 1999d, 1.2; Wood 1988, 122–23). Although philosophers eschew the statesmen's morally ambiguous methods, Cicero concludes that statesmen, because they lead people to act, bring about greater good than philosophers (1991a, 1.70).

Habermas does not require that deliberation terminate in decision making (Chambers 2009, 333; Mansbridge 1999, 212; Mansbridge et al. 2012, 9–10). That political communication does not necessarily conclude in action, however, is not in and of itself a problem for some deliberative democrats.[23] Chambers, for example, argues for a view of deliberation in which "participants are interested in bringing about a 'change of heart,'" in which "communicative actors are primarily interested in mutual understanding *as opposed to external behavior*" (Chambers 1996, 99; emphasis added). But while mutual under-standing is admirable, the lack of action, in politics, has political consequences. For example, a discussion about racism may culminate with a change of heart for some participants, but unless we concern ourselves with translating ideas into action, then the external racism will continue untouched.

Gutmann and Thompson, however, maintain that philosophically oriented discussion—"moral argument"—*can* culminate in action because such dis-cussion often induces interlocutors committed to opposing philosophies (i.e., who are in "moral disagreement," as they term it) to change their views. Although Gutmann and Thompson argue that their study of deliberative de-mocracy reflects actual deliberation rather than preconstructed hypothetical agreement (1996, 16), they create agreement by excluding moral positions from deliberation because *they*—not citizens engaged in actual discussion—decide a priori which moral perspectives do or do not meet the standards of delibera-tive democracy.[24] For example, they exclude deliberative arguments based on fundamentalist interpretations of the Bible because they conclude (without the need of actual deliberation) that fundamentalist conclusions "are impervious, in principle as well as practice, to the standards of logical consistency or to reli-able methods of inquiry that themselves should be mutually acceptable" (56).[25] Utilitarians, at least those advocating a forceful account of utilitarianism, are also barred from deliberative democracy. As they explain, "If utilitarians are to re-main deliberative democrats, then they must let deliberation put utilitarianism in its place. If the aim is to find a perspective that all citizens can accept, citizens should make sure that utilitarianism and its ally policy analysis remain under the firm control of deliberative democracy" (196). Similarly, Gutmann and Thompson reject libertarian moral claims as logically incoherent and, there-fore, unacceptable from a deliberative perspective—unless potential libertarian deliberators "allow room for democratic decisions about some redistributive policies" (206–7).[26] Gutmann and Thompson also reject egalitarian arguments concerning health care when these arguments are grounded on too robust a version of Rawls's "Fair Equality of Opportunity Principle." Thus, they con-tend: "A deliberative democracy . . . needs to limit the demands of egalitarian opportunity. . . . A principle of egalitarian opportunity that requires (or appears to require) normalization across the entire range of basic opportunity goods should . . . not be part of the constitution of deliberative democracy" (214–16). As these examples suggest, rather than presenting moral agreement derived from real-life deliberations (which might include biblical fundamentalists, utili-tarians, libertarians, neo-Rawlsians, and other interlocutors who do not meet Gutmann and Thompson's deliberative democratic criteria), Gutmann and

Thompson offer solutions to moral disagreements attained through thought experiments in which the only moral outlooks represented are those they deem satisfactory according to their interpretation of deliberative democracy. Without their restricting the range of moral disagreement, interlocutors with substantial philosophical or ideological divisions would not arrive, conversationally, at a reasoned agreement leading to political action. Walzer's criticism of philosophical conversation (in Habermas, Rawls, and Bruce Ackerman) applies equally to Gutmann and Thompson: "they are armed, one way or another, against the indeterminacy of natural conversation. The talk proceeds by design to its designated end" (Walzer 1989, 187).

Another reason why Cicero opts for oratory, concomitantly discounting conversation, as the primary means of political speech is because oratory sanctions not only rational argument but also emotional appeals, which are essential to mass political communication. In contrast to Cicero, deliberative democracy has traditionally excluded or demoted emotional appeals, an important element in wariness toward, often explicit opposition to, rhetoric.[27] Even pro-rhetorical deliberative democrats, who have abandoned their theory's traditional hostility toward emotional appeals, generally rule out such appeals from deliberation itself, relegating the use of emotions to an ancillary role in the process of rational argumentation. Contra the deliberative democrats, however, Cicero adopts a rhetorical approach to political speech that affirms the interdependence of the three rhetorical means of persuasion (*ethos, pathos,* and *logos*), denying the categorical superiority of one proof (*logos*) over that of the others. He views human beings as complex creatures—rational and emotional—who must be addressed, depending on the context, by employing the range of *pisteis.*[28] Rhetoric, for Cicero, involves a balancing of rational and emotional proofs.

The appeal to passions is necessary in political speech, according to Cicero, because political speech often takes place in a public setting. Reason alone is insufficient in a large group, regardless of its social or class composition. This insight is familiar to many professors, who perceive that teaching styles will differ between a large introductory lecture and a small seminar, even if the quality of students are identical in each; the lecture will require more performance and showmanship than the seminar.

Despite his occasionally voiced disdain for the masses in relation to the upper classes, the public, for Cicero, is not synonymous with the lower classes, and deliberative oratory is not identical to speech before the ignorant masses. When members of the elite gather in numbers unsuitable for conversation, that is, when it becomes a public audience, then it also must be approached in an oratorical manner. Even in his idealized account of speech in the Senate (with three hundred members before Sulla's reforms circa 80 BCE and six hundred afterward), Cicero observes that when the "topic is so important," then copiousness (*copia*), the nonrational use of stylistic abundance, is needed "either to urge or to explain the case" (1999e, 3.40; 1928a, 3.40). And Cicero does not generally present the orator as artfully condescending toward his public audience. Rather, the true orator, Cicero maintains, must have "gained a knowledge of all important subjects and arts"; "unless the orator has firmly grasped the underlying subject matter, his speech will remain an utterly empty, yes, almost childish verbal exercise" (Cicero 2001a, 1.20).

As we saw in chapter 1, rational argument and emotional appeals need not be at odds with each other. Like Aristotle, who adopts a cognitive approach to emotions, Cicero recognizes that emotions can be rationally based.[29] Emotions can also provide greater awareness of political issues than unalloyed reason. Thus, a growing number of political thinkers have come to accept that political debate should be resolved through some mixture of reason and the emotions.[30] As Martha Nussbaum argues, we would not be better off if decisions were made by calculating intellects lacking empathy. Intellect without emotions "lacks the sense of the meaning and worth of persons" needed to deliberate about less visible human concerns, like far-off famines, homelessness, and safety standards.[31]

But even irrational appeals, for Cicero, are an inescapable part of politics. As he declares, "the greater part of a [political] speech must be devoted to exciting the emotions of the audience, at times *inciting* them, by direct exhortation or by some reminder" (2001a, 2.337; emphasis added). The significance of passionate appeals in political speech is due, to a great extent, to another difference between *contentio* and *sermo*, the agonistic character of the former and the collaborative nature of the latter. In philosophical conversation, the ideal is to arrive at the truth without an unshakeable commitment to any particular position.[32] Likewise, in deliberative democratic discourse, speakers are expected to be open to modifying their original opinions by the "unforced force of the better argument." In contrast, real-life political speakers aim at besting their opponents. Politicians use speech "strategically for the purposes of winning, which deliberative democrats condemn as anti-deliberative and plebiscitary" (Chambers 2009, 337). They seek to move the audience to one side or another because that is the side to which they are committed. As we saw in chapter 1, Cicero recognizes that the degree of irrational appeals will vary with context. In *De legibus*, he imagines an improved Roman Republic—which never materialized—a republic in which political speech would be conducted with moderation. But it seems unlikely that Cicero, a master of emotional appeals, believed that political speech could completely forego negative emotions.

Most empirically oriented political scientists appreciate the widespread use and effectiveness of strategic emotional appeals. For example, Lawrence Jacobs and Robert Shapiro have analyzed the common use of "priming" to move audiences (2000). As Jacobs and Shapiro explain, politicians "carefully track public opinion in order to identify the words, arguments, and symbols that are most likely to be effective in attracting favorable press coverage and ultimately 'winning' public support for their desired policies" (7). This approach to changing public opinion, which Jacobs and Shapiro (in line with social psychologists) refer to as "priming," "concentrates on raising the priority and the weight that individuals assign to particular attitudes already stored in their memories" (50). By crafting their arguments and rhetoric "to change public opinion and create the *appearance* of responsiveness as they pursue their desired goals," politicians, according to Jacobs and Shapiro, "manipulate public opinion . . . to move Americans to 'hold opinions that they would not hold if aware of the best available information and analysis'" (xv; emphasis in original). Although Jacobs and Shapiro do not describe priming as *emotional* manipulation per se, politicians who adopt a priming approach seek to highlight themes the electorate finds more appealing, in the sense of having greater emotional resonance. A priming strategy can also be used to oppose a policy by highlighting emotionally aversive themes—for example, opponents of Bill Clinton's health plan linked the policy to "big government," which "raised the salience of governmental *dread* as a yardstick for evaluating health reform" (51; emphasis added).

Although Jacobs and Shapiro date the beginnings of the priming approach to the 1970s (44), we can easily identify Cicero's use of this strategy in his contional oratory. For instance, Cicero identifies himself and his policies before the common people as *popularis* (i.e., favorable to the *populus*), the sole legitimate ideology in the *contio* of the late Republic (Morstein-Marx 2004; Morstein-Marx 2013, 43). Cicero elicits the audience's backing by employing the terms, themes, and symbols that appeal to the listeners' emotions, bypassing any real assessment of the laws and policies in question. Such is the case in *De lege agraria oratio secunda*, where Cicero, speaking *in contione*, seeks to defeat a measure for land reform promoted by Publius Servilius Rullus. Rather than address the real strengths and weaknesses of Rullus's agrarian measure—Morstein-Marx claims that Cicero "avoid[s] the policy issue entirely" (2004, 201)[33]—Cicero misrepresents the measure as a scheme to transform the ten land commissioners into "ten lords of the whole world" (1930a, 2.15). He further misrepresents himself as a *popularis*, "adopt[ing] for himself the paradoxical title *consul popularis*, that is, 'the People's consul'" (Morstein-Marx 2004, 194–95), thereby effecting an emotional bond between himself and his audience.

Elsewhere, in writings and speeches aimed at the elite, he attacks agrarian distribution as "subversion of the most fundamental bond of society" and justifies the killing of the most prominent champions of land reform, the Gracchi brothers, as enemies of the Republic (Morstein-Marx 2004, 195; Cicero 1977b, 1.3–4; Cicero 1991a, 2.43). Cicero is a principled opponent of agrarian reform that entails the extensive redistribution of land, viewing agrarian reform as the robbing of one man to enrich another (Wood 1988, 202–4). In the *Second Oration*, however, Cicero asserts his belief in true popular agrarian laws, like those proposed by the Gracchi, now described before a popular audience as "two of the most illustrious citizens" (1930a, 2.10–11). He declares that he is not against agrarian redistribution per se but only opposed to bad agrarian laws: "if the [agrarian] law seemed to me likely to be useful to the Roman plebeians, I would support and help to pass it" (1930a, 2.11). While posing as a *popularis*, Cicero concomitantly tars Rullus as a false *popularis* who endangers the freedom of the Roman people, *libertas populi Romani*—a central slogan of the *popularis* (Morstein-Marx 2004, 217; Seager 1972, 331–32).[34] Cicero inspires fear and anger toward Rullus by characterizing the proposed legislation as a dangerous agrarian law whose goal is to steal away "the *freedom* and patrimony *of the Roman People*" (Morstein-Marx 2004, 195; emphasis added). In the end, Cicero succeeds in killing the proposal with the people's presumed support, albeit against their apparent interests, by having the land bill withdrawn without coming to a vote (193). Although Cicero's opposition to the Rullan land bill reflects his belief that it and similar legislation "weaken the foundation of the state, disrupt the essential *otium*, foment dissension among the orders, and subvert equity" (Wood 1988, 203), he defeats Rullus's bill by masking his general conservatism on land measures—which would have alienated many members of the lower classes—by presenting Rullus's proposal as endangering the freedom of *all* Romans.

Despite Cicero's use of priming and other emotionally driven rhetorical techniques, nonrational political speech is commonly presented as a relatively recent problem that stands in contrast to the overall rational, argument-based political discourse of the good old days. In his seminal work *The Structural Transformation of the Public Sphere* (1989), Habermas contrasts the bourgeois public sphere of the late seventeenth and the eighteenth centuries, a period of "rational-critical public debate," with the consumer-driven, non-rational-critical interactions that succeeded the bourgeois public sphere.[35] For Habermas, the degeneration of the bourgeois public sphere is characterized, in part, by the transformation of the media from a locus of rational-critical argument to a purveyor of entertainment, which substitutes "stimulating relaxation" for the "public use of reason" (170). According to Habermas, the decline of the historical public sphere also witnesses the rise of such emotionally manipulative communicative forms as public relations (193–95) and political propaganda (203, 219–20), which are directed to a passive, consumerist public.

Kathleen Hall Jamieson distinguishes between the golden ages of oratory (at some indeterminate time before our own[36]) and the current era of degraded speech. In the golden ages, public speakers concluded their speeches "[o]nly after showing the flaws in the alternative opinions, weighing the objections to their proposals, and arguing the comparative advantages of the course they favored" (Jamieson 1988, 11). Today, however, rational argument and evidence are largely absent from political discourse. And while then, as now, emotionally driven narrative was "the stuff of poignant, powerful speech," that sort of "dramatization was formerly *an* element in a speech, often one that amplified a point already made in other ways"; but "[d]ramatically illustrated discursive argument has given way to dramatically bodied assertion" (13; emphasis in original).

Closer inspection of these golden ages of political speech, though, reveals the deliberative democratic quality of early political communication to be primarily fictive. Accounts of past political speech do not bear out the view that emotional appeals were significantly less pervasive. Even discourse in Habermas's paradigms of the bourgeois public sphere—the English coffee houses and the press—which he portrays as conversational not oratorical, were dominated by emotional rhetoric. The English coffee houses, which for Habermas formed a center of political criticism during "their golden age between 1680 and 1730" (1989, 32) were, actually, not noted in their day for their civil conversation but for "irrational, abusive, and manipulative" discourse (Cowan 2007, 1186, 1189).[37] Habermas appeals to the Whig historians' reimagining of the coffee house as "good-natured, egalitarian and sociable," which stands opposed to the "recalcitrant complexity of coffee-house history, where the coffee-house was equally the home of . . . incendiary rhetoric, dissension and discord" (Ellis 2006, xxiii–xxiv; Laurier and Philo 2007). And the eighteenth-century press, which Habermas describes as the "public sphere's preeminent institution" (1989, 181) is suffused with "appeals to fear and, its opposite, hope—perennials among classical rhetoricians" (Remer 2000, 78–84).

Irrational appeals to the emotions are an integral element of political communication dating back to the dawn of popular politics. For example, Peter Hunt demonstrates how pro-war orators in democratic Athens gained support for their policies by appealing to listeners' passions "based on the intimate and emotionally laden relationships" within the Greek household. Pro-war speakers played on their freeborn, male listeners' aversion to slavish and womanly (cowardly) behavior and their respect for (courageous) ancestors, employing metaphors derived from household relationships—metaphors that tended "to have more emotional force than intellectual structure"; their oratory expressed the simple message: "'Don't be a sissy. Vote for war'" (Hunt 2010, 108–33). Even Aristotle, despite his cognitive appraisal theory of emotions, advises speakers to uses pathos against reason, although such irrational appeals conflict with the norms of artful rhetoric.

Cicero's own speeches and rhetorical works, the best source on rhetoric during the Roman Republic, suggest how wide the gap is between political speech as he observes it practiced and the communicative rationality to which Habermas aspires. As Robert Morstein-Marx notes, with some degree of understatement: "We may safely conclude, even without further investigation, that Republican Rome was not a 'deliberative democracy'" (2004, 23). The twinning, in Cicero's Rome, of the best orator's "capacity to arouse emotion" with "the fickle passions of the audience" points to this putative golden age of oratory as the antithesis of a deliberative democracy; in Joy Connolly's hyperbolic description, the Roman rhetorical scene is "a terrifying spectacle of the republican citizenry as a collective of unreason" (2007, 234). Although Cicero and his fellow Roman orators employ rational argumentation, they do not abjure the exploitation of emotions to manipulate their listeners (Hall 2007, 227–29). Our cursory glance at the ostensible high points of political speech—democratic Athens, republican Rome, and the bourgeois public sphere—implies that deliberative democracy's model of rational communication remains an ideal far removed from the reality of political communication, a matter discussed later in the chapter's conclusion.

Yet another difference between oratory and conversation, which leads Cicero to favor the former as the paradigm of political speech, is the structural inequality of mass political communication. This rhetorical hierarchy is exhibited, during the Roman Republic, in the division between the minority of active speakers and the majority of passive listeners, embodied most visibly in the *contio* (Morstein-Marx 2004, 7–12).[38] Rhetorical inequality also reigned in the smaller, more egalitarian Senate: "only the leading senators . . . , as defined by their rank as ex-office holders and seniority were given an opportunity to speak. . . . Those farther down the ladder, especially junior senators who had risen no higher than the quaestorship, participated largely as silent members" (Ramsey 2007, 124–25).

This communicative inequality, however, is not peculiar to Cicero's Roman Republic but is the structural norm, by and large, for all popular political speech. For example, although Athenian citizens had the freedom of debate (*isēgoria*) in the *ekklesia* (Ober 1989, 104–12, 72–73, 78–79; Sinclair 1988, 32–33), the assembly in democratic Athens was informally divided between the relatively few *rhētores* (orator/politicians), who spoke, and the great majority of *idiōtai* (ordinary citizens), who listened (Ober 1989, 78–79, 104–12). Over two thousand years later, we see that the deliberative democratic demand for discursive equality was not met in the presumably "deliberative" ratification debates over the US Constitution. A study of one state ratification convention, in Massachusetts, for instance, demonstrates how the few spoke to the many. Three hundred fifty-five delegates voted in the Massachusetts convention, but only seventy-two are recorded as having spoken at all. Even fewer spoke with any frequency, with fewer than fifteen recorded as speaking six or more times (Riker 1996, 193). The democratization of the United States and Great Britain during the nineteenth century did not eliminate the division between speaker and audience, though the speech, whether oral or written, became less ritualized and more informal (Robertson 1995). As for democracies today, notwithstanding a multitude of popular political associations, Chambers herself concedes that "the size and unruliness of the mass public dictate that . . . deliberation [among the mass public] will often be asymmetrical, highly mediated, and distorted by the structural inequalities in society" (2009, 339).

In Ciceronian Rome, this inequality was determined, to a significant extent, by one's political position. With few exceptions, speakers were drawn from the political elite (Morstein-Marx 2004, 16; Polo 2011, 288–89). But the unequal structure of political speech, even for Cicero, is not simply the product of republican Rome's sociopolitical hierarchy. If that were the case, Cicero's choice of unequal oratory over egalitarian conversation would be less relevant both for elucidating current politics, in which public speaking and office are not solely the domain of the rich and powerful, and for the critique of deliberative democracy, which would be severely weakened by assuming an inexorable link between class and public speech.

Cicero identifies other reasons, more acceptable (and familiar) to us, for the structural inequities of public speech. Cicero recognizes ability, both natural and learned, as a source for the division between speaker and listener. In *De oratore*, Cicero has Crassus argue that native ability, "not knowledge of the principles and methods of speaking," accounts for an orator's excellence in speaking (2001a, 1.113).[39] But, while Crassus dismisses the possibility of eloquence without natural capabilities, he does not discount the role of training in forming the orator, as "art can kindle and stimulate" native capacities (2001a, 1.114). Therefore, Cicero has Crassus detail, through much of book 1 of the dialogue, what the orator must learn if he is to fulfill his potential. He must gain: "a thorough understanding of human character and the whole range of human nature" (1.53); a comprehensive knowledge of public affairs (1.48); knowledge of philosophy (1.52–57); expertise in all the noble arts (1.71–73). Besides acquiring this general knowledge, the orator must study the rules of rhetoric and consistently practice speaking well, exercising his memory, and training himself in proper delivery (1.134–59).

Although Cicero's Herculean demands are meant only for the ideal orator (2001, 1.78–79, 1.118–19), his basic assumption that only a minority of citizens are, for whatever reasons, likely to become effective political speakers is as true today as it was in ancient Rome. Lynn Sanders (1997) attributes the differentiation between better and worse speakers, as judged by deliberative democratic standards, to power inequalities in society.[40] Gutmann and Thompson respond to Sanders by unwittingly confirming Cicero's claim that most people, whatever their background, are ineffective public speakers and that only a relative few are capable public communicators: "Disadvantaged groups have usually found representatives from their own ranks who could speak for them, and who could articulate their interests and ideas, at least as reasonably and effectively as representatives of established groups. . . . [W]hen the representatives of disadvantaged groups are less successful in politics, it is rarely because of any disadvantage in deliberation" (1996, 132–33). Oratory captures this differentiation of abilities; conversation, including deliberative democratic discourse, does not.

The communicative division between active speaker and passive listener is also generated by citizens' differing levels of interest in political issues. People who are less concerned with politics are less likely to engage in political conversations. And many people want little to do with politics. Disinterest in politics is not restricted to the less powerful but also includes members of the social elite. The Roman Republic included a significant number of citizens who were part of the nonpolitical upper classes (Crawford 1993, 188–89). A case in point during the late Republic is Cicero's closest friend, Atticus. Although Atticus was qualified for a political life by education (being educated as a young man together with Cicero) and rank (born, like Cicero, to the equestrian order), he rejected the *vita activa* for himself. He held no political office and evinced little interest in politics, apart from his concern with how political outcomes might affect his financial interests—he was a man of extraordinary wealth—and physical security (Welch 1996).[41]

The varying levels of political interest among ancient Romans, even among their social elites, find their parallels in today's democracies. In *The Civic Culture*, the classic study of political attitudes in five democracies,[42] Gabriel Almond and Sidney Verba (1963) find that the levels of political cognition, feelings about voting and elections, and attitudes toward political participation span a broad spectrum in all five nations. Almond and Verba also present data about the frequency of direct, face-to-face communication about politics: talking politics is more common in the United States and Great Britain, rarer in Italy and Mexico, and somewhere in between in Germany (115–22).[43] Although they conclude that levels of political awareness, political affect and participation, and political communication are highly correlated with levels of education, the correlation is far from perfect. Many highly educated persons have little interest in politics, including talking politics.

Contemporary research in American politics recognizes a wide gap between a minority of politically informed and concerned citizens and a majority, who have minimal interest in and awareness of politics (Converse 1964; Berelson, Lazarsfeld, and McPhee 1954; Milbrath 1965; Zaller 1992; Hibbing and Theiss-Morse 2002; and Green 2010). Although the estimates vary from study to study, the authors generally suggest low political involvement by the vast majority of citizens. For example, W. Russell Neuman finds that the American citizenry can be divided into three "publics": the bottom stratum (approximately 20 percent) "do not monitor the political realm at all"; the top stratum (approximately 5 percent) is composed of "active and attentive individuals"; and the large middle mass (about 75 percent) "monitor the political process half-attentively" but can be moved to greater attentiveness at critical moments. Thus, Neuman states that "the mass public is for the most part uninterested and unsophisticated" (Neuman 1986, 186). Although low levels of political interest and political awareness do not preclude political conversation, little interest in and awareness of politics suggest (consistent with Almond and Verba's study) limited public discussion about politics. For example, Neuman's research demonstrates that "the behavior of participation in political discussion is strongly, positively, and linearly associated with levels of [political] sophistication" (93).[44] Like Almond and Verba, Neuman observes that education correlates positively with political sophistication (1986, 113). Nevertheless, again like Almond and Verba, the correlation is highly imperfect, meaning that many highly educated citizens are politically unsophisticated and display little concern with discussing politics.[45]

Deliberative democrats expect more political participation from citizens—specifically, political conversation—than most citizens themselves desire. If deliberative democrats simply asserted the formal right of every citizen to participate, their position would be unexceptional, consistent with the empirical evidence supporting minimal public involvement in politics. But, then, they would not be saying anything new: such a right is protected in the United States by the First Amendment. Theorists of deliberative democracy, however, assert more than a citizen's formal right to enter public discourse;[46] they demand a substantive right. Instead of equality of opportunity to participate, they call for equality of fact in participation. As Gutmann and Thompson contend, "a well-ordered democracy requires extensive deliberation" (1996, 37). Such widespread popular discourse, as empirical studies confirm, is not typical of American mass politics.

Popular political discussion in America falls short of deliberative democratic demands not only quantitatively but also qualitatively; most Americans are ill equipped to engage in rational-critical debate about political issues. Therefore, a growing number of deliberative democrats have lowered their expectations for popular political conversation. Thus, Mansbridge espouses the inclusion of "everyday talk" as a "crucial part of the full deliberative system," despite such talk "not always [being] self-conscious, reflective, or considered," that is, "not meet[ing] all the criteria implicit in the ordinary use of the word 'deliberation'" (Mansbridge 1999, 211).[47] Likewise, although deliberative democrats have excluded technical and scientific argumentation from deliberation because deliberation is engaged in by ordinary citizens, not experts (Manin, Stein, and Mansbridge 1987, 355), many deliberative democrats now acknowledge that deliberation among experts, not only deliberation among the citizenry-at-large, is an essential part of the deliberative system: "Deliberative stages include the selection of experts and the appropriate delegation of authority to them, [as well as] the expert deliberation itself" (Mansbridge et al. 2012, 15; see also Brown 2014).

Despite Cicero's esteem for the political life above all others—for example, he states that "virtue is most conspicuously displayed in eminent services to the commonwealth" (2001c, letter 377.5 [X.12.5])[48]—the Roman orator does not insist on the citizenry's (including members of the socioeconomic elite's) political involvement. Cicero reassures his intimate, Atticus, that he is thoroughly justified in avoiding the political life: "I have never felt any difference between us except in the modes of life we have chosen. What may be called ambition has led me to seek political advancement, while another and entirely justifiable way of thinking has led you to an honourable independence. In the things that really matter—uprightness, integrity, conscientiousness, fidelity to obligation—

I put you second neither to myself nor to any other man" (Cicero 1999a, letter 17.5 [I.17.5]). Vocations cannot be evaluated solely in the abstract. They must ultimately be judged by how they comport with one's nature: "let us follow our own nature, so that even if other pursuits may be weightier and better, we should measure our own by the rule of our own nature" (Cicero 1991a, 1.110).[49] Ironically, although deliberative democrats distance themselves from republican conceptions of civic virtue as too demanding (Habermas 1996, 27, 23; Chambers 1996, 184), Cicero's republicanism requires less of citizens than does deliberative democracy.

Although even critics of deliberative democracy have mostly accepted the deliberative democratic understanding of deliberation—if only to reject deliberation (Sanders 1997, 347–76; Shapiro 1999, 28–38)—the concept need not be delineated along deliberative democratic lines. The origins of "deliberation" are ancient, and its traditional meaning does not comport well with the deliberative democratic interpretation of the concept. The English "deliberation" is derived from the Latin verb *dēlīberāre*. Both English and Latin terms are defined similarly: the *Oxford English Dictionary* (3rd ed.) defines "deliberation" as "the action of deliberating, or weighing a thing in the mind"; the *Oxford Latin Dictionary* (1st ed.) defines the infinitive *dēlīberāre* as "to engage in careful thought (usu. in consultations with others)," to "weigh the pros and cons," and "to consider (a matter) carefully, ponder, think over." Although the Latin verb's initial connotation of consulting with others anticipates the deliberative democratic understanding of deliberation, its definition as thinking a matter over—suggesting mental reflection—is inconsistent with deliberative democracy's deliberation.

Deliberation, when used in the context of political speech in classical Rome, is linked to political oratory. Thus, in *De inventione*, Cicero refers to the genre of political oratory as *deliberativum* (1949, 1.7, 2.155; see also 1942c, 69–70). And, contrary to deliberation as rendered by deliberative democrats, deliberation in political oratory lacks face-to-face discussion. But where then is the deliberation in deliberative oratory? Not in the speech of orators, who refrain from considering the merits of the other side, at least in any genuine sense. (If they present both sides of an argument in their speeches, they do so to best their political adversaries by attacking their arguments, not to consider their opponents' arguments, which may then lead to their own change of opinion.) Cicero emphasizes the absence of deliberation among orators by terming political oratory in *De oratore* as a *suasio* or advisory speech (1942a, 2.333–34), which points up the orator's role in exhorting the audience to his point of view but does not suggest his participation as a deliberator.[50] At least in oratory, deliberation takes place among the listeners. Therefore, when discussing the *contio* in *De oratore*, Cicero has Antonius speak of *deliberation*—referring to the deliberation of listeners—being terminated when the audience realizes something is impossible or inevitable (1942a, 2.336; see also 1942c, 83). Given the absence of discussion in the *contio* and even the Senate, listeners do not deliberate, as deliberative democrats would have it, in face-to-face conversations. In the *Orator*, Cicero indicates once again that the public speaker does not engage in deliberation. He refers to the *illusion of deliberation*, where "[the orator] *will seem* to consult [*quasi deliberet*] with the audience, and sometimes even with the opponent" (1939b, 138; emphasis added), not actual deliberation. (This passage from the *Orator*, however, also implies that deliberation can take place in face-to-face speech, although the fact remains that no such direct speech occurred in either the *contio* or the Senate.) For Cicero, deliberation in public speech generally occurs in the minds of the listeners, what Robert Goodin describes as the "internal-reflective" aspect of deliberation, as opposed to deliberation's "external-collective" aspect (Goodin 2000, 81–84).[51] Accordingly, in writing of philosophical thinking in *De finibus*, Cicero uses *deliberare* to refer to the *mental act* of deciding the nature of the supreme good (1914, 2.115), not the external act of debate between exponents of the different philosophical schools.

The precedent for deliberation defined as internal reflection is found, centuries before Cicero, in another rhetorical society, democratic Athens. In a dissertation chapter on democratic deliberation in ancient Athens, Daniela Cammack (2013) shows that the general assumption that the Athenian *demos* engaged in external-collective deliberation in the assembly is mistaken. Although English translations have translated verbs associated with debates in the Athenian assembly with some form of the verb "deliberate"—implying external-collective deliberation engaged in by the assembly as a whole—Cammack argues that careful examination of the Greek terms associated with deliberation points out that different verbs were used to distinguish between speaking and listening. Two verbs were commonly used to denote speaking, usually arguing for or against a proposed action: first, *symbouleuō*, meaning "advise" or "counsel"; second, *dēmēgoreō*, meaning "speak before the people," which was almost always used to indicate speaking in the *ekklesia*. The verb used for listening to speeches was *bouleuomai*, the middle voice of the verb "*bouleuō*," which usually meant internal-reflective deliberation. The first set of verbs characterizes the speech of *rhētores* or orators, who assumed the role of advisors rather than deliberators. In contrast, the verb *bouleuomai* denotes ordinary citizens listening to speeches in the assembly. These citizens deliberated between the speakers' proposals before deciding, by majority vote, on a course of action, but their deliberation took place in their own minds, not in discussion with others.

Although deliberative democrats define "deliberation" as external-collective discussion, eschewing the possibility of deliberation as an act of internal reflection, the language of republican Rome and democratic Athens suggests that deliberation occurred almost solely—at least in the *contiones* and *ekklesia* of these polities—"within the head of each individual" (Goodin 2000, 81). Athens, in its day, was a mass democracy. With its approximate citizenship of thirty thousand adult males during the fourth century, decisions based, primarily, on public conversation were not realistic. External-collective deliberation was even less likely in Rome, with a probable citizen body of over nine hundred thousand during the late Republic. In this mass republic, most citizens, living too far from the city of Rome, were incapable of attending *contiones* and voting assemblies. The difficulties of external-collective deliberation are greater yet in today's mass democracies than in antiquity. As Goodin argues of contemporary democratic states, "it is simply infeasible to arrange face-to-face discussions across the entire community in today's mass democracies" (Goodin 2000, 82).

Given that large sections of the citizenry in republics and democracies, both present and past, do not engage in political discussion, popular deliberation that meets deliberative democracy's standards of deliberation is an unattainable ideal for most citizens. Habermasian deliberation stems from the "ideal speech situation," which is subject to the "unforced force of the better argument." But the ideal speech situation, although a standard toward which we can aspire, can never be achieved. Even Habermas maintains that idealized conversation may only "*perhaps* [be] . . . a form of life to be realized in the future," while he concedes that "there is no historical society that corresponds to the form of life that we anticipate in the concept of the ideal speech situation" (Habermas 2001, 102–3; emphasis added; xv–xvi; 1993, 54–55). (He also refers to the ideal speech situation as "fictitious" and a "constitutive illusion.") Similarly, Joshua Cohen speaks of an "ideal deliberative procedure," which is "a model for deliberative institutions" to mirror (1989, 21–22) but a model that is unrealizable in practice. But as Plato has Socrates explain about the role of ideals in the *Republic*, "our purpose is not to demonstrate the possibility of the realization of these ideals" but to "approximate to [them] as nearly as possible and partake of [them] as more than others" (Plato 1961b, 472b–d). Cannot the ideal of deliberation, as delineated by deliberative democracy, serve a similar purpose, and, if so, why does it matter—as I suggest it does—that deliberation qua deliberative democracy is unrealizable? We turn our attention to these and related matters in the chapter's conclusion.

Conclusion: Realistic Ideals

Although Plato presents his ideal state, the *kallipolis*, as unattainable—so unattainable that, like his other ideals, it is envisioned as a Form in a realm distinct from our own material world—not all thinkers conceive of ideals as impossible to achieve. Thus, C. A. J. Coady states that though most of those who write on ideals treat them as absolutely unrealizable (2008, 53),[52] some writers speak of "achievable ideals" or, at least, ideals that are not absolutely unrealizable (Coady 2008, 53–54). For example, Kimberly Brownlee stops short of identifying unrealizability as a necessary feature of ideals by claiming that ideals exist in varying degrees of unrealizability; "ideals as a class," she maintains, "can be distinguished . . . from deep impossibilities." As she conceives them, ideals "lie within what is possible in principle, though they often may sit at the outer limits thereof" (Brownlee 2010, 246).

I do not dismiss the utility of conceiving of ideals as unattainable. Thus, it seems reasonable to argue, as does Nicholas Rescher, that ideals can "play a positive and productive role in human affairs," even when they are unrealistic or unachievable, because of their capacity to guide thought and action in beneficial directions (Rescher 1987, 1). Utopian ends, however, may not only encourage progress toward an ideal but also impede forward movement when ideals distort the sense of reality necessary to improve on the status quo. Without a clear sense of what is realistically possible, the terrain ahead may be difficult, if not impossible, to traverse. This distortion of reality, with its attendant difficulties, is a salient characteristic of the deliberative democratic ideal.

Early theoretical defenses of deliberative democracy, which were largely unaffected by accurate empirical analyses of the practice of deliberative democracy, were sometimes overly optimistic in their assessments of the "deliberativeness" of communicative spaces. Thus, Benhabib describes the deliberative model of democracy as "elucidating the already implicit principles and logic of existing democratic practices." For Benhabib, "the deliberative theory of democracy is not a theory in search of practice; rather it is a theory that claims to elucidate some aspects of the logic of existing democratic practices better than others" (Benhabib 1996b, 84). Benhabib further points to the bright future of deliberative democracy by citing John Dryzek's work "show[ing] that incipient forms of discursive design already obtain" in a variety of societal institutions and associations (86).[53]

Overall, the growing scholarly literature on the quality and quantity of popular political discourse in advanced democracies, however, has only highlighted the gap between current reality and ideal. In recent years, Chambers and Mansbridge, among other deliberative democrats, have acknowledged that rational, noncompetitive, face-to-face discussion of politics in mass democracies is often impossible. Therefore, to avoid the pitfalls of a utopianism in which significant advances cannot be made toward their ideal, deliberative democrats have increasingly chosen one of two options: first, to create deliberative minipublics, thereby abandoning their ideal for mass democracy but retaining it for smaller bodies; and, second, to mitigate the importance of nondeliberative political communications by viewing them as being offset by the deliberative components of the larger system—in the words of Mansbridge et al., "an institution that looks deliberatively defective on its own can look beneficial in a systemic perspective" (Mansbridge et al. 2012, 3).

Both responses, however, are problematical. The problems caused by substituting deliberative minipublics for broad-based deliberations have been elaborated upon more fully by other writers (Mitofsky 1996; Sanders 1999; Lustig 1999; Chambers 2009), and, therefore, I do not offer a detailed critique of minipublics. Several criticisms of minipublics—specifically, Fishkin's version, the "deliberative poll"—however, include the minipublic's alienation of politics from place, its removal of political discussion "from the everyday loyalties and moral universes in which people live," and the inability of statistically random samples (required for deliberative polls) to "fulfill the job of political representation" (Lustig 1999, 18). Moreover, Jeff Lustig argues: "Fishkin's participants do not select themselves for this deliberative polling. They do not pick their own issues or prepare their background materials. They do not establish their own deliberated zone. They remain the playthings of highly capitalized, mysterious powers, reinforced in the hunch, no doubt, that independent, grassroots activity in the modern world is a futile dream" (1999, 20). The other attempt to deal with deliberative democracy on a mass scale, the systemic approach, appears to involve a leap of faith that deliberative and nondeliberative institutions interact with each other to "produce a healthy deliberative system" (Mansbridge et al. 2012, 2). But little hard evidence exists to substantiate the belief that nondeliberative practices, which had previously been considered adverse to deliberative democracy, should now be viewed as consistent with, even as promoting, a good deliberative system.

In contrast to deliberative democrats, however, Cicero's political ideals are attainable. Cicero instantiates his conception of an attainable ideal in his discussions of the model constitution in *De republica* and of Roman law in *De legibus*. In *De republica*, Cicero has Scipio Aemilianus contend: "I will state my own opinion and belief and judgment that no commonwealth, in either its organization or its structure or its conduct and training, can be compared to the one our fathers received from their ancestors and have passed on to us. . . . My description of our commonwealth will serve as the pattern [*exemplum*] to which I will tailor what I have to say concerning the best form of state" (1999d, 1.70). As Elizabeth Asmis interprets this passage, Cicero uses the Latin term *exemplum* to suggest that the Roman ancestral constitution serves as a model of excellence, "an 'ideal' in the sense of being a historically real model that is superior to all other models." Thus, Cicero idealizes the Roman Constitution, but "view[s] this ideal as a practical goal that can be realized" (Asmis 2005, 393).

In *De legibus*, Cicero proposes an improved code of laws, an ideal (or a near ideal) that is realistic. This proposed code of laws is in agreement with natural law, an unreachable ideal for almost all people, but is not identical to natural law (Asmis 2008, 3). Consistent with the Stoic definition of law, Cicero identifies natural law with perfect rationality, understood and obeyed only by the wise person (Asmis 2008, 12, 15). Because imperfect (i.e., nonwise) human beings, who account for all (or nearly all) humans, do not recognize the commands of natural law adequately, they are expected to obey only intermediate duties (not the perfectly appropriate actions required of the wise person), which are manifested in Cicero's law code (28). By distinguishing between the perfect duties commanded by natural law and the imperfect duties commanded by the best codified laws, Cicero creates two legal ideals—an ideal unreachable by all except the wise person and an ideal within reach of regular persons.

Cicero includes in his code of laws, as discussed in chapter 1, the obligation that "those things which are brought before the people or the senate be moderate" (1999e, 3.10). Although this law does not reflect the law or practice of Cicero's own day, it is proposed as a feasible ideal—in contrast to the unachievable speech ideal of Habermas and the deliberative democrats. Cicero does not provide a plan of how to achieve his ideal. Writing during the political instabilities of the late days of the Republic, it is unreasonable to expect him to delineate how his ideal might be put into practice. It is sufficient that he offers us an ideal that—given the proper conditions—*can* be put into practice.

CONCLUSION

I have argued in *Ethics and the Orator* that Cicero began a tradition of pragmatic political morality that still has implications for contemporary politics. The present-day relevance of the Ciceronian tradition of political morality, however, appears uncertain once we appreciate (as I maintain in the introduction) that one of the hallmarks of an intellectual tradition is the presence of an ongoing virtual conversation between members of the tradition—especially a dialogue between members of the tradition and its founder. But how can we speak of the continuing relevance of the Ciceronian tradition when Cicero, the founder of the tradition, is largely unknown today? Not that long ago, before the latter part of the nineteenth century,[1] Cicero's prominence as a classical political thinker and rhetorician was second to none: "[I]n the period of our past that gave rise to distinctly modern institutions and attitudes, he of all ancients was possibly the most esteemed and influential" (Wood 1988, 1–2). But now, as Neal Wood asks near the beginning of his study of Cicero: "Who today troubles to read Cicero, save a handful of Latinists and ancient historians, and an ever-diminishing number of students?" (1988, 1).

Although the past decade has seen a revived scholarly interest in Cicero's views on the relationship between politics, rhetoric, and morality—of which I count this work a part—he still remains little known among political scientists and philosophers, even among political theorists and political philosophers. Therefore, strictly speaking, the Ciceronian tradition of political morality is no longer an active tradition. But if we focus more on the wide-ranging acceptance of key elements of the tradition than on the pervasive ignorance of the tradition's provenance, the tradition is alive and well. Thus, many today accept the core truth of Cicero's approach, that is, that politics and politicians—to be effective— must be governed by a standard of morality that is, at times, distinct from the ordinary morality that regulates the private lives of the electorate. And in this book's introduction, we also see that a growing number of scholars oppose absolutist moralism in politics—consistent with Ciceronian political morality.

An example out of American history demonstrates how Cicero's conception of political morality was put into practice without the political practitioner knowing of Cicero's arguments for a pragmatic political morality. The example is that of Abraham Lincoln, whose actions at a time of political crisis find important parallels in Cicero's words and deeds. We have little or no evidence that Lincoln was familiar with Cicero's ideas, though he was probably aware, indirectly, of Cicero's oratory through Caleb Bingham's *The Columbian Orator* (1797), a schoolbook text, possessed by Lincoln, in which Cicero figures prominently in the book's speaking exercises. Nevertheless, wittingly or not, Lincoln's political practices hark back to those of Cicero. Like Cicero, who tries to save the Roman Republic from destruction, Lincoln seeks to prevent the Union from dissolution. Both men believe the safety of the Republic is their foremost moral obligation.[2] And, in pursuit of their ends, the two engage in ordinarily immoral and possibly illegal actions during extraordinary circumstances: Cicero kills the Catilinarian conspirators without a formal trial; Lincoln unilaterally suspends the writ of habeas corpus, as well as "proclaiming a blockade, extending the period for volunteer enlistment to three years, increasing the size of the regular army and navy, and entrusting public funds to private persons for the purchase of arms and supplies"—all initiated without authorization from Congress, although these actions would normally call for Congress's prior approval (Donald 1995, 303–4).

Lincoln also adheres to Ciceronian decorum by adapting his speeches to different audiences. In campaigning against Stephen A. Douglas for the Illinois seat in the US Senate, Lincoln accommodates his words to the context: "His speeches were noticeably more receptive to antislavery sentiment in northern Illinois. As he moved to central and southern portions of the state, his manner of expression appeared to correspond to the conservative attitudes of these peoples" (Heckman 1967, 104).[3] In Chicago, he decries "all this quibbling about this man and the other man—this race and that race and the other race being inferior" (Basler 1953, 2:501). But in Charleston, two hundred miles to the south, Lincoln affirms his opposition to "bringing about in any way the social and political equality of the white and black races." The physical differences between the races, Lincoln explains, "will ever forbid the two races living together on terms of social and political equality" (Basler 1953, 3:145–46).

Again, like Cicero, Lincoln defends the morality of his position by adverting to the deeply rooted values of the community. Thus, he condemns slavery as immoral by reading the Declaration of Independence as an assertion of America's permanent ideal of the equality of *all* men, despite the US Constitution's guarantees protecting the South's "peculiar institution"—the Constitution, for Lincoln, representing merely a "provisional embodiment of that ideal" (Wills 1992, 101).[4]

Lincoln's unconscious adoption of Cicero's morally pragmatic politics is, I think, not exceptional among politicians; I compare Lincoln (and not other, later politicians) with Cicero because, unlike most political leaders, Lincoln, like Cicero, confronted an existential threat to the Republic, and Lincoln reacted to the threat with Ciceronian moral pragmatism. But if Cicero's pragmatic politics is not uncommon—maybe even be the norm—among today's politicians, then what does the Ciceronian tradition contribute to contemporary political practice? I focus now on how that tradition's relevance for today lies in its recognition of a distinct morality for politicians, while also circumscribing the power associated with that morality by vesting the electorate with the power to determine decorum.

By recognizing a separate role morality for politicians, Cicero avoids the Scylla of absolutist moralism and the Charybdis of amoral expediency. Ordinary citizens are well aware that politicians act differently than they do. Politicians sometimes engage in actions that are normally deemed morally unacceptable but that the Ciceronian tradition finds justifiable. At one end of the spectrum are those actions that politicians usually justify because they promote state security—for example, drone strikes in which innocents are killed, extraordinary rendition, invasions of citizens' privacy, and torture or torture-like activities. Although these actions are often viewed as exceptional, they are, especially after the beginning of the War on Terror, a common feature of the political landscape. At the other end of the spectrum are actions decried by most citizens, but which the electorate also views as, de facto, an unavoidable part of politics—emotional manipulation of voters, deception, insincerity, abandoning or compromising of principles, and the like. Both ends of the spectrum and the range of morally dubious actions in between are proscribed by a morally absolutist approach. Because politicians cannot live up to the same standards demanded of ordinary citizens—standards that often tend toward moral absolutism—the imposition of such standards, as Stuart Hampshire warns in chapter 2, increases the danger of "set[ting] the politicians free to ignore morality altogether" (Hampshire 1989, 12).

In addition to its effect on politicians' actions, the choice of moral absolutism over moral pragmatism in politics has implications for ordinary citizens' attitudes toward politicians. The gap between our expectations of how politicians *ought* to act and how they *do* act gives rise to popular cynicism about public officials—that "piece of conventional wisdom to the effect that politicians are a good deal worse, morally worse, than the rest of us" (Walzer 1973, 162). I have personally encountered this attitude in the past few years after being questioned about the topic of my book. "The Ciceronian tradition of political morality," I respond, with the inquirer usually retorting with some version of "Isn't political morality a contradiction in terms?" The upshot of such cynicism is popular alienation from politics, including, I believe, a diminished sense that there is much to be gained by public oversight of politicians' actions: "If politicians are all crooks and cheats," the public asks, "why bother keeping an eye on their behavior?"

For some, the alternative to an unattainable morality is a politics devoid of all morality—"the insistence by some theorists that politics and morality are distinct and autonomous realms of judgement and decision" (Coady 2008, 25). Hampshire paints a bleak picture of the (possible) consequences of factoring morality out of politics: "A sufficient contempt for moral scruples in powerful governments, and an unclarity about the moral limits on violence, could possibly contribute to a universal, or at least to a very widespread, destruction of life in many parts of the world. Philosophical confusion, and general skepticism resulting from it, can lead to despair, to a sense that there is no solid ground to stand on when one is thinking of political conciliation and of the decencies of public life" (Hampshire 1989, 12–13). Setting aside the actual consequences of separating out morality from politics, however, I comment here only on the apparent inconceivability of a politics freed from moral restraints—an inconceivability suggested by the inability of political theorists famous (or infamous) for excluding the moral from the political to consistently sustain this exclusion. Two such examples are Machiavelli and Thomas Hobbes.

Machiavelli, the political theorist most often associated with splitting politics and morality into autonomous realms, cannot avoid injecting morality into his discussion of the prince. Thus, he counsels the prince "not [to] deviate from right conduct if possible" (Machiavelli 1988, 62) and refers to the prince's deviations from conventional morality in moral terms, characterizing the prince's necessary breaks with Christian morality as immoral (55), "mean" and "miserly" (56–57), "cruel" (58), skillful deceit, treacherous, ruthless, inhumane, and irreligious (62).

Similarly, Hobbes is generally interpreted (including by me) as grounding his political theory in rational self-interest, not morality. Nonetheless, Hobbes's *Leviathan* is replete with moral terminology. Thus, in the *Leviathan*, he defines a law of nature in ethical terms as "a Precept, or general Rule, found out by

Reason, by which a man is *forbidden to do*, that, which is destructive of his life, or taketh away the means of preserving the same" (Hobbes 1991, 91; emphasis added). Reinforcing the reader's sense that the law of nature is a moral obligation, Hobbes states that "The Lawes of Nature oblige in *foro interno*; that is to say, they bind to a desire they should take place" (110)—thereby implying that the law of nature is something more than the result of rational self-interest. Likewise, although Hobbes's sovereign, like his subjects, is motivated and restricted by self-interest, Hobbes repairs again to moral language in describing the sovereign's obligations: "The Office of the Soveraign . . . consisteth in the end, for which he was trusted with the Soveraign Power, namely the procuration of *the safety of the people* [emphasis in original]; *to which he is obliged by the Law of nature, and to render an account therefor to God, the Author of that Law, and to none but him* [emphasis added]" (231).[5] Although neither Machiavelli nor Hobbes ground their political theory in moral assumptions, they cannot avoid using moral language when delineating their political theory, suggesting the difficulty, if not impossibility, of conceiving of political activity as totally detached from morality.

If Cicero's pragmatic morality affords politicians greater latitude in their actions, it also sets limits on them. Politicians seek to curry favor with the public for reasons of expediency: they wish to be elected; they want popular support for their proposals; many, probably most, pursue public acclaim. These motivations prompt Plato to disparage rhetors as flatterers and panderers of the hoi polloi. But Cicero's decorum-based political morality obligates the orator-statesman to heed the public on moral, not only expediential, grounds. As we saw in chapter 1, Cicero sometimes suggests that the orator's duty to act with decorum is tantamount to following the public's current opinions. For instance, in *De oratore*, Cicero charges orators with knowing the character of the community, so that they may alter their mode of speaking to fit with the public's frequently changing *mores* (Cicero 2001a, 2.337). We also saw in the first chapter, however, that Cicero often portrays decorum as less transitory, with the "sense of the community"—which the orator-statesman must obey—reflecting the fundamental values of the political community; Cicero presumably conceives of decorum in this second, more stable sense when he pursues and receives the people's ex post facto approval for his actions in the Catilinarian conspiracy, which is investigated in chapter 2.

If, however, we interpret the decorum of the community in the second sense, that is, as indicating the community's original or authentic values—whether in Cicero's Rome or in modern democracies—does the politicians' duty to abide by communal decorum not bind them (and us) to the status quo? One means of determining a political community's values (or decorum) is to infer these values from the long-standing institutions and practices of a political community. But if this is the case, then the moral criticism of existing institutions and practices would depend on the very same institutions and practices on which we base our values. Such is the opinion of present-day critics of communitarianism who argue that, to the extent that "the values of the political community *are identified through its practices*" (Cohen 1986, 463; emphasis in original), then the "norms subsequently 'derived' from those values will not serve as criticisms of existing practices" (464).[6] Searching for the genuine values of the community through the evidence presented by archaic institutions and practices, as opposed to more contemporary institutions and practices, would seem even less satisfactory, as it appears to shift us from the conservatism of the status quo to the reactionary point of view that true communal values must be retrieved from some bygone age, which may or may not have existed.

Although Cicero's adherence to decorum often confirms the conservatism that anticommunitarians attribute to deriving moral values from particular historical communities—for example, he generally opposes political change that would weaken the ruling elite—the grounding of morality on communal norms is not inherently conservative, and Cicero does not always employ it as a means of forestalling change. (Thus, as delineated in chapter 1, Cicero envisions a future decorum that will bar the emotional manipulation he currently uses.) Rather, as one scholar contends, for Cicero, our best chance of altering the status quo is to appeal to the hearers' communal values: according to Cicero, "all ethics is local [and] ethical theory has to take account of the values and traditions of those whom it addresses, not in order to leave everything as it is, but to have a chance of inducing change" (Woolf 2015, 159). That the moral values embodied in a society's institutions and practices are not innately conservative is further supported by the fact that social critics, as Walzer explains, "commonly don't, and certainly needn't, invent the principles they apply; they don't have to step outside the world they ordinarily inhabit. They appeal to internal principles, already known, comprehensible to, somehow remembered by, the people they hope to convince" (Walzer 1983).[7]

I do not present here some empirically verifiable method of determining what a particular political community's moral values are. Maybe that is impossible. Nevertheless, I think citizens of a political community can recognize that they share certain values (and emphasize the significance of some values over others) that distinguish them from other, even similar, political communities (Walzer 1994, 17). We are aware of our community's values through a kind of intuition, the result of our conscious and unconscious socialization into these values—but not through intuition alone. We also infer our morality from the history, institutions, practices, and underlying ideas of our political community. For example, when Lincoln argues for the equality of all Americans, regardless of race, he turns to the history of the United States and its ideas as embodied in the Declaration of Independence and the meaning of equality he finds there. In his "Speech on the Dred Scott Decision," delivered on June 26, 1857, he asserts: "I think the authors of that notable instrument [the Declaration of Independence] intended to include all men, but they did not intend to declare all men equal in all respects. They did not mean to say all were equal in color, size, intellect, moral developments, or social capacity. They defined with tolerable distinctness, in what respects they did consider all men created equal—equal in 'certain inalienable rights, among which are life, liberty and the pursuit of happiness.'"[8] Lincoln's interpretation of equality is not so authoritative that it precludes debate about how to put this ideal of equality into practice. For some, slavery needed to be abolished immediately. For others, like Lincoln before the Emancipation Proclamation, slavery was a moral wrong that would ultimately disappear. A consensus existed among most white Northerners, however, that slavery was at odds with America's fundamental value of equality. That most white Southerners did not view equality as inimical to slavery points up the degree to which the North and South were becoming (or had already become) by the beginning of the Civil War distinct moral communities, which would only be reunited by force.

Even nation states whose political values are similar to each other, for example, advanced Western-style democracies, exhibit different moralities concerning politics. Thus, Ronald Krotoszynski Jr. demonstrates how several contemporary democracies (the United States, Canada, Germany, Japan, and the United Kingdom) interpret the right to free speech differently even though, superficially at least, they all embrace the same right (2006). The societies that defend the right to freedom of speech do so not only as a matter of law but also as a matter of morality, that is, these societies accept that it is morally wrong for their governments to deny their citizens the opportunity to voice their opinions about politics and, more generally, to express themselves creatively. Each society, however, construes free speech according to its distinct norms. As Frederick Schauer argues, "rights do not come into existence in a cultural vacuum; rather, rights exist in part because they incorporate and reflect preexisting community norms" (Krotoszynski 2006, 185, paraphrasing Schauer 2000, 328–36). For example, according to Krotoszynski, because of the greater value the United States places on individual self-actualization or liberty, American citizens are free to exercise their free speech right even when exercising this right adversely affects the community. Krotoszynski shows how other countries, by contrast, place greater emphasis on the communal ends of free speech. Thus, free speech is at times limited in Germany for the purpose of advancing "an overarching civility project" (Krotoszynski 2006, 137), with restrictions on free expression justified because speech, in Germany, is "valued according to its utility in promoting desirable social ends" (Eberle 1997, 805). Similarly, the Japanese Supreme Court's unwillingness "to prohibit government action aimed at restricting speech that is demonstrably harmful to the community or potentially disruptive of normal political processes" is consistent with Japan's character as "a group-oriented society that functions on the basis of establishing community consensus" (Krotoszynski 2006, 162–63).

Although political communities *differ between* each other in their political moralities, individual political communities also *differ from within* on matters of political morality. The meaning of "difference" in these two categories, however, is not identical. When discussing difference between communities, difference stems from the distinct values that are particular to each political community. True, it is possible to eliminate the moral differences between countries by artificially constructing a "thin" or "minimal" morality—a sort of lowest common denominator of moralities, at least of the moralities of liberal societies. This thin morality "consists in principles and rules that are reiterated in different times and places, and that are seen to be similar even though they are expressed in different idioms and reflect different histories and versions of the world" (Walzer 1994, 17). The disadvantage of this common minimal morality, however, is that "what is recognized [here] is just . . . (partial) commonality, not the full moral significance [or 'thick' morality] of the other cultures" (17).

In the second category—difference within a political community—disagreement is inevitable not because each particular society lacks a common moral culture, but because members of that shared culture—so long as it is democratic—will interpret its common principles, especially the application of those principles, differently.[9] For example, political leaders who must decide how to act in morally troubling circumstances should reflect on what political morality demands of them. Presumably, this process of reflection begins with an account of what ordinary morality would require and, then, considering their present circumstances, deliberation about how far the community's distinctively political morality sanctions their departures from the dictates of ordinary morality in any given situation. Ideally, the electorate will then, in turn, evaluate the political morality of their leaders' actions and decide whether or not to ratify them. Though both politicians and citizens will consult the moral values of their political community, neither will arrive at the same answer;

politicians will disagree with each other and citizens, as citizens will differ with each other and with politicians.

Cicero acknowledges this point when he concedes that well-intentioned politicians will dispute with each other on the implementation of moral principles. As we have seen, Cicero identifies the safety of the Republic as the highest moral good. Yet, in *De officiis*, he avers that we should "not [consider as enemies] those who want to protect the republic in the way each judges best. It was in this way that Publius Africanus and Quintus Metellus used to disagree with one another, without bitterness" (Cicero 1991a, 1.87). In his "Second Philippic against Antony," Cicero extends the same tolerance toward politicians who give precedence to different moral values in their decision making. Speaking of his disagreement with Pompey the Great during Caesar's civil war, in which Cicero wishes to sue for peace with Julius Caesar and Pompey to continue the war against him, Cicero declares: "That was no small thing, that two men, though holding divergent views on the great question affecting the Republic, remained on their old friendly footing." In Cicero's telling, he and Pompey each adopted a different Roman value as preeminent. Cicero's "concern was for the survival of our countrymen first and foremost; dignity could be considered later." Pompey, however, gave pride of place to "dignity in the present." Cicero never implies that their disagreement on applying moral principles made either less moral. They both adopted sound ends. "The fact that each of us had a reasonable aim," Cicero writes, "made our disagreement easier to bear" (2009, 2.38–39)

Cicero's dispute with Pompey about the best course of action in Caesar's civil war is presented as a disagreement about which Roman value should be regarded as dominant, which is consistent with my exposition of Ciceronian morality as based on norms internal to his own society. But as I have noted earlier, there is another aspect to Cicero's morality, discussed intermittently in this book, which is universalistic, that is, natural law. Although, as I contend in chapter 2, Cicero does not, in practice, give precedence to the universalism of the natural law over the Roman Constitution and the morality inherent in it, he consistently defends traditional Roman norms as naturally just.

The cosmopolitanism of natural law, however, plays a part, albeit limited, in Cicero's account of political morality. Although Cicero expects politicians to conform to the political norms of the community, not to the transnational morality of natural law, he holds up the moral principles of natural law as aspirational norms for politicians and ordinary citizens. Aligning Roman laws with natural law—even though Roman laws in their present state were, according to Cicero, consistent with and therefore morally legitimated by nature (Asmis

2008, 31)—would result in a more perfect morality. Nevertheless, neither the Roman Republic nor any other individual political community can draw specific moral rules from universal nature to enhance the substance of its political morality. Instead, natural law requires of us that we act according to "right reason" (Cicero 1999d, 3.33), the "highest reason, rooted in nature" (1999e, 1.18). But *how* we improve our morality in accordance with natural law is left to us humans because reason is part of our nature, "and as such is not some eternal metaphysical entity" (Alonso 2013, 31). Thus, when Cicero declares that "[n]ature's reason itself [is] divine *and* human" (1991a, 3.23; emphasis added), he recognizes humans as autonomous legislators (Alonso 2013, 31), who derive their sense of divine reason inwardly because, though the god is "the author, expounder, and mover of this law" (Cicero 1999d, 3.33), natural law is inherent in human nature itself.

Although natural law can serve as a goad to improving political morality, to helping us enhance our morality in line with our sense of what reason requires of us, it will not create an eternal unchangeable moral standard the same in Rome as in Athens (1999d, 3.33)—at least as long as our system of nation states with their own values, customs, and traditions continues to predominate. The creation of transnational bodies like the United Nations or the European Union—even with their own courts of justice—has not yet superseded the particular moral communities we identify with the nation state. Perhaps a cosmopolitan political morality will develop, probably piecemeal rather than en bloc. But that time has not yet arrived. If and when it does, critics of communitarianism will be able to draw on those universalistic elements of Cicero that might make natural boundaries morally irrelevant (in line with Martha Nussbaum's [2000b, 185] reading of Cicero). Until then, Cicero's rhetorical, community-based political morality will remain the prevailing model in our interpretation of Cicero and his tradition of pragmatic political morality.

NOTES

INTRODUCTION

1. For Wolin (and, according to Wolin, for Plato as well), "politics is (a) a form of activity centering around the struggle for competitive advantage . . . ; (b) a form of activity conditioned by . . . [circumstances of] change and relative scarcity; and (c) a form of activity in which the pursuit of advantage produces consequences [that] . . . affect in a significant way the whole society or a substantial portion of it (2004, 11, 39).

2. "Thus the Platonic conception of political philosophy and ruling was founded on a paradox: the science as well as the art of creating order was sworn to an eternal hostility towards politics, towards those phenomena, in other words, that made such an art and science meaningful and necessary" (Wolin 2004, 39).

3. Although opinion polls show exceptional public mistrust of politicians today, I believe that there coexists a more deeply rooted (and enduring) understanding among the people that politicians cannot engage in politics effectively by strictly adhering to conventional standards of morality, which I argue in chapter 2. Much of the public's current mistrust of their political leaders has to do with politicians acting more in their own self-interest—for example, lying to cover up their own selfishly motivated misdeeds—or in a partisan manner than in the interest of the general welfare, which may require departing from generally accepted norms.

4. A Pew Research Center Poll finds: "Just 24% say they can trust the government in Washington to do what is right just about always or most of the time; far more (75%) say they trust government only some of the time or never" (http://www.people-press.org/2014/06/26). Similarly, a CNN/ORC International poll "indicates that the public's trust in government is at an all-time low. Just 13% of Americans say the government can be trusted to do what is right always or most of the time, with just over three-quarters saying only some of the time and one in 10 saying they never trust the government, according to the poll" (http://politicalticker.blogs.cnn.com/2014/08/08).

5. See chapter 2.

6. I follow C. A. J. Coady's understanding of "absolutism" as "the view that some moral prohibitions hold come what may." Moral absolutists, Coady contends, deny that some serious

prohibitions, "such as those against lying, promise-breaking, and violations of confidentiality are open to exception" (2008, 43).

7. In chapter 3, I maintain that Machiavelli upholds political expediency at the expense of moral commitment.

8. In *Public and Private Morality*, see Hampshire's essay with the same title as the book, Bernard Williams's "Politics and Moral Character," and Thomas Nagel's "Ruthlessness in Public Life." In *Cruelty and Deception: The Controversy over Dirty Hands in Politics*, see the essays in part 1 and Kai Nielsen's essay in part 2.

9. Machiavelli is the single political thinker most often adduced, mistakenly I argue, on behalf of a pragmatic political morality.

10. Judith Shklar inaugurated the current reappraisal of hypocrisy as an intolerable vice in *Ordinary Vices* (1984). Shklar, however, does not systematically investigate the roots of her viewpoint, though she adverts to a wide range of, primarily, literary figures in elaborating her viewpoint.

11. A noteworthy exception is John Parrish's *Paradoxes of Political Ethics: From Dirty Hands to the Invisible Hand* (2007), "an analytical history of philosophical reflection on [dirty hands] from antiquity to the Enlightenment" (2). Parrish also discusses Plato, Cicero, and the early Christians in some detail when examining the premodern origins of dirty hands.

12. Concerning the blurring of the political and the judicial, Fergus Millar writes: "All trials before *iudicia* [judicial assemblies] were by their nature 'political,' because they took place in the same public space as did *contiones* [public meetings] and meetings of the *comitia tributa* [tribal assemblies]; because they tended to involve persons engaged on political careers, careers that were profoundly affected by a person's conduct in such cases and by the good or bad reputation gained; and because they were exposed to and much affected by crowd reactions and . . . were often disturbed by outright violence" (1999, 87–88).

13. On the importance of political oratory vis-à-vis legal oratory in Cicero, see Fantham (2004, 210).

14. I subsume the related concept "dissimulation" under the broader heading "deception."

15. Dissimulation is the "concealment of what really is, under a feigned semblance of something different" (*Oxford English Dictionary*, 3rd. ed.)—the major difference between deception and dissimulation being that deception denotes speech or action to mislead or lie, and concealment denotes speech or action designed to conceal the truth.

16. For contemporary critiques of manipulation, see Goodin (1980) and several essays in Le Cheminant and Parrish (2011), such as those by Klemp and Fishkin. The contemporary classic critique of deception and dissimulation is Bok (1979). For recent criticisms of violence qua dirty hands, see Shugarman (1990) and (2000), Shue (2006), and Brecher (2007).

17. In *Strong Democracy: Participatory Politics for a New Age* (1984), Benjamin Barber defends participatory politics against representative or "thin" democracy, which weakens the role of citizens in democratic governance. See also *The Local Politics of Global Sustainability* by Thomas Prugh, Robert Costanza, and Herman Daly (2000). See my discussion of deliberative democrats calling for equality of popular deliberation in chapter 6.

18. Plato's later dialogue on rhetoric, the *Phaedrus*, has been read both as a critique and defense of rhetoric. Therefore, I focus instead on the unambiguously critical *Gorgias*.

19. See Plato's discussion of the sophists, the teachers of rhetoric, in the *Republic* (written 380–360 BCE). The sophist who associates "with the motley multitude in their assembly . . . and grants the mob authority over himself more than is unavoidable, the proverbial necessity of Diomedes will compel him to give the public what it likes, but that what it likes is really good and honorable, have you ever heard an attempted proof of this that is not simply ridiculous?" (Plato 1961b, 493d).

20. The *Gorgias*'s attack on rhetoric as deceptive is echoed in the liberal tradition by John Locke, for whom rhetoric is "that powerful instrument of Error and Deceit." Like Socrates, Locke distinguishes between "Truth and Knowledge," which rhetoric cannot discern, and "Pleasure and Delight," which eloquence offers. "All the Art of Rhetorick," Locke writes, is "for nothing else but to insinuate wrong *Ideas*, move the Passions, and thereby mislead the Judgment; and so indeed are perfect cheat" (Locke 1975, 508).

21. For recent discussions of Kant on rhetoric and morality, see Dostal (1980), Abbott (2007), and Stroud (2014).

22. The sophist and rhetorician Gorgias of Leontini anticipates this view of persuasion as denying autonomy. In the *Encomium of Helen*, Gorgias denies that Helen is responsible for her adultery with Paris because she was captivated "by means of [his] words, inspired incantations [that] serve as bringers-on of pleasure and takers-off of pain. . . . For discourse was the persuader of the soul, which it persuaded and compelled." Gorgias then affixes guilt: "He who persuaded (as constrainer) did wrong; while she who was persuaded (as one constrained by means of the discourse) is wrongly blamed" (Gorgias of Leontini. *Encomium of Helen*, translated by Brian R. Donovan, 1999, http://classicpersuasion.org/pw/gorgias/helendonovan.htm, par. 10, 12). Likewise, it may be argued that politicians who whip a crowd into an emotional frenzy are morally culpable not only because of the bad results of their manipulation but also because they deprive their listeners of reaching freely chosen decisions.

23. On lying, see also *The Doctrine of Virtue* in the *Metaphysics of Morals* (Kant 1996a, 6:429–31); and "On a Supposed Right to Lie from Philanthropy" (Kant 1996b, 611–15).

24. According to Seyla Benhabib, for example, "egalitarian reciprocity" is a moral principle maintaining that "each individual has the same symmetrical rights to various speech acts, to initiate new topics, to ask for reflection about the presuppositions of the conversations" (Benhabib 1996b, 78; see also 69–70).

25. Unlike the asymmetry of rhetoric, which distinguishes between the public speaker and the largely silent masses, Socrates's dialectic is structured as a one-on-one conversation. He assumes in the *Gorgias* that individual citizens can be reasoned with and can arrive at truth: "My expertise is restricted to producing just a single witness in support of my ideas—the person with whom I'm carrying on the discussion—and I pay no attention to large numbers of people; I only know how to ask for a single person's vote, and I can't even begin to address people in large groups" (Plato 1979, 474a).

26. Socrates believes that "all members of a community are regarded as sufficiently well qualified to participate in making binding collective decisions on all issues that significantly affect their good or interest." Further, "though Socrates proposes the idea of expert political knowledge, the dialogue he has with his interlocutors in the *Gorgias* neither illustrates nor claims it" (Euben 1997, 208).

27. In my book title, I include both "ethics" and "morality." Although these terms are sometimes accorded different meanings—see, for example, Annas (1992) and Dworkin (2011)—I use the two interchangeably in the book title and throughout this book. I employ a form of "moral" more often than a form of "ethics," primarily, because morality is based on Latin (Cicero's language) and ethics on Greek. As the *Oxford English Dictionary* (3rd ed.) explains, the English adjective "moral" is ultimately derived from the classical Latin *mōrālis*, which Cicero formed to render the ancient Greek ἠθικός ("ethic," adj.), *mōrēs* (habits, morals) already being the accepted Latin equivalent of ἦθη (customs, manners, habits).

28. Isocrates was probably the greatest Greek influence on Cicero's rhetorical outlook (Leff 2012; Smethurst 1953), on which Cicero's conception of political morality is based. Nevertheless, as Eric Laughton observes (1961), Cicero's emphases on the orator's "practical importance in public life" and on his true fulfillment through exercising his oratory "for the good of the commonwealth" are distinctly Roman (27–29). In addition, although S. E. Smethurst stresses the similarities between Cicero and Isocrates, he concedes that Cicero adapts from the Stoics, not Isocrates, two concepts central to his rhetorical *Weltanschauung*—the *honestum* and decorum (310–14).

29. Modern scholars disagree about the affinity between Aristotle and Plato on rhetoric: some see Aristotle as rejecting Plato's views on rhetoric; others read Aristotle as building on Plato's critique and conception of rhetoric, especially as presented in the *Phaedrus*, where Plato assumes a milder position toward rhetoric than in the *Gorgias* (Leff 1993, 315–16). Although Cicero venerated Plato as "virtually a philosopher's god" (1933b, 2.32; Long 1995a, 43–50), he, not surprisingly, rejects Plato's moral condemnation of rhetoric. Rather than concede that Socrates's critique of rhetoric (in the *Gorgias*) had merit, Cicero has Catulus, one of the interlocutors in *De oratore*, assert that if Gorgias was defeated by Socrates, it was because "Socrates was obviously more eloquent and a more skillful speaker and . . . a better and more copious orator" (2001a, 3.129). Thus, Socrates could only have bested the rhetor through rhetoric. Similarly, in describing his careful reading of the *Gorgias*, Cicero writes: "I particularly admired Plato for the way in which, while making fun of orators, he appeared to be a supreme orator himself" (2001a, 1.47). Cicero's attitudes toward Plato's views on rhetoric in the *Phaedrus* are more ambiguous, with Cicero taking "comfort from its positive approach to excellence in speaking," but also describing Plato in the *Phaedrus* as a denouncer of all rhetoricians (Cicero 1939b, 42; Fantham 2004, 69–70). For a fuller discussion of Cicero on Plato and rhetoric, see Fantham (2004, 52–71) and Long (1995a, 50–52).

30. McCabe offers, what I consider, a more explicit claim for rhetoric's morality based on its argumentative focus than either Garver or Garsten. True rhetoric, she observes, is focused on the enthymeme, the rhetorical proof. Arguments that do not adhere to the rules of the enthymeme "are not arguments at all but mere attempts at manipulation. But arguments focused on the enthymeme are not therefore devoid of ethical or political content." Rather, these arguments are "naturally best suited to presenting the truth" (1994, 162).

31. "The excellence of the good man is identified with the excellence of the prudent person operating in a political role" (Bodéüs 1993, 44).

32. I contrast Aristotle's *phronesis* with Cicero's prudence in chapter 5.

33. Like Allen, Thomas Farrell interprets Aristotle's rhetoric as taking place among a community of friends. In line with this interpretation, Farrell (1993) conceives of the Aristotelian

speaker as working to negate any differences between himself and his audience (71). Allen's and Farrell's views of the Aristotelian rhetorical context as symmetrical between speaker and audience, however, is not the dominant understanding of Aristotle. More common is Ekaterina Haskin's position that "Aristotle repeatedly emphasizes the asymmetrical relationship between the rhetor and the audience" (2004b, 133).

34. Garsten acknowledges that he draws different elements of his defense of rhetoric from Aristotle and Cicero (2006, 13–14). Despite their different emphases, however, he does not describe them as in conflict with each other in their general attitude to rhetoric.

35. On the limited influence of Aristotle's rhetoric through the ages, see George Kennedy's discussion of Aristotle in his entry on "Classical Rhetoric," in the *Encyclopedia of Rhetoric*: "Although published in the first century BCE . . . , Aristotle's treatise on rhetoric was little-read throughout antiquity and the Middle Ages." Kennedy notes that it was not until the twentieth century "that the originality and brilliance of the treatise came to be fully appreciated" (2001, 100). In contrast, Cicero has been the dominant influence on the Western tradition of rhetoric. On Cicero's rhetorical legacy, see Kennedy (2002). On the influence of Cicero's rhetorical ideas on politics, see Hauser (1999): Roman rhetorics, especially Cicero's, "endured as the principal vehicle by which rhetorical thought was transmitted in the Western tradition and retained influence on political thinking until the Enlightenment" (19). I would argue that this influence continued until the late nineteenth century, when Cicero came under increasing criticism for lacking originality.

36. Likewise, Garsten describes the *Rhetoric* as a "book [that] could never be mistaken for a work of political ethics" (2006, 118).

37. By "rhetorical emotions," I mean those emotions that serve as means of persuasion in oratory. For purposes of this article, I equate "rhetorical emotions" with the more popular "political emotions," for example, those analyzed in Sokolon's *Political Emotions: Aristotle and the Symphony of Reason and Emotion* (2006) and Koziak's *Retrieving Political Emotion: Thumos, Aristotle, and Gender* (2000).

38. As I do with "rhetorical" and "political" emotions, I equate "rhetorical" and "political" morality. In the classical period, the *rhetor* (orator) *was* the politician. When I speak of "political morality" in relation to Cicero I mean a morality that derives from the rhetorical/political context, not from an a priori philosophical system (see Leff 1998, 63).

39. Nicgorski (1978), Leff (1998, 64), Nederman (2000b), Garsten (2006), Connolly (2007), and Kapust (2011a).

40. "Taken as a whole, Cicero's letters and speeches provide a skeptical view of morality that his theory does not so much reject as dissimulate by adopting euphemism" (199). Zerba further contends: "Cicero's rhetorical styles, both those he extols in *De Oratore* and those he uses, dissimulate the hypocrisy of the *viri boni*, who could never rise to the status they enjoy without feigning the morality they seem to possess. This is duplicity at two levels—that of the subjects discussed and of the one discussing them. Because the text of *De Oratore* protects an interest by using terms not incisive enough to critique it thoroughly, its rhetoric verges on cunning" (204). Finally, comparing Cicero and Machiavelli, Zerba concludes that Cicero can be seen as "more Machiavellian than Machiavelli. . . . The entire drama of strife and pantomimic morality in Machiavelli's politics is oriented toward a less scandalous teaching than the one we have identified in *De Oratore*" (205).

41. Because Dean Hammer's *Roman Political Thought: From Cicero to Augustine* (2014) is, as the title suggests, a broader analysis of ancient Roman political thought, I do not discuss it (in the body of the text) as a recent work concerning the relationship between rhetoric, politics, and morality in Cicero. Nevertheless, *Roman Political Thought* (which is organized by author) contains an excellent chapter on Cicero's political ideas that touches on several themes that I delineate in *Ethics and the Orator*: the connection between speech, morality, and decorum (44–45); morality and political emergency (67–69; although, in contrast to *Ethics and the Orator*, Hammer unreservedly condemns Cicero's use of the *senatus consultum ultimum* against the Catilinarian conspirators); the morality of rhetoric (69–76); the troubling role of manipulation in Ciceronian rhetoric (72); and Cicero's attempts to defend against the immoral use of rhetoric (75–76).

42. For example, Garsten argues that Cicero adopts the *honestum*, the moral or honorable, from the Stoics as a means of insulating orator and public from "the standard of public opinion," as opposed to deriving the concept—or at least justifying its legitimacy—from the values of the people, which (as I argue) reflects Cicero's rhetorical approach that looks to the assumptions of the audience (170–71). Moreover, Garsten does not justify Cicero's prorhetorical use of Stoicism based on inherently rhetorical principles, like decorum.

43. Cicero's "philosophic orators could protect themselves against [the danger of bowing to their audience's assumptions] by guarding carefully the conditions in which they could gain and maintain private beliefs different from the ones they had to propound in public" (164–65), and citizens could "preserve some measure of intellectual independence, some perspective on currents of public opinion, and some psychological space in which to evaluate their impulses" (170).

44. Connolly also maintains that "examining the body in Ciceronian rhetorical discourse unlocks his contribution to ancient and early modern virtue theory" (120).

45. "While [Cicero] does not intend to signal agreement with the excluded, it is key to his success as a speaker in the republican agon that he acknowledges dissent or 'thinking otherwise,' that he recognizes . . . other's sense of alienation, conflict, difference, and loss, accepting these experiences into his own ethos and thus welcoming the excluded back into the body politic" (164).

46. Connolly acknowledges that consensus involves "agreements among members of the senatorial order and between that order and the *populus Romanus* about the rules of the political game." This consensus, however, is not about morality and is necessary only "during the actual [electoral] competition" (41).

47. Cicero's political morality evolves over time, as I explain in chapter 2, where I discuss argument *in utramque partem* (in both directions) as a means Cicero employs to adapt his political morality to changing conditions.

48. "One criterion of the non-existence of *res publica* in a regime or set-up is the dissolution of the mutuality and moral consensus which bind society together" (Schofield 1995, 71).

49. The *contio* was the nonvoting informal assembly in which the orator spoke before the people. The *contio* met before formal, voting political assemblies were convened or at any time a presiding magistrate decided to convene such a meeting (Morstein-Marx 2004, 7–12).

50. Although I speak of the basic characteristics of Cicero's theory and the Ciceronian tradition of political morality, I propose these characteristics with the understanding that others studying the Ciceronian tradition will probably arrive at a different account of its essential elements. I omit the balancing of the power of the electorate and of politicians as a characteristic

of the Ciceronian tradition of political morality in nonrepublican or nondemocratic political systems, where popular political liberty is absent.

51. My claim for the ongoing relevance of Cicero's political thought is consistent with Connolly's stance in *The Life of Roman Republicanism*. The *optimates*, also known as the *boni* (the good men), were those who upheld the special guardianship and leadership functions of the Senate. The *optimates* were opposed to the *populares*, who advocated the rights and the privileges of the common people.

52. The reason why I have added a substantive element to "tradition" is that the absence of such an element can leave "tradition" with almost no meaning. Take the question of the Aristotelian tradition as an example. Notwithstanding their attachment to Aristotle's ethical-political tradition, MacIntyre and Martha Nussbaum concede that elements fundamental to it are unacceptable today. Both also reject what they contend are *inessential* elements of Aristotle's political and ethical philosophy (MacIntyre 1984, 162; Nussbaum 2000a, 114–15; 1990, 239). MacIntyre and Nussbaum justify their connections to Aristotle, even as they distance themselves from basic Aristotelian tenets, by identifying themselves with Aristotelianism or the Aristotelian tradition, rather than with Aristotle himself (MacIntyre 1984, 146–48, 196–97; Nussbaum 1990, 206–7). What seems to make MacIntyre and Nussbaum Aristotelians or neo-Aristotelians, in their minds, is that each takes part in Aristotelianism as an evolving tradition, which is in conversation with Aristotle but not always in agreement with him (MacIntyre 1984, 146–48; Nussbaum 2000a, 104–5) But when their versions of the Aristotelian tradition are often only marginally related to Aristotle's own positions—with Aristotle acting as an initial stimulus to conversations with anti-Aristotelian conclusions—the label "Aristotelian" is drained of its meaning. I have borrowed the term "borrower" from Nussbaum's discussion of neo-Aristotelianism and the many different philosophers who "have used Aristotle as a conversation partner" (Nussbaum 2000a, 104–105).

PROLOGUE

1. As I note at the beginning of chapter 4, the existence of a Ciceronian pragmatic political morality even during the Renaissance and early modernity is doubted by scholars who consider Cicero a moral purist (based on their readings of *De officiis*) whose political moralism was supplanted by Tacitus's realism in the late Renaissance.

2. Several Renaissance and early-modern authors who espouse a Cicero-based, morally pragmatic approach to politics include: Leon Battista Alberti (1404–72), who points up both the necessity of, and the complexities associated with, dissimulation in his *Momus* (Alberti 2003); Giovanni Gioviano Pontano (1426–1503), who justifies dissimulation along Ciceronian lines, in the Preface to *De immanitate* (Pontano 1518, 311), in *De obedientia* (1518, 1–48), and in *De prudentia* (1518, 147–226), especially book 4; Baldassar Castiglione (1478–1529), who assents to the courtier's use of dissimulation in *Il Libro de Cortegiano* (1981); and Pedro de Ribadeneyra (1527–1611), who in *Tratado de la religion y virtudes que deue tener el principe christiano, para gouernar y conseruar sus estados* (1595) recognizes the legitimacy of deceit on Ciceronian grounds of public safety. Although the scholarly literature does not discuss these authors as part of a Ciceronian tradition of political morality per se, some writers have analyzed Cicero's influence on their attitudes to political morality. In a chapter entitled "The Figure of Cicero," Peter Miller, in his *Defining the Common Good: Empire, Religion, and Philosophy in Eighteenth-Century Britain*

(1994, 21–87), focuses on Cicero's view of the common good as the highest moral duty, as well as on the Roman rhetorician's interweaving of the *honestum* and the *utile*—both elements I have associated as part of the Ciceronian tradition of pragmatic morality. Miller includes in this chapter a discussion of late-Renaissance and early-modern thinkers who, according to Miller, accept the Ciceronian claim that conserving a state ruled by law sometimes requires the performance of "ostensibly extra-legal measures" (1994, 39, 51). Miller's emphasis on the Ciceronian roots of these thinkers, however, is often overstated. For example, he highlights Cicero's influence on these thinkers to the neglect of other important classical influences, and he ignores the ways in which some of these "Ciceronian" authors reject fundamental features of Cicero's thought. For two accounts of Cicero's effect on Alberti's views on dissimulation, see Pearson (2011), Kircher (2012, especially 1–33, 225–56). On Cicero's influence on Castiglione's advocacy of dissimulation, see Richards (2001, 460–86). For a concise analysis of Ribadeneyra's use of Cicero to justify dissimulation and inconstancy for the conservation of the community, see Miller (1994, 53–54).

3. Quintilian describes eloquence as *honesta ac rerum pulcherrima*, "honourable [moral] and the fairest thing in the world" (2001a, 1.12.16).

4. On a related matter, Quintilian distinguishes between the decorum of rulers and ordinary citizens: "Some things are becoming [*deceat*] for rulers, which one would not allow in others" (2001d, 11.1.36). See discussion of roles in chapter 2.

5. See also Birger Munk Olsen's observation that John adopts the Ciceronian balancing of the *utilitas* and the *honestas*. "This equilibrium of *honestum* and *utile,* studied long in Cicero's *De Officiis*, is at the center of the ethical and political doctrines of the *Policraticus*" (Olsen 1968, 63).

6. Reflecting Cicero's imagery, in *De inventione*, of eloquence as the effective cause of civilization (Cicero 1949, 1.3)—giving rise to the moral life and benefitting humanity—John describes rhetoric's "delightful and fruitful union of reason and speech" as that "which gave birth to so many glorious cities, brought together and made allies of so many kingdoms, and united and bound so many peoples in the bonds of charity, that whoever strives to put asunder what God has joined together for the common benefit of all [*ad utilitatem omnium*] would rightly be accounted the common enemy of all" (John of Salisbury 2013, 1.1.13, 126).

7. In the *Policraticus*, John illustrates the moral use of flattery and deception to kill a tyrant. In the deuterocanonical Book of Judith, the title character tricks the tyrant Holofernes into making himself vulnerable to her, which allows Judith to strike him on the neck and chop off his head. John recognizes that "the woman would not have been accorded access to the tyrant unless she had concealed her hostile purpose in a pious deception" (John of Salisbury 1990, 8.20, 207–209).

8. Likewise, John maintains that when Judith misleads Holofernes, she does not sin, for "that which maintains the faith and serves charity is not deceitful" (1990, 8.20, 207).

CHAPTER ONE

1. See also Aristotle (1991, 1.9.1). *Ethos* helps the hearer decide whether he or she finds the speaker reliable or not, which is a decision the hearer arrives at "from the speech, not from a previous opinion that the speaker is a certain kind of person" (1.2.4).

2. Aristotle's analysis of the emotions in his works on ethics or psychology is less complete. Concerning the limited discussion of the emotions in these writings, see Cooper (1996, 238–39), Striker (1996, 286), and Sokolon (2006, 14–15).

3. Some scholars enumerate up to fifteen emotions treated by Aristotle. Cooper (1996) explains the reasons for enumerating the emotions differently (242).

4. That Aristotle adopts a cognitive approach, but does not maintain this approach throughout, is supported in the secondary literature. Richard Sorabji (2000), for example, states that "Aristotle's accounts of emotions are shot through with cognitive terms, but they are not yet tidied in the way that the Stoics were later to tidy them" (22).

5. These two examples are from the third book, which some argue was written independently of the rest of the *Rhetoric*. Even if composed separately, however, "its development seems to have been roughly parallel to that of books 1–2" (Aristotle 1991, 304).

6. Cicero retains the threefold means of persuasion found in Aristotle, although Cicero situates the *pisteis* in the larger framework of the "tasks" or "activities of the orator," of which Cicero designates five: "*invention* (thinking out of the material), *arrangement* (ordering it), *style* (putting the ordered material into words), *memory* (memorizing the speech), and *delivery*" (Cicero 2001a, 29). (Aristotle is less clear about these activities; he treats, less explicitly, invention, arrangement, and style [Cicero 2001a, 29–32].) For Cicero, the three means of persuasion are subsumed under the first activity, invention. Cicero defines "invention" in his juvenile *De inventione* as "the discovery of valid or seemingly valid arguments to render one's cause plausible" (Cicero 1949, 1.9).

7. I use the terms "*ethos*" and "*pathos*" here, though Cicero does not designate these *pisteis* with specific names.

8. In speaking of goodwill toward the client, Cicero has judicial oratory in mind.

9. On Ciceronian *ethos* as an emotional appeal, see Fantham (1973), Fortenbaugh (1988), and Wisse (1989, 233–49).

10. The more detailed discussion of vehement and gentle emotions in *De oratore* (2.178–216a), upon which I have relied, is written primarily for judicial oratory. But in *De oratore*, we are presented with a comparable division, in a discussion of political oratory, between the rhetoric of the Senate, where "matters must be handled with less display," and the public meeting (*contio*), which "gives all the force of oratory" (Cicero 2001a, 2.333).

11. "Cicero does not . . . go to the length of giving precise definitions" (Solmsen 1938, 397).

12. In *Tusculan Disputations*, however, where Cicero (1971) assumes a Stoic position on the emotions, he views them as derived from cognitions, albeit false beliefs inconsistent with the Stoic conviction that only virtue matters (3.61; Graver 2002, xix–xxxiii; Knuuttila 2004, 53n114). On the contradiction between Cicero's view of the emotions in *De oratore* and later in *Tusculan Disputations*, see Narducci (1997, 77–96).

13. "Commonplaces" has two overlapping meanings: "commonplace observations, and common *sources* of arguments" (Lanham 1991, 169.)

14. In the prologue to *De oratore*, Cicero, speaking in his own persona, argues that "in soothing or in exciting the feelings of the audience the full force of oratory and *all its available means* must be brought into play" (Cicero 1991a, 1.17; emphasis added). Presumably, "all its available means" includes rational argumentation.

15. See Broadie (1991, 190–98) for a similar distinction between given and guiding ends, and MacIntyre (1984, 188) for the distinction between goods "internal" to a "practice" and those "externally and contingently attached to it."

16. For several interpretations of this apparent inconsistency in Aristotle, see Sprute (1994, 117–28), Aristotle (1991, 28), and Solmsen (1929).

17. Aristotle provides another example of how to mislead an audience in the *Rhetoric* (Aristotle 1991, 1.9.28–29).

18. When Athena, as head of the Areopagus, justifies her decision in the *Eumenides* (in favor of Orestes and Apollo against the Furies), she speaks outside the subject, relying on an irrelevant argument: she is "always for the male" because "[t]here is no mother anywhere who gave me birth" (Aeschylus 1953, 739–42; Garver 1994, 105–106). Thus, Athenians themselves seem to have entertained doubts about whether any institution can forbid speaking outside the subject. Robert Wallace (1985) cites the view that speakers did not limit themselves to speaking only on the crime before them (258n111).

19. The audience's desire to be charmed, however, is an insignificant part of Aristotle's analysis of rhetoric, in contrast to Cicero's.

20. The information about the Willie Horton advertisements is primarily based on Jamieson (1992, 15–42) and Mendelberg (2001, 134–68).

21. On psychoanalysis as a means of understanding racial prejudice, see Clarke (2003, 59–175).

22. The voters, Garver (1994) concludes, were not deceived but rhetorically manipulated (161). In general, Garver claims that because emotional appeals in Aristotle "are intentional and argumentative, they do not rely essentially on deception" (134).

23. Although the Bush campaign almost certainly intended to play the race card, I do not think it possible to distinguish artistic from inartistic rhetoric based on speaking outside the subject. In the Willie Horton commercials, as in other examples of speech purportedly outside the subject, there is no practical way to determine the line between what is inside and outside the subject. Thus, Garver (1994) states that external regulations that distinguish speech inside and outside the subject are impossible to formulate. "What is 'outside the subject' is a judgment only the audience can make" (39), and therefore will vary with the audience. Whether an argument exists or not, however, *can be* discerned.

24. Wayne Rebhorn (1995) acknowledges that Cicero portrays the orator as dominating the judges, but considers this portrayal "a kind of 'minority view.'" More common, Rebhorn argues, is Cicero's placing "the judge metaphorically above the competing speakers" (34–35, 38–39). Given the prevalence, in *De oratore,* of statements supporting the orator's use of emotions to direct the audience, I think Cicero's emphasis on the oratorical domination of listeners is more than a minority view, but an important side of his more complete view.

25. See also Cicero (1923a): "[O]n the stage, I mean on the platform [*in contione*], where there is the greatest opportunity for deception and disguise, truth yet prevails, provided it is made plain and brought into the light of day" (97).

26. This belief that the audience will see through rhetorical manipulation is supported by Robert Morstein-Marx's more recent work (2013) and Alexander Yakobson's research (2010), which shows that the *populus* was better able to ascertain their own interests than has often been acknowledged.

27. I am not arguing that Cicero structures his case for a rhetoric that is not emotionally manipulative in the manner of the examples and quotations I present. Rather, I maintain that the responses I attribute to him are consistent with the positions he takes.

28. Aristotle varies his conception of specific emotions based on the intellectual category

of his analysis, for example, ethics, rhetoric, dialectic, or psychology. In the *Rhetoric,* for instance, Aristotle (1991) defines the emotion "anger" as "desire, accompanied by distress, for conspicuous retaliation because of a conspicuous slight" (2.2.1). In *De anima* (Aristotle 1984a, 403a25–b1), where Aristotle is interested in a physical definition, he defines it as a boiling of the blood or warm substance around the heart. These definitional differences derive from distinct intellectual aims, however, and are not determined by decorum.

29. Decorum is the fourth cardinal virtue (after wisdom, social virtue, and greatness of spirit) Cicero lists in *De officiis* (1991a, 1.93–151). It is a duty in the sense that it is "an act that is ethically required and the omission of which is ethically forbidden," a description of duties (*officia*) (like decorum) derived from justice (Dyck 1996, 7–8).

30. Formally, the Senate was composed of three hundred members before Sulla's reforms circa 80 BCE and six hundred afterward.

31. Although I disagree with Sprute, who argues that Aristotle recognizes in the *Rhetoric* two levels of rhetoric, ideal and normal, Sprute's account of Aristotle's ideal rhetoric differs from Cicero's superior oratory (1994, 118–21). For Sprute, Aristotle excludes all emotional appeals in ideal rhetoric; Cicero, even in his superior rhetoric, does not.

32. Dyck cites Powell's expectation of Cicero's train of thought in our passage, as indicated in a letter to Dyck (2004, 538). Although Aristotle lauds the Athenian Areopagus for barring irrelevant emotional appeals from its judicial decisions, as noted above, the Areopagus was a judicial body restricted to Athens' highest classes, originally based on birth and later on wealth (*Oxford Classical Dictionary*, 3rd rev. ed., s.v. "Areopagus."). Aristotle does not envisage a popular judicial body in which manipulative emotions are actually excluded. In addition, it is doubtful whether the Areopagus, like other Athenian criminal courts, restricted argumentation to the charge at issue (Wallace 1985, 124).

33. See ensuing passage where Cicero (1999e) condemns violence in politics because "[t]here is nothing more destructive for states, nothing more contrary to right and law" (3.42).

34. Cicero meant legislation for the best type of government to be lasting. "In his *Laws,* Cicero aims to compose just such a body of law" (Asmis 2008, 24–25).

35. That the Roman Constitution is in accordance with nature, that is, natural law, does not mean that it is identical to natural law, which is "perfectly in accordance with nature" (Asmis 2008, 26–31).

36. Cicero believes, however, that the exemplarity of good men will more likely effect change in the "character of states" than the reform of the people through formal education (1999e, 3.29–32).

37. See Goodin (1980, 122), for example, where he writes of "a pretty innocent form of manipulatory politics."

38. The claim that different professions have their own distinct moralities, often referred to as "professional ethics," is discussed in Applbaum (1999).

CHAPTER TWO

1. Similarly, Max Weber argues over fifty years before Walzer that politicians who adopt, what he calls, "an ethic of responsibility" must judge their actions—even when they violate

fundamental norms—by the foreseeable results on the political community. The mature politician who adopts this ethic, Weber maintains, "is aware of a responsibility for the consequences of his conduct and really feels such responsibility with heart and soul" (Weber 2009, 127).

2. For a broad discussion of dirty hands, see Parrish (2007).

3. Although Walzer (1973) denies that the need for dirty hands, i.e., the necessity to violate ordinary moral rules, leads to two separate moralities, public and private, in a later essay on emergency ethics (2004), Walzer emphasizes the moral obligation of political leaders, as representatives of the political community, to engage in immoral actions to save the community (41–43). As Tony Coady observes: "It is surely plausible to see [Walzer's later defense of dirty hands in the face of radical risk to our deepest values] as the claim that superior moral considerations of a distinctively political kind have defeated other moral considerations that would more normally be compelling" (2008, 80). In contrast to Walzer's earlier treatment of dirty hands, Nagel argues that there is a separate morality for the public realm (Walzer 1980, 130–31). In addition, Hampshire distinguishes between public and private morality, arguing that "the assumption of a political role, and of powers to change men's lives on a large scale" entails "a withholding of some of the scruples that in private life would prohibit one from using people as a means to an end and also from using force and deceit" (Hampshire 1978b, 52).

4. Unlike most dirty-hands thinkers, however, Cicero rarely acknowledges that the conventionally immoral but politically and (under the conditions) morally necessary act is, in any sense, a moral wrong. In some editions of a letter to his friend Atticus, however, Cicero describes his decision to accompany Pompey to Spain as the lesser of two evils, "the best in evil circumstances" (Cicero 1984, 7.18).

5. For sympathetic analyses of role-based morality, see several essays in Luban (1983), including Held (1983, 60–79) and Williams (1983, 259–69). See also Hardimon (1994). In the Luban volume, Wasserstrom (1983, 25–37) is more critical of, although not entirely unsympathetic to, role-based morality. Applbaum (1999) discusses the morality of roles at length but ultimately rejects it as unpersuasive. See also Markovits (2008, 1–2, 155). Like Cicero, for whom role morality must be consistent with generic morality, Markovits contends that "the ethics of role can never *displace* impartial morality, [although] role-based ideals may *complement* impartiality" (161).

6. As Applbaum observes, John Searle apparently holds the view that "morality itself is an institution created by constitutive rules," suggesting that morality as a whole, whether ordinary or role-based, has a single origin in collective acceptance (1999, 96).

7. For the difference between Cicero's own views and those of the Renaissance or early modern neo-Ciceronians on the value of the community vis-à-vis the individual, see my discussion of Justus Lipsius in chapter 4. Cicero's decorum-based morality can also accommodate the changes in attitudes toward the guilt of politicians with dirty hands. Although Cicero does not suggest that good politicians who violate conventional morality (in the interests of the state) should experience guilt, most contemporary moral thinkers who discuss dirty hands expect, like Walzer, that the moral politician will experience guilt for his necessary, but generally objectionable, actions. (David Konstan has suggested to me that the modernity of Walzer et al.'s sense of guilt over dirty hands is grounded, in part, on the modern conflict between practical necessities and Kantian principles of absolute morality.) Basing themselves on changing decorum, Ciceronian moral theorists may argue (contra Cicero himself) that when political morality

demands certain regrettable actions of a politician, the politician may, even should, feel guilt without actually being morally culpable. This standpoint would be consistent with Nielsen's position that, although politicians with dirty hands may have committed no moral crime, "[a]nyone in such a circumstance with an ounce of humanity will feel anguish in so acting and very deep remorse for having so acted. . . . Indeed, someone who did not feel anguish and remorse in such situations would hardly count as a moral agent. . . . But to *feel* guilty is not necessarily to *be* guilty" (2000, 139–40).

8. Dworkin's goals, however, differ from my own. Most fundamentally, Dworkin is interested in how moral principles embedded in the Constitution aid us in interpreting the Constitution (and how constitutional interpretation should guide future legal decision making); I am concerned with what the American constitutional tradition tells us about our moral principles. For Dworkin's particular understanding of a moral reading of the Constitution, see Dworkin (1996, 10–11; 1986, 239, 254–58).

9. Although the most prominent instances of the divergence between ordinary morality and political morality occur under emergency conditions, politicians may be subject to a distinct morality even under regular circumstances. For example, although private citizens are liable for defamatory statements despite (in the United States) their First Amendment right to freedom of speech, the Constitution, article 1, section 6, bars legislators from being criminally prosecuted and civilly sued for basely defaming the character of a private citizen when fulfilling the responsibilities of their office (Cella 1968, 40–41). The courts have further extended "the law of privilege as a defense by officers of government [judicial and executive] . . . , although the Constitution itself [specifies] an absolute privilege [only] to members of both Houses of Congress in respect to any speech, debate, vote, report, or action done in session" (*Barr v. Matteo*, 360 U.S. 564, 569). The speech and debate of legislative representatives in the United States are constitutionally protected above and beyond the speech and debate of private citizens because the privileges granted to members of Congress, including the protection of their speech and debate, and the free speech rights of ordinary citizens are based on different principles. The moral source of the doctrine of legislative privilege is the norm of self-rule or liberty as instantiated in the American form of representative government. To facilitate the functioning of representative government or, as the Court has stated, "to protect the integrity of the legislative process," legislative privilege must ensure "the independence of individual legislators" (*U.S. v. Brewster*, 408 U.S. 501, 507 [1972]; Killian and Costello 1996, 127–33).

10. See also Jefferson's defense of the Louisiana Purchase, which he considered unconstitutional but necessary as a natural emergency (Franklin 1991, 45). For similar comments, see Gross (2003, 1106–7).

11. On April 27, 1861, following the Confederate firing on Fort Sumter, President Lincoln authorized the suspension of the writ of *habeas corpus* (Farber 2003, 158). Chief Justice Roger Taney took up the constitutionality of Lincoln's suspension in *Ex parte Merryman*. For Taney, the questions surrounding Lincoln's action were both legal, i.e., whether the president can unilaterally suspend the writ of *habeas corpus*, and moral, i.e., whether Lincoln was imperiling America's fundamental values. In his decision, Taney found that Lincoln's suspension of the writ was unconstitutional—arguing that the suspension power is in article 1, which lists the powers of Congress, not in article 2, which lists executive powers—and contrary to the value of

personal liberty, a fundamental norm of the Anglo-American peoples (*Ex parte Merryman*, 17 F. Cas. 892 [1861]). According to Taney, the executive branch has no power to suspend the writ of *habeas corpus*, even in cases of emergency; no argument supporting the president's suspension can "be drawn from . . . the necessities of government for self defense in times of tumult and danger" (892). Lincoln rejected Taney's ruling and directed his officers to defy the chief justice. His response to Taney's opinion in his July 4 special message to Congress, however, was ambiguous. As Richard Fallon notes, Lincoln distinguished between two levels of constitutional legality; the first is the domain "of the strictly legal," the second, what the Constitution authorizes under extraordinary circumstances. Although Lincoln concluded that his actions were strictly legal, his focus on the practical necessity of suspending the writ when faced with "a dangerous emergency" suggests that he was, simultaneously, relying on the claims of exigent circumstances, i.e., the second (not "strictly legal") level of constitutional permissibility. For a fuller discussion of the constitutional history and issues surrounding Lincoln's suspension of the writ of *habeas corpus*, see *Ex parte Merryman*, 17 F. Cas. 144 (1861); Farber (2003), and Fallon (2013, 358–62).

12. Although Taney ruled against Lincoln's suspension of the writ of *habeas corpus*, judges, in general, have not entangled themselves in constitutionally questionable presidential actions taken in the name of preserving the Republic. The courts have largely shied away from deciding on most national security cases, defending their reticence on procedural grounds—the courts' silence redounding to the benefit of presidents. Most commonly, the Supreme Court justifies not intervening in matters of war powers and foreign affairs because of procedural and jurisdictional obstacles like standing, nonjusticiability (i.e., the political question doctrine), ripeness, and mootness (Entin 1997, 1305–13). And when the courts do consider cases that significantly confront the exercise of emergency powers, the decision almost inevitably favors the government (May 1989, 261).

13. Cicero defines "*officium*" as relating to both public and private morality: "I don't feel any doubt that what the Greeks call *kathekon* is our 'duty' [*officium*]. Why do you doubt that it would apply perfectly well to public, as well as private, life?" (1999c, 425.3).

14. Cicero's own conception of *personae* is influenced by Panaetius, the Stoic philosopher from Rhodes, who develops the concept *personae* in his treatise *Peri tou kathekontos*, or *On Duties*. Panaetius's work was Cicero's main external source for the first two books of his own *De officiis*, a work divided into three books. We cannot ascertain with any certainty what is original to Cicero and what is derived from Panaetius. My argument for Cicero's relevance to political morality, however, is not based on Cicero's personal innovativeness, which, in any event, cannot be measured given that we no longer have Panaetius's work. I maintain Cicero's significance, here, because he is the first political theorist who defines general and more particular obligations as part of a single moral theory. For a discussion of Panaetius as Cicero's source, see Dyck (1996, 17–29).

15. Orators include politicians, as deliberative or political oratory is one of the three main rhetorical genres.

16. Cicero identifies statesmanship with the highest virtue: "True dignity lies in virtue; and virtue is most conspicuously displayed in eminent services to the commonwealth" (2001c, 377.5). The politician is even godlike: "And there is nothing in which human virtue approaches the divine more closely than in the founding of new states or the preservation of existing ones"

(1999d, 1.12). In his account of *personae*, however, Cicero promotes the obligation to fulfill the second role, i.e., selecting our vocation by how it comports with our nature, above any responsibility to choose a higher position: "let us follow our own nature, so that even if other pursuits may be weightier and better, we should measure our own by the rule of our own nature" (Cicero 1991a, 1.110). See further discussion of Cicero's approving the freedom (even of "better men") to eschew political roles in chapter 6.

17. In *De officiis*, however, Cicero condemns Romulus for killing his brother so that he could rule alone rather than share power with Remus (1991a 3.41). But as Andrew Dyck explains, "it was doubtless Caesar's emphasis on Romulus at a time when he was striving for the kingship" that caused Cicero to assail Romulus in *De officiis*, which was composed in 44, the year of Caesar's assassination (Dyck 1996, 545).

18. Thus, the *persona* theory explains Cicero's condemnation of Romulus's fratricide in *De officiis*; he killed Remus not for the public welfare but for his own good, and he did so viciously.

19. "The Senate was set up as a Council over the State for ever. . . . The Senate was set up as the guardian, the president, the defender of the State" (Cicero 1958a, 137).

20. The morality of the orator's use of emotional manipulation, however, was the central concern of the previous chapter.

21. In *De republica*, Cicero has Scipio state that "the consuls were to have power that lasted only for one year but was in form and law like royal power" (1999d, 2.56).

22. The tribunes of the *plebs*, who eventually numbered ten, were also elected public officials who held extraordinary powers. Unlike regular magistrates, however, they were elected by the plebeians. Their bodies were considered sacrosanct and possessed a general right of veto (Lintott 1999b, 32–33, 120–28; Vishnia 2012, 73–75).

23. As we shall soon see, Cicero acknowledges the ordinary citizen's obligation to act for the state's welfare, even to undertake extreme actions, but only when politicians are unable to act and not as an obligation of their fourth *persona*.

24. On freedom as a Roman concept precluding the possibility of arbitrary interference by others, see Pettit (1997, 2001).

25. Last believes that the substance of the *senatus consultum ultimum* "was not more than an exhortation to the executive to attend to the business which it was appointed to perform." Last implies that this interpretation is also Cicero's (Last 1932, 84, 86). Similarly, Lintott argues that Cicero believed that magistrates had the power to kill the Catilinarian conspirators even without the *senatus consultum ultimum*, but that it was a vote of confidence "for carrying out an action whose propriety should not be disputed" (1999a, 171). Contra Last and Lintott, Thomas Mitchell maintains that, for Cicero, "it was the senate, and not the consuls, which was placed in supreme command as a result of the ultimate decree." According to Mitchell, magistrates received their power from the Senate and, even after issuing its ultimate decree, the Senate, as the supreme deliberative body, "continued as the director of the consul's subsequent actions" (Mitchell 1971, 54–55). Mitchell accurately points out that Cicero, while conceding that he *proposed* the punishment of the Catilinarian conspirators—"that beneficent and conscientious proposal"—identified their punishment and sentence as "the work of the senate." Cicero, however, emphasizes the Senate's role against the Catilinarians so that he may deflect an attack against him for cruelty against the Catilinarians (Mitchell 1971, 55; Cicero 1953b, 14; see also

Cicero 1926, 2.18). For a critique of Mitchell's interpretation of Cicero's thinking on the *senatus consultum ultimum*, see Lintott (1999b, 92–93).

26. Cicero further endorses the priority of magistrates over private citizens in his account of the killing of Spurius Maelius by Gaius Servius Ahala for aiming at sole rule. According to the oldest tradition, Ahala killed Maelius with the Senate's advice but as a private citizen, not a magistrate. Cicero, however, cites an altered version of the story in which Ahala killed Maelius as a magistrate—the master of the horse (*magister equitum*)—second in command to Lucius Quinctius Cincinnatus, who was appointed dictator. By adopting this revised account of the story, Cicero implies that he prefers that this "irregular" killing be considered the work of a magistrate, not a private citizen (Cicero 1923c, 56; Lintott 1999b, 55–56).

27. In *Pro Rabirio*, Cicero proclaims that it is the "duty of good and courageous citizens . . . to block every crisis in our history, to block all the approaches of revolution, to strengthen the bulwarks of the Republic." But when Cicero explains how citizens can protect the Republic, he centers on their support for the established leadership: "to hold supreme the executive power of the consuls, the deliberative power of the Senate, and by your verdict to declare that he who has followed their guidance deserves praise and honour rather than condemnation and punishment" (2000b, 3).

28. In *De officiis*, Cicero includes in the *honestum* incumbent on ordinary citizens elements of the *utile*, particularly the safety of the state. Colish goes so far as to argue that Cicero reformulated the Stoic conception of the relationship between the *honestum* and the *utile*—in which the *honestum* constitutes the *only* good—to the extent of assimilating the *honestum* to the *utile* (1990, 148–50).

29. Although Cicero describes here general decorum as opposed to the decorum of the *personae*, he does not differentiate between this decorum and the decorum of the first *persona*, which applies to human nature most generally. See Cicero (1991a, 1.107) and Schofield (2012, 48).

30. Cary Nederman's distinction (2000a, 247–59) between "two different and competing theoretical defenses of republicanism within the body of [Cicero's] work"—(1) rhetorical republicanism and (2) rational republicanism—largely aligns with my emphasis on (1) Cicero's rhetorically based political morality and (2) the focus on Cicero as a proponent of natural law.

31. "Indeed, the requirements of the Roman constitution appear to trump the requirements of natural law at the most basic level of civic organization, the laws concerning magistrates" (Asmis 2008, 26).

32. Cicero's norms of legal advocacy and of political activity may be said to be constitutive rules, "which constitute (and also regulate) an activity the existence of which is logically dependent on the rules" (Searle 1969, 34). Practicing law and practicing politics are not activities that preexist the community's creation of (or at least agreement to) these professions' norms.

33. Politics as a vocation would not exist without the political community. Politicians also depend on the community's approbation: orators must persuade their audience, if they are to succeed; magistrates must be elected by the appropriate popular assemblies to gain their jobs. On the selection process for Roman officials, see Lintott (1999b).

34. Searle writes of "institutional facts" here, not politicians per se.

35. John Glucker describes how Cicero also adopted the views of the "Old Academy," associated with his teacher, Antiochus of Ascalon. Glucker, however, distinguishes between Cicero's

affiliation with the Old Academy and his switch, later in life, to the views of the skeptical New Academy. See Glucker (1988, 34–69).

36. Cicero illustrates his procedure of adapting Greek philosophy to Roman context in *De oratore*: "although [*De oratore*] is thoroughly imbued with Greek philosophy and rhetorical theory, the dialogue deliberately and insistently subordinates its models and sources to the practical purposes of Roman statesmen. We have not rhetoric but the Roman orator; not Socrates . . . but Crassus; a textbook of rhetoric (*ars rhetorica*) that is both formally included within the dialogue and constantly distorted and deferred in favour of Roman law and Roman exempla" (Zetzel 2003, 135).

37. Cicero (1991a, 1.35) permits an enemy army to surrender unharmed even after the battering ram has crashed against their wall—more humanitarian behavior than traditional Roman practice.

38. Cicero maintains in his rhetorical works that "the natural law has no actual binding force in Roman jurisprudence" (Colish 1990, 97).

39. Likewise, Cicero accounts for the development of the Roman Constitution, in the second book of *De republica*, as rooted in Rome's own experience, not the product of any philosophers' ideas, whether indigenous or foreign.

40. Quintus rejects the *tribunate* here for expanding the leadership roles of the plebeians at the expense of the patricians. Quintus does not directly address popular political participation more generally.

41. Further justifications of popular participation can be found in Cicero (1999d, 2.57, 1.47, 1.69). The last citation, in particular, reflects Peripatetic sources (Frede 1989, 89–90).

42. For possible penalties, see Gross (2003, 1126).

43. The problems of *ex ante* approval discussed here are not altogether peculiar to current politics. Additionally, we are evaluating *ex ante* authorization by the people (or their representatives), not *ex ante* approval by nonpopular institutions, like the courts and bureaucracies. For example, we do not consider *ex ante* approval of governmental surveillance by the FISA Court—a US federal court established under the Foreign Intelligence Surveillance Act of 1978 (FISA)—which oversees requests submitted by the US government for approval of electronic surveillance, physical search, and other investigative actions for foreign intelligence purposes.

44. Cicero goes so far as to describe his support as global: "I forbear to mention the unanimity of judgement and opinion with regard to my services displayed by communities, tribes, provinces, kings, and, in a word, by all the world." (1923b, 75).

45. Likewise, Cicero states to the Senate: "Can I ever adequately manifest my gratitude towards *Gnaeus Pompeius for having stated not merely in the presence of you, who were united in sentiment, but also before the whole people, that the safety of the Roman people had been secured by me, and stood or fell with my own*" (1923e 29; emphasis added).

46. In the *Merryman* case, Lincoln's suspension of the writ of *habeas corpus* was specifically affirmed by Congress, the people's representatives (Farber 2003, 159; Friedman 2009, 445n143). In addition, Lincoln was strongly supported by public opinion. As the *North American Review* observed regarding the *Merryman* decision, "the Chief Justice . . . failed to secure the support of the people . . . because there were circumstances of no ordinary character involved in the case" (*North American Review* 1861, 475; Friedman 2009, 123–24). Eventually, Lincoln's actions

were arguably affirmed by the citizenry in his 1864 reelection, where he carried twenty-two states against his opponent General George B. McClellan's three. That Lincoln's actions were affirmed by the people, however, does not imply that all politicians' actions have been, or will be, popularly ratified. And we should not infer popular ratification from popular inaction. Just as the courts' silence during periods of national danger is not tantamount to their approval, so too public inactivity should not be equated with the people's *ex post* authorization of normally immoral political acts. Only public affirmation justifies political actors in violating the political norms that hold sway during less urgent situations. Reelection of officials who conceal their morally dubious behavior from the electorate cannot be considered popular ratification. Thus, Gross writes that "the returning to office of elected officials who have acted extralegally" indicates public *ex post* ratification only when the elected officials "have openly and candidly disclosed the nature of the actions to the public" (2003, 1114). The reelection of George W. Bush in 2004 should not be considered popular ratification of his administration's use of torture against enemy prisoners because the administration concealed the full extent of its policy of torture. See Siems (2012).

CHAPTER THREE

1. He endeavors in book 3 of *De officiis* to demonstrate how, in practice, the *honestum* and the *utile* are reconciled or balanced. See also Cicero (2001a, 2.334).

2. Although Barlow does not speak explicitly of Machiavelli's rhetorical politics, his description of Machiavelli's politics "as unlimited by considerations outside politics itself (1999, 637)," like the *honestum*, is consistent with Kahn's (1994, 24) conception of the rhetorical Machiavelli. Eugene Garver (1987, chap. 3) uses the term *rhetorical politics* to describe Machiavelli's prudential approach to politics. Garver writes that "only a politics in which prudence is fundamental can be called a *rhetorical politics*" (1987, 65).

3. Like Kahn and Barlow, Mark Hulliung juxtaposes Cicero and Machiavelli on the relationship between the *honestum* and the *utile*: "Cicero's argument was that since goodness is useful for the soul, no conflict is possible between the *honestum* and the *utile*." But Machiavelli subordinates goodness to utility (1983, 195). In contrast to Kahn, Barlow, Hulliung, and others, including myself, John McCormick (2011) maintains that though Machiavelli inverts Cicero's understanding of *honestas* (*onestà*) by attributing it to the people, i.e., the vulgar instead of the nobles, the Florentine still maintains its compatibility with the *utilitas* (24–25, 194n4).

4. Isaiah Berlin suggests the distance between Machiavelli and his contemporaries when he states that Machiavelli "completely ignores the concepts and categories—the routine paraphernalia—in terms of which the best known thinkers and scholars of his day were accustomed to express themselves" (1972, 160). Paul Rahe accepts Leo Strauss's argument that Machiavelli breaks with classical political philosophy, including "Plato, Aristotle, and the political philosopher Cicero" (Strauss 1958, 290). Thus Rahe concludes: "If a genuine admiration for classical antiquity was the distinguishing feature of the Renaissance, Machiavelli was the man who killed it once and for all." Rahe admonishes his readers to "cease speaking of Machiavelli as a civic humanist, classical republican, or neo-Roman" (2000, 308, 306). By contrast, Felix Gilbert notes that despite a seeming "abyss" separating them, "there is some connection between

the humanists and Machiavelli." According to Gilbert, those chapters in *The Prince* in which Machiavelli "falls most foul of conventional morality . . . were by a consequence of pushing to its logical conclusion the argument that first appeared in the writings of the humanists" (1939, 464). Quentin Skinner denies the belief that "in the *Discourses* no less than in *The Prince*, Machiavelli's outlook is entirely sui generis." Rather, Skinner maintains that Machiavelli shares basic political assumptions with his contemporaries, while simultaneously mounting "a direct attack" on their political theories (1978, 1:128–38, 180–86).

5. Paul Oskar Kristeller writes that "the ancient writer who earned [the humanists'] highest admiration was Cicero. Renaissance humanism was an age of Ciceronianism in which the study and imitation of Cicero was a widespread concern, although the exaggeration of this tendency also found its critics" (1961, 18). Similarly, Marc Fumaroli (1980, 40) has argued that the Renaissance could be called the *aetas ciceroniana*, the Age of Cicero.

6. Leslie Walker, SJ, for example, denies Cicero's influence on Machiavelli: "It would seem, then, to be almost certain that Machiavelli had read the *De Officiis*, but the result was not that he found himself in agreement with Cicero's doctrine, . . . but that he took up on the main issue a diametrically opposite position" (see Machiavelli 1975, 2:278). Rahe (2000, 301) denies Cicero's influence on Machiavelli, as part of a larger argument that Machiavelli is a "modern" breaking from the past. By contrast, Marcia Colish argues that Cicero's "*De officiis* could supply Machiavelli . . . with a way of defining his ethical terminology and a structural framework for the analysis of the ethics of public life." Although Colish concedes that "Machiavelli could, and . . . did apply this Ciceronian bequest in a positive as well as in a negative way," she focuses more on the parallels between Cicero and Machiavelli than on the differences (1978, 82).

7. Barlow writes, "Cicero has been presented as a predecessor whom Machiavelli either followed in his analysis, or rejected entirely. Both of these positions prove to have elements of truth, but each is incomplete" (1999, 644). According to Kahn, Machiavelli "does not so much abandon the resources of humanist rhetoric as use them against humanism itself" (1994, 19).

8. As Paul Oskar Kristeller argues, rhetoric is central to the thought of the humanists. Renaissance humanism, he writes, "must be understood as a characteristic phase in what may be called the rhetorical tradition in Western culture" (1961, 11–13). And as Eugene Garver contends, "Machiavelli too was part of the Renaissance rhetorical tradition" (1987, 26). For a bibliography of recent work on the rhetorical dimension of Machiavelli's political thought, see Kahn (1994, 254n9) and Cox (1997, 1110n3). Maurizio Viroli (1998) links Machiavelli to the classical rhetorical tradition, including the Ciceronian strain. Viroli concedes Kahn's and Barlow's position, that Machiavelli may have "been submitting to a severe critique the conventional view repeated [from Cicero's *De officiis*] by the humanist writers on political affairs that honour must always have priority over advantage." Nevertheless, Viroli recognizes that when Cicero's *oeuvre* is examined, the Roman rhetorician's own stand on the relationship between *honestas* and *utilitas* is more complex than his "euphoric . . . view that honour must always have precedence over interest" found in *De officiis* (88–91).

9. Garver describes Machiavelli similarly: Machiavelli "concludes that no principle guarantees success. Therefore, practical intelligence must be prudent, suited to deliberation about shifting particulars, not the logical derivation of acts from ethical first principles" (2003, 68).

10. Machiavelli understood that "the criterion of correct action" for the orator "is not moral

goodness or the intrinsically moral judgment of prudence but the functional excellence or effectiveness of *virtù*—"a *virtù* . . . that demonstrates its own excellence in being effective" (Kahn 1994, 32).

11. *Virtù* is often translated, depending on context, as "ability," "skill," "energy," "determination." See Machiavelli (1988, 103–04).

12. Garver (1987, 60–62) offers a detailed list of Machiavelli's contradictoriness in both *The Prince* and the *Discourses*.

13. Colish, who emphasizes the parallels between Machiavelli and Cicero, acknowledges "Machiavelli's advocacy of dissimulation" as a "striking departure from Cicero" (1978, 90–91). Like Colish, Michelle Zerba finds important similarities between Cicero and Machiavelli but, in contrast to Colish, Zerba reads Cicero as a dissimulating proto-Machiavellian: "For both thinkers, the *utile* controls considerations of politics. . . . Cicero and Machiavelli alike concede that it would be nice if rulers could both seem and be good. But since greed and envy prevent this ideal from being realized, the ruler must retrench: he must appear to be good, whatever else he might be" (2012, 201).

14. Tarcov, however, maintains that Machiavelli's attitude toward glory is more ambiguous than what is suggested here. Although Machiavelli holds out the promise of eternal glory for great men, he acknowledges that "the names of most excellent men who deserve more praise than Alexander the Great have been forgotten" (Tarcov, forthcoming; see also Machiavelli 1975, 1:1.4).

15. Machiavelli (see 1975, 1:1.11) also treats Numa Pompilius, successor to Romulus and founder of the Roman religion, in political terms.

16. Garver, however, argues that Machiavelli defends a new prince and politics against a traditional prince and politics. Machiavelli, according to Garver (1987, 103–05), uses the appearance of tradition to justify the rejection of tradition.

17. The Stoics' tendency was to regard "the essence of a human being, the real self, as identical to the *hēgemikon*" (Long 1996, 248), that is, "the mind, which represents a rational and unified consciousness" (Reydams-Schils 2005, 15–16), and it is we, as rational beings who determine the correct course of action in concrete situations, based on the demands of virtue.

18. On Cicero's ambivalence about glory as the moral good on the one hand and as public acclaim on the other, see Griffin: "The Stoics themselves differed over whether *eudoxia* (good repute) had any value even as a positive indifferent, and Cicero himself was prepared to accept that only true *gloria* based on solid virtue and accorded by good men was worth pursuing (*Off.* 2.43). But Cicero's own choice of *honestum* . . . reveals an assumption that he makes explicit in the first of the *Paradoxa Stoicorum*: there, after saying that our ancestors agreed with the Stoics that only *quod rectum et honestum et cum virtute est* (what is right and honorable and accompanied by virtue) is good, he enumerates deeds of these Roman paragons that demonstrate their beliefs that the only thing in life worth seeking is what is worthy of praise and renown (*quod laudabile esset et praeclarum*). The Romans could not accept that the conduct of the individual should not be governed in any way by the estimate of others" (1996, 196). Not only Cicero but also the Romans of his time conceived glory as honorable deeds and associated glory with public praise as is manifested in the way they vested *honestum* and related terms like *laus, dignitas*, and *decus* with "strong connotations of reputation as well as of simple virtue" (Miles 1996, 23–24).

19. See also St. Augustine (1998, 5.8): In *De republica*, Cicero, having spoken of the education of the city's ruler, "says that he should be nurtured on glory." Augustine further cites Cicero as claiming that "his own ancestors had done many marvelous and famous deeds because of their passion for glory."

20. Cicero also contends that ignoble actions should be avoided not because of external threats, but because it would be unjust to do otherwise. Thus Cicero states that one must keep one's oaths not because of the anger of the gods, "which does not exist, but [because of] justice and faith" (1991a, 3.104; cf. Machiavelli 1975, 1:1.11). Similarly, Cicero relates Plato's myth of Gyges's ring, where Gyges's invisibility allowed him to act with impunity. The honorable man, Cicero argues here, would not do something "for the sake of riches, power, despotism, or lust, [even] if it would be always unknown by gods and by men alike." Good men "concede that everything dishonorable should on its own account be avoided" (Cicero 1991a, 3:38–39).

21. See Hariman 2001, 205.

22. Berlin's own position on Cicero is more complicated as he links Cicero with the pagan morality that Machiavelli defends.

23. Cicero, however, restricts natural law's applicability, as seen in the previous chapter, by focusing more frequently on the imperfect duties relevant to ordinary citizens than on the perfect duties embodied in natural law, attainable only by the wise man. Thus, "[i]mperfect humans cannot obey the commands of [natural] law, but they can nonetheless be guided by law by obeying part of its commands—that is, the part that demands an intermediate action" (Asmis 2008, 15).

CHAPTER FOUR

1. Besides Tacitus, Lipsius is closely linked with the Stoic Seneca and is seen as a founder of Neostoicism. Lipsius wrote several works on Stoicism, most famously the dialogue *De constantia* (1583). In addition, he published, late in his life, an edition of Seneca's philosophical writings and manuals on Stoic doctrine and physics. Nevertheless, because of the near ubiquity of Tacitus in the *Politica*, Lipsius's political theory is most often described as Tacitist, not Neostoic. In his *Neostoicism and the Early Modern State*, however, Gerhard Oestreich (1982) argues that Lipsius's political thought "derived from the Neostoic philosophy of the state" (70). Christopher Brooke (2012) has argued, more cautiously, for a Stoic influence on Lipsius's political ideas, so that the *Politica* can be viewed, to some extent, as constructed in "a modified Senecan framework" (27). For other views supporting Lipsius's political ideas as Neostoic, see McCrea (1997, 3–39) and Senellart (1995, 211–42; 1999, 117–39). For claims of Machiavelli's influence on Lipsius, see n. 2. Although Diana Stanciu argues for Aristotle's influence on Lipsius's later political work *Monita et exempla politica*, she also makes the case for the Stagirite's influence on the *Politica* (2011, 233–62).

2. Waszink is the translator and editor of the first edition of the *Politica* to appear in almost 250 years and the first English translation of the work to be published in more than 400 years. Not surprisingly, given his defense of princely deceit, Lipsius has often been linked (alongside Tacitus) with Machiavelli. For example, see van Gelderen (1990, 209–10). Waszink (2004) describes Tacitus and Machiavelli as complementing each other, with Machiavelli's *Prince*

contributing to Lipsius "the realistic analysis and explicit precepts of statecraft," and Tacitus's *Annals* and *Histories* adding "elements of a critical re-assessment of political morality" (102). I focus on Tacitus, not Machiavelli, because Lipsius himself criticizes Machiavelli for pursuing political advantage without morality.

3. Peter Miller (1994) argues even more vociferously for the continued Ciceronian influence on Lipsius and other thinkers who are identified as Tacitists. He grants that although "Tacitus surely gained in importance and certainly took on a specific role in contemporary political and social thought, Cicero, far from disappearing was correspondingly reevalutated" (21).

4. I use Lipsius's *Politica* as the model of his mature political thought. Although his later political work, the *Monita et exempla politica* (1605), which Lipsius describes as an illustration and confirmation of, and a commentary to, the *Politica* (De Bom et al. 2011, 9), may seem an obvious source of Lipsius's later political views, he defends a more traditional conception of morality in the *Monita*: "Contrary to the *Politica*, much more credit is given in the *Monita* to justice in relation to prudence, while the hotly debated and often condemned concept of so-called *prudentia mixta* is not mentioned at all" (De Bom et al. 2011, 16). Thus, the *Monita* does not reflect the political morality Lipsius upholds in book 4 of the *Politica*. For the view that the *Monita* espouses an unconventional morality, albeit more subtly than the *Politica*, see Braun (2011, 135–62).

5. I support my claim that Cicero is the primary influence on Lipsian prudence in this chapter by demonstrating Lipsius's reliance on Ciceronian prudence from his early days through maturity. For example, I show how Lipsius defines prudence, in the *Politica*, as adapting oneself to context—a definition almost identical to Cicero's definition of decorum in the *Orator*. A significant difference between Aristotle's and Cicero's conceptions of prudence, which indicates that Lipsius relies on the Ciceronian, not Aristotelian, conception in making his case for mixed prudence is that, for Aristotle, prudence is enacted by choosing the intrinsically good over the instrumentally good (Depew 2004a, 172). Cicero, however, blurs the line between the intrinsic good (*honestum*) and the instrumental good (*utile*), as does Lipsius in mixed prudence (see chapter 5).

6. Although Jon Snyder does not distinguish, as does Tuck, between two humanisms with Lipsius initiating the new humanism, he credits Lipsius with triggering the revival of Tacitism (with its legitimation of dissimulation) throughout Europe. See Snyder (2009, 14–15).

7. This task of refuting the greatly exaggerated reports of Ciceronianism's death, to paraphrase Mark Twain, has already been taken up by Peter Miller (1994, 21–87), who attempts to demonstrate the widespread references to Cicero's moralization of the common good in early modern political writings, albeit with some exaggeration. But Miller chooses breadth rather than depth in his account of Cicero's "post-Tacitean" influence, with little detailed analysis of any early modern "Ciceronian" thinker. I choose, instead, to analyze Lipsius extensively because of his iconic status as the political theorist who "breaks" with Cicero.

8. Although Lipsius applies this citation from the *Agricola* to princely behavior, Tacitus himself intends it to recommend the young Agricola's virtues as a subordinate, "*peritus obsequi*, trained to habits of deference" (Tacitus 1970a, 8.1; Morford 1993, 148).

9. Lipsius expresses this view of Machiavelli in the marginal notes of his *De consilio et forma nostri operis*, part of the preliminary matter of the *Politica*.

10. Waszink (2004) states: "The attack on Ciceronian morality is conspicuous and explicit: the quote from *De Officiis* is marked as such, with the result that the main person to be called naïve

(*puer*) is indeed Cicero himself. Given the fact that the defence of good uses of *prudentia mixta* is one of the major elements of the *Politica*, it is clear that Lipsius with respect to his political theory may indeed be called a clear and conscious 'anti-Ciceronian' (for lack of a better term)" (144).

11. Additionally, when Tacitus describes Agricola, his father in law, as naturally prudent, he suggests that Agricola possessed a sense of propriety that enabled him to adapt to context—akin to Cicero's decorum: "When the business of assize courts demanded he was serious, keen, strict, yet more than merciful; when he had fulfilled the demands of office he dropped the official mask" (1970a, 9.2–4).

12. Cicero is the author cited most often, after Tacitus, in the *Politica* (Waszink 2004, 138).

13. Although Lipsius published his first edition of Tacitus in 1574, he makes little use of Tacitus's political writings in his early works. See Waszink (2004, 93–95, especially 95 and n. 32). For Tuck (1993, 40), Lipsius's major contribution to the "new humanism" does not take place until the 1580s. By contrast, Morford (1993) states that by 1572 "Lipsius had already found in Tacitus the source of *prudentia*" (137).

14. Like Plato, Cicero uses the ship of state metaphor (particularly in *Pro Sestio*) to condemn demagogues (or *populares*). See May (1980) and Vasaly (2013, 155).

15. Although, as noted in the previous chapter, Cicero sometimes includes self-interest in his conception of the moral, he emphasizes the significance of (and discusses more frequently) the common interest as a central element of the *honestum*.

16. Though Cicero links morality to motivation, this belief is not unique to Cicero.

17. See also letter 18 (1999a) for Cicero's description of Cato as displaying more consistency and honesty than prudence or ability.

18. Lipsius demands constancy, however, from the subject, as he argues in *De constantia* and the *Politica*. See Brooke (2012, 30).

19. Cicero defends the Spaniard Lucius Cornelius Balbus in this speech against charges that his Roman citizenship was illegally conferred on him by Pompey.

20. For the view that Lipsius distinguishes between the lower morals demanded of the prince and the higher morals required of the counselor (who, in Stoic terms, is closer to the wise man), see Stanciu (2011, 235–36).

21. "Wine does not stop being wine when it is mixed with a little water, nor does Prudence stop being Prudence when it is mixed with a little drop of deceit" (Lipsius 2004, 509). See also Vasaly (2013, 155n31).

22. Lipsius (2004) still balks at fully accepting that "departing [partially] from the Honourable" (*honestum*) is not tantamount to "depart[ing] from Virtue" (509).

23. Lipsius's advice that the prince must sometimes play the fox when dealing with a fox, although cited from Erasmus, almost certainly suggests agreement with Machiavelli's position in *The Prince* (chapter 18), where the Florentine counsels the ruler to adopt foxiness, i.e., feigning and dissembling. Lipsius, however, parts ways with Machiavelli in maintaining, unlike Machiavelli but like Cicero, that deceit is morally legitimated when it "serves public profit and well-being."

24. "[E]ven if no one praises [moral goodness], it is by nature [*natura*] worthy of praise" (Cicero 1991a, 1:14).

25. I wish to thank Professor Roger Ulrich for his help in translating Lipsius's *"labella et linea"* as "level and plumb line" and for his aid in explaining the function of these tools.

26. See also Lipsius (2004, 311–13), for a statement on the inseparability (and indispensability) of prudence and virtue for a prince's legitimacy and independence.

27. Likewise, the link between the honorable and the beneficial distinguishes Cicero from Machiavelli, as argued in the previous chapter.

28. In this chapter, the citations from Cicero are arranged as follows: four in a row (two pro, then two contra), followed by a citation from Perseus's *Satires*; a single (pro) citation, followed by selections from Aristotle's *Politics* and Erasmus's *Adagia*; five (pro) consecutive quotations from Cicero, followed by five maxims from Tacitus's *Agricola*, Sallust's *Histories*, Seneca's *Thyestes* and *Phoenissae*, and Vergil's *Aeneid*; and then a single (pro) citation of Cicero, followed by quotations from five classical authors—Lucretius, Pacuvius, Plutarch, Pindar, Aristotle—and the Church Father, Basil of Caesarea.

29. On Lipsius's departure from an author's original meaning to constitute a new text and meaning, see Tucker 2011. One likely explanation for Lipsius's (2004) quoting an author out of context is his manifest concern with finding those maxims that most effectively and coherently convey his *own* argument: *"just as the Phrygians make one single tapestry out of a variety of coloured threads, so I make this uniform and coherent work out of a myriad of parts"* (233). Although Lipsius may cite statements that are taken out of their specific context—because these statements function best in his cento—he does not necessarily use these statements contrary to their authors' more general perspective.

30. Lipsius's faithfulness to Tacitus is in even greater question. See Waszink (2004, 150–55). Lipsius's fidelity to the actual Tacitus, as supporters of the dominant account themselves acknowledge, is problematical: he cites him most frequently, but his citations are often at odds with what Tacitus's words mean in context (Morford 1993, 143–45). (I do not reject Tacitus's influence here but only point up the problem of identifying Tacitus as *the* source of any one of Lipsius's arguments.) Morford acknowledges, for example, that "Tacitean *prudentia* . . . is the foundation of doctrines that are those of Lipsius, not necessarily of Tacitus" (151).

31. I do not attempt here to solve the apparently intractable problem of making sense of when and why Lipsius remains faithful to the authorities cited as opposed to "riding roughshod over the quotation indicators" (Moss 1998, 422). Waszink (2004) offers a fairly thorough account of the difficulties related to interpreting the *Politica*, i.e., the extent to which it primarily reflects Lipsius's own views and citations are "emptied of their original meaning" (58–79).

32. Lipsius (2004, 233) states in the preliminary matter to the *Politica* that he views the words and phrases of the ancient writers cited as "solid and established," carrying greater force and authority than his own.

33. In making this claim about Lipsius's use of Cicero, I rely on Waszink's sensible observation about the *Politica*'s correctly cited quotations more generally. According to Waszink (2004), when "Lipsius' context and the original context are not at conflict," then "knowledge of, or reference to, the original context contributes [some of the time] in a simple and unproblematic way to a deeper understanding of Lipsius' argument" (60). Waszink, however, contends that ultimately "the reader must more or less decide for himself which ['notions and meanings included in or corrected with the citation must be included in Lipsius' argument'] and which must not" (61–63).

34. In the preliminary matter to the *Politica*, Lipsius (2004) includes the admonition: "That you always consult the notes which are at the side of the text. Which you will find build into an

interconnected whole, and, to your great profit, always contain a summary of the entire content; you will even find that the content is often somewhat more closely circumscribed by them and explained" (237).

35. In context, Cicero speaks to the relationship between virtue and pleasure, not virtue and political necessity. Cicero, however, often criticizes the Stoics for their impracticality and for alienating their audiences. Thus, he describes the unyielding Stoics here as "now left almost deserted in their lecture-rooms" (Cicero 1958b, 41).

36. Because Lipsius is commenting on the morally degraded condition of his own day, not that of late republican Rome, his "misrepresentation" of Cicero is further mitigated.

37. "Because custom is so corrupted," Cicero (1991a) acknowledges that deceptive sales may not be prohibited by statute or civil law, but are "forbidden by the law of nature" (3.69).

38. Regulus's example should be understood as supporting Cicero's belief that the welfare of the *res publica* is supreme. As Andrew Dyck (1996) notes in his commentary on *De officiis*, "Regulus is regarded as a model because he subordinated his personal (apparent) interest to the larger interest of the state" (620).

39. Lipsius added to the maxim, on his own, "not only against reason." Because Cicero adopts a Stoic-influenced viewpoint here, Lipsius's addition does not change the original meaning. For the Stoics, nature and reason are identical.

40. In situ, the two quotations Lipsius appropriates from Cicero are part of a broader claim that benefiting the Republic is not only a moral duty but one that supersedes all other moral duties, even the protection of innocent life itself.

41. Cicero (*Letters to His Brother Quintus* 1.1.15, as cited in Lipsius 2004, 515, 517; *Letters to Atticus* 2.20.1, as cited in Lipsius 2004, 515).

42. Cicero (2000a) also acknowledges in *Pro Cluentio* that prosecutors, including himself, mislead their audiences by quoting "from current rumour" (139).

43. On Cicero's use of *conciliare* as a term of rhetorical persuasion, see Fantham (1973, 262–75) and Fortenbaugh (1988, 259–73).

44. Lipsius was the first to deny Tacitus as author of the *Dialogus* because of, what he believed to be, stylistic differences between this work and other writings of Tacitus. But "after centuries of debate, external evidence appears to affirm Tacitus as the author, and scholars now generally agree in attributing the work to him" (Saxonhouse 1975, 67n1).

45. See also Cicero (1991a, 3.96).

CHAPTER FIVE

1. See also Hoffman (1974, 32–34, 38–47, 118), Podlech (1984, 509–10), and Urbinati (2006, 231n23). Although Bernard Manin (1997) acknowledges that Athenian democracy assigned powers to "separate, smaller bodies" other than the assembly, he declines to identify these bodies as representative because "their members were mainly appointed by lot." Moreover, Manin contends, "[w]hat makes a system representative is not the fact that a few govern in the place of the people, but that they are selected by election only" (41).

2. Pitkin (1967, 120–21) discusses the use of "rival terms" that suggest analogies in "some contexts or in certain ways like a representative" but concludes that "none of them is synonymous

in meaning with 'representative.'" Nevertheless, though Pitkin may be right in denying that any single term is synonymous with "representative," she does not explore the possibility that a number of these terms taken together would indicate a modern conception of representation.

3. Although Rehfeld affirms that political representation has a long history, he does not try to prove the claim in this article.

4. Rehfeld contends that the trustee-delegate dilemma is not peculiar to political representation, but is a normative concern for decision making more generally (2009, 215–16). For purposes of this chapter, however, I choose not to address this point, but focus on the trustee-delegate distinction as it has historically been viewed, i.e., as most pertinent to representation. Like Rehfeld, Jane Mansbridge also supports "retiring the concept of 'trustee' completely from legislative theory" (2011, 621), although Mansbridge is troubled, specifically, by the hierarchical implications of "trustee" (621–24). Although I agree with Mansbridge that the concept of trustee connotes the representative's greater competence than the constituent's, the trustee-delegate distinction, taken as a whole, presupposes a dynamic relationship between representative and voter, in which neither occupies a static position at the top of the hierarchy.

5. I recognize that the thinkers examined in this article may not consistently use the terms "trustee" and "delegate," as Cicero did not speak of "political representative." Nonetheless, just as Cicero vests other words with the characteristics of the representative, these theorists, including Cicero, similarly distinguish between trustee and delegate by employing other nomenclature.

6. Rehfeld also recognizes this shifting as characteristic of a lawmaker choosing between his threefold set of distinctions (222), but he never provides a coherent justification for the decision maker's movement from one category to the next.

7. The main source for the terms signifying the ideal orator-statesman in *De oratore* (*auctor, procurator, princeps,* and *rector*) is 1.211, 1.215, and 1.216. These words derive from a speech by M. Antonius, the trial lawyer, in which Antonius rejects L. Licinius Crassus's position that the ideal orator must be a man of broad wisdom acting for the common good of society. Although Antonius's standpoint implies opposition to the ideal of the orator-statesman, he later admits in the dialogue (2.41) that he does not believe the case he is arguing and approves of Crassus's broader concept of the orator (Fantham 2004, 313).

8. "Cicero may have been the first to associate eloquence with the authority to determine public policy. To make this claim of leadership for the orator, . . . he had to redefine and expand the basis of eloquence to include both practical prudence and moral wisdom. Thus Crassus himself is described by Antonius in 1.105 as 'preeminent in judgement and speech'" (Fantham 2004, 313).

9. *Oxford Latin Dictionary,* s.v. "rector," shows that the word originated as a synonym of *gubernator* (steersman). Although Cicero's use of "rector" appears first (and only once) in *De oratore,* it appears in *De republica* 5.5, 5.6, and 6.13, besides *De republica* 2.51.

10. *Auctor* is "the traditional term . . . to define the statesman" (Fantham 2004, 312). *Auctor* in *De oratore* 1.211 is a paraphrase for "an [extraordinary] politician" (Leeman, Pinkster, and Nelson 1985, 134).

11. Although Cicero's orator embodies the Republic, he is not described as representing the "will of the people," which Hobbes understands the sovereign to do. In *De cive,* Hobbes

(1982, 68) writes: "A city therefore . . . is one person, whose will . . . is to be received for the will of them all."

12. See also "Cicero not only identifies himself with the republic, he sees its health as depending directly on his proximity to Rome, ability to speak, and similar circumstances" (Hariman 1995, 111).

13. For further evidence of how the Roman *procurator* is a representative, but not of the "strong variety" that Pitkin finds an inapt model for the political representative, see Crook (1995, 158–59).

14. On the role of the people as master, see Millar's argument that the Roman people are the sovereign power of the Republic and are recognized as such by Cicero (Millar 1998, 173–74).

15. Although there was no formal system for popular discussion of the laws between the *contio* and voting, there also was no ban on such speech as there was in Sparta (Millar 1998, 46–47).

16. See also Millar's (1998, 220) remarks on Cicero's comments in *Pro Flacco* about the discussion of laws before voting.

17. As opposed to his *Topics* and *Rhetoric*, in the *Nicomachean Ethics* Aristotle treats *endoxa* philosophically, not rhetorically, which allows him to link *endoxa* to the truth. Aristotle's ethical *endoxa*, however, differ from the *sensus communis* of Cicero and later thinkers on representation by being confirmed through logical testing ("thereby function[ing] as a springboard to launch the philosopher toward the truth") and by standing, ultimately, independent of public beliefs (Most 1994, 175–85).

18. Millar (1998, 173–74) cites Cicero in *Pro Cnaeo Plancio* 11 to prove that the people were viewed as sovereign, because they had the right to elect magistrates *and* vote on the laws.

19. See also Cicero (1999d,1.51), where he argues that nature secures this hierarchy by not only ensuring "that men outstanding for virtue and courage rule over weaker people, but that the weaker people willingly obey the best."

20. On the political nature of criminal trials, see Millar (1998, 88).

21. See Connolly (2015, 170).

22. Although Burke appears to conceive of prejudices as universal—mirroring the sense of *mankind* not *community*—he locates their development in distinct polities not universal humanity (Burke 1989, 244, 137). Cicero uses *sensus communis* similarly in *De oratore* (Cicero 1942a, 1.12, 2.68) to refer to the sense of a particular community *and* to "the common sentiments of humanity."

23. Cicero states that the "guide of the [ideal] commonwealth aims at the blessedness of the life of his citizens, that they should be solid in their resources, rich in property, well endowed with glory, honorable in virtue" (1995, 90).

CHAPTER SIX

1. Similarly, Gutmann and Thompson define "deliberative democracy as a form of government in which free and equal citizens (and their representatives), justify decisions in a process in which they give one another reasons that are mutually acceptable and generally accessible, with the aim of reaching conclusions that are binding in the present on all citizens but open to challenge in the future" (Gutmann and Thompson 2004, 7).

2. See also Manin et al. (1987, 359): "The decisions that will be made by the elected officials will come from the candidates and the points of view that have won a majority. These decisions are legitimate because they are, in the last analysis, the outcome of the deliberative process taking place before the universal audience of all citizens."

3. In this chapter, however, I do not single out any particular construction of deliberative democracy as true or authentic.

4. See Gutmann and Thompson (1996), Benhabib (1996b), Cohen (1989, 1996), Dryzek (1994), Sunstein (1993, 133–45), and Fishkin (1991). For other elaborations of deliberative democracy, see Bessette (1994), Bohman (1996), and Chambers (1996).

5. See also Chambers (2009, 329): "Deliberation as dialogue, especially face-to-face dialogue, initiates a process of reason giving that enhances the epistemic status of the outcomes. The demand for reasons brings weak arguments to light, forces interlocutors to revise indefensible claims, publicizes unacceptable premises, generally facilitates the exchange of information and knowledge, and encourages participants to be reflective. At the heart of many deliberative models is an ideal of dialogic accountability in which high levels of reasoning and reflectiveness are encouraged by the process itself."

6. "More than any other theorist, Jürgen Habermas is responsible for reviving the idea of deliberation in our time, and giving it a more thoroughly democratic foundation" (Gutmann and Thompson 2004, 9). On Kant as a forerunner of deliberative democracy, see O'Neill (2002). Deliberative democrats seeking ancient precursors of their dialogic theory have increasingly turned to Socrates (Euben 1996; Mara 1997). As should be clear in the body of this chapter, Cicero's conception of conversation anticipates deliberative democratic discourse more closely than the dialogic models of any other ancient thinker.

7. I do not intend this list to be exhaustive. I only list those characteristics relevant to my argument.

8. Quintilian (2001b, 3.5.5–7). For further discussion of the differences between theses and hypotheses, see May and Wisse (2001, 25–26).

9. Quintilian (2001b, 3.5.14–15) notes Cicero's change of heart.

10. An exception is the deliberative oratory appropriate to a smaller audience, like the Senate.

11. Although epideictic oratory is mainly celebratory, not contentious, it has also been used agonistically in both legal and political settings (Quintilian 2001b, 3.7.2).

12. Cicero argues that epideictic oratory is less important than deliberative or forensic, partly because the Romans "do not generally use laudatory speeches that much" (Cicero 2001a, 2.341).

13. Cicero's rhetorical dialogues include *De oratore, De partitione oratoria*, and *Brutus* (46 BCE); and his philosophical dialogues include *De republica, De legibus, Academica, De finibus, Tusculanae Disputationes, De natura deorum, De senectute, De amicitia*, and *De divinatione* (44 BCE).

14. For further discussion of the differences between philosophical and political conversations—and why deliberative democratic discourse is more akin to the former—see Remer (2013).

15. See also Cicero (1942a, 2.41–43; 1942b, 3.109) and Michel (1960, 219).

16. Although Cicero structured his philosophical work *De officiis* as a letter from the elder Cicero to his son, the letter was often categorized, classically, as a form of dialogue in which one of the participants is absent. See Grube (1961, 111), Libanius (1903–27, 27), and Erasmus (1985, 20).

17. *De republica* and *De legibus* were his only philosophical dialogues written earlier.

18. Cicero's *otium* was not sought; it came as a consequence of his forced political retirement, his being "released from taking part in the government of the country" (1933a, 1.11). Cicero still preferred the life of the statesman to that of the philosopher, and it was his reentry into political life in 44, with his attack on Mark Antony, that led to his proscription and death in December 43.

19. In *Tusculan Disputations*, Cicero asks the question, "is there anything more like unsoundness of mind than anger?" (1927c, 4.52).

20. Quintilian states that "*pathos* is almost entirely concerned with anger, hatred, fear, envy, and pity" (2001c, 6.2.20).

21. See also Cohen (1996, 99).

22. Garsten writes, concerning Dryzek's endorsement of emotional appeals: "The functions he gave rhetoric—calling attention to arguments and transmitting them—preserve the basic distinction between rhetoric and reasoning" (2011, 163).

23. Some deliberative democrats like Gutmann and Thompson argue that deliberation should conclude in action. Thus, they state that "the deliberative process is not like a talk show or an academic seminar. The participants do not argue for argument's sake. . . . They intend their discussion to influence a decision the government will make, or a process that will affect how future decisions are made" (Gutmann and Thompson 2004, 5).

24. Other deliberative democrats seek to resolve disagreements in actual but artificially created and monitored groups (Fishkin 2009). Proponents of deliberative democracy, however, should not expect to find such change among real-life, ideologically opposed interlocutors engaged in unregulated conversations.

25. A similar critique of Gutmann and Thompson is made by Shapiro (1999).

26. "Deliberative democracy should accept a principle of basic liberty, but should resist the libertarian tendency to favor an overextended conception of liberty and an underdeveloped conception of opportunity" (Gutmann and Thompson 1996, 208).

27. An example of classical deliberative democracy's hostility toward rhetoric, is Benhabib's contention that rhetoric limits, rather than enhances, social justice "because rhetoric moves people and achieves results without having to render an account of the bases upon which it induces people to engage in certain courses of action rather than others" (Benhabib 1996b, 83). See also Chambers (1996, 206).

28. See Arena (2013).

29. Scholars critical of deliberative democracy's traditional exclusion of emotions, however, have relied on Aristotle, not Cicero, in supporting the rationality of emotions. See, for example, O'Neill (2002, 264–68; 2007, 163–66), Abizadeh (2002), and Garsten (2011, 173–74).

30. Amélie Rorty contends that the emotions involve evaluation and appraisal and are not, as such, either rational or irrational (Rorty 1985). Similarly, Nussbaum maintains that the emotions can be rational or irrational and that they are appropriate in deliberation (Nussbaum 1995).

31. Nussbaum (1995, 381–82).

32. As Cicero's philosophical dialogues suggest, even philosophers are not generally as open to changing their opinions as would seem (see Remer 2013, 16–20). "Most speakers quite honestly think that their own arguments are the better ones" (Walzer 1989, 188).

33. Morstein-Marx notes that Cicero avoids analysis of the proposed agrarian law by

"bury[ing] his audience in an avalanche of misrepresentations and distortions of various clauses of the proposal . . . , while giving the impression of undertaking a painstaking and detailed refutation of its provisions" (2004, 195–96). On information overload as a form of manipulation, see Goodin (1980, 58–61), Klemp (2011, 66).

34. *Libertas* appears twenty-two times in Cicero's second speech against Rullus (Morstein-Marx 2004, 217).

35. Habermas's English translation of *The Structural Transformation of the Public Sphere* first appeared in 1989, but it was published in the original German as *Strukcturwandel der Öffentlicheit* in 1962.

36. Jamieson writes of "the golden ages of American, British, Roman, and Greek oratory" (1988, 11), without delineating the birth or death of these ages.

37. Habermas's account of the English coffee house as a locus of rational-critical debate was based on the essays of Joseph Addison and Richard Steele in the *Spectator*. As Brian Cowan, one the foremost scholars of English coffee houses, writes: "But the coffeehouse public sphere described in the Spectator essays was an imagined construct: it was an expression of the desire by 'polite' Whigs such as Addison and Steele to reform early eighteenth-century coffeehouse society" (2007, 1189).

38. Listeners in the late Roman Republic, however, were not altogether passive: members of the audience often responded to orators in *contiones*, both positively and negatively; listeners might converse with each other concerning the political issues spoken about in *contiones*; and, in the final analysis, listeners acted through their votes.

39. According to Crassus, "quickness of the mind and intellect . . . , flexibility of the tongue, the sound of the voice, powerful lungs, physical vigor, and a certain build and shape of the face and body as a whole"—required of the best orator—"cannot be implanted or bestowed by art, for they are all gifts of nature" (2001a, 1.113–15).

40. "Some citizens [read 'the elite'] are better than others [i.e., women; racial minorities, especially Blacks; and poorer people] in articulating their arguments in rational, reasonable terms . . . discrediting on seemingly democratic grounds the views of those who are less likely to present their arguments in ways that we recognize as characteristically deliberative" (Sanders 1997, 348–49).

41. If Atticus exhibited scant interest in politics, why did Cicero seek Atticus's political advice in his letters? Peter White argues that although Cicero framed many of his letters to Atticus (and other correspondents) as requests for political advice, he did not actually desire counsel about which policy to pursue. Rather, what he wanted from Atticus (and other friends) were "forecasts about his public image. The underlying question, which sometimes becomes explicit, is, 'How will you and others regard me if I take such-and-such a step'" (White 2010, 130–31).

42. The five democracies are: the United States, Great Britain, Germany, Italy, and Mexico.

43. Almond and Verba report the following frequencies of talking politics with other people: in the United States, 24 percent never talk politics and 76 percent sometimes talk politics; in Great Britain, 29 percent never talk politics and 70 percent sometimes talk politics; in Germany, 39 percent never talk politics and 60 percent sometimes talk politics; in Italy, 66 percent never talk politics and 32 percent sometimes talk politics; and, in Mexico, 61 percent never talk politics and 38 percent sometimes talk politics (1963, 116).

44. Bruce Ackerman, a constitutional theorist and deliberative democrat of sorts, captures the rarity of widespread political conversation by dividing between (1) periods of normal politics, which comprise the bulk of American history, and (2) rare "constitutional moments," when the American people speak. The first is characterized by a poorly informed and politically disengaged public. The second, which is when "higher lawmaking" takes place, is distinguished by heightened public involvement, when "both the elites and the people come to a considered judgment through a kind of continuing 'deliberative plebiscite'" (Ackerman 1998; Fishkin 2001). Ackerman emphasizes the infrequency of these constitutional moments, with their heightened popular attention to politics, by identifying only three such occasions: the Founding, Reconstruction, and the New Deal.

45. Larry Bartels, a noted political scientist, concedes in his preface to *Unequal Democracy: The Political Economy of the New Gilded Age* that he began his study on the ramifications of economic inequality on the American political system as an apolitical political scientist, who had not voted since 1984—when he voted for Ronald Reagan (2008, xi). That Bartels, a world renowned political scientist, did not vote in any election for a prolonged period suggests, anecdotally, that high levels of education do not *always* correlate with even the most minimal political participation. I thank Russell Neuman for bringing Bartels's account to my attention.

46. The First Amendment right to freedom of speech, as interpreted by the US Supreme Court, protects not only the right *to* speak but also the freedom *not to* speak. See *Wooley v. Maynard*, 430 U.S. 705 (1977), where the Court held that New Hampshire could not constitutionally require citizens to display its state motto, "Live Free or Die," on their vehicle license plates when they found the state motto morally objectionable.

47. Mansbridge et al. also identify "informal talk among politically active or less active individuals whether powerful or marginalized" as a mode in the deliberative system (2012, 10).

48. See Wood (1988, 120–23).

49. Although Cicero himself values the political life above all other paths, his emphasis on "the rule of our own nature" anticipates an even greater acceptance of livelihoods as matters of personal choice.

50. Cicero, however, has Crassus identify political speech with *deliberatio* in *De oratore* without distinguishing between speaker and listener (1942a, 1.141; see also 1942b 3.109), as Cicero does in *De inventione*.

51. Goodin himself argues that internal-reflective deliberation should be viewed as supplementary to external-reflective deliberation. He concedes that the internal-reflective variety can be useful; nonetheless, he does not doubt that, from a democratic perspective, it is inferior to its external-collective cousin. "Invariably modeled upon, and thus parasitic upon, our interpersonal experiences of discussion and debate," internal-reflective deliberation cannot "substitute for" but only "supplement" the "exchange of reasons" that is the hallmark of external-collective deliberation (Goodin 2000, 81, 84; Chambers 2009, 232).

52. For Coady, "the unrealizability of ideals [is] a feature that most theorists who have considered the matter at all have treated as providing a vital distinction between ideals and ordinary goals or values" (2008, 52).

53. Another response to utopian visions of deliberative democracy disconnected from facts is to bemoan the current distance from the ideal, while contrasting the current era of nondeliberative

speech with an earlier golden age. As discussed earlier in this chapter, however, scrutiny of these supposedly earlier golden ages demonstrates that they also fell well short of the deliberative democratic ideal.

CONCLUSION

1. Cicero's "downfall and discredit" (Wood 1988, 6) in the late nineteenth century is due, in part, to the increasing attacks on him by late nineteenth-century German classicists. Foremost among these classicists is Theodor Mommsen, who condemns Cicero as a coward (Cole 2013, 338), "a second-rate, indecisive, disruptive politician and muddled thinker who paled beside the clear-minded, purposeful and magnetic Caesar" (Wood 1988, 7–8). On Cicero's continuing decline in the twentieth century, see Wood (1988, 8–13). On the decline of scholarly interest in Cicero's political thought, as well as Roman political thinking more generally, see Hammer (2008, 13–37).

2. In his First Inaugural Address, Lincoln addresses the enemies of the Union: "You have no oath registered in Heaven to destroy the government, while I shall have the most solemn one to 'preserve, protect, and defend it'" (http://www.abrahamlincolnonline.org/lincoln/speeches/1inaug.htm).

3. Lincoln appears to allude to decorum in his Gettysburg Address, where he refers to dedicating a portion of the battlefield as a final resting place for the fallen soldiers as "altogether fitting and proper (Wills 1992, 263)," both terms that connote decorum.

4. Although Lincoln viewed the Declaration's ideal of equality as thoroughly American, inasmuch as the Declaration reflected the new country's founding principles (Wills 1992, 98–100), he also saw its ideal as "so general and time-free that it does not merely affect Americans—rather, its influence radiates out to *all* people *everywhere*" (103).

5. Hobbes's use of moral language through the *Leviathan* has led some scholars to argue that Hobbes did have a theory of moral obligation. See, for example, Taylor (1938), Warrender (1957), and Hood (1964).

6. "When social practices support a particular, coherent value interpretation—that is, when we have determinate values—it is conservative" (Cohen 1986, 466).

7. On the radical possibilities of social criticism based on communal values, see Walzer (1988, 1993).

8. "Speech on the Dred Scott Decision," June 26, 1857, Ashbrook Center at Ashland University, http://teachingamericanhistory.org/library/document/speech-on-the-dred-scott-decision.

9. Even if we maintain "that in a particular case, in a particular culture, there is, in principle, a right decision . . . , [t]here will be different interpretations and . . . no final and definitive interpretation. But that is not to say that we can't mark off better from worse arguments, deep and inclusive accounts of our social life from shallow and partisan accounts" (Walzer 1983).

Abbott, Don Paul. 2007. "Kant, Theremin, and the Morality of Rhetoric." *Philosophy and Rhetoric* 40: 274–92.

Abizadeh, Arash. 2002. "The Passions of the Wise: Phronêsis, Rhetoric and Aristotle's Passionate Practical Deliberation." *Review of Metaphysics* 56: 267–96.

Ackerman, Bruce. 1980. *Social Justice in the Liberal State*. New Haven, CT: Yale University Press.

———. 1998. *We the People 2: Transformations*. Cambridge, MA: Harvard University Press.

Aeschylus. 1953. *Oresteia*. Translated by Richard Lattimore. Chicago: University of Chicago Press.

Alberti, Leon Battista. 2003. *Momus*. Translated by Sarah Knight. Edited by Sarah Knight and Virginia Brown. Cambridge, MA: Harvard University Press.

Allen, Danielle S. 2000. *The World of Prometheus: The Politics of Punishing in Democratic Athens*. Princeton, NJ: Princeton University Press.

———. 2004. *Talking to Strangers: Anxieties of Citizenship since Brown v. Board of Education*. Chicago: University of Chicago Press.

Almond, Gabriel A., and Sidney Verba. 1963. *The Civic Culture: Political Attitudes and Democracy in Five Nations*. Princeton, NJ: Princeton University Press.

Alonso, Fernando Llano. 2013. "Cosmopolitanism and Natural Law in Cicero." In *The Threads of Natural Law: Unraveling a Philosophical Tradition*, edited by Francisco José Contreras, 27–36. Dordrecht: Springer.

Annas, Julia. 1992. "Ancient Ethics and Modern Morality." *Philosophical Perspectives* 6: 119–36.

Applbaum, Arthur Isak. 1999. *Ethics for Adversaries: The Morality of Roles in Public and Professional Life*. Princeton, NJ: Princeton University Press.

Arena, Valentina. 2013. "The Orator and His Audience: The Rhetorical Perspective in the Art of Deliberation." In *Community and Communication: Oratory and Politics in Republican Rome*, edited by Catherine Steel and Henriette van der Blom, 195–209. Oxford: Oxford University Press.

Arendt, Hannah. 1958. *The Human Condition.* Chicago: University of Chicago Press.

Aristotle. 1926. *"Art" of Rhetoric.* Translated by J. H. Freese. Loeb Classical Library. Cambridge, MA: Harvard University Press.

———. 1984a. *On the Soul.* Translated by J. A. Smith. In *The Complete Works of Aristotle,* edited by Jonathan Barnes, 1: 641–92. Princeton, NJ: Princeton University Press.

———. 1984b. *Nicomachean Ethics.* Translated by W. D. Ross. Revised by J. O. Urmson. In *The Complete Works of Aristotle,* edited by Jonathan Barnes, 2: 1729–1867. Princeton, NJ: Princeton University Press.

———. 1984c. *Politics.* Translated by B. Jowett. In *The Complete Works of Aristotle,* edited by Jonathan Barnes, 2: 1986–2129. Princeton, NJ: Princeton University Press.

———. 1991. *On Rhetoric: A Theory of Civic Discourse.* Translated by George A. Kennedy. New York: Oxford University Press.

Asmis, Elizabeth. 2005. "A New Kind of Model: Cicero's Roman Constitution in *De Republica."* *American Journal of Philology* 126: 377–416.

———. 2008. "Cicero on Natural Law and the Laws of the State." *Classical Antiquity* 27: 1–33.

Augustine. 1998. *The City of God against the Pagans.* Edited and translated by R. W. Dyson. Cambridge: Cambridge University Press.

Balot, Ryan. 2006. *Greek Political Thought.* Malden, MA: Blackwell.

Barber, Benjamin R. 1984. *Strong Democracy: Participatory Politics for a New Age.* Berkeley: University of California Press.

Barlow, J. J. 1999. "The Fox and the Lion: Machiavelli Replies to Cicero." *History of Political Thought* 20: 627–45.

Bartels, Larry M. 2008. *Unequal Democracy: The Political Economy of the New Gilded Age.* Princeton, NJ: Princeton University Press.

Barton, Carlin A. 2001. *Roman Honor: The Fire in the Bones.* Berkeley: University of California Press.

Basler, Roy P., ed. 1953. *The Collected Works of Abraham Lincoln.* 9 vols. New Brunswick, NJ: Rutgers University Press.

Bayer, Thora Ilin. 2008. "Vico's Principle of *Sensus Communis* and Forensic Eloquence." *Chicago-Kent Law Review* 83: 1131–55.

Beiner, Ronald. 1983. *Political Judgment.* Chicago: University of Chicago Press.

Benhabib, Seyla. 1992. *Situating the Self: Gender, Community and Postmodernism in Contemporary Ethics.* New York: Routledge.

———. 1996a. "The Democratic Moment and the Problem of Difference." In *Democracy and Difference: Contesting the Boundaries of the Political,* edited by Seyla Benhabib, 3–18. Princeton, NJ: Princeton University Press.

———. 1996b. "Toward a Deliberative Model of Democratic Legitimacy." In *Democracy and Difference: Contesting the Boundaries of the Political,* edited by Seyla Benhabib, 67–94. Princeton, NJ: Princeton University Press.

Berelson, Bernard R., Paul F. Lazarsfeld, and William N. McPhee. 1954. *Voting: A Study of Opinion Formation in a Presidential Campaign.* Chicago: University of Chicago Press.

Berlin, Isaiah. 1972. "The Originality of Machiavelli." In *Studies on Machiavelli,* edited by Myron Pl. Gilmore, 147–206. Florence: G. C. Sansoni.

Bessette, Joseph M. 1994. *The Mild Voice of Reason: Deliberative Democracy and American National Government*. Chicago: University of Chicago Press.

Olsen, Birger Munk. 1968. "L'Humanisme de Jean de Salisbury, un Ciceronien au 12e siècle." In *Entretiens sur la Renaissance du 12e siècle*, edited by Maurice de Gandillac and Edouard Jeauneau, 53–69. Paris: La Haye.

Bodéüs, Richard. 1993. *The Political Dimensions of Aristotle's Ethics*. Translated by Jan Edward Garrett. Albany, NY: SUNY Press.

Bohman, James. 1996. *Public Deliberation: Pluralism, Complexity, and Democracy*. Cambridge, MA: MIT Press.

Bok, Sissela. 1979. *Lying: Moral Choice in Public and Private Life*. New York: Vintage.

Botsford, George Willis. 1909. *The Roman Assemblies: From Their Origin to the End of the Republic*. New York: Macmillan.

Braun, Harald E. 2011. "Justus Lipsius and the Challenge of Historical Exemplarity." In *(Un) Masking The Realities of Power: Justus Lipsius and the Dynamics of Political Writing in Early Modern Europe*, edited by Erik de Bom, Marijke Jansssens, Toon van Houdt, and Jan Papy, 135–62. Leiden: Brill.

Brecher, Bob. 2007. *Torture and the Ticking Bomb*. Malden, MA: Blackwell.

Brinton, Alan. 1983. "Quintilian, Plato, and the '*Vir Bonus*.'" *Philosophy and Rhetoric* 16: 167–84.

Broadie, Sarah. 1991. *Ethics with Aristotle*. Oxford: Oxford University Press.

Brooke, Christopher. 2012. *Philosophic Pride: Stoicism and Political Thought from Lipsius to Rousseau*. Princeton, NJ: Princeton University Press.

Brown, Mark B. 2014. "Expertise and Deliberative Democracy." In *Deliberative Democracy: Issues and Cases*, edited by Stephen Elstub and Peter McLaverty, 50–68. Edinburgh: Edinburgh University Press.

Browne, Stephen H. 1993. *Edmund Burke and the Discourse of Virtue*. Tuscaloosa: University of Alabama Press.

Browning, Reed. 1984. "The Origins of Burke's Ideas Revisited." *Eighteenth-Century Studies* 18: 57–71.

Brownlee, Kimberley. 2010. "Moral Aspirations and Ideals." *Utilitas* 22: 241–57.

Brunt, P. A. 1988. *The Fall of the Roman Republic and Related Essays*. Oxford: Oxford University Press.

Bugter, S. E. W. 1987. "*Sensus communis* in the Works of M. Tullius Cicero." In *Common Sense: The Foundations for Social Science*, edited by Frits van Holthoon and David R. Olson, 83–97. Lanham, MD: University Press of America.

Burke, Edmund. 1962. *An Appeal from the New to the Old Whigs*. Edited by John M. Robson. Indianapolis: Bobbs-Merrill.

———. 1981. *The Writings and Speeches of Edmund Burke*. Vol. 2. Edited by Paul Langford. Oxford: Oxford University Press.

———. 1989. *The Writings and Speeches of Edmund Burke*. Vol. 8. Edited by L. G. Mitchell. Oxford: Oxford University Press.

———. 1996. *The Writings and Speeches of Edmund Burke*. Vol. 3. Edited by W. M. Elofson. Oxford: Oxford University Press.

Burke, Peter. 1969. "Tacitism." In *Tacitus*, edited by T. A. Dorey, 149–71. New York: Basic Books.

———. 1991. "Tacitism, Scepticism, and Reason of State." In *The Cambridge History of Political Thought 1450–1700*, edited by J. H. Burns with the assistance of Mark Goldie, 479–98. Cambridge: Cambridge University Press.

Cammack, Daniela. 2013. "Rethinking Athenian Democracy." PhD diss., Harvard University.

Cape, Robert W., Jr. 2003. "Cicero and the Development of Prudential Practice at Rome." In *Prudence: Classical Virtue, Postmodern Practice*, edited by Robert Hariman, 35–55. University Park: Pennsylvania State University Press.

Castiglione, Baldassar. 1981. *Il libro del cortegiano*. Milan: Garzanti.

Cella, Alexander J. 1968. "The Doctrine of Legislative Privilege of Freedom of Speech and Debate: Its Past, Present and Future as a Bar to Criminal Prosecutions in the Courts." *Suffolk University Law Review* 2: 1–43.

Chambers, Simone. 1996. *Reasonable Democracy: Jürgen Habermas and the Politics of Discourse*. Ithaca, NY: Cornell University Press.

———. 2009. "Rhetoric and the Public Sphere: Has Deliberative Democracy Abandoned Mass Democracy?" *Political Theory* 37: 323–50.

Cicero, Marcus Tullius. 1913a. *De officiis*. Translated by Walter Miller. Loeb Classical Library. Cambridge, MA: Harvard University Press.

———. 1913b. *Letters to Atticus*. Vol. 2. Translated by E. O. Winstedt. Loeb Classical Library. Cambridge, MA: Harvard University Press.

———. 1914. *De finibus*. Translated by H. Rackham. Loeb Classical Library. Cambridge, MA: Harvard University Press.

———. 1923a. *De amicitia*. Translated by W. A. Falconer. Loeb Classical Library. Cambridge, MA: Harvard University Press.

———. 1923b. *De domo sua*. Translated by N. H. Watts. Loeb Classical Library. Cambridge, MA: Harvard University Press.

———. 1923c. *De senectute*. Translated by W. A. Falconer. Loeb Classical Library. Cambridge, MA: Harvard University Press.

———. 1923d. *Post reditum ad Quirites*. Translated by N. H. Watts. Loeb Classical Library. Cambridge, MA: Harvard University Press.

———. 1923e. *Post reditum in Senatu*. Translated by N. H. Watts. Loeb Classical Library. Cambridge, MA: Harvard University Press.

———. 1923f. *Pro Archia Poeta*. Translated by N. H. Watts. Loeb Classical Library. Cambridge, MA: Harvard University Press.

———. 1926. *Philippics*. Translated by Walter C. A. Kerr. Loeb Classical Library. Cambridge, MA: Harvard University Press.

———. 1927a. *Pro lege manilia*. Translated by H. Grose Hodge. Loeb Classical Library. Cambridge, MA: Harvard University Press.

———. 1927b. *Pro Rabirio Perduellionis*. Translated by H. Grose Hodge. Loeb Classical Library. Cambridge, MA: Harvard University Press.

———. 1927c. *Tusculan Disputations*. Translated by J. E. King. Loeb Classical Library. Cambridge, MA: Harvard University Press.

———. 1928a. *De legibus*. Translated by C. W. Keyes. Loeb Classical Library. Cambridge, MA: Harvard University Press.

———. 1928b. *De republica.* Translated by C. W. Keyes. Loeb Classical Library. Cambridge, MA: Harvard University Press.

———. 1930a. *De lege agraria.* Translated by J. H. Freese. Loeb Classical Library. Cambridge, MA: Harvard University Press.

———. 1930b. *Pro Sexto Roscio Amerino.* Translated by John Henry Freese. Loeb Classical Library. Cambridge, MA: Harvard University Press.

———. 1933a. *Academica.* Translated by H. Rackham. Loeb Classical Library. Cambridge, MA: Harvard University Press.

———. 1933b. *De natura deorum.* Translated by H. Rackham. Loeb Classical Library. Cambridge, MA: Harvard University Press.

———. 1939a. *Brutus.* Translated by G. L. Hendrickson and H. M. Hubbell. Loeb Classical Library. Cambridge, MA: Harvard University Press.

———. 1939b. *Orator.* Translated by G. L. Hendrickson and H. M. Hubbell. Loeb Classical Library. Cambridge, MA: Harvard University Press.

———. 1942a. *De oratore.* Vol. 1. Translated by E. W. Sutton and H. Rackham. Loeb Classical Library. Cambridge, MA: Harvard University Press.

———. 1942b. *De oratore.* Vol. 2. Translated by H. Rackham. Loeb Classical Library. Cambridge, MA: Harvard University Press.

———. 1942c. *De partitione oratoria.* Translated by H. Rackham. Loeb Classical Library. Cambridge, MA: Harvard University Press.

———. 1949. *De inventione.* Translated by H. M. Hubbell. Loeb Classical Library. Cambridge, MA: Harvard University Press.

———. 1953a. *In Pisonem.* Translated by N. H. Watts. Loeb Classical Library. Cambridge, MA: Harvard University Press.

———. 1953b. *Pro Milone.* Translated by N. H. Watts. Loeb Classical Library. Cambridge, MA: Harvard University Press.

———. 1953c. *Verrine Orations.* Vol. 2. Translated by L. H. G. Greenwood. Loeb Classical Library. Cambridge, MA: Harvard University Press.

———. 1958a. *Pro Caelio.* Translated by R. Gardner. Loeb Classical Library. Cambridge, MA: Harvard University Press.

———. 1958b. *Pro Sestio.* Translated by R. Gardner. Loeb Classical Library. Cambridge, MA: Harvard University Press.

———. 1971. *Tusculan Disputations.* Translated by J. E. King. Loeb Classical Library. Cambridge, MA: Harvard University Press.

———. 1977a. *In Catilinam* I–IV. Translated by C. Macdonald. Loeb Classical Library. Cambridge, MA: Harvard University Press.

———. 1977b. *Pro Murena.* Translated by C. Macdonald. Loeb Classical Library. Cambridge, MA: Harvard University Press.

———. 1984. *Letters to Atticus.* Vol. 2. Translated by E. O. Winstedt. Loeb Classical Library. Cambridge, MA: Harvard University Press.

———. 1991a. *On Duties.* Translated and edited by M. T. Griffin and E. M. Atkins. Cambridge: Cambridge University Press.

———. 1991b. *Speech of Thanks to the Citizens.* In *Back from Exile: Six Speeches upon His Return,* translated by D. R. Shackleton Bailey. Atlanta: Scholars Press.

———. 1991c. *Speech of Thanks in the Senate*. In *Back from Exile: Six Speeches upon His Return*, translated by D. R. Shackleton Bailey. Atlanta: Scholars Press.

———. 1995. *De re publica: Selections*. Edited by James E. G. Zetzel. Cambridge: Cambridge University Press.

———. 1997. *The Nature of Gods*. Translated by P. G. Walsh. Oxford: Oxford University Press.

———. 1999a. *Letters to Atticus*. Vol. 1. Translated and edited by D. R. Shackleton Bailey. Cambridge, MA: Harvard University Press.

———. 1999b. *Letters to Atticus*. Vol. 2. Translated and edited by D. R. Shackleton Bailey. Loeb Classical Library. Cambridge, MA: Harvard University Press.

———. 1999c. *Letters to Atticus*. Vol. 4. Translated and edited by D. R. Shackleton Bailey. Loeb Classical Library. Cambridge, MA: Harvard University Press.

———. 1999d. *On the Commonwealth*. Translated and edited by James E. G. Zetzel. Cambridge: Cambridge University Press.

———. 1999e. *On the Laws*. Translated and edited by James E. G. Zetzel. Cambridge: Cambridge University Press.

———. 2000a. *Pro Cluentio*. Translated by H. Grose Hodge. Loeb Classical Library. Cambridge, MA: Harvard University Press.

———. 2000b. *Pro Rabirio Perduellionis*. Translated by H. Grose Hodge. Loeb Classical Library. Cambridge, MA: Harvard University Press.

———. 2001a. *Letters to Friends*. Vol. 1. Edited and translated by D. R. Shackleton Bailey. Loeb Classical Library. Cambridge, MA: Harvard University Press.

———. 2001b. *Letters to Friends*. Vol. 3. Translated and edited by D. R. Shackleton Bailey. Loeb Classical Library. Cambridge, MA: Harvard University Press.

———. 2001c. *On the Ideal Orator*. Translated by James M. May and Jakob Wisse. New York: Oxford University Press.

———. 2009. *Philippics 1–6*. Edited and translated by D. R. Shackleton Bailey. Revised by John T. Ramsey and Gesine Manuwald. Loeb Classical Library. Cambridge, MA: Harvard University Press.

Clarke, Simon. 2003. *Social Theory, Psychoanalysis and Racism*. London: Palgrave.

Coady, C. A. J. 2008. *Messy Morality: The Challenge of Politics*. Oxford: Oxford University Press.

Cohen, Joshua. 1986. Review of *Spheres of Justice: A Defense of Pluralism and Equality*, by Michael Walzer. *Journal of Philosophy* 83: 457–68.

———. 1989. "Deliberation and Democratic Legitimacy." In *The Good Polity*, edited by A. Hamlin and P. Pettit, 17–34. Oxford: Blackwell.

———. 1996. "Procedure and Substance in Deliberative Democracy." In *Democracy and Difference: Contesting the Borders of the Political*, edited by Seyla Benhabib, 95–119. Princeton, NJ: Princeton University Press.

Cole, Nicholas P. 2013. "Nineteenth-Century Ciceros." In *The Cambridge Companion to Cicero*, edited by Catherine Steel, 337–49. Cambridge: Cambridge University Press.

Colish, Marcia L. 1978. "Cicero's *De officiis* and Machiavelli's *Prince*." *Sixteenth Century Journal* 9: 81–93.

———. 1990. *The Stoic Tradition from Antiquity to the Early Middle Ages*. Vol. 1. Leiden: E. J. Brill.

Conley, Thomas M. 1990. *Rhetoric in the European Tradition*. New York: Longman.

Connolly, Joy. 2007. *The State of Speech: Rhetoric and Political Thought in Ancient Rome.* Princeton, NJ: Princeton University Press.

———. 2015. *The Life of Roman Republicanism.* Princeton, NJ: Princeton University Press.

Converse, Philip E. 1964. "The Nature of Belief in Mass Publics." In *Ideology and Its Discontents*, edited by David E. Apter. New York: Free Press.

Cooper, John M. 1994. "Ethical-Political Theory in Aristotle's *Rhetoric.*" In *Aristotle's Rhetoric: Philosophical Essays*, edited by David J. Furley and Alexander Nehamas, 193–210. Princeton, NJ: Princeton University Press.

———. 1996. "An Aristotelian Theory of the Emotions." In *Essays on Aristotle's Rhetoric*, edited by Amélie Oksenberg Rorty, 238–57. Berkeley: University of California Press.

Cowan, Brian. 2007. "Publicity and Privacy in the History of the British Coffeehouse." *History Compass* 5: 1180–213.

Cox, Virginia. 1997. "Machiavelli and the *Rhetorica ad Herennium*: Deliberative Rhetoric in *The Prince.*" *Sixteenth Century Journal* 28: 1109–41.

Crawford, Michael. 1993. *The Roman Republic.* 2nd ed. Cambridge, MA: Harvard University Press.

Croll, Morris W. 1969. "Justus Lipsius and the Anti-Ciceronian Movement at the End of the 16th and Beginning of the 17th Century." In *"Attic" and Baroque Prose Style*, edited by J. Max Patrick, Robert O. Evans, with John W. Wallace, 7–44. Princeton, NJ: Princeton University Press.

Crook, J. A. 1995. *Legal Advocacy in the Roman World.* Ithaca, NY: Cornell University Press.

De Bom, Erik, Marijke Janssens, Toon Van Houdt, and Jan Papy. 2011. "Introduction: Towards a More Balanced View of Justus Lipsius's Political Writings and Their Influence." In *(Un)Masking the Realities of Power: Justus Lipsius and the Dynamics of Political Writing in Early Modern Europe*, edited by Erik de Bom, Marijke Janssens, Toon Van Houdt, and Jan Papy, 3–22. Leiden: Brill.

Depew, David. 2004a. "The Inscription of Isocrates into Aristotle's Practical Philosophy." In *Isocrates and Civic Education*, edited by Takis Poulakis and David Depew, 157–85. Austin: University of Texas Press.

———. 2004b. Review of *Prudence: Classical Virtue, Postmodern Practice*, edited by Robert Hariman. *Philosophy and Rhetoric* 37: 167–75.

Donald, David Herbert. 1995. *Lincoln.* New York: Simon and Schuster.

Dostal, Robert J. 1980. "Kant and Rhetoric." *Philosophy and Rhetoric* 13: 223–44.

Drummond, Andrew. 1995. *Law, Politics, and Power: Sallust and the Execution of the Catilinarian Conspirators.* Stuttgart: Franz Steiner Verlag.

Dryzek, John S. 1994. *Discursive Democracy: Politics, Policy, and Political Science.* Cambridge: Cambridge University Press.

———. 2000. *Deliberative Democracy and Beyond: Liberals, Critics, Contestations.* Oxford: Oxford University Press.

———. 2010. *Foundations and Frontiers of Deliberative Governance.* Oxford: Oxford University Press.

Dworkin, Ronald. 1986. *Law's Empire.* Cambridge, MA: Harvard University Press.

———. 1996. *Freedom's Law: The Moral Reading of the American Constitution.* Cambridge, MA: Harvard University Press.

———. 2011. "What Is a Good Life?" *New York Review of Books*, February 10.

Dyck, Andrew R. 1996. *A Commentary on Cicero, De Officiis*. Ann Arbor: University of Michigan Press.

———. 2004. *A Commentary on Cicero, De Legibus*. Ann Arbor: University of Michigan Press.

Eberle, Edward J. 1997. "Public Discourse in Contemporary Germany." *Case Western Reserve Law Review* 47: 797–901.

Ellis, Markman. 2006. "General Introduction." In *Eighteenth-Century Coffee-House Culture*, edited by Ellis Markman, 1:xi–xxxi. London: Pickering and Chatto.

Engberg-Pedersen, Troels. 1996. "Is There an Ethical Dimension to Aristotelian Rhetoric?" In *Essays on Aristotle's Rhetoric*, edited by Amélie Oksenberg Rorty, 116–41. Berkeley: University of California Press.

Entin, Jonathan L. 1997. "The Dog That Rarely Barks: Why the Courts Won't Resolve the War Powers Debate." *Case Western Reserve Law Review* 47: 1305–13.

Erasmus, Desiderius. 1985. *De conscribendis epistolis*. In *Collected Works of Erasmus*, edited by A. H. T. Levi. Vol. 25. Toronto: University of Toronto Press.

———. 1986. "The Ciceronian: A Dialogue on the Ideal Latin Style." In *Collected Works of Erasmus*, edited by A. H. T. Levi. Vol. 28. Toronto: University of Toronto Press.

Euben, J. Peter. 1996. "Reading Democracy: Socratic Dialogues and the Political Education of Democratic Citizens." In *Demokratia: A Conversation on Democracies, Ancient and Modern*, edited by Josiah Ober and Charles Hedrick, 327–59. Princeton, NJ: Princeton University Press.

———. 1997. *Corrupting Youth: Political Education, Democratic Culture, and Political Theory*. Princeton, NJ: Princeton University Press.

Fallon, Richard H., Jr. 2013. "Interpreting Presidential Powers." *Duke Law Journal* 63: 347–92.

Fantham, Elaine. 1973. "Ciceronian Conciliare and Aristotelian Ethos." *Phoenix* 27: 262–75.

———. 2004. *The Roman World of Cicero's* De oratore. Oxford: Oxford University Press.

Farber, Daniel A. 2003. *Lincoln's Constitution*. Chicago: University of Chicago Press.

Farrell, Thomas B. 1993. *Norms of Rhetorical Culture*. New Haven, CT: Yale University Press.

Fishkin, James S. 1991. *Democracy and Deliberation: New Directions for Democratic Reform*. New Haven, CT: Yale University Press.

———. 2001. Review of *We the People: Transformations*, by Bruce Ackerman. *Ethics* 111: 614–17.

———. 2009. *When the People Speak: Deliberative Democracy and Public Consultation*. Oxford: Oxford University Press.

Fortenbaugh, W. W. 1970. "Aristotle's Rhetoric on Emotions." *Archiv für die Geschichte der Philosophie* 52: 40–70.

———. 1975. *Aristotle on Emotion*. London: Duckworth.

———. 1988. "*Benevolentiam conciliare* and *animos permovere*: Some Remarks on Cicero's *De oratore* 2.178–216." *Rhetorica* 6: 259–73.

Fox, Matthew. 2007. *Cicero's Philosophy of History*. Oxford: Oxford University Press.

Franklin, Daniel P. 1991. *Extraordinary Measures: The Exercise of Prerogative Powers in the United States*. Pittsburgh, PA: University of Pittsburgh Press.

Frede, Dorothea. 1989. "Constitution and Citizenship: Peripatetic Influence on Cicero's Political Conceptions in the *De re publica*." In *Cicero's Knowledge of the Peripatos*, edited by William W. Fortenbaugh and Peter Steinmetz, 77–100. New Brunswick, NJ: Transaction.

Friedman, Barry. 2009. *The Will of the People: How Public Influence Has Shaped the Supreme Court and Shaped the Meaning of the Constitution*. New York: Farrar, Straus and Giroux.

Fumaroli, Marc. 1980. *L'âge de l'éloquence: Rhetorique et "res literaria" de la Renaissance au seuil de l'époque classique*. Geneva: Droz.

Garsten, Bryan. 2006. *Saving Persuasion: A Defense of Rhetoric and Judgment*. Cambridge, MA: Harvard University Press.

———. 2011. "The Rhetoric Revival in Political Theory." *Annual Review of Political Science* 14: 159–80.

Garver, Eugene. 1987. *Machiavelli and the History of Prudence*. Madison: University of Wisconsin Press.

———. 1994. *Aristotle's Rhetoric: An Art of Character*. Chicago: University of Chicago Press.

———. 2003. "After *Virtù*: Rhetoric, Prudence, and Moral Pluralism in Machiavelli." In *Prudence: Classical Virtue, Postmodern Practice*, edited by Robert Hariman, 67–97. University Park: Pennsylvania State University Press.

———. 2006. *Confronting Aristotle's Ethics: Ancient and Modern Morality*. Chicago: University of Chicago Press.

Gilbert, Felix. 1939. "The Humanist Concept of the Prince and *The Prince* of Machiavelli." *Journal of Modern History* 11: 449–83.

Gill, Christopher. 1984. "The Ethos/Pathos Distinction in Rhetorical and Literary Criticism." *Classical Quarterly* 34: 149–66.

———. 1988. "Personhood and Personality: The Four-Personae Theory in Cicero, *De Officiis* I." *Oxford Studies in Ancient Philosophy* 6: 169–99.

Glucker, John. 1988. "Cicero's Philosophical Associations." In *The Question of "Eclecticism": Studies in Later Greek Philosophy*, edited by John M. Dillon and A. A. Long, 34–69. Berkeley: University of California Press.

Goodin, Robert E. 1980. *Manipulatory Politics*. New Haven, CT: Yale University Press.

———. 2000. "Democratic Deliberation Within." *Philosophy and Public Affairs* 29: 81–109.

Goodman, Rob, and Jimmy Soni. 2011. "How the Filibuster Wrecked the Roman Republic and Could Wreck Ours." *The Atlantic*, March 24. http://www.theatlantic.com/politics/archive/2011/03/.

Görler, Woldemar. 1992. "Ein sprachlicher Zufall und seine Folgen: 'Wahrscheinliches' bei Karneades und bei Cicero." In *Zum Umgang mit fremden Sprachen in der griechisch-römischen Antike*, edited by Carl Werner Müller, Kurt Sier, and Jürgen Werner, 159–71. Stuttgart: Franz Steiner.

Grant, Ruth W. 1997. *Hypocrisy and Integrity: Machiavelli, Rousseau, and the Ethics of Politics*. Chicago: University of Chicago Press.

Graver, Margaret. 2002. *Cicero on the Emotions: Tusculan Disputations 3 and 4*. Chicago: University of Chicago Press.

Green, Jeffrey Edward. 2010. *The Eyes of the People: Democracy in an Age of Spectatorship*. New York: Oxford University Press.

Greenridge, A. H. J. (1901) 1971. *The Legal Procedure of Cicero's Time.* London: Oxford University Press. Reprint. New York: Augustus M. Kelley.

Griffin, Miriam. 1996. "Cynicism and the Romans: Attraction and Repulsion." In *The Cynics: The Cynic Movement in Antiquity and Its Legacy,* edited by R. Bracht Branham and Marie-Odile Goulet-Cazé, 190–204. Berkeley: University of California Press.

Grimaldi, William, S. J. 1972. *Studies in the Philosophy of Aristotle's Rhetoric.* Wiesbaden: Franz Steiner.

———. 1978. "Rhetoric and Truth: A Note on Aristotle, 'Rhetoric' 1355a 21–24." *Philosophy and Rhetoric* 11: 173–77.

Gross, Oren. 2003. "Chaos and Rules: Should Responses to Violent Crises Always Be Constitutional?" *Yale Law Review* 112: 1011–134.

Grube, G. M. A. 1961. *A Greek Critic: Demetrius on Style.* Toronto: University of Toronto Press.

Gutmann, Amy, and Dennis Thompson. 1996. *Democracy and Disagreement.* Princeton, NJ: Princeton University Press.

———. 2004. *Why Deliberative Democracy?* Princeton, NJ: Princeton University Press.

———, eds. 2006. *Ethics and Politics: Cases and Comments.* Belmont, CA: Wadsworth.

Habermas, Jürgen. 1979. *Communication and the Evolution of Society.* Translated by Thomas McCarthy. Boston: Beacon Press.

———. 1989. *The Structural Transformation of the Public Sphere: An Inquiry into a Category of Bourgeois Society.* Translated by Thomas Burger, with assistance of Frederick Lawrence. Cambridge, MA: MIT Press.

———. 1993. *Justification and Application: Remarks on Discourse Ethics.* Translated by Ciaran Cronin. Cambridge, MA: MIT Press.

———. 1995. *Moral Consciousness and Communicative Action.* Translated by Christian Lenhardt and Shierry Weber Nicholsen. Cambridge, MA: MIT Press.

———. 1996. "Three Normative Models of Democracy." In *Democracy and Difference: Contesting the Boundaries of the Political,* edited by Seyla Benhabib, 21–30. Princeton, NJ: Princeton University Press.

———. 2001. *On the Pragmatics of Social Interaction: Preliminary Studies in the Theory of Communicative Action.* Translated by Barbara Fultner. Cambridge, MA: MIT Press.

Habicht, Christian. 1990. *Cicero the Politician.* Baltimore: Johns Hopkins University Press.

Hall, Jon. 2007. "Oratorical Delivery and the Emotions: Theory and Practice." In *A Companion to Roman Rhetoric,* edited by William Dominik and Jon Hall, 218–34. Malden, MA: Blackwell.

Hamilton, Alexander, James Madison, and John Jay. 2004. *The Federalist.* Edited by Terence Ball. Cambridge: Cambridge University Press.

Hammer, Dean. 2008. *Roman Political Thought and the Modern Theoretical Imagination.* Norman: University of Oklahoma Press.

———. 2014. *Roman Political Thought: From Cicero to Augustine.* Cambridge: Cambridge University Press.

Hampshire, Stuart. 1978a. "Public and Private Morality." In *Public and Private Morality,* edited by Stuart Hampshire, 23–53. Cambridge: Cambridge University Press.

——, ed. 1978b. *Public and Private Morality*. Cambridge: Cambridge University Press.

——. 1989. *Innocence and Experience*. Cambridge, MA: Harvard University Press.

Hardimon, Michael O. 1994. "Role Obligations." *Journal of Philosophy* 91: 333–63.

Hariman, Robert. 1995. *Political Style: The Artistry of Power*. Chicago: University of Chicago Press.

——. 2001. "Decorum." In *Encyclopedia of Rhetoric*, edited by Thomas O. Sloane, 199–209. Oxford: Oxford University Press.

——. 2003. "Theory without Modernity." In *Prudence: Classical Virtue, Postmodern Practice*, edited by Robert Hariman, 1–32. University Park: Pennsylvania State University Press.

Haskins, Ekaterina V. 2004a. "Endoxa, Epistemological Optimism, and Aristotle's Rhetorical Project." *Philosophy and Rhetoric* 37: 1–20.

——. 2004b. *Logos and Power in Isocrates and Aristotle*. Columbia: University of South Carolina Press.

Hauser, Gerald A. 1999. *Vernacular Voices: The Rhetoric of Publics and Public Spheres*. Columbia: University of South Carolina Press.

Heckman, Richard Allen. 1967. *Lincoln vs. Douglas: The Great Debates Campaign*. Washington, DC: Public Affairs Press.

Held, Virginia. 1983. "The Division of Moral Labor and the Role of the Lawyer." In *The Good Lawyer: Lawyers' Roles and Lawyers' Ethics*, edited by David Luban, 60–79. Totowa, NJ: Rowman and Allanheld.

Hibbing, John R., and Elizabeth Theiss-Morse. 2002. *Stealth Democracy: American Beliefs about How Government Should Work*. Cambridge: Cambridge University Press.

Hill, Thomas E., Jr. 1997. "A Kantian Perspective on Political Violence." *Journal of Ethics* 1: 105–40.

Hobbes, Thomas. 1982. *De cive or The Citizen*. Edited by Sterling P. Lamprecht. Westport, CT: Greenwood Press.

——. 1991. *Leviathan*. Edited by Richard Tuck. Cambridge: Cambridge University Press.

Hoffmann, Ross J. S., and Paul Levack, eds. 1967. *Burke's Politics: Selected Writings and Speeches of Edmund Burke on Reform, Revolutions, and War*. New York: Alfred A. Knopf.

Hofmann, Hasso. 1974. *Repräsentation: Studien zur Wort- und Begriffsgeschicte von der Antike bis ins 19. Jahrhundert*. Berlin: Duncker & Humblot.

Hood, F. C. 1964. *The Divine Politics of Thomas Hobbes: An Interpretation of Leviathan*. New York: Oxford University Press.

Hulliung, Mark. 1983. *Citizen Machiavelli*. Princeton, NJ: Princeton University Press.

Hunt, Peter. 2010. *War, Peace, and Alliance in Demosthenes' Athens*. New York: Cambridge University Press.

Ignatieff, Michael. 2004. *The Lesser Evil: Political Ethics in an Age of Terror*. Princeton, NJ: Princeton University Press.

Ijselling, Samuel. 1976. *Rhetoric and Philosophy in Conflict: An Historic Survey*. Translated by Paul Dunphy. The Hague: M. Nijhoff.

Jacobs, Lawrence R., and Robert Y. Shapiro. 2000. *Politicians Don't Pander: Political Manipulation and the Loss of Democratic Responsiveness*. Chicago: University of Chicago Press.

Jamieson, Kathleen Hall. 1988. *Eloquence in the Electronic Age: The Transformation of Political Speechmaking*. New York: Oxford University Press.

———. 1992. *Dirty Politics: Deception, Distraction, and Democracy*. New York: Oxford University Press.

Jefferson, Thomas. 1984. *Writings*. Edited by Merrill D. Peterson. New York: Library of America.

John of Salisbury. 1987. *Entheticus Maior and Minor*. Vol. 1. Edited by Jan van Laarhoven. Leiden: E. J. Brill.

———. 1990. *Policraticus: Of the Frivolities of Courtiers and the Footprints of Philosophers*. Cambridge: Cambridge University Press.

———. 1991. *Metalogicon*. Edited by J. B. Hall with K. S. B. Keats-Rohan. Turnhout: Brepols.

———. 2013. *Metalogicon*. Translation by J. B. Hill. Introduction by J. P. Haseldine. Turnhout: Brepols.

Johnstone, Christopher Lyle. 1980. "An Aristotelian Trilogy: Ethics, Rhetoric, Politics, and the Search for Moral Truth." *Philosophy and Rhetoric* 13: 1–24.

Jossa, Giorgio. 1964. "*L'Utilitas rei publicae* nel pensiero di Cicerone." *Studi Romani* 12: 269–88.

Kahn, Victoria. 1985. *Rhetoric, Prudence, and Skepticism in the Renaissance*. Ithaca, NY: Cornell University Press.

———. 1994. *Machiavellian Rhetoric: From the Counter-Reformation to Milton*. Princeton, NJ: Princeton University Press.

Kant, Immanuel. 1991. Appendix I to *Perpetual Peace: A Philosophical Sketch*. In *Kant: Political Writings*, edited by Hans Reiss, translated by H. B. Nisbet, 116–24. Cambridge: Cambridge University Press.

———. 1996a. *The Metaphysics of Morals*. Translated and edited by Mary Gregor. Cambridge: Cambridge University Press.

———. 1996b. "On a Supposed Right to Lie from Philanthropy." In *Practical Philosophy*, translated and edited by Mary Gregor, 605–16. Cambridge: Cambridge University Press.

———. 2000. *Critique of the Power of Judgment*. Edited by Paul Guyer. Translated by Paul Guyer and Eric Matthews. Cambridge: Cambridge University Press.

———. 2011. *Groundwork of the Metaphysics of Morals*. Edited by Jens Timmerman. Translated by Mary Gregor. Cambridge: Cambridge University Press.

Kapust, Daniel J. 2011a. "Cicero on Decorum and the Morality of Rhetoric." *European Journal of Political Theory* 10: 92–112.

———. 2011b. *Republicanism, Rhetoric, and Roman Political Thought: Sallust, Livy, and Tacitus*. Cambridge: Cambridge University Press.

Kaster, Robert. 1982. "Decorum." Paper presented at the annual meeting of the American Philological Association, Philadelphia, PA.

Keats-Rohan, K. S. B. 1986. "John of Salisbury and Education in Twelfth-Century Paris from the Account of His Metalogicon." *History of Universities* 6: 1–45.

Kelly, Gordon P. 2006. *A History of Exile in the Roman Republic*. Cambridge: Cambridge University Press.

Kennedy, George A. 1969. *Quintilian*. New York: Twayne.

———. 2001. "Classical Rhetoric." In *Encyclopedia of Rhetoric,* edited by Thomas O. Sloane, 92–115. Oxford: Oxford University Press.

———. 2002. "Cicero's Oratorical and Rhetorical Legacy." In *Brill's Companion to Cicero: Oratory and Rhetoric,* edited by James M. May, 481–501. Leiden: Brill.

Killian, Johnny H., and George A. Costello, eds. 1996. *The Constitution of the United States of America: Analysis and Interpretation.* Washington, DC: Government Printing Office.

Kircher, Timothy. 2012. *Living Well in Renaissance Italy: The Virtues of Humanism and the Irony of Leon Battista Alberti.* Tempe: Arizona Center for Medieval and Renaissance Studies.

Klemp, Nathaniel. 2011. "When Rhetoric Turns Manipulative: Disentangling Persuasion and Manipulation." In *Manipulating Democracy: Democratic Theory, Political Psychology, and Mass Media,* edited by Wayne Le Cheminant and John M. Parrish, 59–86. New York: Routledge.

Knuuttila, Simo. 2004. *Emotions in Ancient and Medieval Philosophy.* Oxford: Clarendon Press.

Konstan, David. 2006. *The Emotions of the Ancient Greeks: Studies in Aristotle and Classical Literature.* Toronto: University of Toronto Press.

Koziak, Barbara. 2000. *Retrieving Political Emotion: Thumos, Aristotle, and Gender.* University Park: Pennsylvania State University Press.

Kristeller, Paul Oskar. 1961. *Renaissance Thought: The Classic, Scholastic, and Humanist Strains.* New York: Harper.

Krotoszynski, Ronald J., Jr. 2006. *The First Amendment in Cross-Cultural Perspective: A Comparative Legal Analysis of the Freedom of Speech.* New York: New York University Press.

Lanham, Richard A. 1991. *A Handlist of Rhetorical Terms.* Berkeley: University of California Press.

———. 1993. *The Electronic Word: Democracy, Technology, and the Arts.* Chicago: University of Chicago Press.

Last, Hugh. 1932. "Gaius Gracchus." In *The Cambridge Ancient History,* vol. 9, edited by S. A. Cook, F. E. Adcock, and M. P. Charlesworth, 40–101. Cambridge: Cambridge University Press.

Laughton, Eric. 1961. "Cicero and the Greek Orators." *American Journal of Philology* 82: 27–49.

Laurier, Eric, and Chris Philo. 2007. "'A parcel of muddling muckworms': Revisiting Habermas and the English Coffee-Houses." *Social and Cultural Geography* 8: 259–81.

Leeman, A. D., H. Pinkster, and H. L. W. Nelson. 1985. *M. Tullius Cicero, De oratore libri III: Kommentar.* Heidelberg: Universitätsverlag Winter.

Le Cheminant, Wayne, and John M. Parish, eds. 2011. *Manipulating Democracy: Democratic Theory, Political Psychology, and Mass Media.* New York: Routledge.

Leff, Michael. 1993. "The Uses of Aristotle's Rhetoric in Contemporary American Scholarship." *Argumentation* 7: 313–27.

———. 1998. "Cicero's *Pro Murena* and the Strong Case for Rhetoric." *Rhetoric and Public Affairs* 1: 61–88.

———. 2012. "Tradition and Agency in Humanistic Rhetoric." *Philosophy and Rhetoric* 45: 213–26.

Leighton, Stephen R. 1996. "Aristotle and the Emotions." In *Essays on Aristotle's Rhetoric*, edited by Amélie Oksenberg Rorty. Berkeley: University of California Press.

Libanius. 1903–27. *Libanii opera*. Vol. 9. Edited by Richard Foerster. Leipzig: B. G. Teubner.

Liebeschütz, Hans. 1950. *Mediaeval Humanism in the Life and Writings of John of Salisbury*. London: Warburg Institute, University of London.

Lintott, Andrew. 1994. "Political History, 146–95 B.C." In *The Cambridge Ancient History*, edited by J. A. Crook, Andrew Lintott, and Elizabeth Rawson, 2nd ed., 9:40–103. Cambridge: Cambridge University Press,.

———. 1999a. *The Constitution of the Roman Republic*. Oxford: Oxford University Press.

———. 1999b. *Violence in Republican Rome*. Oxford: Oxford University Press.

Lipsius, Justus. 1585. *Variarum Lectionum Libri III*. Antwerp: Christophe Plantin.

———. 1726. *Orationes octo: Jenae potissimum habitae*. Jena: Heinrich Christoph Cröcker.

———. 2004. *Politica: Six Books of Politics or Political Instruction*. Edited and translated by Jan Waszink. Assen, The Netherlands: Royal Van Gorcum.

Locke, John. 1975. *An Essay Concerning Human Understanding*. Edited with a foreword by Peter H. Nidditch. Oxford: Oxford University Press.

Long, A. A. 1995a. "Cicero's Plato and Aristotle." In *Cicero the Philosopher*, edited by J. G. F. Powell, 37–61. Oxford: Oxford University Press.

———. 1995b. "Cicero's Politics in *De officiis*." In *Justice and Generosity: Studies in Hellenistic Social and Political Philosophy, Proceedings of the Sixth Symposium Hellenisticum*, edited by Andrè Laks and Malcolm Schofield, 213–79. Cambridge: Cambridge University Press.

———. 1996. *Stoic Studies*. Cambridge: Cambridge University Press.

López, Jorge Fernández. 2007. "Quintilian as Rhetorician and Teacher." In *A Companion to Roman Rhetoric*, edited by William Dominik and Jon Hall, 307–22. Malden, MA: Blackwell.

Luban, David, ed. 1983. *The Good Lawyer: Lawyers' Roles and Lawyers' Ethics*. Totowa, NJ: Rowman and Allanheld.

Lustig, Jeff. 1999. "Experiment in Democracy; or, Trouble in the Deliberated Zone." *The Good Society* 9: 17–22.

Machiavelli, Niccolò. 1975. *The Discourses of Niccolò Machiavelli*. Translated by Leslie J. Walker, SJ. 2 vols. London: Routledge and Kegan Paul.

———. 1988. *The Prince*. Edited by Quentin Skinner and Russell Price. Cambridge Texts in the History of Political Thought. Cambridge: Cambridge University Press.

———. 1996. *Discourses on Livy*. Translated by Harvey C. Mansfield and Nathan Tarcov. Chicago: University of Chicago Press.

———. 1999. *The Prince*. Translated by Luigi Ricci. New York: Signet.

MacIntyre, Alasdair. 1984. *After Virtue: A Study in Moral Theory*. 2nd ed. Notre Dame: University of Notre Dame Press.

Mack, D. 1937. *Senatsreden und Volksreden bei Cicero*. Würzburg, Germany: K. Triltsch.

Manin, Bernard. 1997. *The Principles of Representative Government*. Cambridge: Cambridge University Press.

Manin, Bernard, Elly Stein, and Jane Mansbridge. 1987. "On Legitimacy and Political Deliberation." *Political Theory* 15: 338–68.

Mansbridge, Jane. 1999. "Everyday Talk in the Deliberative System." In *Deliberative Politics: Essays on Democracy and Disagreement*," edited by Stephen Macedo, 211–39. New York: Oxford University Press.

———. 2011. "Clarifying the Concept of Representation." *American Political Science Review* 105: 621–30.

Mansbridge, Jane, James Bohman, Simone Chambers, Thomas Christiano, Archon Fong, John Parkinson, Dennis F. Thompson, and Mark E. Warren. 2012. "A Systemic Approach to Deliberative Democracy." In *Deliberative Systems*, edited by John Parkinson and Jane Mansbridge, 1–26. Cambridge: Cambridge University Press.

Mara, Gerald M. 1997. *Socrates' Discursive Democracy: Logos and Ergon in Platonic Political Philosophy*. Albany, NY: SUNY Press.

Marcus, George E. 2010. *Sentimental Citizen: Emotion in Democratic Politics*. University Park: Pennsylvania State University Press.

Margalit, Avishai. 2010. *On Compromise and Rotten Compromises*. Princeton, NJ: Princeton University Press.

Markovits, Daniel. 2008. *A Modern Legal Ethics: Adversary Advocacy in a Democratic Age*. Princeton, NJ: Princeton University Press.

May, Christopher N. 1989. *In the Name of War: Judicial Review and the War Powers since 1918*. Cambridge, MA: Harvard University Press.

May, James M. 1980. "The Image of the State in Cicero's *Pro Sestio*." *Maia* 3: 259–64.

———. 1981. "The Rhetoric of Advocacy and Patron-Client Identification: Variation on a Theme." *American Journal of Philology* 102: 308–15.

———. 1988. *Trials of Character: The Eloquence of Ciceronian Ethos*. Chapel Hill: University of North Carolina Press.

May, James M., and Jakob Wisse. 2001. Introduction to *On the Ideal Orator*, by Cicero, translated by James M. May and Jakob Wisse, 3–48. New York: Oxford University Press.

McCabe, Mary Margaret. 1994. "Arguments in Context: Aristotle's Defense of Rhetoric." In *Aristotle's Rhetoric: Philosophical Essays*, edited by David J. Furley and Alexander Nehamas, 129–65. Princeton, NJ: Princeton University Press.

McCormick, John P. 2011. *Machiavellian Democracy*. Cambridge: Cambridge University Press.

McCrea, Adriana. 1997. *Constant Minds: Political Virtue and the Lipsian Paradigm in England, 1584–1650*. Toronto: University of Toronto Press.

Mendelberg, Tali. 2001. *The Race Card: Campaign Strategy, Implicit Messages, and the Norm of Equality*. Princeton, NJ: Princeton University Press.

Mendelson, Michael. 2002. *Many Sides: A Protagorean Approach to Theory, Practice, and the Pedagogy of Argument*. Dordrecht: Kluwer.

Michel, Alain. 1960. *Rhétorique et philosophie chez Cicéron: Essai sur les fondements philosophiques et l'art de persuader*. Paris: Presses universitaires de France.

Milbrath, Lester. 1965. *Political Participation*. Chicago: Rand McNally.

Miles, Geoffrey. 1996. *Shakespeare and the Constant Romans*. Oxford: Clarendon Press.

Mill, John Stuart. 1977a. "Considerations on Representative Government." In *The Collected Works of John Stuart Mill*, edited by John M. Robson, 19: 371–557. Toronto: University of Toronto Press.

———. 1977b. *On Liberty.* In *The Collected Works of John Stuart Mill*, edited by John M. Robson, 18: 213–310. Toronto: University of Toronto Press.

Millar, Fergus. 1998. *The Crowd in Rome in the Late Republic.* Ann Arbor: University of Michigan Press.

Miller, Peter N. 1994. *Defining the Common Good: Empire, Religion, and Philosophy in Eighteenth-Century Britain.* Cambridge: Cambridge University Press.

Mitchell, Thomas N. 1971. "Cicero and the *Senatus Consultum Ultimum.*" *Historia: Zeitschrift für alte Geschichte* 20: 47–61.

Mitofsky, Warren J. 1996. "The Emperor Has No Clothes." *The Public Perspective* 7.3: 17–19.

Morford, Mark. 1991. *Stoics and Neostoics: Rubens and the Circle of Lipsius.* Princeton, NJ: Princeton University Press.

———. 1993. "Tacitean Prudentia and the Doctrines of Justus Lipsius." In *Tacitus and the Tacitean Tradition*, edited by T. J. Luce and A. J. Woodman. Princeton, NJ: Princeton University Press.

Morstein-Marx, Robert. 2004. *Mass Oratory and Political Power in the Late Roman Republic.* Cambridge: Cambridge University Press.

———. 2013. " 'Cultural Hegemony' and the Communicative Power of the Roman Elite." In *Community and Communication: Oratory and Politics in Republican Rome*, edited by Catherine Steel and Henriette van der Blom, 29–47. Oxford: Oxford University Press.

Moss, Ann. 1998. "The Politics of Justus Lipsius and the Commonplace-Book." *Journal of the History of Ideas* 59: 421–36.

Most, Glenn W. 1994. "The Uses of *Endoxa*: Philosophy and Rhetoric in the *Rhetoric.*" In *Aristotle's Rhetoric: Philosophical Essays*, edited by David J. Furley and Alexander Nehamas. Princeton, NJ: Princeton University Press.

Mouritsen, Henrik. 2001. *Plebs and Politics in the Late Roman Republic.* Cambridge: Cambridge University Press.

Nagel, Thomas. 1978. "Ruthlessness in Public Life." In *Public and Private Morality*, edited by Stuart Hampshire, 75–91. Cambridge: Cambridge University Press.

Narducci, Emanuele. 1997. *Cicerone e l'eloquenza romana: Retorica e progetto culturale.* Rome: Laterza.

Nederman, Cary J. 1988. "Nature, Sin and the Origins of Society: The Ciceronian Tradition in Medieval Political Thought." *Journal of the History of Ideas* 49: 3–26.

———. 1992. "The Union of Wisdom and Eloquence before the Renaissance: The Ciceronian Orator in Medieval Thought." *Journal of Medieval History* 18: 75–95.

———. 2000a. "Rhetoric, Reason, and Republic: Republicanisms—Ancient, Medieval, and Modern." In *Renaissance Civic Humanism*, edited by James Hankins, 247–69. Cambridge: Cambridge University Press.

———. 2000b. "War, Peace, and Republican Virtue: Patriotism and the Neglected Legacy of Cicero." In *Instilling Ethics*, edited by Norma Thompson, 17–29. Lanham, MD: Rowman & Littlefield.

———. 2005. *John of Salisbury.* Tempe: Arizona Center for Medieval and Renaissance Studies.

Nederman, Cary J., and Tsae Lan Lee Dow. 2004. "The Road to Heaven Is Paved with Pious Deceptions: Medieval Speech Ethics and Deliberative Democracy." In *Talking Democracy:*

Historical Perspectives on Rhetoric and Democracy, edited by Benedetto Fontana, Cary J. Nederman, and Gary Remer, 187–211. University Park: Pennsylvania State University Press.

Nelson, N. E. 1933. "Cicero's *De officiis* in Christian Thought: 300–1300." In *Essays and Studies in English and Comparative Literature*, edited by English Department of the University of Michigan, 59–160. Ann Arbor: University of Michigan Press.

Neuman, W. Russell. 1986. *The Paradox of Mass Politics: Knowledge and Opinion in the American Electorate*. Cambridge, MA: Harvard University Press.

Nicgorski, Walter. 1978. "Cicero and the Rebirth of Political Philosophy." *Political Science Reviewer* 8: 63–101.

Nielsen, Kai. 2000. "There Is No Dilemma of Dirty Hands." In *Cruelty and Deception: The Controversy over Dirty Hands in Politics*, edited by Paul Rynard and David P. Shugarman, 139–55. Peterborough, Canada: Broadview Press.

Nisard, Charles. 1852. *Le triumvirat littéraire au XVIe siècle: Juste Lipse, Joseph Scaliger, et Isaac Casaubon*. Paris: Amyot.

Nussbaum, Martha C. 1990. "Aristotelian Social Democracy." In *Liberalism and the Good*, edited by R. Bruce Douglass, Gerald M. Mara, and Henry S. Richardson, 203–52. New York: Routledge.

———. 1995. "Emotions and Women's Capabilities." In *Women, Culture, and Development*, edited by Martha C. Nussbaum and Jonathan Glover, 360–95. Oxford: Oxford University Press.

———. 1996. "Aristotle on Emotions and Rational Persuasion." In *Essays on Aristotle's Rhetoric*, edited by Amélie Oksenberg Rorty, 303–23. Berkeley: University of California Press.

———. 1997. "Kant and Stoic Cosmopolitanism." *Journal of Political Philosophy* 5: 1–25.

———. 2000a. "Aristotle, Politics, and Human Capabilities: A Response to Antony, Arneson, Charlesworth, and Mulgan." *Ethics* 111: 102–40.

———. 2000b. "Duties of Justice, Duties of Material Aid." *Journal of Political Philosophy* 8: 176–206.

Ober, Josiah. 1989. *Mass and Elite in Democratic Athens: Rhetoric, Ideology, and the Power of the People*. Princeton, NJ: Princeton University Press.

Oestreich, Gerhard. 1982. *Neostoicism and the Early Modern State*. Cambridge: Cambridge University Press.

O'Malley, John. 1979. *Praise and Blame in Renaissance Rome: Rhetoric, Doctrine and Reform in the Sacred Orators of the Papal Court, c. 1450–1521*. Durham, NC: Duke University Press.

O'Neill, John. 2002. "The Rhetoric of Deliberation: Some Problems in Kantian Theories of Deliberative Democracy." *Res Publica* 8: 249–68.

———. 2007. *Markets, Deliberation and Environment*. Abingdon, UK: Routledge.

Parrish, John M. 2007. *Paradoxes of Political Ethics*. Cambridge: Cambridge University Press.

Patrick, Patricia Davis. 2007. "Judgment in Early Modern England, 1580–1615." PhD diss., University of North Carolina at Chapel Hill.

Pearson, Caspar. 2011. "Philosophy Defeated: Truth and Vision in Leon Battista Alberti's *Momus*." *Oxford Art Journal* 34: 1–12.

Peltonen, Markku. 1995. *Classical Humanism and Republicanism in English Political Thought, 1570–1640*. Cambridge: Cambridge University Press.

Perry, Matthew J. 2013. "*Provocatio*." In *The Encyclopedia of Ancient History*. Malden, MA: Basil-Blackwell.

Pettit, Philip. 1997. *Republicanism: A Theory of Freedom and Government*. Oxford: Oxford University Press.

———. 2001. *A Theory of Freedom: From the Psychology to the Politics of Agency*. Oxford: Oxford University Press.

Pike, Joseph B. 1938. *Frivolities of Courtiers and Footprints of Philosophers*. Minneapolis: University of Minneapolis Press.

Pitkin, Hannah Fenichel. 1967. *The Concept of Representation*. Berkeley: University of California Press.

Plato. 1961a. *Letters*. Translated by L. A. Post. In *Plato: The Collected Dialogues*, edited by Edith Hamilton and Huntington Cairns, 1560–1606. Princeton, NJ: Princeton University Press.

———. 1961b. *Republic*. Translated by Paul Shorey. In *The Collected Dialogues*, edited by Edith Hamilton and Huntington Cairns, 575–844. Bollingen Series 71. Princeton, NJ: Princeton University Press.

———. 1979. *Gorgias*. Translated by Terence Irwin. Oxford: Oxford University Press.

Podlech, Adalbert. 1984. "*Repräsentation*." In *Geschichtliche Grundbegriffe*, vol. 5, edited by Otto Brunner, Werner Conze, and Reinhart Koselleck. Stuttgart: Klett-Cotta.

Polo, Francisco Pino. 2011. "Public Speaking in Rome: A Question of *Auctoritas*." In *The Oxford Handbook of Social Relations in the Roman World*, edited by Michael Peachin, 286–303. New York: Oxford University Press.

Pontano, Giovanni Gioviano. 1518. *Opera omnia soluta oratione composite*. Vol. 1. Venice: Aldus.

Price, Russell. 1977. "The Theme of *Gloria* in Machiavelli." *Renaissance Quarterly* 30: 588–631.

Prugh, Thomas, Robert Costanza, and Herman Daly. 2000. *The Local Politics of Global Sustainability*. Washington, DC: Island Press.

Quintilian. 2001a. *The Orator's Education, Books 1–2*. Vol. 1. Translated and edited by Donald A. Russell. Cambridge, MA: Harvard University Press.

———. 2001b. *The Orator's Education, Books 3–5*. Vol. 2. Translated and edited by Donald A. Russell. Cambridge, MA: Harvard University Press.

———. 2001c. *The Orator's Education, Books 6–8*. Vol. 3. Translated and edited by Donald A. Russell. Cambridge, MA: Harvard University Press.

———. 2001d. *The Orator's Education, Books 11–12*. Vol. 5. Translated and edited by Donald A. Russell. Cambridge, MA: Harvard University Press.

Rahe, Paul A. 1992. *Republics Ancient and Modern: Classical Republicanism and the American Revolution*. University of North Carolina Press: Chapel Hill.

———. 2000. "Situating Machiavelli." In *Renaissance Civic Humanism*, edited by James Hankins, 270–308. Cambridge: Cambridge University Press.

Ramsey, John T. 2007. "Roman Senatorial Oratory." In *A Companion to Roman Rhetoric*, edited by William Dominik and Jon Hall, 122–35. Oxford: Blackwell.

Rebhorn, Wayne A. 1995. *The Emperor of Men's Minds: Literature and the Renaissance Discourse of Rhetoric.* Ithaca, NY: Cornell University Press.

Rehfeld, Andrew. 2006. "Toward a General Theory of Political Representation." *Journal of Politics* 68: 1–21.

———. 2009. "Representation Rethought: On Trustees, Delegates, and Gyroscopes in the Study of Political Representation and Democracy." *American Political Science Review* 103: 214–30.

Rehg, William. 1997. "Reason and Rhetoric in Habermas's Theory of Argumentation." In *Rhetoric and Hermeneutics in Our Time: A Reader*, edited by Walter Jost and Michael J. Hyde, 358–77. New Haven, CT: Yale University Press.

Remer, Gary. 2000. "Two Models of Deliberation: Oratory and Conversation in Ratifying the Constitution." *Journal of Political Philosophy* 8: 68–90.

———. 2004. "Cicero and the Ethics of Deliberative Rhetoric." In *Talking Democracy: Historical Perspectives on Rhetoric and Democracy,* edited by Benedetto Fontana, Cary J. Nederman, and Gary Remer, 135–61. University Park: Pennsylvania State University Press.

———. 2009. "Rhetoric as a Balancing of Ends: Cicero and Machiavelli." *Philosophy and Rhetoric* 42: 1–28.

———. 2010. "The Classical Orator as Political Representative: Cicero and the Modern Concept of Representation." *Journal of Politics* 72: 1063–82.

———. 2011. "Ciceronian *Ius Gentium* and World Legislation." *International Law Organizations Law Review* 8: 225–39.

———. 2013. "Political Conversations among Friends and Strangers: Cicero and Deliberative Democracy." Paper presented at the annual meeting of the American Political Science Association, Chicago, IL.

Rescher, Nicholas. 1987. *Ethical Idealism.* Berkeley: University of California Press.

Reydams-Schils, Gretchen. 2005. *The Roman Stoics: Self, Responsibility, and Affection.* Chicago: University of Chicago Press.

Ribadeneyra, Pedro de. 1595. *Tratado de la religion y virtudes que deue tener el principe christiano, para gouernar y conseruar sus estados: contra lo que Nicolas Machiauelo y los politicos deste tiempo enseñan.* Madrid: P. Madrigal.

Richards, Jennifer. 2001. "Assumed Simplicity and the Critique of Nobility; or, How Castiglione Read Cicero." *Renaissance Quarterly* 54: 460–86.

Riker, William W. 1996. *The Strategy of Rhetoric: Campaigning for the American Constitution.* New Haven, CT: Yale University Press.

Robertson, Andrew W. 1995. *The Language of Democracy: Political Rhetoric in the United States and Britain, 1790–1900.* Ithaca, NY: Cornell University Press.

Roloff, Heinrich. 1938. *Maiores bei Cicero.* Göttingen: Dieterichsche Universität.

Rorty, Amélie Oksenberg. 1985. "Varieties of Rationality, Varieties of Emotion." *Social Science Information* 24: 343–53.

Ruch, Michel. 1958. *Le préamble dans les oeuvres philosophiques de Cicéron: Essai sur la genèse et l'art du dialogue.* Paris: Belles Lettres.

Runciman, David. 2008. *Political Hypocrisy: The Mask of Power; From Hobbes to Orwell and Beyond.* Princeton, NJ: Princeton University Press.

Rynard, Paul, and David P. Shugarman, eds. 2000. *Cruelty and Deception: The Controversy over Dirty Hands in Politics*. Peterborough, Canada: Broadview Press.

Sallust. 1931. *The War with Catiline*. Translated by J. C. Rolfe. Loeb Classical Library. Cambridge, MA: Harvard University Press.

Salmon, J. H. M. 1980. "Cicero and Tacitus in Sixteenth-Century France." *American Historical Review* 85: 307–31.

Sanders, Lynn M. 1997. "Against Deliberation." *Political Theory* 25: 347–76.

———. 1999. "Poll Envy: An Assessment of Deliberative Polling." *The Good Society* 9: 9–14.

Saxonhouse, Arlene W. 1975. "Tacitus' *Dialogue on Oratory*: Political Activity under a Tyrant." *Political Theory* 3: 53–68.

Schaeffer, John D. 2004. "Commonplaces: *Sensus Communis*." In *A Companion to Rhetoric and Rhetorical Criticism*, edited by Walter Jost and Wendy Olmsted, 278–93. Hoboken, NJ: Blackwell.

Schauer, Frederick. 2000. "The Generality of Rights." *Legal Theory* 6: 323–36.

Schinkel, Anders. 2007. "Conscience and Conscientious Objections." PhD diss., Vrije Universiteit, Amsterdam.

Schofield, Malcolm. 1995. "Cicero's Definition of *Res Publica*." In *Cicero The Philosopher: Twelve Papers*, edited by J. G. F. Powell, 63–83. Oxford: Oxford University Press.

———. 2012. "The Fourth Virtue." In *Cicero's Practical Philosophy*, edited by Walter Nicgorski, 43–57. Notre Dame, IN: University of Notre Dame Press.

Seager, Robin. 1972. "Cicero and the Word Popularis." *Classical Quarterly* 22: 328–38.

Searle, John R. 1969. *Speech Acts: An Essay in the Philosophy of Language*. Cambridge: Cambridge University Press.

———. 1995. *The Construction of Social Reality*. New York: Free Press.

Seigel, Jerrold E. 1968. *Rhetoric and Philosophy in Renaissance Humanism: The Union of Eloquence and Wisdom, Petrarch to Valla*. Princeton, NJ: Princeton University Press.

Self, Lois S. 1979. "Rhetoric and Phronesis: The Aristotelian Ideal." *Philosophy and Rhetoric* 12: 130–45.

Senellart, Michel. 1995. *Les arts de gouverner. Du regimen médiéval au concept de gouvernement*. Paris: Seuil.

———. 1999. "Le stoïcisme dans la constitution de la pensée politique. Les *Politiques* de Juste Lipse (1589)." In *Le stoïcisme aux XVIe et XVIIe siècles. Le retour des philosophies antiques à l'âge classique*, edited by Pierre-François Moreau, 117–39. Paris: Albin Michel.

Shapiro, Ian. 1999. "Enough of Deliberation: Politics Is about Interests and Power." In *Deliberative Politics: Essays on Democracy and Disagreement*, edited by Stephen Macedo, 28–38. Oxford: Oxford University Press.

Sherman, Nancy. 2000. "Emotional Agents." In *The Analytic Freud: Philosophy and Psychoanalysis,* edited by Michael P. Levine, 154–76. London: Routledge.

Shklar, Judith N. 1984. *Ordinary Vices*. Cambridge, MA: Harvard University Press.

Shue, Henry. 2006. "Torture in Dreamland: Disposing of the Ticking Bomb." *Case Western Reserve Journal of International Law* 37: 231–39.

Shugarman, David. 1990. "The Use and Abuse of Politics." In *Moral Expertise: Studies in Practical and Professional Ethics*, edited by Don MacNiven, 198–231. New York: Routledge.

Siems, Larry. "Why We Know the Decision to Torture Prisoners Started at the Top." *Slate. com*, April 20, 2012, http://www.slate.com/articles/news_and_politics/politics/2012/04 /george_w_bush_and_torture_america_s_highest_officials_are_responsible_for_the _enhanced_interrogation_of_prisoners_.html.

Sinclair, R. K. 1988. *Democracy and Participation in Athens.* Cambridge: Cambridge University Press.

Skinner, Quentin. 1978. *The Foundations of Modern Political Thought.* 2 vols. Cambridge: Cambridge University Press.

Sloane, Thomas O. 1997. *On the Contrary: The Protocol of Traditional Rhetoric.* Washington, DC: Catholic University of America Press.

Smalley, Beryl. 1973. *The Becket Conflict and the Schools: A Study of Intellectuals in Politics.* Totowa, NJ: Rowman and Littlefield.

Smethurst, S. E. 1953. "Cicero and Isocrates." *Transactions and Proceedings of the American Philological Association* 84: 262–320.

Snyder, Jon R. 2009. *Dissimulation and the Culture of Secrecy in Early Modern Europe.* Berkeley: University of California Press.

Sokolon, Marlene K. 2006. *Political Emotions: Aristotle and the Symphony of Reason and Emotion.* DeKalb: Northern Illinois University Press.

Solmsen, Friedrich. 1929. *Die Entwicklung der aristotelischen Logik und Rhetorik.* Berlin: Weidmann.

———. 1938. "Aristotle and Cicero on the Orator's Playing upon the Feelings." *Classical Philology* 33: 390–404.

Sorabji, Richard. 2000. *Emotion and Peace of Mind: From Stoic Agitation to Christian Temptation.* Oxford: Oxford University Press.

Sprute, Jürgen. 1994. "Aristotle and the Legitimacy of Rhetoric." In *Aristotle's Rhetoric: Philosophical Essays,* edited by David J. Furley and Alexander Nehamas, 117–28. Princeton, NJ: Princeton University Press.

Stanciu, Diana. 2011. "Prudence in Lipsius's *Monita et exempla politica*: Stoic Virtue, Aristotelian Virtue or Not a Virtue at All?" In *(Un)Masking the Realities of Power: Justus Lipsius and the Dynamics of Political Writing in Early Modern Europe*, edited by Erik de Bom, Marijke Janssens, Toon van Houdt, and Jan Papy, 233–62. Leiden: Brill.

Stanlis, Peter J. 1991. *Edmund Burke: The Enlightenment and Revolution.* New Brunswick, NJ: Transaction.

Stem, Rex. 2006. "Cicero as Orator and Philosopher: The Value of the Pro Murena for Ciceronian Political Thought." *Review of Politics* 68: 206–31.

Strauss, Leo. 1959. *Thoughts on Machiavelli.* Chicago: University of Chicago Press.

Striker, Gisela. 1996. "Emotions in Context: Aristotle's Treatment of the Passions in the *Rhetoric* and His Moral Psychology." In *Essays on Aristotle's Rhetoric,* edited by Amélie Oksenberg Rorty, 286–302. Berkeley: University of California Press.

Stroud, Scott R. 2014. *Kant and the Promise of Rhetoric.* University Park, PA: Pennsylvania State University Press.

Sullivan, Francis A. 1941. "Cicero and *Gloria*." *Transactions and Proceedings of the American Philological Association* 72: 382–91.

Sunstein, Cass. 1993. *The Partial Constitution*. Cambridge, MA: Harvard University Press.

Tacitus. 1937. *Annals Books XII–XVI*. Translated by John Jackson. Loeb Classical Library. Cambridge, MA: Harvard University Press.

———. 1970a. *Agricola*. Translated by M. Hutton. Revised by R. M. Ogilvie. Loeb Classical Library. Cambridge, MA: Harvard University Press.

———. 1970b. *Dialogus*. Translated by W. Peterson. Revised by M. Winterbottom. Loeb Classical Library. Cambridge, MA: Harvard University Press.

———. 1970c. *Germania*. Translated by M. Hutton. Revised by E. H. Warmington. Loeb Classical Library. Cambridge, MA: Harvard University Press.

Tarcov, Nathan. 1988. "Quentin Skinner's Method and Machiavelli's *Prince*." In *Meaning and Context: Quentin Skinner and His Critics*, edited by James Tully, 194–204. Princeton, NJ: Princeton University Press.

———. Forthcoming. "Machiavelli's Modern Turn." In *The Modern Turn*, edited by Michael Rohlf. Washington, DC: Catholic University of America Press.

Taylor, A. E. 1938. "The Ethical Doctrine of Hobbes." *Philosophy* 13: 406–24.

Taylor, Lily Ross. 1966. *Roman Voting Assemblies: From the Hannibalic War to the Dictatorship of Caesar*. Ann Arbor: University of Michigan Press.

Tinkler, John F. 1987. "Renaissance Humanism and the *genera eloquentiae*." *Rhetorica: A Journal of the History of Rhetoric* 5: 279–309.

Tuck, Richard. 1993. *Philosophy and Government, 1572–1651*. Cambridge: Cambridge University Press.

Tucker, George Hugo. 2011. "Justus Lipsius and the *Cento* Form." In *(Un)masking the Realties of Power: Justus Lipsius and the Dynamics of Political Writing in Early Modern Europe*, edited by Erik De Bom, Marijke Janssens, Toon van Houdt, and Jan Papy, 163–92. Leiden: Brill.

Urbinati, Nadia. 2002. *Mill on Democracy: From the Athenian* Polis *to Representative Government*. Chicago: University of Chicago Press.

———. 2006. *Representative Democracy: Principles and Genealogy*. Chicago: University of Chicago Press.

Ussani, Vincenzo Scarano. 2003. "*Romanus Sapiens* and *Civilis Vir*: Quintilian's Theory of the Orator Acting for the Benefit of the Imperial Power." In *Quintilian and the Law: The Art of Persuasion in Law and Politics*, edited by Olga Tellegen-Couperus. Leuven: Leuven University Press.

van Gelderen, Martin. 1990. "The Machiavellian Moment and the Dutch Revolt: The Rise of Neostoicism and Dutch Republicanism." In *Machiavelli and Republicanism*, edited by Gisela Bock, Quentin Skinner, and Maurizio Viroli, 205–23. Cambridge: Cambridge University Press.

Van Holthoon, Frits, and David R. Olson. 1987. "Common Sense: An Introduction." In *Common Sense: The Foundations for Social Science*, edited by Frits van Holthoon and David R. Olson, 1–14. Lanham, MD: University Press of America.

Vasaly, Ann. 2013. "The Political Impact of Cicero's Speeches." In *The Cambridge Companion to Cicero*, edited by Catherine Steel, 141–59. Cambridge: Cambridge University Press.

Vickers, Brian. 1988. *In Defence of Rhetoric*. Oxford: Oxford University Press.

Viroli, Maurizio. 1992. *From Politics to Reason of State: The Acquisition and Transformation of the Language of Politics, 1250–1600*. Cambridge: Cambridge University Press.

———. 1998. *Machiavelli*. Oxford: Oxford University Press.

Vishnia, Rachel Feig. 2012. *Roman Elections in the Age of Cicero: Society, Government, and Voting*. New York: Routledge.

Wallace, Robert W. 1985. *The Areopagos Council, to 307 B.C.* Baltimore: Johns Hopkins University Press.

———. 2006. "The Legal Regulation of Private Conduct at Athens: Two Controversies on Freedom." *Rivista di Storia del diritto greco ed ellenistico* 9: 107–28.

Walzer, Michael. 1973. "Political Action: The Problem of Dirty Hands." *Philosophy and Public Affairs* 2: 160–80.

———. 1980. Review of *Public and Private Morality*, edited by Stuart Hampshire. *Political Theory* 8: 128–31.

———. 1983. Response to Ronald Dworkin's "To Each His Own." *New York Review of Books*, July 21, 1983.

———. 1988. *The Company of Critics: Social Criticism and Political Commitment in the Twentieth Century*. New York: Basic Books.

———. 1989. "A Critique of Philosophical Conversation." *Philosophical Forum* 21: 182–96.

———. 1993. *Interpretation and Social Criticism*. Cambridge, MA: Harvard University Press.

———. 1994. *Thick and Thin: Moral Argument at Home and Abroad*. Notre Dame, IN: University of Notre Dame Press.

———. 2004. *Arguing about War*. New Haven, CT: Yale University Press.

Wardy, Robert. 1996. "Mighty Is the Truth and It Shall Prevail?" In *Essays on Aristotle's Rhetoric,* edited by Amélie Oksenberg Rorty, 56–87. Berkeley: University of California Press.

Warrender, Howard. 1957. *The Political Philosophy of Hobbes: His Theory of Obligation*. Oxford: Clarendon Press.

Wasserstrom, Richard. 1983. "Roles and Morality." In *The Good Lawyer: Lawyers' Roles and Lawyers' Ethics*, edited by David Luban, 25–37. Totowa, NJ: Rowman and Allanheld.

Waszink, Jan. 2004. Introduction to *Politica: Six Books of Politics or Political Instruction*, by Lipsius, edited and translated by Waszink, 3–203. Assen, The Netherlands: Royal Van Gorcum.

Webb, Clement C. J. 1909. *Ioannis Saresberiensis Episcopi Carnotensis Policratici sive De Nugis Curalium et Vestigiis Philosophorum*. 2 vols. Oxford: Clarendon Press.

———. 1941. "Note on Books Bequeathed by John of Salisbury to the Cathedral Library of Chartres." *Medieval and Renaissance Studies* 1: 128–29.

Weber, Max. 2009. "Politics as a Vocation." In *From Max Weber: Essays in Sociology*, edited by H. H. Gerth and C. Wright Mills, 77–128. New York: Routledge.

Welch, Kathryn E. 1996. "T. Pomponius Atticus: A Banker in Politics?" *Historia: Zeitschrift für alte Geschichte* 45: 450–71.

White, Peter. 2010. *Cicero in Letters: Epistolary Relations of the Late Republic*. Oxford: Oxford University Press.

Williams, Bernard. 1978. "Politics and Moral Character." In *Public and Private Morality*, edited by Stuart Hampshire, 55–73. Cambridge: Cambridge University Press.

———. 1981. *Moral Luck*. Cambridge: Cambridge University Press.

———. 1983. "Professional Morality and Its Dispositions." In *The Good Lawyer: Lawyers' Roles and Lawyers' Ethics*, edited by David Luban, 259–69. Totowa, NJ: Rowman and Allanheld.

———. 1987. "Ethical Consistency." In *Moral Dilemmas*, edited by Christopher Gowans, 115–37. Cambridge: Cambridge University Press.

Wills, Gary. 1992. *Lincoln at Gettysburg: The Words That Remade America*. New York: Simon and Schuster.

Winterbottom, Michael. 1964. "Quintilian and the *Vir Bonus*." *Journal of Roman Studies* 54: 90–97.

Wiseman, T. P. 2009. *Remembering the Roman People: Essays on Late-Republican Politics and Literature*. New York: Oxford University Press.

Wisse, Jakob. 1989. *Ethos and Pathos from Aristotle to Cicero*. Amsterdam: Adolf M. Hakkert.

Wisse, Jacob, Michael Winterbottom, and Elaine Fantham. 2008. *M. T. Cicero, De oratore libri III: A Commentary on Book III, 96–230*. Heidelberg: Universitätsverlag Winter.

Wolin, Sheldon. 2004. *Politics and Vision: Continuity and Innovation in Western Political Thought*. Princeton, NJ: Princeton University Press.

Wood, Neal. 1988. *Cicero's Social and Political Thought*. Berkeley: University of California Press.

Woolf, Raphael. 2015. *Cicero: The Philosophy of a Roman Sceptic*. New York: Routledge.

Yakobson, Alexander. 2010. "Traditional Political Culture and the People's Role in the Roman Republic." *Historia* 59: 282–302.

Young, Iris Marion. 2002. *Inclusion and Democracy*. Chicago: University of Chicago Press.

Young, R. V. 2011. *Justus Lipsius' Concerning Constancy*. Tempe: Arizona Center for Medieval and Renaissance Studies.

Zaller, John R. 1992. *The Nature and Origins of Mass Opinion*. New York: Cambridge University Press.

Zerba, Michelle. 2003. "Love, Envy, and Pantomimic Morality in Cicero's *De Oratore*." *Classical Philology* 98: 299–321.

———. 2012. *Doubt and Skepticism in Antiquity and the Renaissance*. Cambridge: Cambridge University Press.

Zetzel, James. 2003. "Plato with Pillows: Cicero on the Uses of Greek Culture." In *Myth, History and Culture in Republican Rome: Studies in Honour of T. P. Wiseman*, edited by David Braund and Christopher Gill, 118–38. Exeter: University of Exeter Press.